THE AFTERLIFE OF SHAKESPEARE'S SONNETS

Why did no one read Sonnet 18 for over one hundred years? What traumatic memories did Sonnet 111 conjure up for Charles Dickens? Which Sonnet did Wilfred Owen find particularly offensive on the First World War battlefront? What kind of love does Sonnet 116 celebrate and why? Filling a surprising gap in Shakespeare studies, this book offers a challenging new reception history of the Sonnets and explores their belated entry into the Shakespeare canon. Jane Kingsley-Smith reveals the fascinating cultural history of individual Sonnets, identifying those which were particularly influential and exploring why they rose to prominence. This is a highly original study which argues that we should redirect our attention away from the story that the Sonnets tell as a sequence, to the fascinating afterlife of individual Shakespeare Sonnets.

JANE KINGSLEY-SMITH is Reader at the University of Roehampton, London. She is author of *Shakespeare's Drama of Exile* (2003) and *Cupid in Early Modern Literature and Culture* (Cambridge University Press, 2010). Dr Kingsley-Smith has a PhD from the Shakespeare Institute, Stratford-Upon-Avon and is a regular lecturer at Shakespeare's Globe.

THE AFTERLIFE OF
SHAKESPEARE'S SONNETS

JANE KINGSLEY-SMITH

University of Roehampton

CAMBRIDGE
UNIVERSITY PRESS

CAMBRIDGE
UNIVERSITY PRESS

University Printing House, Cambridge CB2 8BS, United Kingdom

One Liberty Plaza, 20th Floor, New York, NY 10006, USA

477 Williamstown Road, Port Melbourne, VIC 3207, Australia

314-321, 3rd Floor, Plot 3, Splendor Forum, Jasola District Centre, New Delhi - 110025, India

79 Anson Road, #06-04/06, Singapore 079906

Cambridge University Press is part of the University of Cambridge.

It furthers the University's mission by disseminating knowledge in the pursuit of education, learning and research at the highest international levels of excellence.

www.cambridge.org
Information on this title: www.cambridge.org/9781009060066
DOI: 10.1017/9781316756683

© Jane Kingsley- Smith 2019

First published 2019
First paperback edition 2021

A catalogue record for this publication is available from the British Library

ISBN 978-1-107-17065-0 Hardback
ISBN 978-1-009-06006-6 Paperback

For James

Contents

Figures

Acknowledgements

This book could not have been written without all the extraordinary criticism on the Sonnets that has informed it. I would like to acknowledge in particular the work of Katherine Duncan-Jones, Heather Dubrow and Stanley Wells.

I am grateful to a number of scholars who kindly shared their knowledge with me, specifically Mary Ellen Lamb, Naomi Miller, Penny McCarthy, Maggie Kilgour, Ann Baynes Coiro, Hannah Crawforth and Elizabeth Scott-Baumann. I'd like to thank Sarah Stanton at Cambridge University Press for commissioning this book, and for her ongoing support, and to Emily Hockley, Tim Mason and Carrie Parkinson for their work on it.

This book has also benefited from some wonderful readers and supporters. These include the anonymous reviewers for Cambridge University Press and my lovely Roehampton colleagues. I'd like to thank Andy Kesson and Callan Davies for their helpful comments; Laura Peters for her unwavering support and kindness; and Clare McManus for being such a true friend, and for reading the whole thing with characteristic generosity.

I'm grateful to have had the love and support of my mum, Margaret, whilst writing this book. The memory of my father, Trevor, is diffused throughout it, and he is always in my heart. Finally, I would like to thank James, Roxana and Dash for all their love and grace. They inspire me every day.

Introduction
Why Shakespeare's Sonnets Need an Afterlife

> Probably, more nonsense has been talked and written, more intellectual and emotional energy expended in vain, on the sonnets of Shakespeare than on any other literary work in the world.[1]

Where this situation fills W. H. Auden with dismay, it might equally inspire us with admiration. The creative energy that has gone into re-ordering, re-explicating, rewriting and re-imagining Shakespeare's Sonnets implies something of their plenitude and stimulus to invention. Whilst the attention they have received has much to do with their status as the 'most autobiographical' of Shakespeare's writings, it is also a reaction to the aesthetic and affective power of individual sonnets, lines and phrases. Nevertheless, the partial cause of Auden's dismay, and one of the concerns that drives this book, is the extent to which the autobiographical narrative generated by the 1609 Quarto arrangement or 'sequence' has circumscribed responses to individual Sonnets.[2] As Gary Taylor has observed, 'only a handful of the 154 have ever attracted or rewarded as much enthusiasm as the story told outside and between them'.[3] And yet, alongside the history of the Quarto narrative, with its seductive fictions about Shakespeare, the Dark Lady and the Fair Youth, is a history of individual lyrics, circulating through manuscript, print edition, anthology and literary allusion, which might be just as fascinating and worthy of attention.

To prioritise the sequence over particular Sonnets is not only critically and creatively inhibitive, but anachronistic. Tennyson's *In Memoriam* was

---

[1] Auden, 'Introduction', p. xvii.

[2] I use the capitalised term 'Sonnets' throughout this book to indicate Shakespeare's poems, and to differentiate them from the published text of *Shake-speares Sonnets*. Although critics including Sasha Roberts and Katherine Duncan-Jones have made a case for discussing *A Lover's Complaint* as a 'thematic counterpart to [the Sonnets]', and a 'carefully designed component of the whole [Quarto]', its circulation and reception are generally separate from that of the Sonnets, and therefore beyond the scope of this study. See Shakespeare, *Shakespeare's Sonnets*, ed. Duncan-Jones, p. 92, and Roberts, *Reading Shakespeare's Poems*, pp. 146–53.

[3] Taylor, *Reinventing Shakespeare*, p. 158.

compared in its own time to Shakespeare's *Sonnets* as a sequence idealising male friendship, or one that overstepped the bounds of decency with its excessive effeminate passion. But whilst the elegy's allusions to Sonnet 116 ('Let me not to the marriage of true minds') are informed by this debate, they also draw upon the history of Sonnet 116 as a standalone poem, defining an ideal of constancy that Tennyson used both to romanticise and to deflect homoerotic desire. George Eliot shows no awareness of the fact that the Sonnets quoted in the chapter headings of *Middlemarch* are potentially addressed to a man. She reads Sonnet 93 ('So shall I live supposing thou art true') through the lens of Rousseau, and her own suspicion of *female* beauty. In *To The Lighthouse*, Mrs Ramsay encounters the Sonnets in an anthology, and this allows Virginia Woolf to invoke the history of Sonnet 98 ('From you have I been absent in the spring'), apart from the sequence, and to explore the lyric's Romantic nostalgia.

As suggested above, one of the ways in which the sequence most limits our interpretation of the Sonnets is the understanding that 1–126 are addressed to a man, and 127–52 to a woman – an assumption that dates all the way back to Edmond Malone's editing of the Quarto in 1780. After speculating about the identity of Mr W. H., the *Sonnets*' dedicatee, Malone averred that 'To this person, whoever he was, one hundred and twenty [six] of the following poems are addressed; the remaining twenty-eight are addressed to a lady'.[4] This is a critical orthodoxy so monumental in our time that it has only just begun to be dismantled. In an important re-evaluation of Sonnet criticism in 1993, Margreta de Grazia described some of the motives that might lie behind Malone's decision. These included his desire to make the Sonnets into Shakespearean autobiography (restricting the addressees to two made it easier to uncover their identities), and his unconscious response to the scientific 'discovery' of two discrete sexes at the end of the eighteenth century.[5] But if de Grazia exposed the constructedness of this division, she was not willing to reject it entirely: 'Some kind of binary division appears to be at work'.[6] Three years later, Heather Dubrow would cite de Grazia's findings about how little grammatical support *Sonnets* provides for such a division: 'about five sixths of the first 126 sonnets and a slightly smaller proportion of the entire collection do not specify an addressee through a gendered pronoun'.[7] Dubrow would go on to argue

---

[4] Malone, *Supplement to the edition of Shakspeare's Plays*, p. 529.
[5] De Grazia, 'The Scandal of Shakespeare's Sonnets', 37, 42.
[6] Ibid., 41.
[7] Dubrow, 'The Politics of Plotting Shakespeare's Sonnets', 292.

that the existence of 'subdivisions and clusters' challenges a simple bipartite scheme, and that it is entirely possible 'that some poems intended for one group or the other slipped out of place'.[8] Thus, Sonnet 126 ('O thou my lovely boy'), which is usually thought to complete the first sequence, might equally conclude the 'procreation' poems; the sexual innuendos of Sonnet 128 ('How oft when thou, my music, music play'st') might be directed to the male addressee previously identified with music in Sonnet 8; and the confession in Sonnet 147, 'For I have sworn thee fair, and thought thee bright', suggests that some of the pre-127 poems which praise the beloved could refer to the mistress.[9]

The reasons why we continue to perpetuate a bipartite division are varied but include the fact that 'it is easier to discuss these poems critically if one can determine to whom they refer and what story they tell'.[10] It certainly makes them easier to teach. And yet, as this book will show, to insist on Malone's division estranges us from centuries of readers who did not feel similarly constrained and can lead to an unpleasant kind of intellectual snobbery and moral self-righteousness when 'misreadings' are encountered. Such a target has been John Benson, whose reader-centred edition of Shakespeare's *Poems* in 1640 altered pronouns from male to female in Sonnet 101 and replaced 'boy' with 'love' in Sonnet 108. Benson has been the subject of much critical opprobrium for 'censoring' the Sonnets, but he left most of the male pronouns untouched,[11] and the title he gave to Sonnet 122, 'Upon the Receit of a Table Book from his Mistris', arguably emerged less from a desire to misrepresent or obscure the Sonnet's sexuality, than because he 'assumed that the sonnets were to a female, unless otherwise specified'.[12] More recently, in 2007, a student who uploaded a video of Sonnet 18 ('Shall I compare thee to a summer's day?') to YouTube, featuring a female beloved, found him/herself admonished: 'sonnet 18 is about a man. You probably should have checked that out'.[13] In the context of the 'erasure of the male object of address' which Stephen O'Neill has found in other Sonnet videos,[14] we might welcome this critique, which challenges 'the kind of transcendentalizing long associated with Shakespeare, a problematic phenomenon that is predicated on at best an unwitting presumptive

---

[8] Ibid., 295.

[9] Ibid., 295, 301–2.

[10] Ibid., 303.

[11] See Rollins' critique of Benson in *A New Variorum Edition of Shakespeare*, vol. 2, p. 20. For a defence of Benson's editing, see Shrank, 'Reading Shakespeare's Sonnets', and Acker, 'John Benson's *Poems*'.

[12] De Grazia, 'The Scandal of Shakespeare's Sonnets', 35–6.

[13] See www.youtube.com/watch?v=H-_QlzUJBbU, accessed 2 May 2018.

[14] O'Neill, *Shakespeare and YouTube*, p. 162.

heterosexuality, at worst a silent erasure of non-heterosexual love and desires'.[15] But Sonnet 18 contains no gendered pronouns and could express a variety of desires. The student's plea that they were using 'creative licence' potentially invokes the long tradition of directing Sonnet 18 to a mistress, which may be 'wrong' or inaccurate, but is so only if we believe that the Quarto sequence is Shakespeare's own,[16] and if we subscribe to the theory that authorial intention can and should delimit the ways in which a lyric functions in the world. As it is, the author of this video cannot invoke the creative tradition of Sonnet 18 because s/he does not know it: the only history at play here relates to interpretations of the sequence, not of the Sonnet.

My assertion that Shakespeare's Sonnets (as opposed to the *Sonnets*) deserve a detailed afterlife may seem redundant – surely we have one? But although a number of important, chapter-length studies exist, there is no monograph on the Sonnets' reception.[17] This matters because the failure to explore the critical, editorial and creative afterlife of the Sonnets has led to a number of erroneous assumptions.

At one extreme is the view, prevalent in popular culture, that the Sonnets have always been admired; as a publishing blurb on the Faber & Faber website reads: 'Shakespeare's Sonnets of 1609 are as thrilling and persuasive today as they were when they were first published; perhaps no collection of verses before or since has so captured the imagination of lovers and readers as these.'[18] Necessary hyperbole aside, this overlooks the ominous silence to which the Sonnets emerged in 1609, and the difficulty that centuries of lovers have had in understanding them, and of finding a way to reconcile them with Shakespeare's plays. At the other extreme is the more informed, but still faulty, notion that the Sonnets languished in obscurity from 1609 to 1780 – that they had 'no history' until they were rescued by Malone.[19]

---

[15] Ibid., p. 163.

[16] Whether or not Shakespeare authorised the arrangement and publication of the Quarto is discussed further in Chapter 1. For an argument in the Quarto's defence, see Duncan-Jones, 'Was the 1609 Shakespeare's Sonnets Really Unauthorised?'. For a more agnostic approach, see Shakespeare, *The Complete Sonnets and Poems*, ed. Burrow, pp. 91–7.

[17] See the chapters in Smith's *The Tension of the Lyre*, Roberts, *Reading Shakespeare's Poems*, and Edmondson and Wells, *Shakespeare's Sonnets*, and essays such as Smith's 'Shakespeare's Sonnets and the History of Sexuality', Roberts, 'Reception and Influence', and Matz, 'The Scandals of Shakespeare's Sonnets', discussed further below. Crawforth *et al.*, *The Sonnets*, also brings together a number of critical essays on the Sonnets' afterlife, and testifies much more positively than most criticism has done before to the 'unbroken tradition of reading [the Sonnets], both professional and personal', p. 1.

[18] This statement accompanies Paterson's insightful and irreverent *Reading Shakespeare's Sonnets*.

[19] De Grazia justifies her focus on the Malone and Malone/Boswell editions on the basis that 'it is with them that the modern history of the Sonnets begins, and since no full edition of the 1609 Quarto

Yet the circle of William Herbert, Earl of Pembroke, seems to have been particularly engaged with the Sonnets in the first decades of the seventeenth century,[20] and the Sonnets sustained a 'Cavalier' readership until well into the 1680s. The fact that they were read and adapted in manuscript may mean that they were not 'popular', but it does not mean that their history is a blank. Furthermore, although Malone congratulated himself on being the first to 'separate [Shakespeare's] genuine poetical compositions' from 'the spurious performances with which they have been so long intermixed',[21] he was not the first to favour the 1609 text. Serious critical discussion of the Sonnets emerged in 1709–11, between Charles Gildon and Bernard Lintott, and editions of the Quarto were printed in 1711 and 1766. Moreover, although for modern readers *Shake-speares Sonnets* is 'the Sonnets', the canon of his lyrical verse proved surprisingly fluid well into the nineteenth century, with anthologists incorporating poems from William Jaggard's *The Passionate Pilgrim* (1599) and Benson's *Poems* (1640), often out of personal preference – because these lyrics were what readers wished that Shakespeare had written – rather than from ignorance.[22]

By 2013, the Sonnets can be described as 'the fascinating and frustrating center of Shakespeare's *oeuvre* and, by extension, the corpus of Renaissance poetry [and] the canon of English literature',[23] but for at least two hundred years after publication they occupied a precarious position in the works of Shakespeare, with only a fragile claim to authenticity. They came into print through a counterfeit – Jaggard's pretended single-author volume, *The Passionate Pilgrim* – and their absence from the 1623 First Folio identified them as in some way illegitimate or superfluous – a hint that was taken up by Nicholas Rowe in his edition of 1709, which included all the apocryphal plays but rejected the Sonnets as 'spurious'. Peter Kirwan's *Shakespeare and the Idea of Apocrypha: Negotiating the Boundaries of the Dramatic Canon* (2015) does not, as its title suggests, include the Sonnets, but its compelling account of the fluctuating status of the apocryphal

---

was printed prior to Malone's that belated history can be considered their *only* history' ('The Scandal of Shakespeare's Sonnets', 40). De Grazia does include a footnote here, acknowledging that editions of the Quarto were reprinted in 1711 and 1766, but the damage has arguably been done.

[20] I am partly indebted here to Katherine Duncan-Jones' work on the Sonnets and Pembroke in *Shakespeare's Sonnets*, discussed further in Chapter 1.

[21] Malone, *Supplement to the edition of Shakspeare's Plays*, p. iv.

[22] See Paul D. Cannan's fascinating discussion of stubborn attribution of *The Passionate Pilgrim* lyrics to Shakespeare in 'Edmond Malone, *The Passionate Pilgrim* and the Fiction of Shakespearean Authorship'.

[23] Catherine Nicholson goes on to deconstruct this assumption, tracing the Sonnets' lack of status in the eighteenth century, and exploring ideas about their originality versus their 'commonness' that are extremely suggestive. See 'Commonplace Shakespeare', p. 185.

plays, and its reconsideration of what the Shakespeare canon means, can usefully be applied to the Sonnets. Indeed, for some time these poems were more 'apocryphal' than those plays. In 1738, John Hayward's *The British Muse* gathered together poetry by Daniel, Spenser, Drayton and Donne, but overlooked Shakespeare's Sonnets, though it did find room for extracts from *Locrine, The London Prodigal, The Puritan, Thomas, Lord Cromwell, Sir John Oldcastle* and *A Yorkshire Tragedy*.[24] For anyone interested in the processes of canon-formation, the Sonnets also provide a fascinating test case, given the extent to which they endure and eventually thrive through the overlapping of different canons, including the personal, the critical and the pedagogical.[25] Catherine Stimpson's discussion of the personal or 'paracanon' is particularly pertinent here, as one that 'asks that we systematically expand our theoretical investigations of "the good" to include the "lovable"'.[26] Given the critical opprobrium to which the Sonnets were long subject, this might seem like an odd category for them to fall into, but it is evident from early seventeenth-century responses to Sonnet 116 – perhaps the Sonnet with the strongest historical claim to 'lovability' – that their afterlife is partly shaped by writers returning again and again to the same lyric, and even to individual phrases, as Charles Dickens does to Sonnet 111 ('My nature is subdu'd ... like the dyer's hand'), or W. H. Auden to Sonnet 121 ('I am that I am').

In terms of the history of individual Sonnets, perhaps the most important syllogism this book will challenge is the notion that our selection has not changed:

> the same sonnets from the 1609 Quarto tend to be anthologised over and over again. This is not merely because, since 1780, we have gradually reached a consensus about those of outstanding aesthetic merit. It is because the majority of them make little sense outside a narrative that gives them a living context. Most of them defy the very idea of the anthology.[27]

But even a cursory examination of which Sonnets are anthologised from 1599 to the present shows that this is not true. The very first 'anthology' to feature Shakespeare's Sonnets, *The Passionate Pilgrim*, opens with two of the least adaptable and most narratively titillating: 138 ('When my love swears that she is made of truth') and 144 ('Two loves I have, of comfort

---

[24] See Shakespeare's entry in the 'List of Authors' in Hayward, *The British Muse*, vol. 1.
[25] See Alastair Fowler's identification of six kinds of canon in 'Genre and the Literary Canon', and Wendell V. Harris' 'Canonicity' on the way in which they interact.
[26] Stimpson, 'Reading for Love', 958.
[27] Schalkwyk, *Speech and Performance*, p. 27.

and despair'). By contrast, Sonnet 18 ('Shall I compare thee to a summer's day?'), which is now a staple of anthologies of love poetry, and has arguably become *the* archetypal Shakespeare Sonnet in the sense that it compounds some of their most obvious themes,[28] went missing for more than one hundred years, after being left out of Benson's *Poems*. Once returned to print, it was not one of the Sonnets that Malone lingered over, and it was generally ignored by early nineteenth-century anthologists, until it found a place in Victorian hearts through the agency of Francis Turner Palgrave. Similarly, the pall that fell over the 'Dark Lady' sequence,[29] for reasons both moral and aesthetic, meant that Sonnet 130 ('My mistress' eyes are nothing like the sun') was cheerfully ignored until the beginning of the twentieth century, when the tragedy of Oscar Wilde made even such a mistress as this preferable to the alluring Mr W. H.

A comparison between Palgrave's *Golden Treasury* and the most recent *Norton Anthology of English Literature: The Sixteenth Century and Early Seventeenth Century* (2012) is instructive. Palgrave excludes all of the 'procreation' Sonnets, along with Sonnet 20 ('A woman's face with Nature's own hand painted') for perhaps obvious reasons. He is either uninterested in or disapproving of the 'Dark Lady' Sonnets, featuring only the morally chastising 146 ('Poor soul, the centre of my sinful earth') and 148 ('O me! What eyes hath love put in my head'). The *Norton Anthology* selects, among others, Sonnets 1, 3, 12 and 15 of the 'procreation' series, Sonnet 20, and ten Dark Lady sonnets (including 146 but not 148) but makes its own surprising omissions. It does not include Sonnet 2 ('When forty winters shall besiege thy brow'), although, as Gary Taylor has shown, this was the runaway manuscript success of the early to mid-seventeenth century.[30] It also excludes Sonnet 64 ('When I have seen by Time's fell

---

[28] It praises the beloved's beauty, which it finds beyond compare; it insists upon his/her defiance of Time; it glories in the poet's power to confer immortality through the poem. Sonnet 18 has also become a 'gateway' Sonnet. In a change to Victorian practice, twentieth-century anthologies began to print the Sonnets in sequential order, thereby giving prominence to Sonnet 18 which seems to have been the first Sonnet that editors would alight on. It appears first in three editions of *The Oxford Book of English Verse*, as edited by Arthur Quiller-Couch (1900, 1939), Helen Gardner (1972) and Christopher Ricks (1999).

[29] All references to the Dark Lady or Fair Youth in this book should be understood as having quotation marks around them: these fictional individuals probably contain multiple real-life addressees, and have their own conceptual history, as discussed further in the final chapter. See also Wells, ' "My Name is Will" ', and Paul Hammond's discussion of the terms 'Dark Lady' and 'Friend' in *Shakespeare's Sonnets*, pp. 3–5. I will also refer to the 'procreation' Sonnets (Sonnets 1–17) as a convenient shorthand, and because they do have some internal coherence, but this does not preclude the movement of lyrics in and out of this grouping.

[30] Taylor, 'Some Manuscripts of Shakespeare's Sonnets'. See also Chapter 2.

hand defaced'), despite the impact this had on Romantic poetry, and its recurrence in nineteenth-century anthologies.[31] It might be argued that the *Norton*'s ambition 'to bring together works of enduring value' and 'to give access to many of the most remarkable works written in English during centuries of restless creative effort' would be enriched by a sense of which Shakespeare Sonnets have most inspired this 'restless … effort'.[32]

One critic who *has* usefully engaged with the history of individual Sonnets is Robert Matz. In an article which seeks to survey the Sonnets' history from 1640 to 2007, he maps the differing popularity in anthologies of (in ascending order of popularity) Sonnets 54, 98, 130, 30, 18, 73 and 116, and his conclusions overlap broadly with the findings of my own research.[33] However, the limited scope afforded by a journal article inhibits how useful these conclusions can be. Matz has conducted 'a survey of over 2000 choices in the anthologization of selected Shakespeare sonnets from 1800 to the present',[34] but he cannot list which ones, or explain how those anthologies' self-description and implied audience might influence their choice of Sonnets. He also does not explain why he went looking for these Sonnets in particular: 64 and 129 ('Th'expense of spirit in a waste of shame') are significant omissions, whilst 30 ('When to the sessions of sweet silent thought') and 54 ('O how much more doth beauty beauteous seem') arguably prove less influential. Finally, Matz's focus on anthologies limits his ability not only to trace the influence of particular Sonnets but also to explain what readers found in them.

The Afterlife of Shakespeare's Sonnets represents a new reception history of these lyrics, extending across a period of more than four hundred years and based on the evidence of manuscripts, commonplace books, print editions and anthologies, reviews, critical articles and academic books, the letters, diaries and notebooks of key literary figures, and quotations and allusions in some of the most celebrated literary texts. Whilst I hope to offer a more extensive and detailed account of the *Sonnets*' reception than any before, I am also concerned to trace the cultural history of individual Sonnets. The heading of each chapter quotes from a Sonnet which was particularly resonant at this historical moment, either because it was admired or because it

---

[31] The Norton selection has also changed substantially since the first 1962 volume, which included a section headed 'Songs from the Plays' and then nineteen Sonnets: 18, 29, 30, 55, 56, 60, 71, 73, 97, 98, 106, 107, 116, 118, 129, 130, 138, 144, 146. See *The Norton Anthology of English Literature*, ed. M. H. Abrams *et al.* (1962), vol. 1.

[32] See Greenblatt, 'Preface to the Ninth Edition', in *The Norton Shakespeare*, p. xxii.

[33] Matz, 'The Scandals of Shakespeare's Sonnets', 500.

[34] Ibid., 479.

seems to get to the heart of some larger issue with the Sonnets (as in the case of Sonnet 20). Although tempting, I have tried to refrain from declaring any of these Sonnets to be the most 'popular' in their time. Such a determination is hampered by the absence of any kind of statistics on who was reading what for the majority of the period covered by this book, as well as by the more troubled question of defining who and what we mean by 'popular'.[35] Instead, I focus on the cultural, political and aesthetic influence of particular Sonnets, and suggest those which seem to have been most enabling in terms of allowing readers to articulate their own experiences. In the process, I offer new interpretations of Sonnet allusion in the work of Milton and Suckling, Keats and Wordsworth, Tennyson, George Eliot and Oscar Wilde, Wilfred Owen and Virginia Woolf, William Empson, W. H. Auden and Anthony Burgess. In each case, I am concerned with the particular manuscript, print edition or anthology which mediates the Sonnets. By reading these writers' appropriation of certain Sonnets through the material text, and through the Sonnet's individual history, we gain a deeper understanding of the allusion's resonance for the author and for his/her contemporary readers.[36] As this list suggests, my focus has been on literature written in English by British writers, with limited forays into American literature represented by the work of Laura Riding, Harryette Mullen and Samuel Beadle in the final chapter. A very different but equally rich afterlife might be written about the Sonnets in Continental Europe, and in North American and other post-colonial literatures.[37] The Sonnets' reinvention in other art forms such as music and film cannot be included here but would also be worth further study.

Each of the following five chapters is defined by a significant critical moment or publishing event in the Sonnets' history. Chapter 1 (1598–1622) begins with the first testimony to the Sonnets' existence by Francis Meres, and examines the experience of reading the Sonnets in both Jaggard's *Passionate Pilgrim* and Thorpe's 1609 Quarto, before examining their early manuscript transmission. Chapter 2 (1623–1708) considers the Sonnets' 'omission' from the first Folio, and the ways in which John Benson attempted

---

[35] For a fascinating account of this dilemma in the early modern period, including some key chapters on methodology, see Kesson and Smith, *The Elizabethan Top-Ten*.

[36] Andrew Murphy's work in *Shakespeare in Print* and *Shakespeare for the People* proves particularly important here.

[37] Sonnet 66 ('Tired with all these for restful death I cry'), for example, has a fascinating history during the twentieth century as a response to political tyranny in Europe. See Phfister, 'Route 66 and No End'. Sonnet 29 ('When in disgrace with fortune and men's eyes') influenced Walt Whitman, 'the bardic voice of American individualism, expansiveness and freedom', as explored by Claussen in ' "Hours Continuing Long" ', 131.

to exploit this absence, and to refashion the Sonnets into 'Cavalier' poems. It also explores the Sonnets' strongly Royalist associations as they circulated in manuscript through the period of the English Civil Wars, up until the end of the seventeenth century. In Chapter 3 (1709–1816), we begin with Nicholas Rowe's castigation of the Sonnets as 'spurious', and their struggle to find a secure foothold in the burgeoning Shakespeare industry of the eighteenth century, until Malone's *Supplement* finds them a role in the canon that will bring them both prestige and notoriety. Chapter 4 (1817–1900) opens with the ecstatic re-reading of the Sonnets by John Keats, and a Romantic re-evaluation which not only produces new biographical fictions, but begins the vital process of selection and anthologisation that will increase their familiarity and accessibility by the mid-nineteenth century. Victorian women writers, including Elizabeth Barrett Browning and George Eliot, prove particularly concerned with how Shakespeare loves in the Sonnets, but it is Oscar Wilde's advocacy that destroys their romantic innocence, and brings the chapter to a tragic end. Chapter 5 (1901–1997) sees a new interest in Shakespeare's Dark Lady as a response to the Wilde scandal, but also demonstrates the sustained use of the Sonnets by First World War and modernist poets to give voice to homoerotic desire and to critique heterosexual convention. By the end of the twentieth century, however, the Dark Lady returns, providing a means by which women may write back to Shakespeare, but also prompting the first sustained discussion of the Sonnets' racial politics. Finally, in the Conclusion (1998–2018), we examine the innovations of contemporary poets and scholars in the last twenty years, which have reshaped even Shakespeare's most 'temperate' Sonnet, 'Shall I compare thee to a summer's day?'.

Given that Shakespeare's dramatic canon now looks more collaborative and 'open' than it has for centuries,[38] an insistence on the Quarto's authority and integrity appears somewhat nostalgic, if not reactionary. With what we know about the Sonnets' early fluidity in manuscript,[39] and the errors apparent in Q, so that 'It is impossible entirely to exclude the possibility that the sequence was set from different manuscripts, or from a single manuscript containing different hands',[40] the notion that there are other voices included in this text, and indeed other writers' lyrics, should no longer seem so transgressive. But this is not a study of the Sonnets'

---

[38] See, for example, Shakespeare, *The New Oxford Shakespeare*, ed. Taylor *et al.* (2016), which adds *Arden of Faversham*, *Edward III*, and *Sejanus* to the Shakespearean canon, and extends Shakespeare's collaboration with Marlowe.

[39] See Marotti, 'Shakespeare's Sonnets as Literary Property', pp. 143–73.

[40] Shakespeare, *The Complete Sonnets and Poems*, ed. Burrow, p. 93.

authorship. Rather, I am interested in the processes by which the *Sonnets* fragments and comes together, becomes spurious and then authentic, moves from the margins into the centre, and what happens when individual Sonnets go out into the world and form relationships with their readers. As one of the Sonnets' most sensitive critics, David Schalkwyk, puts it, their very lack of specificity makes them available for appropriation:

> the 1609 sonnets are not works of fiction in the usual sense of the word. Like a series of snapshots, they arise from, respond and refer to a world that they make no attempt to recover, because that world was self-evident to the people who appear in the photographs and to the persons who took them. It can only be glimpsed in the discrete shards of the poems. By an ironic paradox, then, the rootedness of the sonnets in real experiences and relationships leaves them especially abstracted and open to subsequent appropriations and projection: to precisely the 'death of the author' that is the consequence of 'the birth of the reader'.[41]

The invitation to speak through the Sonnets is one that centuries of readers have taken up in intriguingly different ways. That difference is the subject of this book.

---

[41] Schalkwyk, *Speech and Performance*, pp. 26–7.

CHAPTER I

Loved When They Alteration Find, 1598–1622

In 1612, the poet and dramatist Thomas Heywood published a dedication praising Nicholas Okes, at the expense of another stationer, William Jaggard. He claimed that Jaggard had spoilt his book, *Troia Britannica* (1608), by printing it with 'infinite faults', including 'misquotations, mistaking of sillables, misplacing halfe lines, coining of strange and never heard of words'.[1] To support his complaint, Heywood cited another 'Author [whom] I know much offended with M. Jaggard (that altogether unknowne to him) presumed to make so bold with his name' (by attributing to him in print lyrics that were not his) 'and he to doe himself right, hath since published them in his owne name'.[2] This aggrieved Author was apparently Shakespeare, and the story Heywood tells pits William Jaggard's *The Passionate Pilgrim by W. Shakespeare* (1599) against Thomas Thorpe's *Shake-speare's Sonnets* (1609).[3] One is fraudulent, unauthorised, shameful; the other is legitimate, authorised, restorative – and this is how the narrative of the first published texts of the Sonnets has largely played out. And yet, there remain serious questions over whether Shakespeare authorised the Quarto, how involved he was in its production, and whether he wanted to publish at all. Heywood may have made assumptions based on the title *Shake-speares Sonnets*, or he may have cited this example disingenuously. As Adam G. Hooks points out, 'even if this story is true, it demonstrates nothing more than that Shakespeare's reputation was

---

Part of Chapter 1 is reprinted from the following article, '"Let Me not to the Marriage of True Minds": Shakespeare's Sonnet for Lady Mary Wroth', *Shakespeare Survey* 69 (2016), 292–301. This is reproduced with kind permission of the editor.

[1] Heywood, 'To my approved good Friend, Mr Nicholas Okes', in *An Apology for Actors*, sig. G4.

[2] Ibid.

[3] One of the obscurities of Heywood's argument is that he seems to conflate two separate incidents. If Shakespeare was moved by Jaggard to publish the Sonnets in 1609, then he must have been responding to the misattribution of lyrics in the original twenty-poem *Passionate Pilgrim* of 1599. However, Heywood also refers to the attribution of his poems from *Troia Britannica* to Shakespeare in the expanded 1612 *Passionate Pilgrim*. The critique is therefore based on at least two separate offences caused by Jaggard.

determined by stationers, and not by the author'.[4] Moreover, the Quarto text contains some substantive errors which further destabilise the opposition between *The Passionate Pilgrim* and the *Sonnets*:

> Q contains the odd line that does not rhyme … a couplet that is repeated in two poems … a fifteen-line sonnet … a sonnet with a second line which repeats, unmetrically, a phrase from its first line … and a repeated error in which 'their' is printed for 'thy'.[5]

But perhaps the more important question is whether either of these texts served Shakespeare's interests, in terms of generating an admiring audience for his Sonnets.

This chapter argues that both the printed forms in which the Sonnets first appeared did more to alienate readers than to inspire their admiration. Indeed, the paratextual, bibliographical and narrative disappointments produced by these two texts arguably ruined the appreciation of the Sonnets before they had come to be read. This conclusion is important because in rejecting the old condemnations of Jaggard's piracy,[6] emphasising instead *The Passionate Pilgrim*'s 'importance to shaping a public authorial persona for Shakespeare',[7] critics have tended to overlook the fact that the cultural prestige of the poet was achieved at the expense of the Sonnets. Shakespeare became 'Shakespeare' through poems that were not his own, and thus his poetic canon marginalised the 'genuine' Sonnets from the start. It was only in their 'private', manuscript life, where they circulated individually, that the Sonnets achieved any real engagement with their readers, and the evidence suggests that this was focused around William Herbert, Earl of Pembroke – whether or not he was Mr W. H. It was in the writing of Pembroke's circle, and in the lyric verse of Pembroke himself and of his cousin Lady Mary Wroth, that a few Shakespeare Sonnets – most notably 128 and 116 – found an audience. This chapter, then, examines the Sonnets as a canon ostensibly defined by the 1609 Quarto, but not limited to that volume, and reveals the extent to which the Sonnets were forced into competition with both Shakespeare's narrative poems and *The Passionate Pilgrim* to their detriment.

---

[4] See https://shakespearedocumented.folger.edu/exhibition/document/apology-actors-thomas-heywoods-reply-passionate-pilgrim, accessed 28 November 2018.

[5] Shakespeare, *The Complete Sonnets and Poems*, ed. Burrow, p. 92.

[6] The most notorious is A. C. Swinburne who described *The Passionate Pilgrim* in 1894 as 'A worthless little volume of stolen and mutilated poetry, patched up and padded out with dirty and dreary doggrel', *Studies in Prose and Poetry*, p. 90.

[7] Francis X. Connor, '*The Passionate Pilgrim*', in Shakespeare, *The New Oxford Shakespeare*, ed. Taylor *et al.* (2017), p. 621.

1598–1599: Shakespeare's *Passionate* Sonnets

The first extant reference to Shakespeare's Sonnets seems to be that of Francis Meres in *Palladis Tamia. Wits Treasury being the Second Part of Wits Commonwealth* (1598), when he observes that among the moderns

> the sweete wittie soule of *Ovid* lives in mellifluous & hony-tongued *Shakespeare*, witnes his *Venus* and *Adonis*, his *Lucrece*, his sugred Sonnets among his private friends, &c.[8]

Here the Sonnets are placed after the narrative poems chronologically, but there may also be a sense of culmination – that Shakespeare's sweetness crystallises in the Sonnets. At the same time, Meres draws a distinction between the publicly available *Venus* and *Lucrece*, first published in 1593 and 1594 respectively, and the 'private' manuscript Sonnets. As such, the passage may serve as an advertisement for lyrics that have yet to come to light. Meres will subsequently mention Shakespeare among England's most famous sonneteers, Surrey, Wyatt, Sidney, Spenser and Daniel, these being 'the most passionate among us to bewaile and bemoane the perplexities of Love'.[9]

William Jaggard's *The Passionate Pilgrim by W. Shakespeare* was published in approximately 1599,[10] and includes twenty poems, only five of which are now agreed to have been written by Shakespeare. It opens with Sonnet 138 ('When my love swears that she is made of truth') and Sonnet 144 ('Two loves I have, of comfort and despair') – both versions usually judged inferior to those of the 1609 Quarto, but representing the first of Shakespeare's Sonnets to get into print.[11] The other three derive from *Love's Labour's Lost*, which had been published the year before, namely Longueville's sonnet to Maria (the third poem in *The Passionate Pilgrim* or PP3), Biron's sonnet to Rosaline (PP5) and Dumaine's lengthier

---

[8] Meres, *Palladis Tamia*, pp. 281–2.
[9] Ibid., p. 284.
[10] The title-page of the first edition has been lost, but it must have been printed after September 1598 when the printer, Thomas Judson, first set up his business. There was probably little gap between the first and second editions.
[11] Marotti describes the first *The Passionate Pilgrim* lyric as showing signs of being a 'memorial transcription' of Sonnet 138 (see 'Shakespeare's Sonnets as Literary Property', p. 151), a theory endorsed by James P. Bednarz who reminds us of the corruption suffered by Marlowe's 'Come live with me and be my love' in the same volume ('Canonizing Shakespeare', 255). Nevertheless, Edward Snow defends PP1 as 'an early Shakespearean version' of Sonnet 138 ('Loves of Comfort and Despair', 463), and subsequent editors have allowed that PP1 and 2 might 'preserve genuine Shakespearean variants' (Wells *et al.*, *William Shakespeare*, p. 455).

poem to Katherine (PP16).[12] The rest of the collection includes four erotic encounters between Venus and Adonis (PP4, 6, 9 and 11) of which at least one (PP11) was written by Bartholomew Griffin; two brief meditations on the deceptive nature of beauty (PP10, 13); a shepherd's lament for his suffering at the hands of an inconstant mistress (PP17); and a corrupted version of Christopher Marlowe's famous lyric 'Come live with me and be my love', with an abbreviated version of Walter Raleigh's answer (PP19). But although admirers of Shakespeare would have found very little of his work in this volume, they appear not to have recognised this fact, or not to have cared. The book seems to have quickly sold out its first edition, requiring a second in the same year, and a third more than a decade later in 1612. This makes it considerably more successful than most early modern editions of poetry,[13] and certainly more than the Quarto, which was never reprinted during Shakespeare's lifetime.

Jaggard's collection remains enigmatic at many points, but perhaps most frustrating is the difficulty of knowing the principles (and the manuscript) behind it. Jaggard was almost certainly aware that not all the poems he was publishing under Shakespeare's name were by Shakespeare.[14] PP8 ('If music and sweet poetry agree') and 20 ('As it fell upon a day') by Richard Barnfield appear in almost the exact form in which they had been published by Jaggard's brother, John, in *The Encomium of Lady Pecunia: or the Praise of Money* in 1598. PP11 ('Venus, with Adonis sitting by her') had been printed as Sonnet III in Bartholomew Griffin's *Fidessa, More Chaste than Kind* (1596).[15] It seems likely that either Jaggard came across a manuscript miscellany in which he recognised some Shakespeare, or that he 'obtained a hot property in the form of two genuine sonnets by Shakespeare',[16] and compiled a volume to showcase them, choosing accompanying poems either known to be by Shakespeare, or easily mistaken for his.[17] Disputes between

---

[12] Arthur Freeman and Paul Grinke have found evidence of a first 1597 quarto of the play in the private library catalogue of Viscount Conway (1594–1655) in 'Four New Shakespeare Quartos?'. Borrowings from this edition might explain variants between *The Passionate Pilgrim* lyrics and *Love's Labour's Lost* (1598).

[13] Lukas Erne and Tamsin Badcoe have demonstrated that only just over one in four poetry books was reprinted within twenty-five years of its first publication, 'The Popularity of Poetry Books in Print', 11.

[14] See Colin Burrow's more extensive summary of the possibilities in Shakespeare, *The Complete Sonnets and Poems*, ed. Burrow, pp. 76–7.

[15] For a full account of the previous printed and manuscript occurrences of eleven out of the twenty lyrics, see *The New Oxford Shakespeare*, ed. Taylor *et al.* (2017), pp. 620–22.

[16] Shakespeare, *The Complete Sonnets and Poems*, ed. Burrow, p. 76.

[17] Bednarz argues that 'Jaggard apparently copied 8 and 20 from his brother's edition of Barnfield's poetry, primarily because Barnfield admired and imitated Shakespeare and his poems could be passed off as Shakespeare's', 'Canonizing Shakespeare', 257.

authors and stationers recorded in the prefaces of other poetry collections suggest that neither was an unusual occurrence. In 1591, for example, the stationer, Richard Jones, published *Brittons Bowre of Delights*, a collection of lyrics attributed to the poet, Nicholas Breton, who enjoyed considerable success in the late 1590s, and whose work was mentioned favourably in the same breath as Shakespeare's.[18] Jones acknowledged the collection to have been prepared 'in the Authours absence',[19] but emphasised the lyrics' paternity in the titles – 'Brittons vision of Cupids complaint against his fowle father Vulcan for begetting him' and 'Brittons Farewell to Hope' – and by signing the volume off with 'FINIS. N. B. Gent'. However, the following year in a preface to *The Pilgrimage to Paradise* Breton declared:

> Gentlemen there hath beene of late printed in london by one Richarde Ioanes, a printer, a booke of english verses, entituled *Bretons bower of delights*: I protest it was donne altogether without my consent or knowledge, & many thinges of other mens mingled with few of mine, for except *Amoris Lachrimae*: an epitaph upon Sir Phillip Sydney, and one or two other toies, which I know not how he unhappily came by, I have no part with any of them: and so I beseech yee assuredly beleeve.[20]

And yet, rather than just an epitaph and 'one or two other toies', nearly half of the collection has now been attributed to Breton, who emerges as the most likely manuscript compiler and source.[21] His subsequent disavowal of the volume might be the result of a complaint by one of the unacknowledged contributors, or it might be an elaborate marketing ploy, 'a variant on the pervasive early modern *topos* whereby print publication was slighted or disavowed by the author or instigator'.[22] We need to approach with similar caution Francis Davison's distancing of himself from the verse miscellany *A Poetical Rhapsody*, published in 1602:

> If any except against the mixing (both at the beginning and ende of this booke) of diverse things written by great and learned Personages, with our meane and worthless Scriblings, I utterly disclaime it, as being done by the Printer, either to grace the forefront with Sir *Ph. Sidneys*, and others names, or to make the booke grow to a competent volume.[23]

---

[18] See Meres, *Palladis Tamia*: 'As *Pindarus, Anacreon* and *Callimachus* among the Greekes; and *Horace* and *Catullus* among the Latines are the best Lyrick Poets: so in this faculty the best among our Poets are *Spencer* (who excelleth in all kinds) *Daniel, Drayton, Shakespeare, Bretton*', pp. 282–3.

[19] Breton, *Brittons Bowre of Delights*, p. 3.

[20] Breton, *The Pilgrimage to Paradise*.

[21] See Gazzard, 'Nicholas Breton, Richard Jones, and Two Printed Verse Miscellanies', 80.

[22] Ibid., 81.

[23] Davison, 'The Preface', in *A Poetical Rhapsody*.

Yet it was Davison himself who had gathered lyrics by Mary and Philip Sidney, and who dedicated the volume to William Herbert. Moreover, as H. R. Woudhuysen notes, 'Davison acknowledged the importance of his publication of two new poems by Sidney by placing them first in the volume'.[24]

This pattern of a poet incorporating his own lyrics with those of others already familiar in print or manuscript, consulting with the stationer on publication, and then disassociating himself from the volume, might suggest a more collaborative relationship existed between Shakespeare and Jaggard on *The Passionate Pilgrim*.[25] Yet Edwin Willoughby's conjecture in 1934 that Jaggard inherited 'a small manuscript commonplace book of verse, chiefly amorous, such as Elizabethan gentlemen were fond of compiling'[26] is more convincing for a number of reasons. Not only does it require less ingenuity and enterprise on the part of the publisher,[27] and less humility and self-effacement on the part of Shakespeare, it explains why there is such a discrepancy between what *The Passionate Pilgrim* appears to be and what it is.

The compiler of this miscellany was clearly interested in the sonnet form – the first fourteen poems include six lyrics that we would recognise as sonnets, as well as eight that would have fitted the looser Elizabethan definition, thereby 'giv[ing] the impression of a sonnet collection, or even a sequence'.[28] Moreover, *Love's Labour's Lost*, upon which the compiler draws heavily, is a play peculiarly concerned with sonnets. Not only does it suspend the action in 4.3 so that these lyrics may be read aloud, it also refers to the word 'sonnet' more than any other play in the Shakespeare canon, not only in the text but in the stage directions: '*He reads the Sonnet*'; '*Dumaine reads his Sonnet*'.[29] Furthermore, the layout of the 1598 Quarto

24 Woudhuysen, *Sir Philip Sidney and the Circulation of Manuscripts 1558–1640*, p. 291.
25 H. R. Woudhuysen hints that Shakespeare might have worked with Jaggard in 'The Foundations of Shakespeare's Text', 80. For a looser sense of the anthology as a 'collaborative' work, see Connor, 'Shakespeare, Poetic Collaboration and *The Passionate Pilgrim*', 125.
26 Willoughby, *A Printer of Shakespeare*, p. 48.
27 I agree with John Roe: 'as likely as not the common-place book compiler had done Jaggard's work for him, the printer astutely spotting the marketing advantages of the sequence', Shakespeare, *The Poems*, ed. Roe, p. 58.
28 Ibid.
29 Although we cannot be sure of the authorship of Shakespearean stage directions, those in the 1598 quarto (thought to be based on scribal copy of foul papers) are generally vague and lacking in detail, suggesting that Shakespeare included them on the assumption that they would be fleshed out by the company. The fact that the stage directions in *LLL* 4.3 are so specific might reflect Shakespeare's own interest in the sonnet form at this moment in his career. On further sonnets embedded within the play, see Walter Cohen's introduction to the Norton edition of *Love's Labor's Lost* (2015).

text makes these lyrics more accessible (and detachable) by italicising and indenting two out of three, as though offering them up for anthologisation. There is even a ¶ (pilcrow) immediately before 'Did not the heavenly rhetoric', which may have been copied over from the manuscript – perhaps Shakespeare's reminder to himself to go back and insert 'just about any "sugared sonnet" he had to hand'.[30] Finally, we should note the curious existence of a second title-page in *The Passionate Pilgrim*, 'SONNETS to Sundry Notes of Music', which appears three-quarters of the way through, though none of the poems thereafter is a sonnet. The existence of this title-page has never been satisfactorily explained,[31] but it might reflect the title of the original miscellany.

By contrast, the book of *The Passionate Pilgrim* strongly suggests that although Jaggard knew that the name 'Shakespeare' would increase sales, he felt much less confident about the word 'sonnet' – and he may have been right. According to Lukas Erne and Tamsin Badcoe's analysis of the sale of early modern poetry books, sonnets had lost much of their initial purchase on the market at the time Jaggard was preparing *The Passionate Pilgrim*. The early success of Sidney's *Astrophil and Stella* (1591), Constable's *Diana* (1592) and Daniel's *Delia* (1592), which had run into multiple editions, was not sustained by later poetic efforts: 'If we discount reprints in larger collections, only 2 out of 30 sonnet collections published between 1593 and 1615 received a second edition and none a third.'[32] The modern assumption that there was an audience eager for Shakespeare's Sonnets is partly a reflection of our own post-Romantic fascination with them, which we project back into the late sixteenth century by means of Francis Meres, quoted above but worth revisiting:

> As the soule of *Euphorbus* was thought to live in *Pythagoras*: so the sweete wittie soule of *Ovid* lives in mellifluous & hony-tongued *Shakespeare*, witness his *Venus* and *Adonis*, his *Lucrece*, his sugred Sonnets among his private friends, &c.

Duncan-Jones is not alone in assuming that '[t]his passage must have stimulated intense curiosity in the book-buying public, creating a ready market for publication of those "sugred Sonnets"'.[33] Yet it seems unlikely that most book-buyers would ever have seen it. Not only is Shakespeare's name not included in the preliminary list of 'The Authours both sacred

[30] Connor, 'Shakespeare, Poetic Collaboration and *The Passionate Pilgrim*', 128.
[31] See Shakespeare, *The Complete Sonnets and Poems*, ed. Burrow, p. 76.
[32] Erne and Badcoe, 'The Popularity of Poetry Books in Print, 1583–1622', 20.
[33] Shakespeare, *Shakespeare's Sonnets*, ed. Duncan-Jones, p. 83.

and profane, out of which these similitudes are for the most part gathered' (unlike Lyly and Sidney), but the essay which contains these allusions, 'A Comparative Discourse of our English Poets, with the *Greek, Latine, and Italian Poets*', occurs 279 pages in, without any advertisement on the book's title-page. Within this essay, the particular reference comes five pages in, after a succession of paragraphs beginning 'As [classical author] … was … so [early modern author] is …' which certainly strain the reader's pleasure in anaphora.[34] Perhaps Meres was bearing witness to a knowledge of private sonnets which the majority of the book-buying public had never seen, but it could equally be that their privacy meant very few people knew of their existence.

Much more widely known were Shakespeare's narrative poems, and it seems undeniable that Jaggard became interested in publishing poetry by Shakespeare because of the remarkable success of *Venus and Adonis* (1593), which outstripped the publication of any single Shakespeare play during his lifetime.[35] Jaggard probably approached the bookseller, William Leake, with *The Passionate Pilgrim* because the latter had acquired the copyright of *Venus* three years earlier. Not only would the title-pages of the 1599 editions of *Venus and Adonis* and *The Passionate Pilgrim* direct the reader to the same bookseller's stall, 'at the Greyhound in Paules Churchyard', the latter may have been published in octavo format so that it could be bound with the new *Venus*.[36] But more than simply a 'companion volume' to *Venus and Adonis*,[37] or even its material bedfellow, I would argue that *The Passionate Pilgrim* was marketed by Jaggard so as to allow for the possibility of its being Shakespeare's third narrative poem.[38]

---

[34] I am not convinced by MacDonald P. Jackson's theory that Shakespeare read this passage and was moved to write the 'Rival Poet' sequence in response, but even if he had been, that does not mean that the majority of the book-buying public had read this comparison. See 'Francis Meres and the Cultural Contexts of Shakespeare's Rival Poet Sonnets'.

[35] Erne and Badcoe describe it as 'the best-selling poetry book of its time, going through more editions that any other of the 701 poetry books first published between 1583 and 1622', 'The Popularity of Poetry Books in Print, 1583–1622', 21. Erne notes that *Venus* went through ten editions, compared to only six for Shakespeare's most popular play, *Henry IV Part One*, 13.

[36] Tara L. Lyons notes that the change to octavo format strengthened the narrative poems' links with Ovid's poetry, also printed by Richard Field and John Harrison in octavo, and that these little books suggested a greater intimacy between reader and author. See 'Shakespeare in Print before 1623', pp. 8–9.

[37] Shakespeare, *The Complete Sonnets and Poems*, ed. Burrow, p. 75.

[38] The epyllion was considerably more popular than the sonnet in publishing terms. In 1598, five epyllia were published, including two reprints, Marlowe's *Hero and Leander* and R. S.'s *Phillis and Flora,* as opposed to one sonnet sequence, a reprint of *Delia*. In 1599, there were four epyllia (including two reprints of Shakespeare's *Venus*) compared with one edition of sonnets, Jean de Nesme's *The Miracle of the Peace in Fraunce* (Erne and Badcoe, 'The Popularity of Poetry Books in Print, 1583–1622', 18, 22).

Critics have expressed perplexity and not a little annoyance at Jaggard's choice of title. Swinburne described it as 'senseless and preposterous', and Duncan-Jones has suggested that 'Jaggard's inane and irrelevant title may have irritated Shakespeare almost as much as the ascription to him of lyrics by Griffin, Barnfield, Marlowe, and others'.[39] For our purposes, 'The Passionate Pilgrim' is intriguing because it perpetuates ambiguity about the contents. In 1582, Thomas Watson's *Hekatompathia or Passionate Centurie of Love* had described itself as a 'Booke of Passionate Sonnetes', narrating the story of the poet's courtship of the beloved, his disappointment and eventual renunciation of love. The descriptions which accompany each sonnet refer to them as 'passions': for example, no. 1: 'The Author in this Passion taketh but occasion to open his estate in love'; no. 2: 'In this passion the Author describeth in how piteous a case the hart of a lover is'; no. 3: 'This passion is all framed in manner of a dialogue, wherein the Author talketh with his owne heart'. Three years before the publication of Jaggard's collection, 'passionate' had once again appeared in the title of a sonnet sequence: William Smith's *Chloris, or the Complaint of the passionate despised Shepheard* (1596). If 'passionate' implies a central protagonist – a consistent lyric speaker – whose experience provides a narrative structure for the whole work, then the protagonist of *The Passionate Pilgrim* might have been presumed to be Shakespeare, suggesting that fascination with the poet's private experience was already a potential selling-point. Patrick Cheney observes the connections with *Romeo and Juliet*:

> By presenting Romeo as a pilgrim who loves a lady, Shakespeare puts a passionate pilgrim on the stage. Since Romeo co-performs the self-conscious literary form of the sonnet in the theatre, we can note his resemblance to his author, as Juliet entreats: 'You kiss by th'book' (110). Jaggard's 1599 title page, then, presents Shakespeare as a poet of desire within a religious cult of love.[40]

However, this may not be the only amorous pilgrim with which the collection aligned itself.

'The Tale of Dom Diego and Ginevra' is an Italian novella which may have generated additional narrative expectations around Jaggard's title. The tale appeared in Bandello and Belleforest, before being translated

---

[39] See Swinburne, *Studies in Prose and Poetry*, p. 90, and Duncan-Jones, 'What are Shakespeare's Sonnets Called?', 5–6.

[40] Cheney, *Shakespeare, National Poet-Playwright*, p. 156. One of the *Passionate Pilgrim*'s lyrics, 'Good night, good rest, ah, neither be my share' (no. 14) might echo Romeo's emotions after the balcony scene, acting as an imaginative extension of the Shakespearean original, much as the *Passionate Pilgrim*'s Venus lyrics might be said to do for *Venus and Adonis*.

into English by George Whetstone, Geoffrey Fenton and William Painter. In Fenton's version, Dom Diego is unjustly accused of infidelity by his beloved, Genivera, and takes off into the mountains of the Pyrenees to live a life of 'hard pennance', dressed as a pilgrim.[41] He spends his time engraving elegiac lyrics into the trees and rocks until even the narrator loses patience: 'here let us leave our amorous hermit full of passions in his simple cloister or cave'.[42] Dom Diego's poetic potential was recognised by Richard Linche who included a narrative poem on this subject alongside a sonnet sequence in his *Diella, Certaine Sonnets, adioyned to the amorous Poeme of Dom Diego and Ginevra*, published in 1596. Indeed, Linche incorporates the narrative into the sequence, pausing in Sonnet 38 to urge the beloved 'Harken awhile (*Diella*) to a storie', and remarking in the concluding sonnet that he too will turn pilgrim: 'Forced by thee (thou mercy-wanting mayd)/ must I abandon this my native soyle,/ Hoping my sorrows heate wilbe allayd/ by absence, tyme, necessity or toyle.'[43] Three years later, when Jaggard was trying to think of a title, he might possibly have remembered Linche's tale, which uses the same sixain stanza as *Venus and Adonis*, and contains a number of obvious allusions to Shakespeare's poem. Not only does Linche describe Diego as an equally beautiful but more pliant version of Adonis ('Hunting he lov'd, nor did he scorne to love'), he insists on Ginevra's kisses being 'More honny sweete, then *Venus* gave *Adonis*'.[44]

But if a 'Passionate Pilgrim' might be the protagonist of a sonnet sequence or narrative poem, Jaggard's title-page strengthens the expectation of a narrative poem through its very refusal to explain itself.[45] In the case of both sonnet sequences and single-author collections, the title-page conventionally demonstrates the contents' formal variety. We might

---

[41] Fenton, *Certaine Tragical Discourses*, no. 13, p. 281.

[42] Ibid., p. 295.

[43] Linche, *Diella, Certaine Sonnets, adioyned to the amorous Poeme of Dom Diego and Ginevra*, lines 5–8, last page.

[44] Ibid., p. F2r.

[45] The strangeness of the title-page not describing what kind of poems it contains has been unfortunately obscured by what may be a mistake in the *Short Title Catalogue* which reads: '22341 – [Anr ed.] The passionate pilgrim. Or certaine amorous sonnets. (Sonnets to sundry notes of musicke). 8°. [T. Judson?] f. W Jaggard, sold by W. Leake, 1599', p. 327. However, on neither of the title pages for the two surviving copies of the 1599 edition do we find this phrase 'certaine amorous sonnets', nor does it appear in the Stationers' Register, since Jaggard did not gain permission for any of these volumes. Not until the 1612 edition of *The Passionate Pilgrim* do we find the title including the phrase 'Or certaine amorous sonnets'. This causes confusion in Burrow's excellent edition of the poems, where he refers to the second 1599 edition of *The Passionate Pilgrim* under this title, which it never possessed in the sixteenth century, Shakespeare, *The Complete Sonnets and Poems*, ed. Burrow, p. 75.

consider Thomas Lodge's *Phillis: Honoured with Pastoralls, Sonnets, Elegies and amorous delights* (1593), Richard Brathwait's *The Poet's Willow: or, The Passionate Shepherd: With sundry delightfull, and no lesse Passionate Sonnets* (1614) or even *Brittons Bowre of Delights* (1591, 1597) which boasts of *Many, most delectable and fine devices, of rare Epitaphes, pleasant Poems, Pastorals and Sonets*. Ceri Sullivan has argued for more critical engagement with the extended titles of early modern books, whose generic descriptor acts 'not as a classification of the text by the reader for its formal qualities, but as an instruction to the reader to take up a series of appropriate positions before the text as it progresses … genre, everyone agrees, is an effect of expectation'.[46] On this basis, the title-page of *The Passionate Pilgrim* is strikingly blank. And yet, its appearance was familiar from the layout of early modern erotic epyllia, such as Marlowe's *Hero and Leander* (1598) or Shakespeare's *Lucrece* (repr. 1600), where the identification of the narrative subject matter is apparently all that is required.

The indeterminacy of *The Passionate Pilgrim*'s title-page – its refusal to categorise what kind of work by Shakespeare this is – may have been a deliberate marketing strategy by Jaggard. Poets in the 1590s often complained of the bookstall-browser's laziness in engaging with anything more than a few words on a title-page. As Thomas Churchyard put it in his dedication to *The Mirror of Man, and Manners of Men* (1594):

> Some reades awhile, but nothing buyes at all,
> For in two lines, they give a pretty gesse,
> What doth the boke contayne such schollers thinke,
> To spende no pence, for paper, pen and inke.[47]

Moreover, Tiffany Stern has pointed out examples of playbooks where the genre of the play was deliberately kept from the title-page in response to changing theatrical fashions.[48] Perhaps Jaggard withheld 'sonnets' from his title-page 'to sell a product and have the buyer read the book at home'.[49] If we imagine *The Passionate Pilgrim*'s readers taking their copies home in this expectation, what must the first reading experience of Shakespeare's Sonnets in print have been like?

Upon turning past the title-page, the reader was surprised to find – nothing. No authorial dedication, address to the reader or supporting eulogy by an admiring fellow poet. Not only were these standard

[46] Sullivan, 'Disposable Elements?', 647.
[47] Churchyard, *The Mirror of Man, and Manners of Men*, A2v.
[48] Stern, *Documents of Performance in Early Modern England*, p. 57.
[49] Voss, 'Books for Sale', 755.

Hen my Loue ſweares that ſhe is made of truth,
I do beleeue her (though I know ſhe lies)
That ſhe might thinke me ſome vntutor'd youth,
Vnſkilful in the worlds falſe forgeries.
Thus vainly thinking that ſhe thinkes me young,
Although I know my yeares be paſt the beſt :
I ſmiling, credite her falſe ſpeaking toung,
Outfacing faults in loue, with loues ill reſt.
But wherefore ſayes my loue that ſhe is young ?
And wherefore ſay not I, that I am old :
O, Loues beſt habit's in a ſoothing toung,
d Age in loue, loues not to haue yeares told.
herefore I'le lye with Loue, and loue with me,
Since that our faultes in loue thus ſmother'd be.

Figure 1.1 Sonnet 138 in *The Passionate Pilgrim* (1599), A3r
© Folger Shakespeare Library, STC 22341.8

features of published sonnet sequences and single-authored collections, but Shakespeare's 'other' two narrative poems had both appeared with dedications to Southampton, signed by the poet. The impression of anonymity would have become more intense when the reader moved beyond *The Passionate Pilgrim*'s silent paratext and found a single sonnet, untitled and unnumbered (see Figure 1.1), followed by a blank verso page, and a further discrete sonnet on the recto. At this point, the reader probably assumed s/he was reading a sonnet sequence. The prestige afforded by the abundance of space on the page, as well as the decorative borders top and bottom, recalls the layout of the most fashionable sequences of the 1590s, including Daniel's *Delia* and Lodge's *Phillis*.[50] Upon this assumption, rather different narrative expectations would have come into play. As Carol Thomas Neely has observed:

> Sonnet sequences do not 'tell a story' if to do so implies a straightforward narrative progression from sonnet to sonnet throughout. Neither are they 'prolonged lyric meditation', collections of random poems on related themes. They are something in between.[51]

And yet, opening sonnets are expected to introduce the poet-lover and his beloved, and to present the lyrics inspired by the former's passion. They are also where the sequence is most explicit about its narrative structure: 'often describ[ing] the author's infatuation prospectively and retrospectively, looking forward to the experiences recorded in the sequence and backward on the outcome of the affair'.[52] This was a strategy made famous by Petrarch in the *Rime Sparse*, and the most obvious narrative expectations that the title 'The Passionate Pilgrim' sets up are based on this archetype: a frustrated lover attempts to overcome his beloved's indifference, her cruelty and her chastity through passionate persuasion. But the reader who came to PP1 (Sonnet 138) for the familiar Petrarchan narrative would have found his/her expectations vertiginously disappointed:

> When my love swears that she is made of truth,
> I do believe her (though I know she lies),
> That she might think me some untutored youth,
> Unskilful in the world's false forgeries.
> Thus vainly thinking that she thinks me young,
> Although I know my years be past the best,

---

[50] See Marcy L. North's description of the standard sonnet sequence of the 1590s in 'The Sonnets and Book History', p. 207.

[51] Neely, 'The Structure of English Renaissance Sonnet Sequences', 362.

[52] North, 'The Sonnets and Book History', pp. 207–8.

> I, smiling, credit her false-speaking tongue,
> Outfacing faults in love with love's ill rest.
> But wherefore says my love that she is young?
> And wherefore say not I that I am old?
> O, love's best habit's in a soothing tongue,
> And age, in love, loves not to have years told.
> > Therefore I'll lie with love, and love with me,
> > Since that our faults in love thus smothered be.[53]

Rather than expressing the male speaker's deepest truth, 'unclasp[ing] the book of [his] charged soul',[54] the poem focuses obsessively on the lies that the lovers tell one another, and on the woman's rhetorical manipulation of the man, characterised by 'false forgeries' and 'her false-speaking tongue'. This re-gendering of amorous persuasion may have been even more surprising than the fact that, as Michael R. G. Spiller puts it, 'for the first time in the entire history of the sonnet, the desired object is *flawed*'.[55] This is not the chaste Petrarchan mistress one was expecting, but a woman forced to swear oaths that she is 'made [maid] of truth', whose sexual submission is taken for granted in the couplet: 'Therefore I'll lie with love, and love with me', and whose genitalia may be alluded to in a pun on 'fault'. But if these are not the familiar protagonists of the sonnet sequence, there is also something discombobulating about the plot. We have begun *in medias res*, with the beloved already won. The expected *impasse* is an erotic one – they will continue to have sex with one another, without gaining any greater intimacy or understanding – rather than a Petrarchan one in which the male speaker obsessively articulates his feelings, but the fulfilment of his desire recedes ever further into the distance.

The movement from PP1 to PP2 not only affirms the impression that this is not what an opening sonnet is supposed to do, but provokes questions about whether this is a sonnet sequence at all, for the characters of the first lyric do not obviously recur in the second:

> Two loves I have, of comfort and despair,
> That like two spirits do suggest me still:
> My better angel is a man (right fair),
> My worser spirit a woman (coloured ill).
> To win me soon to hell, my female evil
> Tempteth my better angel from my side,

---

[53] All quotations from *The Passionate Pilgrim* are taken from *Shakespeare's Poems*, ed. Duncan-Jones and Woodhuysen.

[54] Daniel, *Delia*, B1r, Sonnet 1.

[55] Spiller, *The Development of the Sonnet*, p. 156.

And would corrupt my saint to be a devil,
Wooing his purity with her fair pride.
And whether that my angel be turned fiend,
Suspect I may (yet not directly tell):
For being both to me, both to each, friend,
I guess one angel in another's hell.
   The truth I shall not know, but live in doubt,
   Till my bad angel fire my good one out.

Initially, the two lyric voices might seem to resemble one another: they share a fondness for direct address through arresting monosyllables: 'When my love swears …'; 'Two loves I have …' Both refer to a particular situation in the present which seems unlikely to be resolved, due to the speaker's refusal to confront reality: 'The truth I shall not know, but live in doubt'. Yet there is very little resemblance between the naively garrulous first mistress, and the devious beloved of PP2, and no explanation of who the 'better angel' might be. The Sonnets' tone is also significantly different: PP1 recalls the urbanity of the Ovidian epyllion, with its pleasure in making pronouncements about love ('O, love's best habit's in a soothing tongue'); PP2 reaches back to a medieval, psychomachic tradition which explores the terrible moral and spiritual consequences of lust. The sense of disorientation created by the printing of Sonnets 138 and 144 at the start of a collection seems likely to have troubled its early readers, as it does readers today. The title of the book would seem to imply 'a continuous persona … mak[ing] his amorous pilgrimage',[56] but there is no obvious narrative, dramatic or even lyric continuity between PP1 and PP2.

That said, there are clearly benefits to reading the poems in this new context. Sasha Roberts has argued that *The Passionate Pilgrim* reveals 'how the homoerotic and misogynist tones of Shakespeare's sonnets are dependent on their specific structure and sequencing in the 1609 quarto'.[57] In the latter, 138 would follow 137, 'Thou blind fool love', in which the lover condemns his own poor judgement for having assumed virtue and chastity ('fair truth') from an appearance of beauty, when morally and sexually this face is 'foul'. The crude assertions of the woman's promiscuity – 'the bay where all men ride' – inevitably infect the opening line of 138, and that mistress' declaration of 'truth'. Divorced from this context, PP1 has a lighter and more comic tone. Similarly, PP2 opens up a greater range of interpretations for 'coloured ill' than can be afforded by 144, where it is

---

[56] Duncan-Jones, 'What are Shakespeare's Sonnets Called?', 5.
[57] Roberts, *Reading Shakespeare's Poems*, p. 154.

dominated by preceding associations of blackness with moral turpitude. These alternatives include that she wears cosmetics and that she has been 'put in a false light or represented unfairly'.[58] Substantive variants between PP and Q versions also suggest that Shakespeare may have intensified the misogyny of these poems in the process of revision. Where PP1 acknowledges the speaker's part in his self-deception ('Although I know my years be past the best'), Q blames the woman: 'Although she knows my days are past the best'. Both poems begin with the same pun on 'made'/'maid', but PP1 does not pursue the notion of her unchastity, offering 'But wherefore says my love that she is young' in place of Q's 'But wherefore says she not she is unjust?'. This might be an effect of inaccurate memorial transcription, which 'ruins Shakespeare's witty differentiation of lies involving her unfaithfulness and his vanity',[59] but it also represents an interesting challenge to the Quarto's juxtaposition of male fidelity and female betrayal. In the case of PP2, the mistress stands accused of 'fair pride', the latter term suggesting 'splendor; show of finery; gorgeousness',[60] rather than Q's 'foul pride'. The tone of the couplet is also subtly different, with PP2 gesturing towards a past in which they were all three united (and rendered equivalent) by affection: 'For being both to me, both to each, friend …', as opposed to Q's 'But being both from me …'.

And yet, if encountering Sonnets 138 and 144 in *The Passionate Pilgrim* enables modern readers to re-think their potential and to encounter them in a less misogynistic mood, Shakespeare's original readers seem hardly to have thought of them at all. Commonplace books and verse miscellanies published in 1600 demonstrate a total lack of interest in these two Sonnets, despite their prominent position at the front of the volume. For example, when Nicholas Ling sat down to compile the verse miscellany *England's Helicon*, he appears to have had *The Passionate Pilgrim* open before him, but he overlooks 138 and 144 in favour of four lyrics printed after the inset title-page 'SONNETS. To Sundry Notes of Music'.[61] Other selections are drawn from Elizabethan songbooks, suggesting that Ling favoured *The Passionate Pilgrim*'s more lyrical verse over the two Sonnets which lack any

[58] Bell, 'Rethinking Shakespeare's Dark Lady', p. 302.
[59] Bednarz, 'Canonizing Shakespeare', 255.
[60] Booth, *Shakespeare's Sonnets*, p. 498.
[61] These are PP16 ('On a day'), PP17 ('My flocks feed not'), PP19 ('Live with me') and PP20 ('As it fell'). PP16 is the only one that Ling attributed to Shakespeare. He corrected the false attribution of the others, citing the authors of PP17 and PP20 as 'Ignoto', and PP19 as Marlowe and Raleigh. For further discussion of Ling's alterations, see Bednarz, 'Canonizing Shakespeare', 260–2.

history of musical setting in the seventeenth century.[62] The fact that they do not fit the collection's pastoral theme may also have been problematic, though this was not an insuperable obstacle in the case of PP16, from *Love's Labour's Lost*, in which Ling replaces the word 'lover' with 'Sheepheard' (line 7). Perhaps most telling is Ling's eye for poems which were already popular. 'My flocks feed not' had been published anonymously in Thomas Weelkes' *Madrigals to 3, 4, 5 and 6 Voices* (1597), and could be found in a manuscript miscellany, dated *c.* 1596–1601.[63] 'Come live with me and be my love' survives in three manuscript copies, potentially predating Jaggard's collection.[64] It had also been alluded to in *The Jew of Malta* (*c.* 1590) and *The Merry Wives of Windsor* (*c.* 1597),[65] and would appear in a further seven manuscripts, dated *c.* 1600–1660s. 'As it fell' had already been printed in *Poems: In divers Humors* (1598) and was subsequently reprinted as a ballad *c.* 1625, and included in a manuscript belonging to Katherine Packer *c.* 1638.[66] All of these poems were considerably more popular than Sonnets 138 and 144, whose restricted circulation may have prevented them from being copied before 1599, but which had almost no influence *after* publication. Only 138 is extant in manuscript before *c.* 1640, in a single miscellany where it is copied from *The Passionate Pilgrim* with five other poems from that collection.[67]

Not only were Shakespeare's Sonnets competing with more popular contemporary lyrics, they were overshadowed by his own narrative poems. In John Bodenham's commonplace book, *Belvedere* (1600), Shakespeare is the fourth most frequently quoted author after Drayton, Spenser and Daniel, with a total of 214 entries. Of this number, 112 are taken from the

---

[62] On the later MS settings of two other *Passionate Pilgrim* lyrics, PP4 and PP11, by John Wilson (*c.* 1630–40), see *The New Oxford Shakespeare*, ed. Taylor *et al.* (2017), pp. 643–7.

[63] See BL Harley MS 6910. Centuries later this poem would become the occasion for Swinburne's excoriation of *The Passionate Pilgrim*, when he found it included in *Lyra Elegantiarum* (1891) under Shakespeare's name.

[64] These are the copy included in Simon Forman's alchemical papers (*c.* 1598), Bodleian MS Ashmole 1486, 2, f.6v; a copy in the miscellany of John Lilliat *c.* 1589–99, Bodleian, MS Rawl. Poet, 148, f. 96v; and the miscellany once owned by John Thornborough, Bishop of Limerick, which appears to be late sixteenth to early seventeenth century, Folger MS 2.e.28, f. 100v. See Beal, *Index of English Literary Manuscripts*, vol. 1, Part 2, 325.

[65] There may also be an allusion in John Donne's poem, 'The Bait', whose date could be as early as 1593.

[66] See Harvard b MS Eng 1107. A further popular lyric from *The Passionate Pilgrim*, though excluded from *England's Helicon*, is no. 18, 'When as thine eye hath chose the dame', which offers witty advice about women to an implied male friend. Of this poem, three extant manuscript copies remain: one in a verse miscellany compiled by Anne Cornwallis *c.* 1580s–90s; one roughly contemporary with *The Passionate Pilgrim*; and one in a miscellany owned by Joseph Hall, *c.* 1640, Folger MS V.a.339.

[67] See Hall's miscellany, f197v.

plays, with *Richard II* (47), *Edward III* (23) and *Romeo and Juliet* (13) the most popular, but these are outstripped by excerpts from the narrative poems, with *Lucrece* appearing ninety-one times and *Venus* thirty-four. In Robert Allot's *England's Parnassus* (1600), Shakespeare appears as the ninth most popular poet, but we search in vain for any lyrics from *The Passionate Pilgrim*, his poetic output being represented by thirty-nine extracts from *Lucrece* and twenty-six from *Venus*, as opposed to thirty from the plays.

It is easy to see why the narrative poems should have found favour in commonplace books, for they were stuffed with aphorisms and naturally lent themselves to thematic organisation. *Venus and Adonis* includes such truisms as 'Affection is a coal that must be cooled;/ Else, suffered, it will set the heart on fire',[68] and extracts from the poem are anthologised in *England's Parnassus* under the heading 'Affection', but also 'Audacitie', 'Danger', 'Griefe', 'Iealousie', 'Lechery', 'Love', 'Miserie', 'Dalliance' and 'Feare'.[69] Moreover, the impulse to quote from *Venus and Adonis* was driven by its reputation as 'a sex manual or handbook for wooers'.[70] In *The Return from Parnassus, Part One* (1600), a play performed by students at St John's College, Cambridge, the foolish courtier, Gullio, rehearses both Venus' lines and the narrator's ironic commentary in his attempted seduction: 'Pardon faire lady, thoughe sicke thoughted Gullio maks a maine unto thee, and like a bouldfaced sutore gins to woo thee … Thrise fairer than my selfe, thus I began,/ The gods faire riches, sweete above compare,/ Staine to all Nimphes, [m]ore lovely then a man/ More white and red than doves and roses are.'[71] Less commented on, but arguably more significant, is the fact that Gullio then asks aspiring poet, Ingenioso, to write him lyrics in the style of the three poets he most admires: Chaucer, Spenser and Shakespeare. Ingenioso produces close parodies of *Troilus and Criseyde* and *The Faerie Queene*, but the poem he offers as Shakespearean betrays no obvious source:

> Faire Venus, queene of beutie and of love,
> Thy red doth stayne the blushing of the morne,
> Thy snowie neck shameth the milke white dove,

[68] *Venus and Adonis* in *Shakespeare's Poems*, ed. Duncan-Jones and Woudhuysen, lines 387–8.
[69] PP1's 'love's best habit's in a soothing tongue' seems the most likely quotation, though it was not particularly stable, appearing in Q as 'love's best habit is in seeming trust'. The couplet pun on 'lie/ lie' had appeared in a brief epigram attributed to John Donne in a miscellany dated *c.* 1630 ('You say I lye, I say you ly, iudg whether,/ But if we both ly, lets ly both together'), but no records of Shakespeare's version survive. See Bishop, *Robert Bishop's Commonplace Book*, no. 42, p. 29.
[70] Duncan-Jones, 'Much Ado with Red and White', 496.
[71] Leishman, *The Three Parnassus Plays (1598–1600)*, ll 983–5, 995–8.

> Thy presence doth this naked worlde adorne;
> Gazinge on thee all other nymphes I scorne.
> When ere thou dyest slowe shine that Satterday,
> Beutie and grace must sleep with thee for aye.[72]

J. B. Leishman remarks that 'These lines, intended as an imitation of Shakespeare, are presumably original',[73] but the joke depends upon the audience being able to recognise the verse that is being parodied. Perhaps Ingenioso was referring to a Shakespeare Sonnet familiar to university students in manuscript, but one that was never printed in the Quarto.[74] C. H. Hobday has argued that the Venus and Adonis sonnets in *The Passionate Pilgrim* (4, 6 and 9) were early efforts by Shakespeare, rendered obsolete by the narrative poem.[75] More specifically, Ingenioso's lyric bears some resemblance to PP9: 'Fair was the morn, when the fair queen of love/ .../ Paler for sorrow than her milk-white dove.'[76] It seems a fair assumption that the missing second line would have contained some allusion to red and/or blushing – the opposition of red and white being one that Shakespeare plays on relentlessly in both the narrative poems. If PP9 was indeed the source for Ingenioso's parody, it serves to reiterate the fact that Shakespeare's Venerian poetry was more admired than his non-mythological Sonnets.

Another important witness to contemporary taste at the end of the century is John Weever's eulogy, 'Ad Gulielmum Shakespeare', in *Epigrammes in the oldest cut, and newest fashion* (1599):

> Honey-tongued Shakespeare, when I saw thine issue,
> I swore Apollo got them, and none other;
> Their rosy-tainted features, clothed in tissue,
> Some heaven-born goddess said to be their mother:
> Rose-cheeked Adonis, with his amber tresses,
> Fair fire-hot Venus charming him to love her;
> Chaste Lucretia, virgin-like her dresses,
> Proud lust-stung Tarquin, seeking still to prove her;
> Romeo, Richard – more, whose names I know not –
> Their sugared tongues and power-attractive beauty

---

[72] Ibid., 1191–7.

[73] Ibid., 192, fn. 1191–7.

[74] Sasha Roberts describes St John's College as 'a literary hotbed in the late sixteenth century; a centre for new writing and manuscript transmission', *Reading Shakespeare's Poems*, p. 66. It may not be a coincidence that a copy of Sonnet 2 would be found in a manuscript miscellany belong to St John's in the 1630s–40s (see Chapter 2).

[75] See Hobday, 'Shakespeare's Venus and Adonis Sonnets'.

[76] *Shakespeare's Poems*, ed. Duncan-Jones and Woudhuysen, p. 396.

> Say they are saints, although that saints they show not,
> For thousands vows to them subjective duty;
> They burn in love; thy children, Shakespeare, het them,
> Go, woo thy muse, more nymphish brood beget them.[77]

Just like contemporary miscellanists, Weever prioritises the narrative poems over the plays, and places a surprising emphasis on the *characters* of Venus and Adonis, Lucrece and Tarquin, ahead of the dramatic ('Romeo, Richard – more whose names I know not').

Traces of hostility are detectable in phrases such as 'rosie-tainted features' and 'Rose-checkt Adonis' in the original spelling (usually taken as misprints), whilst 'sugared tongues' and 'saints they show not' implicitly condemn the seductive power of Shakespeare's poetry.[78] Given that this is the only sonnet in a collection of epigrams, and one that repeats the Shakespearean rhyme scheme, Ernst Honigmann suggests that Weever was having a dig at the Sonnets, which he had read in a manuscript provided by Francis Meres.[79] And yet, Meres shows no familiarity with the Sonnets directly, and this poem is probably more valuable as evidence that in 1599 what readers wanted from Shakespearean poetry were tales of seduction and a language to make the reader 'burn in love'. This is not the kind of response that 138 and 144 were likely to produce.

It would be another decade before book-buyers would gain access to a wider range of Shakespeare Sonnets, including a few that might satisfy their taste for bawdy. There is, however, one tantalising hint of an earlier intervention. On 3 January 1600, 'A booke called *Amours* by J. D. with certain *other sonnetes* by W. S.' was entered into the Stationers' Register, but no copies have been found, suggesting that it may never have reached print. This 'W. S.' might have been William Smith, the author of the sonnet sequence *Chloris* (1596), who had also managed to get a poem into *England's Helicon*,[80] but it might also be Shakespeare, who hereby 'took immediate measures to put right the wrong done to him by Jaggard in 1599'.[81] Which Sonnets would have been made available through this book is a matter of pure conjecture. Duncan-Jones suggests that 138 and 144 would have been there:

---

[77] Quoted by Honigmann, *John Weever*, p. 110.
[78] For further discussion of Weever's critique of Shakespeare, see Jones, ' "Say They Are Saints Although That Saints They Show Not" ', 93–6.
[79] Honigmann, *John Weever*, p. 90.
[80] This was suggested by Sidney Lee in his *Life* (1923), 166ff, cited by Rollins, *A New Variorum*, vol. 2, p. 55.
[81] Shakespeare, *Shakespeare's Sonnets*, ed. Duncan-Jones, p. 3.

> Both poems, but especially the second, seem to call for a fuller poetic and narrative context in which the speaker's treacherous lust and triangular passion are more fully analysed … Perhaps, then, these 'certain *other sonnetes*' included or comprised the 'dark lady' sequence.[82]

There is, however, no evidence that readers wanted to find out more about the opening sonnets of *The Passionate Pilgrim*, and Shakespeare might equally have chosen to publish lyrics more in keeping with the rest of that collection, and with his reputation as one of those 'most passionate among us to bewaile and bemoan the perplexities of Love'.

It is not until 1612 that we find more concrete evidence of Shakespeare's desire to redeem his reputation. As discussed above, Thomas Heywood argued that Shakespeare was 'much offended' with Jaggard for having '(altogether unknowne to him) presumed to make so bold with his name' and therefore, 'to doe himselfe right, hath since published them in his owne name'.[83] The text Heywood is presumably referring to is the 1609 Quarto, which blazed Shakespeare's name across the title page and the running title, and which presented a collection of 154 sonnets to transform his poetic reputation. And yet, rather than displace *The Passionate Pilgrim* in the public imagination, the Quarto seems only to have strengthened its hold, inspiring Jaggard to go for a third, expanded edition in 1612: *The passionate pilgrime, Or Certaine amorous sonnets, betweene Venus and Adonis, newly corrected and augmented. By W. Shakespere. Where-unto is newly added two loue-epistles, the first from Paris to Hellen, and Hellens answere backe againe to Paris.* Jaggard may have decided to risk including the word 'sonnets' in the title for the first time, but the poems upon which he confers this are still not Shakespeare's Sonnets, but lyrics which recall his famous narrative poem: '*Certaine amorous sonnets, betweene Venus and Adonis*'. We find no additional Shakespearean Sonnets in the collection.

Although Erne and Badcoe have tried to temper the perception that the 1609 Quarto was a publishing disaster, observing that it was quite usual for a poetry book not to be reprinted,[84] the evidence that it was a failure is compelling. There are thirteen copies of the original Quarto extant, as opposed to only one of *Venus* which was apparently read to destruction.[85] Moreover, Leonard Digges, an ardent admirer of Shakespeare, referred in a copy of Lope de Vega's *Rimas* (1613) to 'this book of sonnets, which with

---

[82] Ibid., p. 6.
[83] Heywood, *An Apology for Actors*, 'To my approved good Friend, Mr Nicholas Okes'.
[84] Erne and Badcoe, 'The Popularity of Poetry Books in Print, 1583–1622', 21.
[85] Murphy, *Shakespeare in Print*, p. 20.

SHAKE-SPEARES

SONNETS.

Neuer before Imprinted.

AT LONDON
By *G. Eld* for *T. T.* and are
to be solde by *William Aspley.*
1609.

Figure 1.2 Title page of *Shake-speares Sonnets* (1609)
© Folger Shakespeare Library, STC 22353

Spaniards here is accounted of their Lope de Vega as in England we should of our Will Shakespeare'.[86] Katherine Duncan-Jones' suggestion that the silence which greeted the Quarto was 'stunned or disappointed'[87] has never been seriously challenged. What then was wrong with *Shake-speares Sonnets*?

'That Eternity Promised By': The 1609 Quarto

Unlike *The Passionate Pilgrim*, the title-page of the 1609 Quarto (Figure 1.2) seems designed to eliminate any possible confusion about what it is. On a sparse page, the capitals stand out boldly, monumentally, 'SHAKE-SPEARES SONNETS', affirming the authorship of these poems and the use of one poetic form throughout. The claim that they are 'Never before Imprinted' is not strictly true but allows the Quarto to position itself aggressively against *The Passionate Pilgrim*. But along with these promises, the title-page offers something more – and it is here that the Sonnets may have set up expectations they would not be able to fulfil.

Duncan-Jones has demonstrated how a genitive title in early modern literature was often used to suggest 'some sort of cult of personality by a notorious or popular writer', as in the case of *Greenes Groatsworth of Wit*, *Nashes Lenten Entertainment*, *Churchyardes Farewell* etc.[88] In this way, the Quarto invites its readers to anticipate insights into Shakespeare's private thoughts and feelings, and the paratext might have been expected to build on this promise. A useful comparison is William Alexander's collection of sonnets, *Aurora: Containing the first fancies of the Authors youth*, published in 1604. In a dedication to Lady Agnes Douglas, Countess of Argyle, signed by the poet, he bashfully acknowledges these 'unpolished lines' as his own. The opening sonnet then explains the circumstances in which the poems were both written and published:

> Whilst charming fancies move me to reveale
> The idle ravings of my brain-sicke youth,
> My heart doth pant within, to heare my mouth
> Unfold the follies which it would conceale …
> But had not others otherwise advis'd,
> My cabinet should yet these scroles containe,
> This childish birth of a conceitie [*sic*] braine,

---

[86] See Paul Morgan's discovery of this allusion and his more optimistic interpretation of it in ' "Our Will Shakespeare" and Lope de Vega', 118–20.

[87] Shakespeare, *Shakespeare's Sonnets*, ed. Duncan-Jones, p. 69.

[88] Duncan-Jones, 'What are Shakespeare's Sonnets Called?', 3.

Which I had still as trifling toyes despis'd:
Pardon these errours of mine unripe age;
My tender Muse by time may grow more sage.[89]

The conceits of sonnets as childish births and trifling toys, and of being forced into print by importunate friends, are all very familiar from 1590s sequences (see Sidney, Daniel, Barnes), and thereby lessen the distinctiveness of the poet's personality as implied here. Shakespeare might have had to take another approach, being unable to pull off the blushing ingénu role at this point in his career. Yet the fact remains that the Quarto cannot offer anything comparable to the intimacy between poet and reader that is performed by the *Aurora*. For a start, there is no dedication to a noble patron signed by the poet. Thorpe's habitual practice was to sign dedications only when the author was absent or dead,[90] and it may have been an outbreak of the plague that sent Shakespeare hurrying out of London.[91] But this was not necessarily fatal to establishing a text's paternity and sending it 'authorised' out into the world. Consider, for example, Spenser's *Amoretti* (1595) – like the Quarto, a collection of sonnets published by a celebrated writer in his maturity and presented to readers in the poet's absence. The stationer, William Ponsonby, dedicates the volume to Sir Robert Needham, emboldened to do so by the fact that 'these sweete conceited Sonets, [are] the deede of that wel-deseruing gentleman, maister Edmond Spenser: whose name sufficiently warranting the worthinesse of the work: I do more confidently presume to publish it in his absence'.[92] Spenser's location 'in forraine landes', and the sonnets' place within his illustrious literary career (alongside *The Shepherdes Calendar* and the first part of *The Faerie Queene*) are established in two succeeding panegyric sonnets by G. W. Senior and Junior, the latter probably Geoffrey Whitney, author of *A Choice of Emblems* (1586).[93]

By contrast, the dedication that Thorpe produced on Shakespeare's behalf was bafflingly obscure: 'TO. THE. ONLY. BEGETTER. OF. THESE. ENSUING. SONNETS. Mr. W. H. ALL. HAPPINESS. AND. THAT. ETERNITY. PROMISED. BY. OUR. EVER-LIVING. POET. WISHETH. THE. WELL-WISHING. ADVENTURER. IN. SETTING. FORTH. T. T.' The 'begetter' of a text was usually assumed to be its author, but the epigraph implies otherwise by identifying a further

---

[89] Alexander, *Aurora: Containing the first fancies of the Authors youth*, lines 1–4, 9–14.
[90] Shakespeare, *The Complete Sonnets and Poems*, ed. Burrow, p. 99.
[91] Shakespeare, *Shakespeare's Sonnets*, ed. Duncan-Jones, pp. 11–12.
[92] Spenser, *Amoretti and Epithalamion*.
[93] See Hadfield, *Edmund Spenser*, p. 302.

protagonist: 'our ever-living poet'. One explanation would be that this is no mortal 'maker' but God himself, described as 'ever-living' in the Book of Common Prayer. This would reinstate Shakespeare as begetter, his identity accidentally obscured by a misprint: 'W. H.' instead of 'W. S.' or 'W. Sh.'.[94] 'Only' – in the sense of 'sole' – 'begetter' might be a jibe at *The Passionate Pilgrim*, with Thorpe avowing that *here* Shakespeare has no unwitting collaborators. If, however, 'Mr W. H.' is accurate, 'begetter' seems more likely to indicate a patron, and the case for William Herbert, Earl of Pembroke is compelling,[95] not least because, as I will show, he was uniquely implicated in the Sonnets' early transmission. And yet, the point of identifying a patron was to offer them literary celebrity by garlanding their name with plaudits, including their full title. Elsewhere, Thorpe had been so anxious to acknowledge the disparity in rank between himself and Pembroke that he had addressed him as ' "your Lordship" six times in a single paragraph'.[96] Perhaps, then, 'begetter' needs to be extended to 'pro-curer'. Geoffrey Caveney has recently argued that Mr W. H. was William Holme, a colleague of Thorpe's who published plays by Ben Jonson and George Chapman. The fact that Holme had recently died (at which point Thorpe and Eld rifled through his stash of manuscripts and took both plays and Sonnets) makes sense of the funereal typography of the dedication.[97]

Whichever reading is correct (and it seems unlikely we will agree about this any time soon), the effect of Thorpe's epigraph was to distance the volume from Shakespeare.[98] As readers moved beyond the paratext to the lyrics themselves, they would have been further justified in asking where the Shakespeare of *Shake-speares Sonnets* had gone. The opening poem not only fails to identify the speaker and his relationship to an imagined beloved, it does not even speak in the first person, beginning with the measured and impartial proposition, 'From fairest creatures we desire increase'. There is, as yet, no suggestion that the speaker himself wishes such a thing, or that he has any desires of his own. It is not until Sonnet 10 that we find the lyric 'I' making its first appearance, and not until Sonnet 135 that we find the first explicit pun on will/Will. It may be that, as Heather Dubrow has

---

[94] This argument was initially made by Donald W. Foster ('Master W. H., R. I. P.'), but has been extended by Lynne Magnusson in 'Thomas Thorpe's Shakespeare: "The Only Begetter" ', pp. 34–7. She amends the epigraph accordingly in the latest Norton edition of the Sonnets.

[95] See Shakespeare, *Shakespeare's Sonnets*, ed. Duncan-Jones, pp. 53–64.

[96] Shakespeare, *The Complete Sonnets and Poems*, ed. Burrow, p. 100.

[97] Caveney, ' "Mr W. H.": Stationer William Holme (d. 1607)', 124.

[98] Magnusson notes 'the respectful distance and careful courtesy' represented by Thorpe's greeting to the poet, which 'suggest[s] neither a close acquaintance between them nor an active collaboration in the venture'. See 'Thomas Thorpe's Shakespeare: "The Only Begetter" ', p. 50.

argued, the *Sonnets* relegate narrative and dramatic elements in order 'to body forth the speaker's own emotions as immediately and intensely as possible', creating a figure 'as subtly realised as the personages in Shakespeare's major plays' or narrative verse.[99] Yet the Quarto's original readers seem to have been unwilling to commit the time and effort required to effect this subtle characterisation, particularly when they were not on first name terms. Unlike Astrophil, whose teasing relationship with Sir Philip Sidney was just sufficiently hinted at to encourage reader speculation, and whom Thomas Nashe imagined as a tragically affective character in his own right ('enter *Astrophel* in pompe'),[100] the anonymous protagonist of *Shake-speares Sonnets* seems not to have lived outside the literary work.

The absence of names under which to collate the characteristics, speech and actions of any of the Sonnets' other imagined persons was also potentially damaging. David Schalkwyk likens the experience of reading the *Sonnets* to 'trying to make sense of a play such as *Romeo and Juliet* from which the speech tags have been removed and in which all references to other characters are entirely pronominal'.[101] Moreover, the labels that editors and critics have invented (and which enable an overarching narrative), such as the 'Fair Youth' and 'Dark Lady', have no early modern counterparts, and are potentially misleading. It seems unlikely that there is only one of each – Stanley Wells points to the multiple lovers hinted at in Sonnet 31: 'Thou art the grave where buried love doth lie,/ Hung with the trophies of my lovers gone'[102] – and the speaker's mistress is nowhere described as a 'lady' or 'dark'.[103]

The absence of any easily discernible plot also does the Sonnets' characterisation no favours. Nashe's preface to the 1591 edition of *Astrophil* suggested that story was key: 'The argument cruell chastitie, the Prologue hope, the Epilogue dispaire.'[104] The plot afforded by Shakespeare was arguably more scandalous than anything that had been seen in the sonnet sequence before: a man who tries to persuade a youth to marriage falls in love with him instead; he is then betrayed by the youth who sleeps with the poet's mistress, who is herself married. But the fact that none of Shakespeare's contemporaries recorded their response to such a plot may reflect how deeply buried it is within the collection. As James Schiffer

---

[99]   Dubrow, *Captive Victors*, pp. 184, 198.
[100] Sidney, 'Somewhat to reade for them that list', *Syr P. S. His Astrophel and Stella*, A3r.
[101] Schalkwyk, *Speech and Performance*, p. 24.
[102] Wells, ' "My Name is Will" ', 102.
[103] Hammond, *Shakespeare's Sonnets*, p. 4.
[104] Sidney, *Syr P. S. His Astrophel and Stella*, A3r.

puts it, 'At most, the sonnets … give hints of a narrative; but they do so sporadically … at times obscurely … inconsistently … and in any case incompletely'.[105]

Moreover, in terms of content, the Sonnets seem to have been too pro-fane/carnal for some readers, and not sexy enough for others. In what is probably the earliest surviving response to the Quarto, in two sonnets included in a letter to his mother (New Year, 1610), George Herbert complains:

> My God, where is that ancient heat towards thee,
> Wherewith whole showls of *Martyrs* once did burn,
> Besides their other flames? Doth Poetry
> Wear *Venus* Livery? Only serve her turn?
> Why are not *Sonnets* made of thee?[106]

The allusion to '*Venus*' might be generic, but coming so close to '*Sonnets*' in the months after Q's publication it suggests a specific barb at Shakespeare's poetic career. George Herbert was a distant cousin of William Herbert, Earl of Pembroke, and his religious poetry emerges partly from his resistance to Sidneian amatory verse, and to the kind of coterie which, as we shall see, may have directly nurtured Shakespeare's Sonnets.[107] In the second sonnet, Herbert redirects to devout purposes the Shakespearean imagery of distillation (Sonnet 5) and crystal tears (Sonnet 46): 'Each Cloud distils thy praise, and doth forbid/ *Poets* to turn it to another use'; 'Why should I *Womens*' eyes for Chrystal take?'.[108] Nor was Herbert alone in his con-demnation of the Sonnets' profanity: in the Steevens copy of Q, now held at the Huntington library, an early seventeenth-century reader has crossed out Sonnet 129 ('Th'expense of spirit in a waste of shame').[109] And yet, if disapproval of the Sonnets' eroticism defined some readers' responses, it does not explain why they had so little appeal for those still enamoured of *Venus and Adonis* and *The Rape of Lucrece*, reprinted in 1608 and 1610, and 1607 respectively.

[105] Schiffer, 'The Incomplete Narrative of Shakespeare's Sonnets', p. 45.
[106] Herbert, *The Works of George Herbert*, p. 206.
[107] Cristina Malcolmson has argued for the importance of the Sidney–Herbert coterie to George Herbert's writing, and also avers that 'there is strong evidence that Shakespeare's Sonnets were important to the Sidney-Herbert circle', *George Herbert: A Literary Life*, pp. 8–15, 12.
[108] Ibid. Duncan-Jones suggests that the allusions to the 'poor invention' and 'low mind' of those who waste poetry on secular subjects rather than praising their Lord recall the 'blunt invention' of Shakespeare's Sonnet 103, *Shakespeare's Sonnets*, ed. Duncan-Jones, pp. 70–1.
[109] Ibid., pp. 69–70.

One further reason why the 1609 Sonnets may have failed to engage readers relates to the physical layout of the volume. Consistency and detail in terms of characterisation and plot would arguably matter less if the poems were set out to encourage a non-sequential reading, enabling the reader to linger and admire a lyric without troubling about its connections to the rest. But where *The Passionate Pilgrim* initially implied a sonnet sequence through the extravagant space around the poems, the opposite is true of the Quarto, where the compression of sonnets suggests the successive verses of a narrative poem. The claustrophobic effect of the book's material appearance may have hindered readers from engaging with lyrics individu- ally and from inserting their own voices in and around the sonnets.[110] Nor should we overlook the structural criticism in the comment inscribed at the end of the Rosenbach copy of Q: 'What a heap of wretched INFIDEL stuff.'[111] The perception of sonnets piled on top of one another relates not only to the way in which the principles of arrangement might be obscure – groupings of poems on the young man's betrayal, for example, recur with no explanation of whether these are discrete occurrences or more of the same – but to the arrangement of sonnets on the page. Coleman Hutchison notes that 'Through a non-uniform, seemingly arbitrary imposition of page breaks, several quarto poems appear clipped, severed, and fractured; others are preserved and monumentalized in the field of the page'.[112] Given the fragility of quartos, which were often sold unbound, the survival of indi- vidual sonnets might be linked to their positioning on the page, and their canonicity related to their being laid out 'in a way conducive to attracting attention'.[113] Hutchison's compelling argument is unfortunately weakened by his examples. Sonnets 18 and 130 are placed in the centre and at the top of their respective pages, and 'remain among the most enduring literary artifacts of the English language',[114] and yet, as noted in the Introduction, Sonnet 18 would be out of print from 1609 to 1711, and neither this nor Sonnet 130 shows any signs of manuscript transmission in the seventeenth century. Hutchison's theory is better supported by Sonnets 116 or 128, both

---

[110] See my 'Shakespeare's Sonnets and the Claustrophobic Reader'.

[111] See Rollins, *Variorum*, vol. 2, p. 348. This comment is not necessarily representative of attitudes during Shakespeare's lifetime: Allardyce Nicoll argued that it was inscribed by an eighteenth-century owner of the Quarto. See 'Shakespeare in the Bibliotheca Bodmeriana', 84. Nevertheless, it resonates with Edward Ravenscroft's criticism of *Titus* in 1687 as 'rather a heap of Rubbish then a Structure', causing him to rewrite the play. See 'To the Reader', in *Titus Andronicus, or The Rape of Lavinia*, sig. A2.

[112] Hutchison, 'Breaking the Book Known as Q', 50.

[113] Ibid.

[114] Ibid.

of which appear 'monumentalised' on the Quarto page and would circulate in seventeenth-century manuscripts, as discussed below.

To whatever we attribute the Quarto's failure, that volume must be substantially to blame for the Sonnets' pitiful impact on English literature during Shakespeare's lifetime. The following list contains all the Sonnet reprintings, transcriptions and allusions I have been able to find between 1598 and 1622:[115]

Sonnet 5 ('Those hours that with gentle work did frame'): possible allusion to distillation imagery in a sonnet of George Herbert, New Year 1610.

Sonnet 13 ('O that you were yourself! But, love, you are'): concluding couplet appears in Richard Brathwait's 'A Threnode occasioned upon the Authors discontent', published in *The Poet's Willow or, The Passionate Shepherd* (1614):

> If every creature thus ordained be,
> For to observe the solemne rites of love:
> Dost thou suppose she hath exempted thee,
> No pensive passions ere thy mind to move?
> O be not so deluded: **dear you know,**
> **You had a father, let your sonne say so.**[116]

Sonnet 21 ('So is it not with me as with that Muse'): Final line, 'I will not praise that purpose not to sell', perhaps echoed in line 6 of George Herbert's poem 'Jordan II' (*c.* 1615–25),[117] 'Decking the sense as if it were to sell', published posthumously in *The Temple* (1633).[118]

---

[115] This list is indebted to Hyder E. Rollins' *Variorum*, *The Shakespeare Allusion Book*, Beal's *Index of English Literary Manuscripts*, Edmondson and Wells' *Shakespeare's Sonnets*, Duncan-Jones (ed.), *Shakespeare's Sonnets*, and Malcolmson, *George Herbert: A Literary Life*. I have not included echoes or anticipations of the Sonnets in Shakespeare's plays, though such can certainly be found in *The Merchant of Venice*, *All's Well That Ends Well*, *Cymbeline*, and most extensively *The Reign of King Edward III* (1596, repr. 1599), which includes phrases from Sonnets 29 ('bootless cries'), 94 ('Lilies that fester, smell far worse than weeds') and 142 ('scarlet ornaments'). Claes Schaar argues that the playwright was writing with a manuscript copy of the Sonnets open before him, and adds possible allusions to 7, 33, 127 and 143 (*Elizabethan Sonnet Themes and the Dating of Shakespeare's Sonnets*). However, it seems unlikely to me that Shakespeare had a complete sonnet sequence written by this date (if he ever did), and I would tend towards Giorgio Melchiori's theory that these phrases are 'suggestions for as yet unwritten poems', *King Edward III*, p. 190.

[116] Brathwait, *The Poet's Willow*, p. 76. Richard Abrams offers an illuminating account of Brathwait's career-long fascination with Shakespeare. As well as the lines lifted from Sonnet 13, he detects 'many more probable echoes' in *The Poet's Willow*, from Sonnets 3, 9, 29 and 73. See Abrams, 'Rereading Shakespeare', 281, fn. 50.

[117] The poem appears in the Williams manuscript (MS Jones B 62 at Dr Williams' Library, London), which has been dated to 1615–25. See Herbert, *The English Poems of George Herbert*, pp. xxxvii, 365.

[118] Malcolmson notes that the line was once even closer to Shakespeare's Sonnet: 'Praising the sense as if it were to sell'. See *George Herbert: A Literary Life*, pp. 11–12.

Sonnet 27 ('Weary with toil, I haste me to my bed'): part of line 8 repeated in William Drummond's 'Madrigal', published in *Poems by William Drummond of Hawthorn-denne* (1616):[119]

> Dear night, the ease of care,
> Untroubled set of peace,
> Time's eldest child, **which oft the blind do see,**
> On this our hemisphere
> What makes thee now so sadly dare to be?'

Sonnet 46 ('Mine eye and heart are at a mortal war'): possible allusion to 'crystal eyes' imagery in a sonnet of George Herbert, New Year 1610.

Sonnet 116 ('Let me not to the marriage of true minds'): phrase 'love is not love' repeated in William Herbert's lyric 'If her disdain ...', *c.* 1602–9, included in British Library, Harley 4064, *c.* 1610–12, and circulated in at least sixteen other manuscripts 1620–30, and printed in editions of 1635 and 1660.[120] The same phrase is repeated in William Barksted and Lewis Machin's *The Insatiate Countess* (1613), based on a draft by John Marston, 3.2.79–83,[121] and Lady Mary Wroth's poem 'As these drops fall', *c.* 1618–20, published in *The First Part of The Countess of Montgomery's Urania* (1621).

Sonnet 128 ('How oft when thou, my music, music play'st'): transcribed in full in verse miscellany, Bodleian MS. Rawl. Poet 152, fol. 34 (*c.* 1613–20).[122] Also possible allusion to lines 3 and 9 in Ben Jonson's *Every Man out of his Humour* (1599, pub. 1600), 3.9.101–6.

Sonnet 129 ('Th'expense of spirit in a waste of shame'): possible allusion in the final line of George Herbert's 'Jordan II' (*c.* 1615–25), where the religious poet is advised to 'Copie out only that, and save expense'.[123]

Sonnet 138 ('When my love swears that she is made of truth'): printed in *The Passionate Pilgrim* (1599, 1599, 1612).

Sonnet 144 ('Two loves I have, of comfort and despair'): printed in *The Passionate Pilgrim* (1599, 1599, 1612). Possible influence on Michael

---

[119] Drummond also refers to *A Lover's Complaint* in Sonnet 11, Part Two.

[120] For further discussion of the Harley MS, see Lamb, ' "Love is not love": A Lyric Exchange'. On the other manuscripts in which it appeared, see Herbert, *The Poems of William Herbert*, ed. Krueger, p. 62.

[121] Barksted was an actor, turned poet and playwright, who openly admired his predecessor Shakespeare. He praised him explicitly in *Mirrha the Mother of Adonis* (1607), and modelled his two narrative poems on *Venus and Adonis* and *Lucrece* respectively. It would not then be a surprise if he got hold of a copy of the *Sonnets*. See Melchiori, 'Barksted, William'.

[122] This is Duncan-Jones' dating which is considerably earlier than Beal's 1625–40s. She describes it as 'probably the earliest surviving transcription of any of Shakespeare's Sonnets'. See *Shakespeare's Sonnets*, ed. Duncan-Jones, pp. 460–1.

[123] See Malcolmson, *George Herbert: A Literary Life*, p. 13.

Drayton's Sonnet 22, 'An evill spirit your beauty haunts me still', first published in *Englands Heroicall Epistles. With Idea* (1599). Both sonnets share the end-rhymes 'still/ill' and 'evil/devil', and Drayton's final line, 'good wicked spirit, sweet Angel devill', recalls the paradox at the heart of Shakespeare's Sonnet 144/PP2.[124]

Three things might immediately strike us about this list. The first is how little evidence it affords of early manuscript circulation. Arthur F. Marotti reminds us that across extant sixteenth- and seventeenth-century manuscripts there have been found 'only eleven whole [Shakespeare] sonnets in twenty different manuscripts', by contrast with John Donne, whose verse 'shows up in some 250 manuscripts'.[125] There are only three possible allusions in this list which predate 1609, two of which are associated with Shakespeare's friends, Ben Jonson and Michael Drayton, who may have had access to Shakespeare's draft papers. The second thing to notice is how little discernible reaction we find to the publication of the 1609 Quarto, apart from George Herbert's allusions in his New Year letter.[126] Subsequent borrowings by Jacobean poets Richard Brathwait, William Drummond and William Barksted are most likely derived from the Quarto, but otherwise that book seems to have had little impact. That said, there are two Sonnets which

---

[124] Drayton and Shakespeare had much in common, not least their Warwickshire origins and theatrical and poetic ambitions, and it seems likely that they shared their work. Shakespeare seems to be borrowing from Drayton's *The Shepheards Garland* (1593), Eclogue 2, in the manuscript version of Sonnet 2 (see Chapter 2) and there are a number of echoes in other procreation Sonnets which suggest he knew Drayton's work, perhaps including Amour 14 (*Idea*, 1594), 'Looking into the glasse of my youths miseries' and Sonnet 43 (*Englands Heroicall Epistles*, 1600), 'Whilst thus my penne strives to eternize thee'. At the same time, debts to Shakespeare's *Venus and Adonis* and *The Rape of Lucrece* have been found in Drayton's complaint poems and his epyllion, *Endimion and Phoebe* (1595), and Meghan C. Andrews makes a compelling case for Shakespeare's *Henry VI* plays influencing Drayton's work in the 1590s. On this basis, it is impossible to tell who borrowed from whom. I would be inclined to think that Shakespeare complicated Drayton's 'Angel devil' mistress by splitting the oxymoron between two protagonists, but it might also be the case that Drayton rendered Sonnet 144/PP2 more conventional to fit his *Idea* sequence. For further discussion, see the notes by Raymond MacDonald Alden in *The Sonnets of Shakespeare: From the Quarto of 1609 with Variorum Readings and Commentary*, pp. 346–7, and Andrews, 'Michael Drayton, Shakespeare's Shadow'.

[125] Marotti, 'Shakespeare's Sonnets and the Manuscript Circulation of Texts in Early Modern England', p. 186. For further discussion, see Chapter 2.

[126] There is a reference to the actor, Edward Alleyn, having purchased a copy on 19 July *c.* 1609 (the year is not specified). On the back of a letter from Thomas Bowker (now in the Dulwich College archive), Alleyn wrote down various payments, including for 'a book Shaksper Sonets 5d.'. This note had been presumed to be a John Payne Collier forgery, but it has since been authenticated. See Alan H. Nelson, 'Shakespeare Documented' at https://shakespearedocumented.folger.edu/exhibition/document/letter-thomas-bowker-edward-alleyn-about-dog-numerous-notes-verso-alleyn, accessed 30 November 2018.

combine manuscript circulation and printed allusion, and these are Sonnets 128 and 116. In the rest of this chapter, I will argue that the relative 'success' of these lyrics offers a fascinating glimpse into what Shakespeare's readers might have wanted from his Sonnets, and that they betray the influence of one particular reader, William Herbert, Earl of Pembroke.

The Enduring Love of Sonnets 128 and 116

Sonnet 128 locates the speaker and the addressee within a familiar courtship scenario – where the virgin plays upon the virginals to enchant a suitor, and the latter makes bawdy innuendos about it.[127] It may thus have seemed more appealing to readers than other Sonnets in the Quarto which lack any such domestic setting or any such straightforward intent.

> How oft when thou, my music, music play'st,
> Upon that blessèd wood whose motion sounds
> With thy sweet fingers when thou gently sway'st
> The wiry concord that mine ear confounds,
> Do I envy those jacks that nimble leap,
> To kiss the tender inward of thy hand,
> Whilst my poor lips which should that harvest reap,
> At the wood's boldness by thee blushing stand!
> To be so tickled, they would change their state
> And situation with those dancing chips,
> O'er whom thy fingers walk with gentle gait,
> Making dead wood more bless'd than living lips.
>> Since saucy jacks so happy are in this,
>> Give them thy fingers, me thy lips to kiss.[128]

Whilst the final line recalls Romeo's amorous plea, 'My lips, two blushing pilgrims, ready stand/ To smooth that rough touch with a tender kiss',[129] this Sonnet's 'sweet' flattery, bawdy innuendo and elaborate conceit would also have appealed to admirers of *Venus and Adonis*. Where the goddess offers to become an inanimate object to achieve erotic satisfaction ('I'll be a park, and thou shalt be my deer ...' (231)), here the speaker offers for his lips to become virginal keys: 'O'er whom thy fingers walk with gentle gait', whilst the 'jacks that ... leap' anticipate his erectile response. Perhaps written and circulated close in time with *Venus* and *Romeo*,[130] like them

---

[127] See Trillini, 'The Gaze of the Listener'.

[128] All quotations from the Sonnets are taken from Duncan-Jones' edition.

[129] 1.5.94–5. All quotations from Shakespeare's plays are taken from *The Norton Shakespeare*, ed. Greenblatt *et al.*

[130] As part of the group 127–54, this is probably one of the earliest Sonnets, certainly no later than 1599.

Sonnet 128 provided a kind of lustful ingenuity that lent itself to parody. Ben Jonson seems to have got hold of a manuscript copy, for in *Every Man out of his Humour*, performed by the Lord Chamberlain's Men in 1599, Fastidius Briske comments on Saviolina's viol-playing: 'You see the subject of her sweet fingers, there? O, she tickles it so … I have wished myself to be that instrument, I think, a thousand times.'[131] Briske is identified in the 1600 Quarto as 'A neat, spruce, affecting courtier, one that wears clothes well and in fashion; practiseth by his glass how to salute; [and] speaks good remnants'.[132] Jonson's suggestion that fragments of Sonnet 128 make up the amorous posturing of an upstart courtier (as was often said of *Venus and Adonis*) is consistent with the play's other satirical references to Shakespeare, in terms of both his personal ambition and his pandering to popular taste.[133]

At the same time, Sonnet 128 is notable for its musical theme. This feature seems to have encouraged manuscript transcription – as later in the case of Sonnet 8 ('Music to hear, why hear'st thou music sadly'), which exists in an MS dated *c.* 1630–50 under the Latin title, '*In laudem Musice et opprobrium Contemptorii eiusdem*' ('In praise of music, and in contempt of its despiser'), though it may have been in circulation much earlier.[134] Whether or not Sonnet 128 was ever set to music, it appears in the company of a song, 'Rest awhile, you cruel cares', by the composer John Dowland (1563–1626), in a miscellany dated *c.* 1613–20. Shakespeare and Dowland had been coupled together in print through *The Passionate Pilgrim*, in which the poem 'If music and sweet poetry agree' (PP8) praises the musician by name. In this miscellany, containing just four poems, the first stanza of 'Rest awhile' describes a familiar Petrarchan scenario in which the speaker appeals to 'Laura, fair queen of love's despight' to 'grant me love'. The song had been in print since 1597,[135] and so, although it bears no title or other musical notation, might have been remembered as a musical performance. It is then followed by Shakespeare's Sonnet 128, which describes performance at a distance, from the perspective of the male spectator whose desire is heightened by the mistress's expert handling of her instrument. This version of Sonnet 128 also corrects a musical solecism: in harpsichord-like instruments, the wooden jacks would never touch the player's fingers, so 'jacks' has been replaced with 'keys', and the bawdy 'tickle' with

---

[131] Jonson, *Every Man Out of Humour*, 3.3.105–10.
[132] Ibid., p. 104.
[133] See Bednarz, *Shakespeare and the Poets' War*, pp. 24–6.
[134] See Shakespeare, *Shakespeare's Sonnets*, ed. Duncan-Jones, p. 457.
[135] Dowland, *The First Booke of Songes or Ayres*.

the more accurate 'touch'.[136] The other two lyrics in the miscellany do not share this musical theme. They are William Browne's 'This is love and worth commending …', printed in *Britannia's Pastorals* (1613, 1616); and 'I bend my wits' by Francis Davison, which appears as sonnet 2 in *A Poetical Rhapsody* (1602, 1608, 1611, 1621). Their effect on the reception of Sonnet 128 is to place it (and by extension Shakespeare) within an imagined literary coterie, dominated by one particular music-lover: William Herbert, third Earl of Pembroke. Dowland, Browne and Davison had all either been employed by Pembroke or had sought his patronage. Dowland was paid by the Earl to adapt his verses to music, published in *The Third Book and Last Book of Ayres* (1602) and *A Pilgrimes Solace* (1612). Browne dedicated the 1616 volume of *Britannia's Pastorals* to Pembroke – most likely after the latter had helped him to the position of Pursuivant of the court of wards and liveries – and has been described as 'the official poet of the Herbert family' in the 1620s and 1630s.[137] Davison's *A Poetical Rhapsody* included poems by Sidney and the Countess of Pembroke, and was dedicated to the Earl in 1602.

To find a Shakespeare Sonnet in such manuscript company might suggest that the poet himself was part of Herbert's artistic circle.[138] The dedication of the first Folio (1623) praises William and Philip Herbert for having 'prosecuted' Shakespeare and his dramatic works 'with so much favour'.[139] That Pembroke was also an enthusiastic reader of Shakespeare's Sonnets, and a worthy 'executor' to his poetry, is implied by the afterlife of Sonnet 116.

> Let me not to the marriage of true minds
> Admit impediments; love is not love
> Which alters when it alteration finds,
> Or bends with the remover to remove.

---

[136] Alternatively, the Rawlinson MS 'may reflect an earlier draft of the poem', with 'keys' and 'touched' reflecting Shakespeare's first thoughts, given that 'Shakespeare describes kisses as the "touching" of lips at *Venus* 115, *Othello* 4.3.317/2699 and *Pericles* 22.64/ 2330'. See Wells and Taylor, *A Textual Companion*, p. 466. Both Dowland's and Shakespeare's lyrics show some alterations from the printed text. Whilst in Dowland's case, this looks more like a case of eyeskip, the opening line of 128 has changed ('how ouft when thow, deere deerest musick plaiest') which strengthens the possibility that it derives from a manuscript source.

[137] M. Brennan, 'The Literary Patronage of the Herbert Family, Earls of Pembroke', qtd in O'Callaghan, 'William Browne'.

[138] We might also note that the opening phrase of Shakespeare's sonnet 27, 'Weary with toil', appears in Browne's *Britannia's Pastorals*, with a slight modification, 'Weary'd with toil', Bk 1, Song 4. This was not an uncommon phrase, hence the fact that I have not included it in the above list, but it might strengthen our hypothesis that the Pembroke circle was familiar with Shakespeare's Sonnets.

[139] Shakespeare, *William Shakespeare: The Complete Works*, ed. Wells and Taylor, p. xliv.

O no, it is an ever fixèd mark,
That looks on tempests and is never shaken;
It is the star to every wandering bark,
Whose worth's unknown, although his height be taken.
Love's not Time's fool, though rosy lips and cheeks
Within his bending sickle's compass come;
Love alters not with his brief hours and weeks,
But bears it out, even to the edge of doom.
   If this be error and upon me proved,
   I never writ, nor no man ever loved.

There are many reasons why this Sonnet might have been singled out for admiration by seventeenth-century readers. It seems already detached from the rest of the collection, sharing 'no obvious thematic connections' with the other poems,[140] and was thus more easily extracted from the Quarto sequence. It expresses an idealised, timeless vision of romantic love, which transcends pleasure in physical beauty ('rosy lips and cheeks') and endures to 'the edge of doom', even as it resonates with a deep strain of melancholy and forced self-abnegation. Its juxtaposition of the union of mere bodies and the 'marriage of true minds' might speak to any reader whose passion had been compromised by the social and fiscal pressures on marriage among the gentry or aristocracy in this period, even as it borrows from the marriage ceremony in the Book of Common Prayer ('… know of any lawful impediment'). At the same time, its chief pleasures are probably sonorous: the rather clipped 'Admit impediment', sealed with a caesura, opens out into the lovely exhalation of 'love is not love', and the use of *epanalepsis* here (the repetition of one word from the beginning of a clause at the end) makes it particularly memorable.[141]

Despite its lack of allusion to musical instruments or song, a three-stanza version of this Sonnet, with some substantial alterations, was set to music by the songwriter Henry Lawes (1596–1662), appearing first anonymously in a seventeenth-century manuscript,[142] and then with attribution in a songbook owned by the composer John Gamble, c. 1630–50.[143] The opening stanza reads:

---

[140] Edmondson and Wells, *Shakespeare's Sonnets*, p. 32.
[141] Obvious examples would be Hamlet's 'To be or not to be' or Macbeth's 'Blood will have blood'.
[142] Bodleian MSS. Ashm. 36/37, f29r, no. 35. John P. Cutts argues that this represents an intermediary text between the Q version and the Drexel in 'Two Seventeenth-Century Versions of Shakespeare's Sonnet 116'.
[143] MS Drexel 4257, no. 33, New York Public Library, Music Division.

Selfe blinding error seazeth all those mindes:
who with falce Appellations call that love
wch alters when it alteration findes
or with the *mouer hath a power to moue*
not much unlike ye hereticks pretence
that scites trew scripture but prevents the sence:[144]

The identity of the adapter remains unknown. Willa McClung Evans admitted that 'with some shaping it may be made to fit Pembroke, Sandy's [*sic*], Donne, Davenant, Carew, Milton or Shakespeare himself',[145] though the latter seems unlikely. Not only is this religious fervour uncharacteristic of the Sonnets, but the terms 'self-blinding', 'appellations' and 'eye-deluding' appear nowhere in the Shakespearean canon. There is a Pembroke connection, however, in the setting if not the adaptation by Henry Lawes, for Lawes was born near Wilton, and may have received his musical education on the Pembroke estate in the 1610s, before being promoted by the Earl to a position within the royal household.[146] He published a musical setting for Pembroke's 'Canst thou love me' in his *Ayres and Dialogues* (1653), and included arrangements of three other Pembroke lyrics in his autograph songbook. Ian Spink has argued that the other poets to be found in the earliest section of this songbook, probably written in the 1620s, suggest '[Lawes'] attachment to the circle surrounding the Earl of Pembroke, and his mother, Mary Sidney, the Dowager Countess – William Browne and Benjamin Rudyerd especially'.[147] Finally, we might recall John Donne the younger's claim in *Poems written by the Right Honorable William Earl of*

[144] This is as transcribed by Willa McClung Evans, with italics for the sections that differ from Shakespeare's version, in 'Lawes' Version of Shakespeare's Sonnet CXVI', 121. The succeeding stanzas are:

Oh noe *Loue* is an ever fixed marke
That lookes on tempests but is never shaken
It is the starr to every wandring barke
Whose worth's vnknowne although his height be taken
Noe mountebanck with eie-deludeing flashes
But flameing Martyr in his holly ashes

Love's not tymes fool though Rosie lipps & Cheekes
Within his *bynding Circle* compas *round*
Loue alters not with his breife howers & weekes
But *holds* it out even to the edge of doome
If this be errour *& not truth approu'd*
Cupids noe god nor Man *nere* lou'd.

[145] Evans, 'Lawes' Version of Shakespeare's Sonnet CXVI', 42.
[146] Waller, *The Sidney Family Romance*, p. 170.
[147] Spink, *Henry Lawes*, p. 14.

Pembroke (London, 1660) that Lawes had many of them in his keeping.[148] Perhaps Pembroke drew Lawes' attention to Sonnet 116 in its revised form, and asked for it to be set to music, or perhaps Lawes undertook the setting himself on the assumption that it would be favourably received. That Sonnet 116 was a particular favourite of Pembroke's is, I would argue, evident in the Earl's own lyric poetry.

'If her disdain least change in you can move' is part of a 'poem-and-answer set' created with his friend, Benjamin Rudyerd, which was probably written in the first decade of the seventeenth century when they were at the Inns of Court together.[149] The allusion to Sonnet 116 appears in the first stanza:

> If her disdain least change in you can move
>   You do not love,
> For while your hopes give fuel to your fire
>   You sell desire.
> Love is not love, but given free,
> And so is mine, so should yours be.[150]

This stanza might be viewed as a loose paraphrase of Sonnet 116's asseveration: 'love is not love/ Which alters when it alteration finds,/ Or bends with the remover to remove', culminating in a direct borrowing of the key phrase itself.[151] However, the differences between the two lyrics have prevented the latter from being taken seriously as a response to Shakespeare's poem. Pembroke emphasises the mistress's 'disdain', thereby placing the lyric within a stronger Petrarchan context than the Shakespeare Sonnet, where love is tested by *alteration*, implying there was once reciprocity. At the same time, as conceived of within a debate structure, Pembroke's lyric stresses the inherent masochism of love, so that Rudyerd can defeat it, and thereby push an anti-Petrarchan, if not Cavalier, agenda: '"Tis love breeds love in me, and cold disdain/ Kills love again.'[152] But for all the

---

[148] 'To the Reader', in Herbert, *Poems*.

[149] Waller, *The Sidney Family Romance*, p. 165.

[150] Herbert, *Poems*, ed. Krueger, p. 2. I am indebted to Duncan-Jones for the observation that Pembroke borrows here from Sonnet 116. See *Shakespeare's Sonnets*, ed. Duncan-Jones, pp. 68–9. Most recently, Mary Ellen Lamb has kindly shared with me her discussion of Sonnet 116 as Shakespeare's response to Pembroke and Rudyerd's debate poem, with 'Selfe blinding error' another Inns of Court poem that combines allusions to both. Although we differ on who was responding to whom, Lamb's analysis of Sonnet 116 within this legal context, and as expressive of Shakespeare's love for Pembroke, is extremely suggestive. See '"Love is not love": A Lyric Exchange'.

[151] Shakespeare liked the phrase so much that he used it again in *King Lear c.* 1606, when France warns Burgundy – placing the phrase after the caesura, as in the Sonnet – 'Love is not love/ When it is mingled with respects that stands/ Aloof from the entire point', 1.230–2.

[152] Herbert, *Poems*, ed. Krueger, p. 3.

differences between this and Sonnet 116, Pembroke's quotation 'Love is not love' need not be dismissed as evidence of his habitual derivativeness. Although Gary Waller is surely right to emphasise Pembroke's verses as ' "coterie social transactions", written for or within a group of friends, perhaps on particular, though relatively common, social or erotic occasions',[153] his lyrics have increasingly been read as personally inflected, acknowledging Pembroke's own painful experiences of betrayal and of female inconstancy.[154]

We might assume that the phrase 'love is not love' was already a cliché; however, a search of the Chadwyck-Healy database to include all phrases beginning 'love/loue is not' between 1590 and 1640 produces only three examples in poetry and these are Shakespeare, Pembroke and Lady Mary Wroth. It is very unlikely that Wroth and Pembroke shared the phrase unthinkingly. Mary Wroth, née Sidney, was Pembroke's cousin, but she was also his mistress, producing two illegitimate children by him some time after the death of her husband, including a son called William.[155] At exactly what point the relationship became romantic and/or sexual remains unknown, but it may have predated their weddings to other people in 1604.[156] Josephine Roberts observes the way in which the relationship between Pamphilia and Amphilanthus in Part Two of Wroth's heavily autobiographical prose romance, *The Countess of Montgomery's Urania*, is sealed by a *de praesenti* marriage, described as 'the knott never to bee untide', although they both subsequently marry other people.[157] Furthermore, a letter by Lady Mary's father dated 10 October 1604 alluded to the new husband's dissatisfaction with the marriage: 'I finde by him that there was some what that doth discontent him: but the particulars I could not get out of him.'[158] Critics have conjectured that either he had discovered the degree of affection between Lady Mary and her cousin, or

[153] Waller, *The Sidney Family Romance*, p. 166.
[154] The autobiographical resonance of Herbert's verse is explored by Garth Bond, Mary Ellen Lamb and Ilona Bell, as referenced below.
[155] Michael G. Brennan suggests a date for the son as early as 1617, 'Creating Female Authorship', p. 83, but Josephine A. Roberts and Margaret P. Hannay make a strong case for 1624 and the birth of twins, based on John Chamberlain's letter of 1624: 'Here is a whispering of a Lady that hath been a widow above seven years, though she had lately two children at a birth. I must not name her though she be said to be learned and in print', Hannay, *Mary Sidney, Lady Wroth*, p. 251.
[156] Bond asserts that 'Mary Wroth's assertion of a premarital relationship with her cousin, William Herbert, 3rd Earl of Pembroke, lies at the heart of her fiction, and by implication of her poetry as well', 'Amphilanthus to Pamphilia', 51.
[157] See Wroth, *The First Part*, p. lxxiv, and Roberts, ' "The Knott Never to Bee Untide" '.
[158] Qtd by Roberts in Wroth, *The Poems of Lady Mary Wroth*, pp. 11–12.

that she was no longer a virgin.[159] There are also strong indications that Pembroke's marriage was affected by his relationship with Wroth. Having delayed his union with the considerable fortune of Lady Mary Talbot for so long that at least one commentator assumed it would never happen, Pembroke finally married just two months after Mary. Like his cousin's union, this also became the subject of gossip, with Rowland Whyte having to reassure the bride's parents that Pembroke was a loving husband and that she was well treated.[160] Moreover, although he had facilitated the marriage by making a substantial contribution to Lady Mary's dowry, Pembroke seems to have acknowledged the suffering it caused him. In the lyric 'Muse get thee to a Cell', the speaker complains:

> Who says that I for things ne'er mine am sad?
> That was all mine which others never had.
> No sighs, no tears, no blood but mine was shed
> For her that now must bless another's bed.

As Mary Ellen Lamb puts it, 'There can be little doubt that Mary Wroth and William Herbert … read and responded to each other's poems … The long-term physical proximity underlying the[ir] familial and later sexual relationship … created the reading of each other's poetry as all but inevitable'.[161] But whilst the autobiographical allusions in Herbert's poetry have proven harder to discern, they lie at the heart of Wroth's literary canon, most nakedly in the relationship between the constant Pamphilia who suffers at the hands of the loving philanderer Amphilanthus, but also discernible in other characters and their romantic histories.

In Book One of the First Part of the *Urania* (pub. 1621, written 1618–20), the character of Bellamira (whose name means 'beautiful Mary')[162] tells Amphilanthus how she was cast off by her beloved, a king, who had at first pursued her so ardently that her father married her off to someone else, but whose affections subsequently waned:

---

[159] See Wroth, *The First Part*, p. xc, and Hannay, *Mary Sidney, Lady Wroth*, pp. 107–8. Two Herbert poems, which inspired answering lyrics by Wroth, also seem to claim that he had taken her virginity: 'Enjoy thou many, or rejoice in one,/ I was before them, and before me none' ('Why with unkindest swiftness …', ll 71–2); 'None had had her but I, she none but me' ('Muse get thee to a Cell', line 12). For further discussion, see Bond, 'Amphilanthus to Pamphilia', and Lamb, '"Can you suspect a change in me?"'.

[160] Hannay, *Mary Sidney, Lady Wroth*, p. 96.

[161] Lamb, '"Can you suspect a change in me?"', pp. 53, 54.

[162] Roberts argues that Bellamira is one of the key fictional self-portraits Wroth created in her work, specifically 'highlight[ing] her private relationship with Pembroke', in Wroth, *The First Part*, p. lxxi.

When I was a Widdow, and suffered so many crosses, my poore beauty decayd, so did his love, which though he oft protested to bee fixed on my worth, and love to him, yet my face's alteration gave his eyes distaste, or liberty from former bands, to looke else where, and so he looked, as tooke his heart at last from me, making that a poore servant to his false eyes, to follow still their change. I grieved for it, yet never lessned my affection.[163]

Bellamira's use of the terms 'fixed', 'worth', 'love' and 'alteration' in close proximity to one another suggests that Wroth was recalling Sonnet 116, whose fantasy of an enduring and unalterable love speaks to one of the overarching themes of her work, namely the desire for constancy,[164] but which may also have struck a chord with her for more personal reasons. Bellamira's claim that once her beauty was lost her lover's affections strayed resonates ironically with the Sonnet's observation that 'Love's not Time's fool, though rosy lips and cheeks/ Within his bending sickle's compass come'. We might speculate that Wroth was here recalling her own private experience. The years 1614–16 had been traumatic, with the deaths of her husband and then her son (at this point her only child), as well as considerable financial pressures, and she might well have considered her beauty to have faded, with a resulting slackening of Pembroke's affections. Wroth appropriates Sonnet 116's romanticisation of unrequited passion, and its celebration of a love that 'bears it out, even to the edge of doom', to ennoble the suffering of Bellamira and herself.

When Bellamira claims the phrase 'love is not love' as her own, however, the effect is more complex. Required to share some of her verses, she expresses a deep sense of alienation from her own poetry:

'Truely Sir,' said she, 'so long it is since I made any, and the subject growne so strange, as I can hardly cal them to memory which I made, having desired to forget all things but my love, fearing that the sight, or thought of them, would bring on the joyes then felt, the sorrowes soone succeeding.'[165]

There may be a trace here of Wroth's own perceived distance from Sonnet 116, whose idealism is a relic of her youth, and may be similarly painful to re-examine.[166] Nevertheless, Bellamira offers up to Amphilanthus the lyric

---

[163] Ibid., p. 390.

[164] See Beilin, ' "The Onely Perfect Vertue" '; Waller, *The Sidney Family Romance*, pp. 208–9; and Hannay, *Mary Sidney, Lady Wroth*, pp. 108–9, for opposing viewpoints on the interpretation of this theme in Wroth's work.

[165] Wroth, *The First Part*, p. 390.

[166] It seems to me entirely possible that Shakespeare wrote Sonnet 116 for Pembroke and Mary Wroth, in 1604, when they were forced apart by their marriages to other people. In this sense, Sonnet 116 is part of Wroth's own personal history, which she revisits here. See my article, ' "Let Me not to the Marriage of True Minds" ', 277–91.

'As these drops fall ...', which she describes as having been written after the king's neglect had begun but before she despaired of ever recapturing his affection: 'one time after he had begun to change, hee yet did visite mee, and use mee somtimes well, and once so kindly, as I grew to hope a little, whereupon I writ these lines'.[167] The poem expresses relief that her lover is softening towards her, but fears that the change may not be lasting. The final two stanzas read:

> But if like heate drops you do wast away
> Glad, as disburden'd of a hot desire;
> Let me be rather lost, perish in fire,
> Then by those hopefull signes brought to decay.
>
> *Sweete be a louer puer, and permanent,*
> *Cast off gay cloathes of change, and such false slights:*
> *Love is not love, but where truth hath her rights,*
> *Else like boughs from the perfect body rent.*[168]

For Bellamira at the time of writing, 'Love is not love' becomes a 'fixèd mark' within the oceanic instability of her relationship with the king – an ideal to aspire to. There might also be an echo of Shakespeare's Sonnet 80 in the desire that she be 'not by those hopefull signes brought to decay' through the same excess of love and hope.[169] As Bellamira recites the lyric now, within the fiction, there is no chance of the quoted Sonnet being able to move the absent lover, but the same cannot be said for Wroth, for whom the key feature of the lyric is that it is performed before Amphilanthus, i.e. Pembroke, as reader of the romance. In this context, the phrase 'Love is not love' potentially forces Pembroke to confront his falling-off from the romantic sentiments that inspired both Sonnet 116 and his own lyric in defiance of change.

What the reception history of Sonnet 116 suggests, then, is that the early circulation of Shakespeare's 'sugred Sonnets among his private friends' was a more emotionally charged experience than has previously been assumed, and that those with access to Shakespeare's Sonnets in manuscript seem to be the ones who returned to the poems creatively. The fact that these were predominantly members of Pembroke's patronage circle or literary coterie – not only Dowland and Lawes, but Mary Wroth and George Herbert – suggests that we have still more to discover about Pembroke's sponsorship of the Sonnets, which extends into the 1630s, as the next chapter will show.

---

[167] Ibid., p. 391.
[168] Wroth, *Poems*, U29, ll 17–24.
[169] 'Then if he thrive and I be cast away/ The worst was this: my love was my decay.'

By contrast, the reading of the Quarto *Shake-speares Sonnets*, if its scant reception history from 1599 to 1622 is to be relied upon, produced very few vibrations. Only a fundamental dismantling of the Quarto sequence, and a more Cavalier approach to individual lyrics, would enable those outside this elite circle to voice their own desires through the Sonnets.

CHAPTER 2

Annals of All-Wasting Time, 1623–1708

The period 1623–1708 is hardly rich in terms of the bibliographic history of the Sonnets: only three Shakespeare poetry books were published between 1640 and 1700 – one each for *Venus*, *Lucrece* and the Sonnets – as opposed to two Folios of dramatic works, and sixteen Quarto playbooks.[1] This seems to have impacted on the Sonnets' creative influence, for 'Milton shows no knowledge of them, nor, indeed, does any of the Cavalier poets except Suckling'.[2] This is, nevertheless, a fascinating and significant moment in the Sonnets' reception. Their absence from the First Folio in 1623 defines them as potentially 'not Shakespeare', and their reputation as apocryphal and/or supplementary begins here, extending well into the eighteenth century. At the same time, the inclusion of a small number of Sonnets in Caroline manuscript miscellanies allows them to develop a distinctively 'Cavalier'[3] identity. Sonnet 2 ('When forty winters shall besiege thy brow') not only fits the *carpe diem* interests of many of those collecting lyric poetry at this time, but also shapes a broader understanding of Shakespeare's Sonnets as 'all at war with time'. One reader who proved particularly responsive to both the Sonnets' absence from the Folio and their obsession with 'Injurious Time' was John Benson, whose *Poems* had a more positive influence on the appreciation of Shakespeare's Sonnets than has yet been acknowledged. This chapter will look again at what Suckling, Milton and the Cavalier poets knew of the Sonnets, and explore those lyrics' Royalist affiliations during the English Civil Wars and the

---

[1] Erne, '*Cupids Cabinet Unlock't* (1662), Ostensibly "By W. Shakespeare", in Fact Partly by John Milton', p. 112.

[2] Rollins, *Variorum*, vol. 2, p. 329.

[3] I use this term 'Cavalier' advisedly, in acknowledgement of its essentially anachronistic nature, and the way in which it has obscured the variety of aesthetic and political attitudes among poets to whom it is applied. Nevertheless, in the context of the reception of Shakespeare's Sonnets it remains a useful term. For further discussion, see Sharpe, *Criticism and Compliment*, pp. 113–14, and Corns, 'Thomas Carew'.

Interregnum, pushing their afterlife further into the seventeenth century than has previously been thought possible.

Not in the Folio: The Sonnets and the *Works*

The First Folio of 1623, the book that defined Shakespeare as 'a single, and singular author, rather than a playwright',[4] did so without including his narrative or lyric verse. The reasons for this decision remain unclear. *Venus* and *Lucrece* were still popular enough to justify reprinting, so the copyright holders would have been unlikely to give them up; however, the 1609 *Sonnets* had not reached a second edition, and it is hard to imagine that John Heminges and Henry Condell could not have acquired the rights had they been so inclined.[5] Given some of the names associated with this publishing venture, it is surprising that the Folio does not at least refer to Shakespeare's Sonnets. William Jaggard, who appears in the colophon as part of the syndicate behind the Folio (though he was dead when it came out), is the stationer responsible for *The Passionate Pilgrim*.[6] William Herbert, Earl of Pembroke, one of the Folio dedicatees, has a strong connection to the Sonnets, as discussed in the previous chapter. Leonard Digges had offered a rare, positive view of the Sonnets in 1613 and contributes a prefatory poem to the Folio, promising Shakespeare that this book, 'When brass and marble fade, shall make thee look/ Fresh to all ages'.[7]

Building on this impression that the Sonnets *ought* to be here, Douglas Lanier has argued that the Folio's translation of theatrical documents into literary works relies on 'self-presentational tropes already established by the Sonnets'.[8] However, the specific allusions to the Sonnets that Lanier discovers vary considerably in persuasiveness. Ben Jonson, who had quoted a Sonnet as early as 1599, might well be rewriting the final couplet of Sonnet 18 ('So long as men can breathe or eyes can see,/ So long lives this, and this gives life to thee') in lines 22–24 of his tribute: 'And art alive still, while thy Booke doth live,/ And we have wits to read, and praise to give.' It does seem significant that Hugh Holland chose to write his eulogy in the form of a sonnet, concluding 'For though his line of life went soon

[4] Kastan, *Shakespeare and the Book*, p. 68.
[5] Alternatively, Edmondson and Wells suggest that Thorpe 'may well not have wished to jeopardise the sale of the remaining copies by making them available elsewhere', *Shakespeare's Sonnets*, p. 117.
[6] For further discussion of Jaggard's role in the printing, see Rasmussen, 'Publishing the First Folio'.
[7] Shakespeare, *William Shakespeare: The Complete Works*, ed. Wells and Taylor, p. xlvi.
[8] Lanier, 'Encryptions', p. 229.

about,/ The life yet of his lines shall never out', which echoes the pun in Sonnet 16, 'So should the lines of life that life repair …'. But Lanier's other discovered allusions in Heminges and Condell's dedication and the Digges poem are harder to accept, and potentially betray not only our need to believe that the Sonnets have always been valued by those who invented Shakespeare as Author, but our assumption that the monument *topos* is predominantly identifiable with Shakespeare's Sonnets.

Both John Kerrigan and Chris Laoutaris have usefully called attention to the posthumous language in which the Folio describes itself. When Heminges and Condell consecrate 'these remaines of your servant *Shakespeare*',

> The mortuary implication of this ('remaines' meaning corpse as well as corpus) is not accidental. Earlier, the actors say that they have 'done an office to the dead … onely to keepe the memory of so worthy a Friend, and Fellow alive, as was our SHAKESPEARE.' It has not been sufficiently recognized that the Folio, like *Loves Martyr*, is a memorial volume, is itself, indeed, a memorial.[9]

It was therefore natural for the preliminary poems to borrow the *scripta manet topos* from classical writers such as Horace and Ovid. Indeed, Digges makes the origin of his source known: 'Nor fire nor cank'ring age, as Naso said/ Of his, thy wit-fraught book shall once invade.'[10] At the same time, Shakespeare was himself the author of a number of epitaphs which use very similar language to that of the Sonnets. John Milton, for example, probably believed that the Stanley epitaph, inscribed on the family tomb at Tong in Shropshire, was by Shakespeare, and it was to this poem that he turned, rather than a Sonnet, when he came to write 'An Epitaph on the Admirable Dramatic Poet, William Shakespeare' (see below).

It may be that the Folio was always conceived of as a volume that would collate and celebrate Shakespeare's plays (*Mr William Shakespeare's Comedies, Histories and Tragedies*), and Peter Kirwan provides some valuable perspective on the expectation that it should represent a 'Complete' Works. As he

---

[9] Kerrigan, 'Shakespeare, Elegy, and Epitaph, 1557–1640', p. 240. Laoutaris has pointed out similar connotations created by the Droeshout engraving, which he likens to 'a death mask', as emphasised by the accompanying text by B. I. which describes its being 'cut' in brass by 'the Graver': 'The suggestion is of a funereal effigy, with "Graver" evoking both an engraver on monumental brass and a grave-maker. The title-page and facing poem together reproduce the function of post-reformation tomb effigies which often looked directly at the viewer rather than upwards towards God and served, in the words of Thomas Fuller, as "monuments to mens merits" instead of aids to intercessory prayer'. See Laoutaris, 'The Prefatorial Material', pp. 51, 52.

[10] Shakespeare, *William Shakespeare: The Complete Works*, ed. Wells and Taylor, p. xlvi.

notes, the Folio's preliminary pages make no claims to completeness, and our modern assumption that a 'Works' will be definitive (reflected in the OED definition '(a person's) literary or musical compositions, considered collectively') is potentially anachronistic: Jonson's 1616 *Workes* omitted early and collaborative plays to represent the author in his best light, and was followed by a second volume.[11] Moreover, Kirwan highlights an intriguing line from Digges' prefatory poem which promises that Shakespeare will live on 'Till these, till any of thy Volumes rest/ Shall with more fire, more feeling be express't':[12]

> Here, Digges acknowledges that the Folio is not in itself complete; it does not replace the 'rest' of Shakespeare's volumes. The implication is that Digges conceptualises Shakespeare as having multiple volumes of which one, the present volume, constitutes his 'Works'. Quite what the volumes are remains unclear – he may be referring to individual texts of plays, or to collections of Shakespeare's poems. However, the point is that the volume of 'Workes' is complete unto itself, but is itself not all of the 'Volumes' of Shakespeare.[13]

But if Kirwan is right that there is a difference between the Sonnets' absence from the Folio and their omission,[14] it would nevertheless come to be read as an 'exclusion', with devastating consequences. Heminges and Condell had 'collected and published [Shakespeare's] writings', and Digges agreed that they had given 'The world thy works';[15] hence the canon was constructed without the Sonnets. Their 'exclusion' was perpetuated by F2 (1632) – although by this point the copyright-holder, Thorpe, was dead – and then by F3 (1663) and F4 (1685), although these volumes had found room for six apocryphal plays. For all the Sonnets' claims to confer monumentality – reflecting 'many of the same qualities … sought in actual funerary structures: permanence, memory, authority'[16] – they themselves were denied it. Even when the Sonnets began to be printed in supplementary volumes to the *Works* in the early eighteenth century, their former omission went against them. In his 'Remarks on the Poems of *Shakespear*' (1710), Charles Gildon acknowledges that some will consider them 'not

---

[11] Kirwan, '"Complete" Works', pp. 88–9.
[12] It is possible to read this another way, depending on how one punctuates. In the *Oxford Complete Works* (Shakespeare, *William Shakespeare: The Complete Works*, ed. Wells and Taylor), the line reads 'Till these, till any of thy volume's rest …', p. xlvi.
[13] Kirwan, '"Complete" Works', p. 90.
[14] Ibid., p. 88.
[15] Shakespeare, *William Shakespeare: The Complete Works*, ed. Wells and Taylor, pp. xlv, xlvi.
[16] Blaine, 'Milton and the Monument Topos', 221.

valuable enough to be reprinted, as was plain by the first Editors of his Works who wou'd otherwise have join'd them altogether'.[17]

But if the Folios failed to preserve the Sonnets, both textually and allusively, a small number of manuscripts bearing individual poems kept them in circulation. Indeed, one of the most surprising aspects of the Sonnets' reception in the seventeenth century is not their obscurity, but their sudden efflorescence. Between 1623 and 1660, at least ten complete Sonnets were circulating in manuscript, half of them singly,[18] and these were numbers 2, 8, 32, 33, 68, 71, 106, 107, 116 (in its heavily adapted version) and 138.[19] Of these, twelve out of twenty-three copies are taken from manuscripts dated in the 1630s, with eight attributed to the early years of that decade.[20] Whether or not this is a matter of Caroline readers taking better care of their miscellanies than Shakespeare's contemporaries, or whether the 1620s and 1630s represent a nostalgic turn to the Sonnets by a new readership, concentrated in the universities and the Inns of Court, has yet to be determined.[21] Debate has centred on Sonnet 2 ('When forty winters shall besiege thy brow'), which was preferred in a variant text in no less than thirteen manuscripts, and whose provenance might help us to determine whether the Sonnets were mislaid and rediscovered, or whether we have simply lost the evidence of their unbroken transmission. Gary Taylor recognises the variant Sonnet 2 as a Shakespearean original, composed *c.* 1597, which circulated independent of the Q text.[22] Duncan-Jones disagrees, pointing out that the Sonnet is found 'largely in the company of late Jacobean and Caroline verse, not with other pre-1609 poems'. She attributes the variants to Caroline admirers who recognised one of

---

[17] Shakespeare, *The Works of Mr. William Shakespear. Volume the Seventh. Containing Venus & Adonis. Tarquin & Lucrece And His Miscellany Poems*, ed. Gildon, p. 446.

[18] Sonnets 33, 68 and 107 appear with excerpts from others in Folger MS. V.a.148, and Sonnets 32 and 71 in Folger MS. V.a.162.

[19] For a full list of MS Sonnets, see *The New Oxford Shakespeare*, ed. Taylor *et al.* (2017), vol. 1, pp. 1436–8. I have excluded 128 (BL Rawlinson Poetical 152), discussed in the previous chapter as dated *c.* 1613–20.

[20] These statistics are based on Beal's *Index*, with the addition of Cutts' discovery of a second copy of 116 (Bodleian MSS Ashm. 36/37, f29r), and excluding 128. These figures otherwise tally with Marotti's discussion of 'eleven whole sonnets in twenty different manuscripts' in 'Shakespeare's Sonnets and the Manuscript Circulation of Texts in Early Modern England', pp. 186–7.

[21] At least three of the Sonnet manuscripts have a Christ Church, Oxford connection. Marotti attributes this college's influence to two factors: '(1) the high percentage of students coming from Westminster School, whose Master, William Osbaldson, encouraged poetic composition; and (2) the poetic activities of Richard Corbet, William Strode, George Morley, and other poets connected to Christ Church' ('Folger MSS V.a.89 and V.a.345', p. 48). See also Roberts, *Reading Shakespeare's Poems*, pp. 178–9.

[22] Taylor, 'Some Manuscripts of Shakespeare's Sonnets'.

their own: 'alongside poems by Carew, Strode, Corbett and Herrick, Shakespeare's speaker's plea for fruition and procreation – implicitly, and sometimes explicitly, addressed to a young girl – comes across as in effect an honorary "Cavalier" seduction lyric'.[23] I will argue here that the two most frequently transcribed Sonnets – 2 ('When forty winters') and 106 ('When in the chronicle of wasted time')[24] – do imply a Shakespearean original, but also show evidence of alteration, as Caroline writers adapted them to their literary and romantic needs.

Caroline Lyrics of Choice: Sonnets 2 and 106 in Manuscript

There are other Sonnets which anticipate the effects of Time upon the addressee's beauty, and urge the begetting of a child, but perhaps none has such a memorable opening as Sonnet 2, with its striking juxtaposition of the martial and the physiognomical:

> When forty winters shall besiege thy brow,
> And dig deep trenches in thy beauty's field,
> Thy youth's proud livery, so gazed on now,
> Will be a tattered weed, of small worth held:
> Then being asked, where all thy beauty lies,
> Where all the treasure of thy lusty days,
> To say, within thine own deep-sunken eyes,
> Were an all-eating shame and thriftless praise.
> How much more praise deserved thy beauty's use
> If thou couldst answer, 'This fair child of mine
> Shall sum my count, and make my old excuse',
> Proving his beauty by succession thine:
> > This were to be new made when thou art old,
> > And see thy blood warm when thou feel'st it cold.

But whilst the Quarto's opening line is accurately repeated in the MS texts,[25] the rest of the Sonnet is transcribed with substantive changes, and the following is the version that Caroline readers mainly preferred:[26]

---

[23] Shakespeare, *Shakespeare's Sonnets*, ed. Duncan-Jones, p. 453.
[24] Reproduced in two manuscripts, 106 arguably comes in third after 116, if we include the inclusion of lines 11–2 of 116 in the Hailstone MS ('Love alters not with his briefe hours & weeks/ But bears It out even to the Edge of Doome' (fol. 23r)). However, the full-text 116 endures in the substantially altered version, adapted for musical performance, discussed in the previous chapter, and so will not be further considered here.
[25] There are two slight variants out of thirteen MSS (including the Hailstone), specifically 'threescore' instead of 'forty', and 'yeares' instead of 'winters'. See Taylor, 'Some Manuscripts of Shakespeare's Sonnets', 212.
[26] Only the St John's College, Cambridge MS S.23 (1630s–40s) is based on the Quarto, and even in this case, there is scope for doubt. Taylor notes the unusual spelling of 'Shakspere' in the MS, in

'Spes Altera. A Song', c. 1630[27]

> When forty winters shal besiege thy brow
> And trench deep furrowes in that louely feild
> Thy youth faire livery so accounted now
> Shal be like rotten weeds of no worth held
> Then being asked where al thy beuty lyes
> Wheres al the lustre of thy youth ful days
> To say within these hollow suncken eyes
> Were an al eaten truth and worthless prayse
> Oh how much better were thy beutyes vse
> If thou couldst say this pretty childe of mine
> Saues my account, and makes my old excuse
> Making his beuty by succession thine.
> This were to be newborne when thou art old
> And see thy blood warme when thou feel'st it cold.[28]

This text represents a less metaphorically dense version of Q, or one 'dilute and conventional' if you will.[29] The Q text favours compression through metaphor, with the forehead lined by 'trenches' rather than 'furrows'; youth's livery being 'a tattered/tottered weed' rather than 'like rotten weeds'; and the phrase 'all-eating shame' more intelligible than 'al eaten truth'. It may be that the MS version lost some of its complexity in the process of musical adaptation, as suggested by the title 'Spes altera A song'. At the same time, as Taylor has shown, the MS version resonates with Shakespeare plays and poems of the 1590s; for example, 'trench deep furrowes in that louely feild' recalls 'help to furrow me with age' in *Richard II*, 1.3.229, and 'trench' as a verb in *Two Gentlemen of Verona* and *Venus and Adonis*. This line also suggests the influence of Michael Drayton's *The Shepheards Garland* (1593), Eclogues 2, 'The time-plow'd furrowes in the fairest field'.[30] Nevertheless, Duncan-Jones is unconvinced, arguing

contrast with the much repeated 'Shake-speare' of Q and suggests that other minor differences might imply an intermediate source. See ibid., 215, fn. 7.

[27] Critics disagree about which version of the variant Sonnet is closest to the imagined original. Duncan-Jones chooses the Bellasys version in BL Add. MS 10309 f. 143, *Shakespeare's Sonnets*, p. 463, and Taylor the Westminster Abbey MS 41 which he dates to 1619–30. Taylor identifies two distinct lines of transmission, accounting for those titled 'Spes altera', and those which take another title, 'To one yt would dye a Mayd' (x4), 'The Benefitt of Mariage' and 'A Lover to his Mistress'. He posits at least two missing MSS to explain these lines of descent but acknowledges that there might be more: 'both branches might be many removes from an autograph original'. See the full diagram and explanation in 'Some Manuscripts of Shakespeare's Sonnets', 219.

[28] Hobbs, 'Shakespeare's Sonnet II', 112.

[29] Shakespeare, *Shakespeare's Sonnets*, ed. Duncan-Jones, p. 456.

[30] Taylor, 'Some Manuscripts of Shakespeare's Sonnets', 228, 232–3. This Drayton allusion was originally noted by Hyder Rollins.

that 'trench deep furrows' cannot be Shakespearean, because it 'deviate[s] from the image of siege warfare' and 'introduces associations with seed-sowing and eventual harvest which are wholly inappropriate, since the dynamic of the sonnet depends upon an absolute contrast between the invasive threat posed to the youth's beauty by "forty winters" if he fails to marry, and the fruitful alternative if he does'.[31] This is certainly true, but it would be consistent with the relationship between Sonnet 138 and its earlier version in *The Passionate Pilgrim* if the variant/draft of Sonnet 2 lacked the contrast which becomes more dynamic and meaningful in Q. I also find myself pausing over the variant text's deictics – a feature which many critics have found characteristic of Shakespeare's Sonnets: not 'thy beauties field' but '*that* louely feild'; not 'thine owne deep sunken eyes', but '*these* hollow suncken eyes' (italics mine).[32] Finally, the MS text is closer to what most critics agree was Shakespeare's source: the trans-lation of Erasmus in Thomas Wilson's *The Arte of Rhetorique* (1553, rev. 1560), specifically 'An Epistle to perswade a young ientleman to Mariage'. As Taylor notes,

> Several passages in one paragraph seem to have influenced this sonnet ... 'you shall have a *pretie* little boie, running up and doune your house, soche a one as shall expresse your loke, and your wiues loke ... by whom you shall seme *to bee newe borne*'. We would not expect scribal error, or authorial revi-sion, to introduce variants which are closer than the Quarto to the poem's unacknowledged source.[33]

But if Caroline readers preferred an earlier Shakespearean draft, it seems likely that they made some revisions of their own. Taylor's argument that the title 'Spes Altera' originates with Shakespeare is less likely than that it was added by one of those university-educated Caroline miscellanists who appended a Latin title to Sonnet 8 ('*In laudem Musice et Opprobrium Contemporii eiusdem*').[34] These readers may also be responsible for the addressee's implied change of gender. Q's 'treasure' in line 6, with its possible pun on 'semen', is replaced in favour of 'lustre', and 'lusty', i.e. sexually vigorous, becomes the gender-neutral 'youthful'. Hence, the Sonnet better befits both the titles bestowed on it, 'To one yt would dye a Mayd' and 'A Lover to his Mistress', and its place in the anthology by

---

[31] Shakespeare, *Shakespeare's Sonnets*, ed. Duncan-Jones, p. 456.

[32] For further discussion of Shakespeare's distinctive use of proximal and distal deixis in the Sonnets see Dubrow, *Captive Victors*, p. 182, and Lanier, 'Encryptions', p. 224.

[33] Taylor, 'Some Manuscripts of Shakespeare's Sonnets', 244.

[34] See British Library Add. MS 15226, f. 4v, discussed by Beal, *Index of English Literary Manuscripts*, ShW20.

Daniel Leare (*c.* 1631–3), where it precedes poems entitled 'On a made not mariagable' and 'On mary w[i]thout a dowry'.[35] The former lyric places Sonnet 2 in a particularly 'Cavalier' context, when Lydia's reluctance is attributed to her youth: 'like a rose new blowne' she 'yeelds no seed', but if the addressee will wait until Autumn, 'Then hir ripeness will be such/ That shee will fall over with a touch' (fol. 19v).[36] Whilst this Sonnet might well have appealed to 'bachelor gentlemen',[37] it was also to be found in the miscellany owned (and partly compiled) by Margaret Bellasys (d. 1624), and Sasha Roberts describes it as 'a *carpe diem* lyric addressed to a female beloved against the denial of sexual pleasure'.[38] That said, it also seems to me to develop a particularly misogynist strain of the Caroline *carpe diem* lyric.

At some point in 1632–7, Sir John Suckling adapted Donne's poem 'Farewell to Love', in a lyric of the same title, but with some striking alterations. Donne's speaker renounces erotic love on the basis of post-coital disgust – and there may be an echo of Shakespeare's Sonnet 129 ('Had, having, and in quest to have, extreme') in the assertion that 'Being had, enjoying it decays' and the promise not 'To pursue things which had endamaged me'. Women come under no particular scrutiny in Donne's poem; the speaker will 'admire their greatness, [but] shun their heat'.[39] By contrast, Suckling's speaker wields his aversion for women like a scalpel, and what he discovers redoubles his disgust:

> If I gaze now, 'tis but to see
> What manner of deaths-head 'twill be,
> When it is free
> From that fresh upper skin,
> The gazers Joy, and sin …
>
> A quick corse me-thinks I spy
> In ev'ry woman; and mine eye,
> At passing by,
> Checks, and is troubled, just
> As if it rose from Dust.[40]

---

[35] BL Add. MS.30982, f. 18. See Roberts, *Reading Shakespeare's Poems*, p. 177.

[36] See the full poem as reprinted by Marotti, 'Shakespeare's Sonnets and the Manuscript Circulation of Texts in Early Modern England', p. 193.

[37] Taylor, 'Some Manuscripts of Shakespeare's Sonnets', 224.

[38] Roberts, *Reading Shakespeare's Poems*, p. 177.

[39] Donne, *John Donne: The Complete English Poems*, pp. 56–7, ll 17, 33, 38.

[40] All quotations from Suckling are taken from *The Works of Sir John Suckling*, pp. 67–8, ll 26–30, 41–50.

Suckling was an avid admirer of *Hamlet* and Jacobean revenge tragedy,[41] but this lyric may also reflect the increasingly dark *carpe diem* lyric which was particular to Cavalier poetry, though indebted to Jonson and Donne.

We find another example in Robert Herrick's 'The Changes to Corinna', perhaps written in the 1620s–1630s, though not published until 1648, in which the beloved's prospective ageing produces a disgust in the spectator that imperils his desire to seize the day:

> You are young, but must be old,
> And, to these, ye must be told,
> Time, ere long, will come and plow
> Loathed Furrows in your brow:
> And the dimnesse of your eye
> Will no other thing imply,
> > But you must die
> > As well as I.[42]

The variant text of Sonnet 2 introduces a similar note of contempt for the (implicitly female) beloved, juxtaposing 'yt louely field' with Herrick's despised 'furrows'. Aged beauty will be 'like rotten weeds of no worth held' as opposed to 'a tattered weed of small worth held'. But perhaps most arresting is the shadowy presence of the skull beneath the skin in that image of 'Hollow suncken eyes', whose 'lustre' is lost. We might recall Thomas Middleton's *The Revenger's Tragedy*, when Hippolito asks of the skull of Gloriana: 'Is this the form that living shone so bright?', and Vindice commands him to 'Place the torch there that his affrighted eyeballs/ May start into those hollows'.[43] In this context, 'al eaten truth' is no longer a nonsense; rather, it echoes the Jacobean/Cavalier obsession with decomposition as proof of woman's falsehood:

> Here might a scornful and ambitious woman
> Look through and through herself; see, ladies, with false forms
> You deceive men but cannot deceive worms.[44]

Although miscellanists did not tend to arrange lyrics thematically, it is interesting to find Sonnet 2 following an epigram 'On an olde woeman' in the Morley MS.[45]

---

41 See Wilcher, *The Discontented Cavalier*, pp. 148–9. Suckling's debt to Shakespeare is discussed further below.
42 Herrick, *The Complete Poetry of Robert Herrick*, p. 92, ll 11–18.
43 Middleton, *The Revenger's Tragedy* in *Thomas Middleton: The Collected Works*, 3.5.68, 145–6.
44 Ibid., 3.5.95–7.
45 See Shakespeare, *Shakespeare's Sonnets*, ed. Duncan-Jones, p. 454.

Sonnet 106 has no such macabre appeal, but it resonates with Sonnet 2 in other ways, not least the fact that it too was preferred in a variant text.[46] The Q version reads:

> When in the chronicle of wasted time
> I see descriptions of the fairest wights,
> And beauty making beautiful old rhyme
> In praise of ladies dead and lovely knights,
> Then in the blazon of sweet beauty's best,
> Of hand, of foot, of lip, of eye, of brow,
> I see their antique pen would have expressed
> Even such beauty as you master now.
> So all their praises are but prophecies
> Of this our time, all you prefiguring,
> And for they looked but with divining eyes,
> They had not skill enough your worth to sing:
>   For we, which now behold these present days,
>   Have eyes to wonder, but lack tongues to praise.

In both the miscellany used by the Holgate family of Saffron Walden *c.* 1630s,[47] and the verse miscellany of Robert Bishop *c.* 1630,[48] the Sonnet begins: 'When in the Annalls of all wastinge Time …' The personification of Time here is much more arresting than the passive 'wasted time' of the Quarto, and recalls the similar construction, 'all-eating shame', in Sonnet 2. The aural effect of 'Ann*alls* of *all* wasting' might also be something that we would want to attribute to Shakespeare, though he uses the term 'annals' only once (see *Coriolanus*, 5.6.114), and its Latinity, and the association with Tacitus, make this a more sophisticated (Caroline?) choice than the Middle English word 'chronicle'.[49] The addition of a title which defines the subject as heterosexual love – 'On his Mistress' (Holgate) and 'On his Mistris Beauty' (Bishop) – similarly reflects Caroline adaptations made to Sonnet 2.

What is truly distinctive about this variant of 106 is the fact of its being conflated with another lyric, 'When mine eyes first admiring of your beauty', whose author was William Herbert, Earl of Pembroke.[50] Both poems appear separately in the Holgate MS, with distinct titles ('On his Mistress' (p. 96) and 'The picture of his Mistris' (p. 140)), but in the Bishop

---

[46] Stanley Wells links the two sonnets on the basis that in both cases 'the variants are so substantial that they amount in effect to a different version of the poem', in Wells *et al.*, *Textual Companion*, p. 444.

[47] Pierpont Morgan Library, MA 1057, p. 96 (Beal ShW25).

[48] Rosenbach Foundation, MS 1083/16, pp. 256–7 (Beal ShW26).

[49] See Shakespeare, *The Complete Sonnets and Poems*, ed. Burrow, p. 592.

[50] This lyric was printed in Pembroke's 1660 *Poems* (ed. Donne), p. 54.

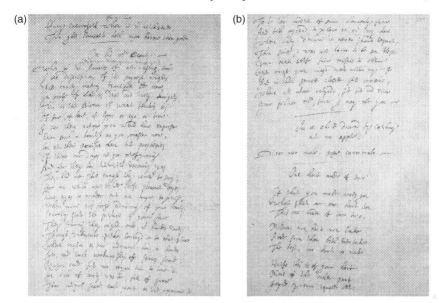

Figure 2.1 Sonnet 106 in Robert Bishop's *Commonplace Book, c.* 1630, pp. 256–7
© Rosenbach Library, MS 1083/16

miscellany, Shakespeare's Sonnet is immediately preceded by Pembroke's, generating a 32-line poem.

Quite how this happened is a matter for speculation. It may have been Pembroke's 'competitive handling of the same topic as Sonnet 106 – perhaps a lyric sent in response to Shakespeare's poem'.[51] This could be supported by the couplet's implied challenge: 'For [w]e which now behold these pleasant dayes/ Have eyes to wonder but noe tongues to praise', which Pembroke disputes by offering a conventional homage of praise based on what *his* eyes see. And yet, the poems are thematically very different. Shakespeare's Sonnet explores the literary depiction of beauty in the past as a means of flattering superlative beauty in the present. Pembroke's poem turns on the familiar conceit of the lover engraving his mistress's image in his heart because she refuses to proffer herself in reality. His use of allegory – where the portrait is judged by Reason and True Judgement – is Sidneian, but distinctly un-Shakespearean. Thus, it seems more likely that the poems were 'contiguous in the source-text' and so conjoined.[52] Whilst this allows for

[51] Marotti, 'Shakespeare's Sonnets as Literary Property', pp. 149–50.
[52] Ibid.

the intriguing scenario of Shakespeare and Pembroke exchanging poems, it also reinforces the notion, discussed in the previous chapter, that at least some of Shakespeare's Sonnets 'belonged' to Pembroke, and interacted with his poetry in the same material space. Furthermore, the Earl's verse enjoyed a modest afterlife in Caroline miscellanies,[53] perhaps because of his thematic and stylistic affinity with 'Cavalier' poetry.[54] Hence, the value afforded to Pembroke's papers (particularly after his death in 1630) may have ensured the transmission of a small number of Shakespeare's Sonnets, if only by accident.

But whilst the 1630s represent the most lively period of Sonnet transcription and circulation we have yet encountered, drawing on a wider range of poems, it is also true that this was only a small fraction of the *Sonnets*. The next most significant publishing venture, which would proffer another 130 or so Sonnets to a wider audience, was John Benson's *Poems* (1640), a volume which strategically positions itself between print and manuscript culture.

'Serene, clear and elegantly plain': John Benson's *Poems*

Benson's *Poems* was not only the first printed edition of the Sonnets for thirty years, it was the first posthumous edition of Shakespeare's poetry.[55] It followed the Caroline fashion for collections of 'Poems' by dead writers, beginning with Donne and Herbert in 1633, and continuing with the work of Thomas Randolph, Thomas Carew, Francis Beaumont and Ben Jonson (1638–40).[56] At the same time, Benson was specifically indebted to that other posthumous collection, the First Folio, and envisaged his octavo as a (diminutive) companion volume. Not only was *Poems* printed

---

[53] The Bishop manuscript, for example, contains four other poems by Pembroke, alongside eighteen by Donne, fifteen by Harington, ten by Jonson, seven by Corbett, and three (not including Sonnet 106) by Shakespeare.

[54] See Waller, *The Sidney Family Romance*, pp. 161, 187. We might take as an example the lyric 'That he would not be beloved' (included in the Holgate MS) which urges the mistress to deny him on the basis that 'Love surfeits with rewards, his nurse is scorn'. This resonates with the key Cavalier theme of the 'pleasure of restraint', as explored by Scodel in 'The Pleasures of Restraint'.

[55] Although the narrative poems were still being reprinted, they remained in the form in which they had first been published, with Shakespeare's dedications to Southampton, despite the fact that in 1636, when the most recent *Venus* had been printed, Southampton had been dead for twelve years and Shakespeare for twenty.

[56] Marotti describes the 1633 Donne and Herbert editions as authorising single-author collections. As a result, 'lyric poems themselves were perceived less as occasional and ephemeral and more as valuable artifacts worth preserving in those monumentalising editions that were among the most prestigious products of print culture' (*Manuscript, Print*, p. 247). For more detailed discussion of Benson's debts to Donne, see Heffernan, 'Turning Sonnets into Poems', 87–97.

by Thomas Cotes, who had worked on F2, it begins with a woodcut of the Droeshout engraving,[57] an eight-line mash-up of Jonson's eulogy, and elegies by William Basse (from F1) and John Milton (from F2). But if the posthumous features of Benson's volume emphasise fixity, monumentality and posterity, 'add[ing] glory to the deserved Author in these his Poems',[58] this volume also locates the Sonnets within a manuscript culture defined by immediacy, flexibility and appropriation.

Poems contains 146 Sonnets, interspersed with the twenty original *Passionate Pilgrim* lyrics, 'A Lover's Complaint', poems from the 1612 *Passionate Pilgrim*, 'The Phoenix and the Turtle' (published in *Love's Martyr* (1601)), a couple of lyrics from the plays, and three elegies for Shakespeare. All of this material was taken from printed sources, with the Sonnets derived from the 1609 Quarto.[59] There follows a section entitled 'An Addition of some Excellent Poems … By other Gentlemen' which includes fifteen lyrics by Jonson, Beaumont, Herrick, Strode, Carew and possibly Milton, none of which had been published before.[60] In his address 'To the Reader', Benson fails to mention the Quarto,[61] or any print history for his collection, perhaps in order to perpetuate the fantasy that the Sonnets are manuscript lyrics. He introduces them as

> Some excellent and sweetely composed Poems, of Master *William Shakespeare*, which in themselves appear of the same purity, the Authour himselfe then living avouched; they had not the fortune by reason of their Infancie in his death to have the due accommodation of proportionable glory, with the rest of his everliving works, yet the lines of themselves will afford you a more authentick approbation than my assurance any way can.

Some of Benson's imagined readers might already know about the existence of the Quarto, but the obvious interpretation is that these are all unpublished poems, 'of the same purity' as those to which Shakespeare had put his name, which would have been included in his 'workes' had the poet

---

[57] This is not extant in all editions of the *Poems*; it is missing from the copy in the British Library and that reproduced on Early English Books Online. See editions held in the Folger and Harvard libraries.

[58] 'To the Reader', in Shakespeare, *Poems*, ed. Benson.

[59] Taking Benson at his word, Sidney Lee concluded that the *Poems* was 'based on some amateur collection of pieces of manuscript poetry, which had been in private circulation' (*Shakespeares Sonnets*, p. 57); however, Benson has since been shown to have relied heavily on Q, with very little consultation of any other printed or manuscript source. See Alden, 'The 1640 Text of Shakespeare's Sonnets', 19.

[60] Shrank, 'Reading Shakespeare's Sonnets', 291.

[61] There are a couple of perhaps unconscious echoes in the hyphenation of Shakespeare's name on the title-page, and the phrase 'everliving workes' which recalls 'our ever-living poet' in Thorpe's dedication.

not died before he could ensure their posterity. This argument is familiar from the Folio dedication, in which Heminges and Condell describe the plays as 'out-living' Shakespeare, who was therefore unable 'to be executor to his own writings' and reliant on them to 'procure his Orphans Guardians'.[62] Where Benson's dedication differs significantly is that Heminges and Condell presuppose the inadequacy of the previous printed texts, 'diverse stolne, and surreptitious copies, maimed and deformed',[63] whilst Benson (who might equally make that argument) focuses instead on the poems themselves, emphasising their 'purity' and 'authentic[ity]'. This strongly implies the taint of illegitimacy which 'exclusion' from the Folio or 'workes' had incurred, anticipating Nicholas Rowe's dismissal of the poetry as 'spurious' in 1709. Furthermore, by insisting that the Sonnets were 'infants' at the time of Shakespeare's death, Benson hints that they are late works,[64] thereby potentially invoking some of the assumptions about late writing explored by Gordon McMullan: 'it is a supplement to the main body of the artist's work which is also a fulfilment of that work ... it has ramifications beyond the personal, expressing a sense of epochal lateness or of a going beyond the possibilities of the current moment or, combining the two, of a certain paradoxical prolepsis in its finality'.[65] The fact that Shakespeare's Sonnets give way to Caroline lyrics in the *Poems* potentially reinforces this prolepsis. Indeed, David Baker has aptly described the *Poems* as 'a publication in the "cavalier mode" ... [which] survived the period between 1640 and 1660 as a cavalier volume'.[66] The title-page drops the word 'Sonnets', which was now not only old-fashioned, but had fallen in status, being most frequently applied to broadside ballads and ditties.[67] The author is specifically 'Wil. Shake-speare. Gent', and the poems themselves are gentrified: 'eligantly plaine', 'gentle straines', which will 'raise your admiration to his praise', implying that the reader will be elevated by the leisurely pursuit of reading them. Although Benson's praise of the poems has been shown to be borrowed from another preface,[68] it also reads

[62] Shakespeare, *William Shakespeare: The Complete Works*, ed. Wells and Taylor, p. xlv.

[63] Ibid.

[64] Other critics who identify the Sonnets as late works focus on their publication date of 1609, but on the assumption that Shakespeare revised for publication and the Sonnets were thereby infected with lateness. Duncan-Jones sees them as 'deeply rooted in an awareness of death, and of the desperate struggle to make one's voice heard before disease destroys both pen and phallus', *Ungentle Shakespeare*, p. 219.

[65] McMullan, *Shakespeare and the Idea of Late Writing*, p. 26.

[66] Baker, 'Cavalier Shakespeare', 153.

[67] Shrank, 'Reading Shakespeare's Sonnets', 276.

[68] See Thomas May's prefatory poem to *The Shepheards Holy-Day* (1635), published by Benson, and discussed by Smith, 'No Cloudy Stuffe to Puzzell Intellect'.

as an attempt to address negative assumptions about the Sonnets that had been generated by the Quarto:

> in your perusall you shall finde them *Seren*, cleere, and eligantly plaine, such gentle straines as shall recreate and not perplexe your braine, no intricate or cloudy stuffe to puzzell intellect, but perfect eloquence.

Cathy Shrank's observation that *Poems* 'offers one of the earliest critical and imaginative responses that we have to a work which otherwise has left scant imprint on the literature of seventeenth-century England'[69] is a compelling one and speaks to some of Q's deficiencies from a reader's point of view, discussed in the previous chapter. In editing the Sonnets, Benson was clearly driven by the need to make them more attractive and accessible to mid-seventeenth-century readers.

Perhaps his most contentious editorial intervention was to reorder the sequence, causing irreparable damage to Q's narrative structure. But this is a narrative which had arguably never served the Sonnets' interests, and Benson had no scruples in dispensing with it, if he even noticed its existence. The 'procreation' Sonnets in which a beautiful nobleman is urged to beget a child no longer open the story; the poet's response no longer evolves from admiration to erotic love.[70] Rather, by starting with 67 ('Ah, wherefore with infection should he live') and 68 ('Thus is his cheek the map of days outworn'), which repeat the imagery of the procreation Sonnets but with a more cynical edge,[71] Benson prioritises the threat of emotional betrayal by a beautiful man, before connecting this with Time's betrayal of Beauty and Youth. He thereby precipitates the reader into a same-sex relationship *in medias res* in a fashion which is arguably more radical than the Quarto, presenting 'an amorous, passionate, doting relationship … that is not tempered by the imperatives of procreation, patrimony or husbandry'.[72] Moreover, if Benson sullies the male beloved's reputation from the start, his failure to uphold the fragile demarcation between Sonnets addressed to the 'Fair Youth' and those to the 'Dark Lady' does much to

---

[69] Shrank, 'Reading Shakespeare's Sonnets', 273.

[70] For a more detailed version of this reading of Q, see Crosman, 'Making Love Out of Nothing at All'.

[71] Sonnet 67 resembles Sonnet 1 in its association of beauty with the 'Rose' (suggestively capitalised as in Q), and also Sonnet 4 in its emphasis on bankruptcy and nature's audit, but where Sonnet 11 had used the idea of nature's store as a positive image, 67 is more reticent: 'the speaker no longer proposes that progeny should perpetuate the stored-up beauty contained in the youth' (Shakespeare, *Shakespeare's Sonnets*, ed. Duncan-Jones, p. 245), perhaps because the infection lives within him.

[72] Roberts, *Reading Shakespeare's Poems*, p. 163.

exonerate the mistress.[73] Poem 86 in Benson's collection combines Sonnets 148–50, which deplore his blind infatuation for someone unworthy (usually taken to be the Dark Lady). But the very next poem, 87, is a conflation of Sonnets 78–9, in which the speaker avers 'sweet love, thy lovely argument/ Deserves the travail of a worthier pen'.

With the impossibility of reading either character or narrative consistently across the Sonnets, Benson's *Poems* places greater emphasis on the discrete lyric. As we have seen, individual titles were a feature of Shakespeare's Sonnets in Caroline manuscripts, though they were also associated with print miscellanies such as Tottel's *Songs and Sonnettes*. Margreta de Grazia describes them as 'a highly abbreviated form of literary criticism that extrapolates meaning, function, or circumstance from texts. The titles give the reader an interpretative threshold from which to enter the poem'.[74] In this case, they encourage ownership and appropriation. Does the reader wish to describe his self-abnegation to the beloved? He may turn to 'The force of love'. Must he urge a mistress to surrender her virginity? Why not try 'An invitation to Marriage'? Has he been meditating on mortality? He will find comfort in 'Injurious Time'. Also familiar from the manuscript tradition, and reflecting the same user-centred approach, is Benson's occasional stipulation of a female subject or addressee. In Sonnet 101, he alters three male pronouns to female; in 104, 'friend' is replaced by 'love'; and in 108 'sweet boy' becomes 'sweet love'. Furthermore, the conflation of Sonnets 113–15 is described as 'Selfe flatterie of her Beauty', 122 as 'Upon the receipt of a table book from his Mistris', and 125 'An Intreatie for her acceptance'. But this is nothing like as extensive as it might have been were it really an attempt to eradicate the homoeroticism of the sequence.[75] Equally of note is the way in which Benson generates new positions for a female subject within the collection. This is partly through the incorporation of *The Passionate Pilgrim*. In the poems which trace Venus' attempt to seduce Adonis, at least two lyrics (PP4, PP11) respond with pleasure, titillation and envy to the 'fair queen['s]' overt sexuality, whilst PP12 is voiced by a woman who defends her preference for youthful male beauty over 'crabbed age'. Benson's labelling of the Sonnets also challenges a misogynist perspective, either by stressing generic Petrarchan situations which dissipate some of the sequence's personal loathing ('Loves crueltie', 'In

---

[73] Benson omits Sonnet 126, 'O thou my lovely boy …' which is often thought to draw a line between the two sequences, perhaps because it appears to be incomplete.

[74] De Grazia, 'The First Reader of *Shake-speares Sonnets*', p. 95.

[75] See de Grazia, 'The Scandal of Shakespeare's Sonnets', p. 36, and my Introduction.

praise of his Love', 'A request to his scornfull love'), or by apportioning blame to the desirer rather than the desired. Sonnet 129 ('Th'expense of spirit in a waste of shame') may still end by associating the vagina with the entrance into the fiery pit of hell, but it is now damned by the title 'Immoderate lust'.

Benson's disregard for the quatorzain, conflating poems into verses of twenty-eight or more often forty-two lines (though with the couplets still indented), was probably a response to a Caroline audience with no particular interest in the sonnet form.[76] But which Sonnets he chose to conjoin and which he allowed to stand alone also implies that he did not expect readers to have any familiarity with these poems. Although those we found most often copied/alluded to in 1599–1622, Sonnets 128 and 116, are distinct, the later seventeenth-century favourites Sonnets 2 and 106 appear as the middle and end of three-poem lyrics, entitled respectively 'Loves crueltie' and 'Constant affection', which would have made it difficult for any reader to find them.

The process of conflation was arguably Benson's strongest tactic in encouraging new readers to engage with the poems, promoting aural pleasure and thematic intensity. Whilst it denies the individual couplet its ironic power, the cumulative effect becomes a refrain, not only repeating the argument, but also enhancing the Sonnets' musical qualities. This is particularly the case with Benson's opening poem, 'The glory of beautie', which includes the couplets of Sonnets 67 and 68: 'O him [Nature] stores, to show what wealth she had/ In days long since, before these last so bad'; 'And him as for a map doth nature store/ To show false art what beauty was of yore'. Poem 80, 'His heart wounded by her eye', reads like a compendium on this theme through its conflation of 137, 139 and 140, moving from Cupid's arrow to the mistress's 'glance', and taking in the eyes' power to bereave the lover of his judgement and his life.

Finally, we should note the larger theme that Benson foregrounds through his rearrangement of the Quarto groups. Poem 2 ('Injurious Time') is one of the longest in the collection (see Figure 2.2), conjoining Sonnets 60, 63, 64, 65 and 66 to create the impression of Time's relentless assault: 'Like as the waves make towards the pebbled shore/ So do our minutes hasten to their end … Against my love shall be as I am now,/ With time's injurious hand crushed and o'erworn … When I have seen by Time's fell hand defaced' and so on. Not only the removal of Sonnets 61 and 62 (which do not contribute to this theme), but the

---

76 For further discussion, see Baker, 'Cavalier Shakespeare'.

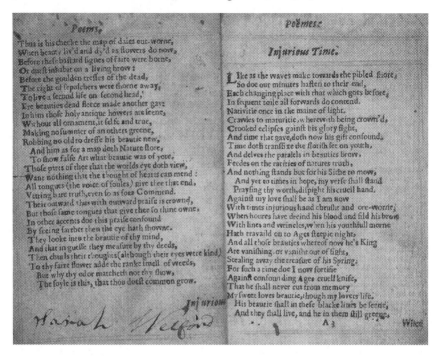

Figure 2.2 'Injurious Time' in John Benson, *Poems* (1640), A2v–A3r
© Folger Shakespeare Library, STC 22344, copy 10

diminution of the white space between each lyric, which prevents the
couplet from generating even a momentary pause or glimpse of consolation, intensifies the experience of 'Injurious Time'. Benson also closes
the gap between the procreation Sonnets (1–18) and the Time-obsessed
60s, by positioning a conflation of Sonnets 1, 2 and 3 ('When forty
winters shall besiege thy brow … Calls back the lovely April of her
prime') as the sixth poem in the volume.

The prominence that Benson afforded to the Sonnets' truisms about
mortality and Time clearly caught the attention of his readers. Copy 2 of the
Poems in the Folger Shakespeare Library includes a variety of annotations
on this theme, for example, 'Injurious Time' is retitled 'Eternity of Verse,
spight of that destroys all things else' (sigs A3–A4). Poem 6, 'Loves crueltie',
is retitled 'Motives to procreation as ye way to outlive Time' (sig A6v). This
writer also underscored the lines in Sonnet 8, 'Looke what an unthrift in
the world doth spend,/ Shifts but his place, for still the world enjoys it' and

Sonnet 9, 'Beauties waste hath in the world an end,/ And kept unus'd the user so destroyes it' (sig. B1).[77]

The immediate success of Benson's *Poems* remains hard to calculate. It never received a second edition, but this was not unusual for one of Benson's publications, and it has been described as a 'modest success', having been 'sold by at least three retail booksellers'.[78] As we will see in the following chapter, it was not until the eighteenth century that Benson's Shakespearean miscellany would really shape the way in which the Sonnets were read, and enable them to vie for a place in the Shakespearean canon. Nevertheless, there are traces of its influence in its own day which have not been acknowledged, most immediately in the work of the poet and playwright Sir John Suckling.

'Beauties waste': Sir John Suckling's *Brennoralt*

Suckling's admiration for Shakespeare's dramatic works has been passed down in anecdote, inscribed through quotation in his plays and lyrics, and visually represented in a portrait by Anthony Van Dyck, in which he is depicted holding a copy of the Folio open at *Hamlet*.[79] His engagement with the Sonnets is less ostentatious. Robert Wilcher notes a quotation from Sonnet 144, 'My better angel', in the unfinished play, *The Sad One* (*c.* 1630–1, 2.1.11), though there is nothing in the context to suggest a conscious allusion. In the lyric poetry (*c.* 1632–7), he finds an echo of the line 'To hear with eyes belongs to love's fine wit' (23.4) in 'To a lady that forbidd to love before company', and possible allusions to Sonnets 127, 130 and 132 in Sonnet II's insistence that black is beautiful if the lover says so.[80] If accepted, these would make Suckling unusual among his contemporaries in engaging with the Dark Lady sequence. Where his knowledge of the Sonnets proves undeniable is in the tragedy *Brennoralt* (*c.* 1639–41), first performed by Shakespeare's old company, the King's Men, at the Blackfriars in 1641.

Discussion of *Brennoralt*'s Sonnet allusions tends to reduce down to two essential points. First, Suckling's familiarity with the Sonnets reveals

---

[77] I am indebted here to Roberts, *Reading Shakespeare's Poems*, pp. 168–9. See also Mayer, 'Transmission as Appropriation', 2–3.

[78] Acker, 'John Benson's *Poems* and Its Literary Precedents', p. 91.

[79] Suckling's advocacy of Shakespeare would be described by Dryden in his *Essay of Dramaticke Poetry* (1668) and incorporated into Rowe's biography of Shakespeare (1709). See Wilcher, *The Discontented Cavalier*, p. 195.

[80] Ibid., pp. 43–4, 145–6.

the depth of his engagement with Shakespeare, for they were not easy to access: he must either have had an original copy of Q (by this point somewhat obscure) or a fairly extensive manuscript collection.[81] The range of Sonnets referred to, and the very limited number which survive in manuscript, makes the latter unlikely, prompting Duncan-Jones to describe Suckling as 'The only early-seventeenth century writer who can be shown to have read Q attentively and appreciatively'.[82] Second, critics have observed that these quotations are mainly spoken by Iphigene, a woman disguised as male since birth, who seduces another woman, Francelia, so that she will not marry Iphigene's true love, Almerin. This is taken to imply that Suckling 'enjoyed [the Sonnets'] unconventionality and gender confusion' and that he intended to point up his own 'piquant variation on the Shakespearian sexual triangle'.[83] But I would argue that both of these assumptions are misleading.

The distribution of allusions in *Brennoralt* has gone unremarked, but of its ten quotations (two of which I identify here for the first time),[84] five are clustered in the final scene – in just over two hundred lines (5.3.5–223). Suckling probably knew the Sonnets already through a copy of Q,[85] but this density of allusion suggests a new source. Although the play is often dated 1639, it could have been written any time between September 1639, when Suckling returned from the Scottish wars, and early summer 1641, given that it was listed in the King's Men's repertoire on 7 August.[86] This means that its composition might well have coincided with the publication of *Poems*, entered on the Stationers' Register in November 1639 and dated 1640. For a Shakespeare enthusiast such as Suckling this would have been a significant publishing event, and his tragedy being nearly completed would not have hindered him from incorporating Sonnets into the final scenes. Unfortunately, there are no clues in the quotations themselves to indicate

[81] Ibid., p. 195.
[82] Shakespeare, *Shakespeare's Sonnets*, ed. Duncan-Jones, p. 72.
[83] Ibid., p. 74, and Wilcher, *The Discontented Cavalier*, p. 289.
[84] I am indebted to Rollins' *Variorum*, L. A. Beaurline's edition of *The Works of Sir John Suckling*, and *Shakespeare's Sonnets*, ed. Duncan-Jones, for the identification of 1, 9, 12, 33, 47, 99, 104 and 140. I am not convinced by Rollins' argument that Suckling also alludes to sonnet 52 (1.140) so have not included this in my tally, though readers may disagree (see 3.4.19–22). To this list I add allusions to Sonnets 87 and 5.
[85] In 1.4, Suckling quotes Sonnet 33 and 'A Lover's Complaint' within eight lines of each other, suggesting that he was relying on Q at this point. The Sonnets and 'A Lover's Complaint' are kept apart in Benson by Heywood's Heroidean poems.
[86] See Suckling, *The Works of Sir John Suckling*, vol. 2, p. 289. Martin Butler suggests a date of summer 1640, based on the play's contemporary allusions to Charles I's wars with Scotland, *Theatre and Crisis 1632–1642*, pp. 76–9.

which text was used. The 1646 edition of *Brennoralt* suggests a reliance on *Poems* rather than Q in only three details: the spelling of 'unthrifts', 'enjoyes' and 'perceiv'd' (5.3.119, 121, 140), but these are corrections that a compositor might easily have made as part of the house style. Nevertheless, the fact that quotations from the Sonnets suddenly become lengthier and more precise strongly suggests that Suckling was writing with a copy of *Poems* (rather than *Shake-speares Sonnets*) in front of him.

In 1.4 and 3.4, we find brief phrases, such as 'glorious Mornings' turned to 'clouds' (Sonnet 33), or 'fresh ornament of the world' (Sonnet 1), but from 4.4 onwards the Sonnets are used more extensively. In a close paraphrase of Sonnet 87 ('Farewell, thou art too dear for my possessing'), identified here for the first time, Iphigene defends herself from Francelia's mistrust, arguing that it is she who ought to feel insecure. The Sonnet reads:

> For how doe I hold thee but by thy granting,
> And for that riches where is my deserving?
> …
> Thy selfe thou gav'st, thy owne worth then not knowing,
> Or me to whom thou gav'st it, else mistaking.
> So thy great guift upon misprision growing
> Comes home againe, on better judgement making.[87]

This is transformed into Iphigene's fearful remonstrance:

> IPHIGENE: I hold thee now but by thy owne free grant,
> A slight securitie, alas it may fall out,
> Giving thy selfe, not knowing thine own worth,
> Or want of mine, thou mayst, like Kings deceiv'd,
> Resume the gift on better knowledge backe.[88]

This exploits the inequality of rank between speaker and addressee implied by the Sonnet, and absorbs its final couplet ('In sleepe a King, but waking no such matter'). It also significantly removes the feminine rhymes, perhaps as part of Iphigene's cross-dressing. At the beginning of the final scene, we find another close paraphrase of a Sonnet, no. 47 ('Betwixt mine eye and heart a league is took'):

> When that mine eye is famisht for a looke,
> Or heart in love with sighes himselfe doth smother;
> With my loves picture then my eye doth feast,
> And to the painted banquet bids my heart.[89]

---

[87] Benson no. 57, 'A Resignation', lines 19–20, 23–6.
[88] *Brennoralt*, 4.4.13–17.
[89] Benson no. 41, 'Two faithfull friends', ll 17–20.

This is borrowed in Iphigene's farewell to Francelia:

> IPHIGENE: Will you not send me neither
> Your picture when y'are gone?
> That when my eye is famisht for a looke,
> It may have where to feed,
> And to the painted Feast invite my heart.[90]

But why should Suckling have turned to the Sonnets for the dénouement of his tragedy? For Robert Wilcher, the Sonnets' relevance is not confined to the conclusion, but is determined by the fact that they are mainly spoken by cross-dressed Iphigene:

> Was Suckling expecting a few witty and well-read members of his audience to appreciate the piquant variation on the Shakespearean sexual triangle of two men and a woman created by his heroine's male disguise? ... Might he even have cherished a hope that fellow enthusiasts for Shakespeare would recall that only a few poems earlier in the 1609 sequence, the young man was feared to be in danger of breaking a 'two-fold troth' – 'Hers, by thy beauty tempting her to thee,/ Thine, by thy beauty being false to me' (Sonnet 41, lines 13–14) – and the speaker was revolving in his mind the complexities of his own predicament, which was very close to that of Iphigene: 'If I lose thee, my loss is my love's gain,/ And losing her, my friend hath found that loss' (Sonnet 42, lines 9–10).[91]

Ingenious as this may be, it is based on an anachronistic understanding of how Suckling encountered the Sonnets. Rather than reading the Quarto sequentially and narratively, Suckling most likely browsed through Benson's miscellany, never referring to consecutive poems; he could not, therefore, expect his audience/readers to remember what happens 'only a few poems earlier'. To argue that Iphigene's situation is implicitly under-pinned by the Sonnets' love triangle, or their exploitation of gender ambi-guity, is also misleading. Suckling has significantly reduced Iphigene's role from his source, Jean-Pierre Camus' romance, *L'Iphigène* (1625), to focus on his invented character, Brennoralt – and the love triangle over which Brennoralt anguishes is that of himself, Almerin and Francelia, which is at no point described in terms of the Sonnets. The truth about Iphigene's gender is not revealed until the end of the play,[92] and there has

---

[90] *Brennoralt*, 5.3.5–8.
[91] Wilcher, *The Discontented Cavalier*, p. 289.
[92] There are various hints, such as her former practice of dressing as a shepherdess, her tendency to weep and to swoon, and her desire to prevent Almerin's marriage. Suckling's audience was prob-ably sufficiently familiar with the main source, *L'Iphigène*, or with the story of Iphis in Ovid's *Metamorphoses*, to anticipate Iphigene's revelation.

been remarkably little allusion to it before then. Not only does Suckling not use those Sonnets cited above by Wilcher, there are no references to the 'Master Mistris of my passion' (Sonnet 20),[93] nor to the 'beautie' that Iphigene 'master[s] now' (Sonnet 106).[94] We might agree with Charles L. Squier that 'Suckling does not seem much interested in the situation itself … There is no attempt to understand in any serious fashion the consequences of such a fate as Iphigene's'.[95] Moreover, for all the aggressive masculinity on display here (and associated with Suckling more generally),[96] *Brennoralt* is surprisingly sympathetic to lesbian desire. In her survey of plays featuring female homoeroticism from 1570 to 1662, Denise Walen finds Suckling's tragedy highly original: 'Iphigene is no reluctant, resisting quarry awkwardly evading pursuit, but the eager lover of a willing impassioned partner … [she] exploits her male disguise and enthusiastically performs the male subject role in a sexual relationship with another woman.'[97] The play features a number of sexually charged scenes between Iphigene and Francelia, which often ask the audience to imagine what kinds of erotic experience they have indulged in offstage, not least when they appear in bed together at the beginning of 5.3 with an aubade which recalls *Romeo and Juliet*.

More fundamental to Suckling's reading of the Sonnets than their sexuality is their musing on the destruction of beauty by Time, and the impossibility of possessing the beloved, even when passion is reciprocal. The *carpe diem/memento mori* theme of the procreation Sonnets clearly fascinated Suckling, and may even have inspired a repeated motif in the play – namely scenes in which a protagonist gazes on the unconscious/dead beauty of his beloved. In 3.2, for example, after bribing his way into Francelia's bedchamber, Brennoralt gazes on her sleeping form:

> Heavens! Shall this *fresh ornament*
> *Of the world*; this precious lovelines
> Passe with other common things
> Amongst *the wasts of time*, what pity 'twere.[98]

---

[93] Here reproduced from Benson, Poem 20, 'The Exchange', line 2.

[94] Poem 63, 'Constant Affection', line 36.

[95] Suckling, *The Works of Sir John Suckling*, p. 91.

[96] Michael P. Parker argues of Suckling the poet that he 'distinguishes himself from Donne and from poets like Carew and Waller in his persistent tendency to dehumanise the mistress … Woman is a force to be placated or an object to be used, never a human equal', '"All are not born (Sir) to the Bay"', 353. See also Gibson, '"'Tis not the meate, but 'tis the appetite"'.

[97] Walen, *Constructions of Female Homoeroticism*, p. 93.

[98] 3.4.25–8, allusions to Sonnets 1 and 12 in italics.

Although the morbid prognostications of *carpe diem* were supposed to sexually invigorate the lover, they could also have the opposite effect. Sarah Gilead offers a brilliant reading of Herrick's 'To the Virgins to make much of time', demonstrating how this 'graceful, easily elegant poem contravenes the fearful urgency of its message … [each stanza] exhibits a contrary "entropic" movement, potential verbal energy reducing to a state of enervation or motionlessness'.[99] Much the same might be said of Brennoralt, whose recollection of Sonnets 1 and 12 results in an ebbing of desire, as his understanding of his own impotence in the face of mortality manifests itself physiologically. The flesh is suddenly weak.

In the final scene, the characters are repeatedly struck by their own helplessness. After Almerin has discovered Iphigene in Francelia's bedchamber, he gives them both a mortal wound, only for Iphigene to reveal that she is a woman. Francelia's response is not shame but envy:

> How like an unthrifts case will mine be now?
> For all the wealth he looses shifts but's place;
> And still the world enjoyes it: so will't you,
> Sweet *Iphigene*, though I possesse you not.[100]

In Sonnet 9, the point was that the addressee's beauty could not endure without some physical transaction on his part: 'Looke what an unthrift in the world doth spend/ Shifts but his place, for still the world enjoyes it/ But beauty's waste hath in the world an end,/ And kept unused, the user so destroys it.'[101] The speaker of the Sonnets ostensibly does not care how the addressee bestows himself, so long as it results in marriage and procreation, but these are the very things that Francelia tacitly fears. At the same time, Suckling fulfils the tragic potential of the Sonnets by denying their conditional tense, specifically their assumption that there *is* still time – your beauty will be lost *unless* you do this. Instead, Suckling emphasises the Sonnets' fatalism by invoking them in a context where it is manifestly too late; for example, Iphigene recalls Sonnet 104 ('Ah, yet doth beauty, like a dial hand,/ Steal from his figure, and no pace perceived') at the very moment of Francelia's death: 'Shee's gone:/ Shee's gone. Life like a Dials

---

[99] Gilead, 'Ungathering "Gather ye Rosebuds"', 134–5. Gilead goes on to explain the conflicting drives of the *carpe diem* poem, one the urge to self-actualisation, and the other the death drive: 'the carpe diem poem thus becomes an internal dialogue between two drives competing for dominance within a single psyche, each defending itself against the other', 134–5, 147.

[100] 5.3.119–22.

[101] Poem 11, 'An invitation to Marriage', lines 23–4. These lines are underscored in the Folger Copy 2 of Benson's *Poems*. Roberts, *Reading Shakespeare's Poems*, p. 169.

hand hath stolne/ From the faire figure e're it was perceiv'd.'[102] Moreover, in the play's final allusion to the Sonnets, Brennoralt kisses the dead Francelia, and remarks: '[Her breath] keeps a sweetnesse yet-/ As stills from Roses, when the flowers are gone.'[103] The poignancy of this moment, which tries to suspend the lovers in the present tense, is enhanced by the fact that in Sonnet 5 the preservation of beauty can still be achieved: 'Then, were not summer's distillation left,/ A liquid prisoner pent in walls of glass,/ Beauty's effect with beauty were bereft.' For Suckling's Brennoralt, however, the sexual consummation anticipated in 3.4 never occurred, and at any moment the sweetness of Francelia's youth and beauty will become the sweetness of putrefaction.

Milton's 'No Knowledge' of Shakespeare's Sonnets

If there is one poet who would seem to have understood the stasis that comes upon Suckling's lover when s/he remembers Shakespeare's Sonnets, that poet would be John Milton. And yet, Milton seems, at first glance, to evince a surprising disregard for the Sonnets. When it came to writing his own, he turned to his Italian predecessors (specifically Giovanni della Casa, whose book of sonnets he annotated) apparently finding their work less old-fashioned and more prestigious.[104] He composed in the Petrarchan form (ABBAABBA CDECDE) and even, initially, in the Italian tongue. Later, he would expand the range of topics addressed by the English sonnet, featuring the names of his addressees in an ostentatiously public fashion,[105] reminiscent of Torquato Tasso but quite opposite to Shakespeare's narrow, private and erotic lyrics.

The lack of explicit allusion to the Sonnets in his work has suggested to most Shakespeare scholars that Milton did not know them. Duncan-Jones observes:

> there is no clear evidence that he ever read *Shakespeare's Sonnets*, unless his dismissal of 'a star-ypointing pyramid' as an adequate monument carries some reference to the speaker's dismissal of 'pyramids' in 123; but this seems rather tenuous.[106]

[102] 5.3.138–40.
[103] 5.3.222–3.
[104] See Prince, *The Italian Element in Milton's Verse*.
[105] On the importance of names in the sonnets, see Patterson, 'Milton's Heroic Sonnets', pp. 84–6.
[106] Shakespeare, *Shakespeare's Sonnets*, ed. Duncan-Jones, p. 70.

Similarly, Paul Stevens, in his extensive work on Milton's debt to Shakespeare, finds no trace of the Sonnets. Comus' warning to the Lady 'If you let slip time, like a neglected rose/ It withers on the stalk with languished head' (742–3) overlaps with the themes of the procreation Sonnets, but echoes *Venus and Adonis*: 'Make use of time, let not advantage slip' (129–33).[107] And yet, in light of revisionist work on Milton and Shakespeare which builds on Stevens' findings, it becomes unthinkable that Milton did not know the Sonnets. Ann Baynes Coiro has described Shakespeare as 'Milton's lodestar … [he] cannot have not known Shakespeare's Sonnets', whilst Maggie Kilgour remarks: 'There is no evidence that Milton knew the sonnets. But then there is no hard evidence that he knew lots of other things he must have known … Shakespeare's preoccupations with art and immortality are Milton's as well.'[108]

Before trying to prove that Milton did know the Sonnets, it is useful to consider what his lack of allusion reveals about the canon of Shakespeare's lyric poetry in the early to mid-seventeenth century. For Milton's idea of a Shakespearean lyric is not ours. In perhaps his earliest original poem in English,[109] 'On the Death of a Fair Infant Dying of a Cough' (*c.* 1625–8), Milton begins with a line that echoes *The Passionate Pilgrim* no. 10 beginning: 'Sweet rose, fair flower, untimely plucked, soon faded,/ Plucked in the bud and faded in the Spring.' Since at least the early nineteenth century, editors have wondered if this inspired the opening of Milton's elegy:

> O fairest flower no sooner blown but blasted,
> Soft silken primrose fading timelessly,
> Summer's chief honour if thou hadst outlasted
> Bleak Winter's force that made thy blossom dry;
> For he being amorous on that lovely dye
> > That did thy cheek envermeil, thought to kiss
> > But killed alas, and then bewailed his fatal bliss.[110]

There is an obvious borrowing from *Venus and Adonis* in the image of Winter killing where it thought to kiss, but for Milton *The Passionate Pilgrim* lyric may have been just as securely Shakespeare's as the narrative poem.

---

[107] Stevens, *Imagination and the Presence of Shakespeare in Paradise Lost*, p. 18.

[108] I am grateful to both Ann Baynes Coiro and Maggie Kilgour for these remarks made in private correspondence. See also Coiro's 'Poetic Tradition, Dramatic' on Milton's debt to Shakespeare's plays, and her discussion of the latter's haunting presence in *Samson Agonistes* in 'Fable and Old Song'. Kilgour explores connections between Milton and Shakespeare in her book *Milton and the Metamorphosis of Ovid*, and in a forthcoming monograph. I am grateful to John Savoie for sharing his essay with me before publication, 'Monuments Men'.

[109] Milton, *The Complete Poetry and Essential Prose*, p. 7.

[110] Ibid.

Indeed, this may have counted for Milton as a citation from a Shakespeare Sonnet (although the lyric is only twelve lines long). Something similar seems to happen in the elegy Milton wrote for Shakespeare, which would be published not only in the 1632 Folio but also in Benson's *Poems*, 'An Epitaph on the Admirable Dramatic Poet, W. Shakespeare':

> What neede my *Shakespeare* for his honour'd bones,
> The labour of an Age, in piled stones
> Or that his hallow'd Reliques should be hid
> Under a starre-ypointing Pyramid?
> Deare Sonne of Memory, great Heire of *Fame*,
> What needst thou such dull witnesse of thy Name?
> Thou in our wonder and astonishment
> Hast built thy selfe a lasting Monument:
> For whil'st to th'shame of slow-endevouring Art,
> Thy easie numbers flow, and that each part,
> Hath from the leaves of thy unvalued Booke,
> Those Delphicke Lines with deepe Impression tooke
> Then thou our fancy of her selfe bereaving,
> Dost make us Marble with too much conceiving,
> And so Sepulcher'd in such pompe dost lie
> That Kings for such a Tomb would wish to die.

Coiro describes this as Milton's 'opening gambit in a career that will repeatedly find inspiration in Shakespeare as well as creative energy in denying him',[111] and part of the epitaph's fascination is its intent *not* to be a sonnet (though it is often still described as such).[112] Ignoring Hugh Holland's use of the sonnet form in F1, Milton aligned himself with Ben Jonson's poem, 'To the memory of my beloved, Master William Shakespeare, and what he hath left us', as suggested by the use of rhyming couplets, the phrase 'my Shakespeare', and the play on being a 'Monument without a tomb'.[113] Furthermore, although Milton's 'Epitaph' might recall for us the imagery of Sonnet 55 ('Not marble nor the gilded monuments/ Of princes shall outlive this powerful rhyme'), this was a much-handled trope, stretching back to Horace and Ovid, and forwards via Spenser and Jonson to Herrick and Cowley.[114] For

---

[111] Coiro, 'Poetic Tradition, Dramatic', p. 58.
[112] Stevens observes this phenomenon in 'Subversion and Wonder', 385. The tendency to describe the poem using the 1645 title 'On Shakespeare' also contributes to this confusion.
[113] On Milton's antagonistic, Oedipal relationship to the Jonson poem, see Lanier, 'Encryptions', p. 237, and Hammond, 'Milton's "On Shakespeare"', 115–16.
[114] See Blaine's important re-contextualisation of the poem within this rich heritage in 'Milton and the Monument Topos', especially 217–19.

early modern readers, the Shakespearean source Milton's tribute alluded to was not a sonnet but an 'epitaph' – specifically that appended to the Stanley tombs in the Collegiate Church of St Bartholomew in the village of Tong, Shropshire. This epitaph was attributed to Shakespeare in three out of five manuscript copies circulating in the seventeenth century, and it seems highly likely that Milton understood it to be his. The first of the two verses has the most overt connections with Milton's tribute:

> Not monumental stone preserves our fame,
> Nor sky-aspiring pyramids our name.
> The memory of him for whom this stands
> Shall outlive marble and defacers' hands.
> When all to time's consumption shall be given,
> Stanley for whom this stands shall stand in heaven.[115]

Here, we find not only Milton's 'name'/'fame' rhyme, but a source for his 'sky-ypointing pyramids'.

If a Shakespearean Sonnet does lie buried in Milton's 'Epitaph' for Shakespeare, it does so in a manner that suggests how troubling Milton found the Sonnets. Emma Smith and Laurie Maguire's approach to source study becomes particularly apt here, avoiding the 'photocopy function' in favour of 'the qualities psychologists attach to traumatic memory':

> Intrusive, detailed, multi-sensory recollections of the stressor; disturbed or partial recall, often unbidden; false or fictive associated memories with a similar effect. The consequence of that redefinition means that the conclusive evidence for the source is not its instant or accurate visibility within the text but rather its distorted and fragmentary emanation.[116]

If the 'Epitaph' implies Milton's interest in other parts of the poetic canon than the Sonnets, it also reveals his 'unbidden' recollection of Sonnet 86, which recurs whenever Milton worries about the failure to bring forth what he has conceived.

---

[115] The case for Shakespearean authorship is strong. Duncan-Jones and Woudhuysen note that all the OED's earliest examples of 'monumental' in three different senses come from Shakespeare; that *Richard II* alludes to 'sky-aspiring and ambitious thoughts' (1.3.130); and that 'defacers' is similarly recurrent in *Richard III* and *Henry VIII* but otherwise rare (*Shakespeare's Poems*, p. 439). I would add that the final line of the first sestet with its use of polyptoton, 'Stanley ... stands ... stand', recalls the pleasure Shakespeare obviously took in that device in *Venus*: 'She's love, she loves, and yet she is not loved'. Gordon Campbell offers a persuasive account of how Milton might have come to know the poem in manuscript through his Stanley connections in 'Shakespeare and the Youth of Milton', 100.

[116] Smith and Maguire, 'What is a Source?', 25.

Was it the proud full sail of his great verse,
Bound for the prize of all-too-precious you,
That did my ripe thoughts in my brain in-hearse,
Making their tomb the womb wherein they grew?
Was it his spirit, by spirits taught to write
Above a mortal pitch, that struck me dead?
No, neither he, nor his compeers by night,
Giving him aid, my verse astonished.
He, nor that affable familiar ghost
Which nightly gulls him with intelligence,
As victors of my silence cannot boast;
I was not sick of any fear from thence;
    But when your countenance filled up his line,
    Then lacked I matter, that enfeebled mine.

Milton seems to have taken the notion of Shakespeare's abortive influence ('Dost make us Marble with too much conceiving') from Shakespeare's own experience of creative stillbirth ('That did my ripe thoughts in my brain inhearse,/ Making their tomb the womb wherein they grew'). Indeed, Louis Schwartz finds in Sonnet 86 an origin for Milton's lifelong preoccupation with the poetic-creation-as-childbirth trope.[117] Kilgour also notes that the Sonnet's language of 'ships, ripeness and abortive creation anticipates the themes of Milton's own early verse'. I would add that this memory of Sonnet 86 not only reflects the anxiety that lies behind the 'Epitaph', namely that Shakespeare's prodigious creativity has made it impossible for other poets to create,[118] it also performs it: to express poetic rivalry is to quote Shakespeare. But perhaps what made Sonnet 86 stand out among Shakespeare's other 'rival poet' Sonnets was its particular concern with publication. The opening line seems to me to contain an obvious pun on 'sail'/'sale' – one that even Stephen Booth has missed. It is not simply that the rival poet has written verses 'Bound for the prize of all-too-precious you' but that he has published them, 'the proud full sail [proudful sale] of his great verse'. Furthermore, the imagery of a ship venturing out for treasure better fits a volume entering the print market than it does the private circulation of lyrics, and incidentally anticipates Thorpe's dedication to the Quarto. To accept this reading of Sonnet 86 might lead us to speculate further about the identity of the rival poet,[119] but for our

---

[117] Schwartz, *Milton and Maternal Mortality*, pp. 85–7.
[118] Two influential Oedipal readings of the poem are Guillory, *Poetic Authority*, and Goldberg, *Voice Terminal Echo*, pp. 127–45.
[119] Duncan-Jones' suggestion that this might be Francis Davison is compelling, given that his father was a spy who might well 'gull' the poet 'with intelligence', *Shakespeare's Sonnets*, p. 65. As we saw in the previous chapter, Davison was part of Pembroke's circle, and his work circulated alongside

purposes here it is significant that Milton was moved by a lyric which not only explores the experience of poetic inhibition due to the superior gifts of a rival, but which also talks about the effect of published work on a poet still (voluntarily) confined to manuscript. The 'Epitaph' famously ignores Shakespeare's life in the theatre to emphasise the experience of reading him, 'that each [heart],[120]/ Hath from the leaves of thy unvalued Booke,/ Those Delphicke Lines with deepe Impression tooke'. If the aspiring poet becomes the paper on which Shakespeare writes, he is also the paper on which his words are printed, 'deep Impression tooke', rendering his own self-expression into illegible palimpsest.

Twenty years later, Milton reworked some of the Epitaph's imagery in the sonnet 'On His Blindness':

> When I consider how my light is spent
> Ere half my days in this dark world and wide,
> And that one Talent which is death to hide
> Lodged with me useless, though my soul more bent
> To serve therewith my Maker, and present
> My true account, lest He returning chide,
> 'Doth God exact day-labour, light denied?'
> I fondly ask. But Patience, to prevent
> That murmur, soon replies, 'God doth not need
> Either man's work or his own gifts. Who best
> Bear his mild yoke, they serve him best. His state
> Is kingly: thousands at his bidding speed,
> And post o'er land and ocean without rest;
> They also serve who only stand and wait.'

Jonathan Goldberg finds a number of echoes between this sonnet and the 'Epitaph': if it is death to hide one's talent, so Shakespeare's 'hallowed relics' should not be 'hid'; just as 'God doth not need' his labour, 'What needs my Shakespeare …/ The labour of an age'? This prompts Goldberg to ask whether there is 'some strange victory here? To be spent, to be extinguished before – this is to displace Shakespeare even further, to deny, by occupying his tomb'.[121] I see less of a victory than a surprising recurrence of youthful fears. Despite the fact that his *Poems* (1645) had now been published, allowing Milton to reframe an anonymous 'Epitaph' for Shakespeare into

---

Sonnet 128 in manuscript. In 1602 and 1608 he published his *Poetical Rhapsody* dedicated to Pembroke. This might explain the reference to 'sail'/'sale', and the notion of the beloved's 'countenance' filling up the rival poet's line in Sonnet 86.

[120] This reading, instead of 'part' from F2, reflects the poem as it appeared in the 1673 edition.

[121] Goldberg, *Voice Terminal Echo*, p. 130.

a poem retitled 'On Shakespeare' and placed in the service of his own reputation, this has not rendered obsolete the fears of creative stillbirth. The phrasing of 'that one talent, which is death to hide/ Lodged with me useless' recalls both Sonnet 86 and the 'Epitaph', given that 'lodged' could be synonymous with 'entombed', and 'death to hide' might allude to maternal mortality.[122] At the same time, Milton's lyric potentially registers a more explicit disavowal of Shakespeare's Sonnets in its recall of the first line of Sonnet 15, 'When I consider everything that grows'.[123] In the wake of Benson's *Poems*, Milton might have been able to assume that some readers would pick up on this allusion, although the phrase had been used more recently by Herrick:

> When I consider (Dearest) thou dost stay
> But here a while, to languish and decay;
> Like to these Garden-glories, which here be
> The Flowrie-sweet resemblances of Thee;
> With griefe of heart, methinks, I thus doe cry,
> Wou'd thou hast ne'er been born; or might'st not die.[124]

By beginning his sonnet 'When I consider', Milton challenged both Shakespeare and the Cavalier poets' misuse of poetry in the service of profane desires, as he had previously coupled them in the figure of Comus, 'a Cavalier poet and spokesman for a life of pleasure and consumption',[125] who also speaks Shakespearean lines. Milton begins his sonnet with the same phrase as Shakespeare and Herrick, but then shifts abruptly to his graver subject, deploying poetry in the service not only of God but of his own self-abasement. The implied contrast not only exposes the egotism and triviality of *carpe diem* poetry, but the particular deficits of Sonnet 15, whose dread of Time is rhetorically useful but emotionally fake; as Anne Ferry observes:

> There are no changes of tense in the poem. 'When I consider' exists in the same expansive present with 'everything that growes' ... The prominent series, 'When ... When ... Then', with which successive quatrains opens, is

---

[122] The gravedigger in *Hamlet* insists that Ophelia 'should in ground unsanctified [have] been lodg'd' (5.1) whilst Marston's *Antonio's Revenge* (1602) refers to those 'departed soules,/That lodge in coffin'd trunkes'. Jonson also uses it in this sense when he promises 'I will not lodge thee by/Chaucer, or Spenser ...'

[123] The connection is discussed by Goldberg, *Voice Terminal Echo*, p. 129, and Patterson, 'Milton's Heroic Sonnets', p. 79.

[124] 'To his Kinswoman, Mistresse Susanna Herrick', in Herrick, *The Complete Poetry of Robert Herrick*, p. 182.

[125] On Milton's rejection of Cavalier poetry, see Guibbory, 'Milton and English Poetry', pp. 77–8.

essentially not a temporal but a logical pattern. 'When' and 'Then' do not mark stages in a narrative of consecutive events but terms in a syllogism whose structure dictates the design of the poem.[126]

By contrast, Milton's sonnet confronts the finality of destruction, 'how my light is *spent*', and its anguish is expressed through the bitter urgency of the enjambement: 'though my soul more bent/ To serve therewith my maker, and present/ My true account' (4–6). The last line, 'They also serve who only stand and wait', has divided critical opinion, but it effectively displaces the *carpe diem* notion of ripeness with an 'attentive waiting upon God's time'.[127] Finally, we might observe the way in which sonnet 16's insistence that God's 'state/Is kingly' revises the image of 'kings' which had closed the 'Epitaph' – the vainglorious secular monarch replaced by the peerless sufficiency of God. Milton's increasing scepticism about the value of Shakespeare's Sonnets may express a mature hostility towards Petrarchan *eros* – the 'serenade/ which the starved lover sings/ To his proud fair, best quitted with disdain'[128] – but it was probably also influenced by the increasingly Royalist associations of the Sonnets.[129]

Shakespeare's Royalist Sonnets

Milton had been required to distance himself from Shakespeare, in public at least,[130] when it became known that one of the books Charles I was reading in prison was *Mr William Shakespeare's Comedies, Histories, Tragedies* (F2 1632), even though this contained a poem by Milton himself.[131] In *Eikonoklastes* (October 1649), Milton's strategy to tear down the false idol that was Charles' *Eikon Basilike* and to destroy its tragic affect was partly to emphasise Charles' theatrical association with Shakespeare. Shakespeare was 'one whom we well know was the Closet Companion of these his solitudes',[132] and the king is guilty not only of plagiarising a

---

[126] Ferry, *All in War with Time*, p. 6.
[127] Lewalski, *The Life of John Milton*, p. 306.
[128] Milton, *Paradise Lost*, 4.769–70.
[129] See also Coiro's discussion of how differently the last lines of the 'Epitaph' would have read when they were republished in 1673 in 'Fable and Old Song', 126. On the presence of embedded sonnets in *Paradise Lost*, see Nardo, *Milton's Sonnets and the Ideal Community*.
[130] The extent to which Milton genuinely turned away from Shakespeare is a matter of much debate. See Zwicker, *Lines of Authority*, p. 39, versus Smith, *Literature and Revolution in England*, pp. 16–17.
[131] This fact was used by other polemicists including John Cook who condemns the frivolous reading habits which have rendered the King morally deficient, wishing he had 'but studied Scripture half so much as *Ben: Johnson* or *Shakespear*', *King Charles His Case*, p. 13.
[132] See Milton, *Complete Prose Works*, vol. 3, p. 361.

passage from *Richard III*, but of performing false piety so as to seduce an unwitting audience. At the same time, Milton is acutely aware that it is a book which has had this effect, and his concern with the power of reading takes us back to the 'Epitaph'. Indeed, Nicholas McDowell perceives a connection between the two:

> *Eikonoklastes* is also in effect an apostrophe to a deceased entity whose post-humous book has overwhelmed its readers' conceptual capacities with its affective rhetoric, turning them into 'blockish' idolaters who lose the liberty of thought and action that defines their humanity.[133]

With the narrative poems and *Pericles*, the Sonnets were now the only Shakespeare works which had not been tainted by association with Charles, given that they were not included in the second Folio. And yet, they were rendered potentially suspect through Shakespeare being 'the Closet Companion of [the King's] solitudes', given the Sonnets' thematic preoccupations with privacy, withdrawal and imprison-ment: Sonnet 46 describes the heart as 'A closet never pierced with crystal eye'.

Shakespeare's perceived Royalism mainly inhered in his association with Stuart patronage and theatrical culture. A preface to the anonymous play, *The Famous Tragedie of King Charles I* (1649), begins:

> ... *Johnson, Shakespeare, Goffe,* and *Davenant,*
> Brave *Sucklin,* Beaumont, Fletcher, *Shurley* want
> The life of action, and their learned lines
> Are loathed, by the Monsters of the times ...

Nevertheless, Shakespeare's poetry also contributed to this reputation and vice versa. *The Rape of Lucrece* was published in 1655 by the Royalist-leaning John Stafford, with a continuation by John Quarles, a writer who had had some success with an elegy for King Charles I in 1649. Quarles condemned Tarquin less for the rape than for having 'cost the lives of many of the Nobility; nay, and the King himself'.[134] Shakespeare's lyric poetry would find itself sharing the same political allegiances, due in part to the associations of the form. As Nigel Smith observes, 'Lyrics kept the gentry and the nobility together during the Civil War and the Interregnum', and the Petrarchan tradition became a form of 'dissent' through amorous sequences such as Nicholas Hooke's *Amanda* (1653).[135] More specifically,

---

[133] McDowell, 'Milton's Regicide Tracts and the Uses of Shakespeare', p. 257.
[134] Quoted by Hooks in 'Royalist Shakespeare', p. 32.
[135] Smith, *Literature and Revolution in England, 1640–1660*, pp. 250–1.

the Sonnets looked 'Royalist' because of the company they were keeping in print.

In 1638, John Benson had published Henry Cary's translation of *Romulus and Tarquin* by Virgilio Malvezzi, dedicated to King Charles, and including preliminary poems by Carew, Suckling and Davenant. His edition of Shakespeare's Sonnets in 1640 lacked a dedication but likewise added lyrics by Carew, Herrick and Strode. The following year, Benson published *A Discourse of the Most Illustrious Prince Henry, Late Prince of Wales … by Sir Charles Cornwallis, Knight* in which Charles is praised as the 'living mirrour … of Piety, Wisedom and Justice'.[136] This may have been fairly standard practice in 1640–1, but it looked considerably more partisan a decade later. When Benson's *Poems* was re-sold by Humphrey Moseley *c.* 1653–60, it came under the auspices of a publisher famed for preserving Cavalier literature and was listed among volumes which celebrated (and implicitly mourned) their royal connections, such as *Poems with a Masque by Thomas Carew Esq Gentleman of the Privy Chamber to his late Majesty*.[137]

Manuscript evidence for the Royalist appropriation of Shakespeare's Sonnets is less compelling. David Baker points out that in the Hailstone MS, dated to the 1650s,[138] Sonnets are found in the vicinity of Henry King's poem, 'A Deepe Groane at the Funerall of Charles I', and Robert Wild's lament for the Royalist martyr, Christopher Love, thereby emphasising the Sonnets' 'imagery invoking the lamentable mortality and collapse of majesty and kingdoms'.[139] However, a closer examination of their context belies any straightforward sense of their political affiliation. Sonnet 60 ('Like as the waves make to the pebbled shore') is one of those included in this manuscript, beginning:

> Nativity once in the maine of light
> Crawls to maturity wherewith being crownd
> Crooked eclipses gainst his glory fight
> And time that gave doth now his gift confound …[140]

[136] I am indebted here to David Baker's 'Cavalier Shakespeare', 163–4.
[137] See the catalogue that appears in *Lusus Serius, or Serious passe-time* (1654), where no. 95 is 'Poems written by Mr *William Shakspeare* Gent. 8°'. Baker lists others in 'Cavalier Shakespeare', 169–70. On the elegiac publishing practices of Moseley, see Chernaik, 'Books as Memorials'.
[138] Folger Shakespeare Library MS V.a.148, pt. 1 (fol. 22v).
[139] Baker, 'Cavalier Shakespeare', 171.
[140] It should be remembered that this Sonnet appeared as the opening of a longer poetic unit, Benson's 'Injurious Time' (no. 2).

The theme of a violent reversal of fortune is associated with kingship through the verb 'crownd', and through the 'eclipses' which were thought to attend the deaths of kings. And yet, this poem is immediately followed by a full text of Sonnet 107 ('Not mine own fears, nor the prophetic soul'), which avers that 'the sad augurs mock their own presage' and celebrates 'this most balmy time', which is usually associated with the accession of James I.[141] Particular Sonnets would lend themselves to mourning the regicide, not least Sonnet 33, which is included in the Hailstone MS, beginning 'Ful many a glorious morning have I seene/ Flatter the mountaine tops with sovereign eye', before tracing the sun's defeat and defacement by 'the basest clouds'. This language anticipates Moseley's description of Suckling as having 'liv'd only long enough to see the Sun-set of that Majesty from whose auspicious beams he derived his lustre, and with whose declining state his own loyal Fortunes were obscured'.[142] Yet there is otherwise very little evidence of the Sonnets being consciously used in this way. The sense in which they were 'Royalist' probably pertains to their moral rather than their political content.

Bawdiness and disregard for moral propriety were characteristic of many mid-century miscellanies and carried a political charge; as Adam Smyth puts it, 'by including verse celebrating, among other things, lust, sex, inconstancy in affection, and general decadence [these miscellanies] were issuing a protest to midcentury Puritanism *and* Interregnum government'.[143] One such miscellany was condemned by William Godwin in the early nineteenth century for its 'conspicuous ingenuity and profligacy', being 'entitled to no insignificant rank among the multifarious productions, which were at that time issued from the press, to debauch the manners of the nation, and bring back the king'.[144] This is *The Mysteries of Love and Eloquence, or the Arts of Wooing and Complementing* (1658) by Edward Phillips, Milton's nephew. It includes 'A Perswasive Letter to his Mistress', which is made up of a series of quotations from Shakespeare's Sonnets, affirming their salacious possibilities.[145] Following 'To his Mistress, desiring Enjoyment' and 'A letter from a Lady with Child' which glories in the couplet: 'Fond man what glory hast thou won,/ Or praise, a Virgin thus to have undone?',[146] 'A Perswasive Letter' appears thus (with Sonnet quotations in bold):

[141] See Shakespeare, *The Sonnets and A Lover's Complaint*, ed. Kerrigan, pp. 313–20.
[142] Qtd Corns, 'Thomas Carew', p. 202.
[143] Smyth, 'Profit and Delight', p. 137.
[144] Godwin, *Lives of Edward and John Philips, Nephews and Pupils of Milton*, p. 52.
[145] Phillips, *The Mysteries of Love and Eloquence*, pp. 138–9.
[146] Ibid., pp. 135, 137.

```
              Sweetest, but read what silent love hath writ
              With thy fair eyes, tast but of loves fine wit, (23.13–4)
              Be not self will'd; for thou art much too fair
              For death to triumph o'er without an heir; (6.13-4)
  5           Thy unused beauty must be tomb'd with thee,
              Which us'd lives thy Executour to be; (4.13-4)
              The Flowers distill'd, though they with winter meet
              Lose but their show, their substance still is sweet, (5.13-4)
              Nature made thee her seal, she meant thereby:
  10          Thou shouldst print more, not let the Copie die. (11.13–4)
              ...
  17          What is so fair that hath no little spot;
              Come, come thou mayst be false yet know'st it not. (92.13–4)
```

The question of which text of the Sonnets Phillips was using seems not to have been asked, but it seems clear that this is another instance of Benson's influence rather than that of the Quarto, for Phillips' reading is more intensive than extensive – and guided by Benson's titles. He begins with a couplet from 'A Bashfull Lover' (Benson's Poem 16, Sonnet 23), then takes three couplets from 'Magazine of Beautie' (Poem 10, a conflation of Sonnets 4–6), one from 'An Invitation to Marriage' (Poem 11, Sonnets 8–12), and finally one from 'A Lovers Affection though his love prove unconstant' (Poem 60, Sonnets 92–5). The effect is an intensification of the Sonnets' *carpe diem* theme, but emphasising the addressee's beauty at the expense of criticism and avoiding the serious threat of 'never-resting time' (Sonnet 5.5). The tone is also more ribald in the way it rewrites the couplet of Sonnet 92, 'But what's so blessed fair that fears no blot?/ Thou mayst be false, and yet I know it not'. Where Shakespeare's speaker suggests that knowledge of the beloved's inconstancy would kill him, Phillips' speaker urges the lady to blot her chastity with impunity, since she is probably already 'false'.

Perhaps the most important information about how Phillips read the Sonnets comes not from the quotations themselves but from the rest of the 'Letter'. Critics have been content to identify the Shakespeare borrowings and leave it at that: '[they are] combined with other lines, perhaps written by compiler Edward Phillips, or perhaps borrowed from some other text';[147] 'adding verses presumably of his own composition'.[148] But once one understands that Phillips is working from a copy of Benson's *Poems*, it becomes clear that the rest of the poem is almost entirely borrowed from

---

[147] Smyth, *'Profit and Delight'*, pp. 97–8.
[148] Rollins, *Variorum*, vol. 2, p. 330.

Thomas Heywood's 'The amorous Epistle of Paris to Hellen', printed in the 1612 version of *The Passionate Pilgrim*, and appearing as the one hundredth poem in Benson.[149]

Phillips may have been struck by the fact that Heywood's poem was already a letter persuading a woman to have sex with the sender. It was therefore a less time-consuming matter to borrow multiple lines from this poem than do any further excavation of the Sonnets. However, this shift of source may also highlight a perceived deficiency in the Sonnets. What Phillips relies on Heywood for is, first, a sense of the divine inevitability of the lovers' passion, based partly on the originary moment when Paris first set eyes on Helen; and second, terms of praise by which to seduce a woman. One of the ways in which Shakespeare's Sonnets are surprisingly un-Petrarchan is their refusal to idealise or remember a first moment of infatuation – for all the wordplay on the interchange of eyes, there is no iconic moment when eyes meet. Similarly, once the implied flattery of the procreation Sonnets has been exhausted, we are left with poems

---

[149] A marked-up copy of the rest of the letter looks like this:

What hast thou vow'd an aged Maid to die?
Be not a fool; lovers may swear and lie.
Forswear thy self, thou wilt be far more wise
To break an oath than lose a Paradise. (PP3, LLL 4.3)
15   For in the midst of all loves pure protesting,
All Faith, all Oaths, all Vows should be but jesting:
What is so fair that hath no little spot;
Come, come thou mayst be false yet know'st it not. (92.13–4)
I wish to you, what hath been wish'd by others,
20   **For some fair Maids by me would have been Mothers; (Paris, ll 163–4)**
Pardon me not, for I confess no error,
Cast not upon these Lines a look of terror, (Paris, ll 19–20)
Nor vainly Lady think your beauty sought
For these instructions are by Loves self wrought; (Paris, ll 31–2)
25   **Venus her self my Pen to this theam lead,**
And gives thee freely to my longing bed. (Paris, ll 37–8)
I saw thee in my thoughts fair beauteous Dame,
When I beheld thee with the eyes of fame
I lov'd thee, ere I saw thee long ago,
30   **Before my eyes did view that glorious shew (Paris, ll 69–70, 67–8)**
Imagin not your face doth now delight me,
Since seen, that unseen did invite me. (Paris, ll 177–8)
Believe me, for I speak butt what's most true,
Too sparingly the world hath spoke of you;
35   **Fame that hath undertook your worth to blaze,**
Plai'd but the envious Huswife in your praise; (Paris, ll 251–4)
'Tis I will raise thy name, and set thee forth,
Enjoy thy riches; glorifie thy worth;
Nor with vain scribbling longer vex my head
40   **To fancy love, but leap into thy bed. (Paris, 495–6)**

which seem acutely uncomfortable with the act of praise. It is always either inadequate (and faintly embarrassing) or so hyperbolic as to be obviously undeserved.[150]

The persuasiveness of this letter is clearly an effect of accumulation rather than of reasoning. The carefully enumerated argument of each Sonnet is abandoned in favour of their witty final couplets, which the reader is encouraged to sprinkle generously into his own compositions. Smyth finds *Love and Eloquence* typical of 'a flourishing in popular print of this interest in pieces of language, what Dekker calls "small parcels" of discourse, which one might "fling about", in the combining and recombining of chunks into new combinations'.[151] The effect of Phillips' 'Letter' is to destroy the Sonnets as literary artefacts with their own integrity and argumentation, producing a set of detachable maxims which are not only liberated from any narrative, but from poetry itself.

A more extreme example of this fragmentation would be Josua Poole's *The English Parnassus, or, A Helpe to English Poesie* (1657, 1677). Poole was a Cambridge graduate, who became a schoolmaster in Hadley, Middlesex, and compiled the book for his students, describing Part 3 in which the Sonnet quotations are found as 'an ample treasury of *phrases*, and elegant expressions, gathered out of the best esteemed English Authors' ('The Preface'). The way in which not only author but poetic form is lost in the listing of choice epithets is apparent from the following example:

> *The resolved fair Virgin.*
> Which contracted to her own bright eyes,
> Feeds her lights flame with self substantiall fewell,
> Making a famine where abundance lies, (Sonnet 1.5–7)
> Whose uneard womb
> Disdains the tillage of good husbandry. (Sonnet 3.5–6)
> Unthrifty lovelynesse. Beauteous niggardnesse.
> Profitlesse usurer, that trafficks with her self alone. (Sonnet 4.1, 5, 7, 9)
> The seal that stamps no print, (Sonnet 11.13–4)
> Natures Apostate. June in her eyes, in her heart January,
> The cruell fair one. Venus Anchorite.
> That will leave the world no copy of her graces.
> Fair cruelty clasp'd in her own embraces ...[152]

We might also note the recurrence of Sonnet 2 (and 60 and 12) in an extract entitled 'Old':

---

[150] See Dubrow, *Captive Victors*, on the problem of praise in the Sonnets.
[151] Smyth, 'Commonplace Book Culture', pp. 97–8.
[152] Poole, *The English Parnassus*, p. 541.

> Envious time
> Hath delv'd her parallels within her brow,
> Forty winters have besieg'd the brow,
> And dig'd deep trenches up in beauties field.[153]

Duncan-Jones suggests that 'Such unacknowledged pillaging did little for Shakespeare's reputation as a non-dramatic poet, and may have contributed to the steady decline of interest in or appreciation of *Sonnets* during the eighteenth century'.[154] But before we rush to agree with this sentiment, we should consider one last seventeenth-century admirer of Shakespeare's Sonnets.

William Chamberlayne (1619–89) was a physician and poet in Shaftesbury, Dorset, whose career was interrupted by the outbreak of the Civil Wars. He fought with the king's forces in the second battle of Newbury in 1644, and he was also involved in at least one planned uprising to defeat the Commonwealth and bring back King Charles.[155] Chamberlayne drew upon his experiences of fighting for the king in the long heroic poem, *Pharonnida* (1659), which he later abbreviated and adapted into prose as *Eromena: or, the Noble Stranger: A Novel* (London, 1683). There is no reference to Shakespeare in the dedication to *Pharonnida*, which was addressed to Sir William Portman, Baronet, whose father had been captured at the battle of Naseby and died in the Tower of London in 1645.[156] Portman was only sixteen at the time of the dedication – Chamberlayne refers to 'the pregnant hopes of your blooming Spring', and describes the current work as fit for 'the April of your Age', phrases which conjure up the relationship between the speaker of Shakespeare's Sonnets and the Fair Youth.[157] Chamberlayne is also much concerned with the transitoriness of earthly glory, even as he expects the youth's fame to endure:

> When the splendid Beauties of your most glorious *Palace,* and the lasting *Structure* of your *Marble Domitory,* time shall have so levigated, that the wanton winds dally with their Dust: I doubt not but to find you so much a *Maecenas,* as to affect the Eternizing of your Name …[158]

---

[153] Ibid., p. 431. Rollins identified allusions to Sonnets 1, 2, 3, 4, 8, 11, 12, 53, 54, 60, 98, 99 and 102 (*Variorum,* vol. 2, pp. 329–30), but they are clearly more extensive than this. My cursory glance at the sections on 'Beauty' and 'Beautiful' revealed four lines from Sonnet 67, and a further fragment from Sonnet 2. I have no doubt that many more could be found, though they would offer little further insight into what the Sonnets represent to the mid-seventeenth-century reader.

[154] Shakespeare, *Shakespeare's Sonnets*, ed. Duncan-Jones, p. 75.

[155] See Jagger, 'William Chamberlayne'. See also Parsons, 'A Forgotten Poet'.

[156] See Clifton, 'Sir William Portman'.

[157] Parsons suggested that Chamberlayne may even have been Portman's tutor in 'A Forgotten Poet', 297, fn. 5.

[158] Chamberlayne, *Pharonnida*, 'The Epistle Dedicatory'.

However, these thoughts do not take on any recognisably Shakespearean form until Chamberlayne adapted them for his novel, *Eromena*, some twenty years later.[159] In the dedication 'To Madam Sarah Monday', that lady is urged to give the protagonists 'a candid and a gracious Entertainment':

> I dare be security enough, they'll be grateful and ingenious; and wherever they shall for the future happen to come, I doubt not but they will make good that of the incomparable *Shakespear*;
>
> Not Marble, nor the gilded Monument
> Of Princes shall out-live this powerful Line;
> But you shall shine more bright in this Content,
> Than dusty Trophies soil'd with sluttish Time.
> Gainst Death and all oblivious Enmity,
> Still shall you live, your Praise shall still find room
> Ev'n in the Eyes of all Posterity;
> Were this frail World sunk to its final Doom.
> So till in Judgment you again shall rise,
> You live in this, and dwell in Lovers Eyes.[160]

Chamberlayne's choice of Sonnet 55 is intriguing because we have no evidence for its circulation in seventeenth-century manuscript, and no powerful argument for its literary influence. It is usually assumed that Chamberlayne was drawing on the Benson text rather than the Quarto; however, there are some intriguing substantive changes which suggest that Sonnet 55, along with Sonnets 2 and 106, might also have been circulating in a variant (and perhaps Shakespearean) manuscript version which Chamberlayne knew. For example, *Eromena* reads 'shall out-live this powerful Line', where Q and Benson end with 'rime'. This might be a Shakespearean original, given that Sonnet 63 promises that the beloved's beauty 'shall in these black lines be seen', and Sonnet 16 plays on 'lines of life'. We might also linger over line 4, 'Than dusty Trophies soil'd with sluttish Time', which is a more heroic but simpler version of Q/Benson's 'Then unswept stone, besmeer'd with sluttish time'. 'Besmeer'd' is a favourite Shakespearean term to describe the blackening effects of both sin and warfare,[161] suggesting either that Chamberlayne was reading an early Shakespeare draft which became more sophisticated through authorial revision, or that something was lost through Caroline translation. That

---

[159] G. Thorn-Drury first noted this citation in *Some Seventeenth Century Allusions to Shakespeare* (1920), cited by Rollins.
[160] *Eromena*, dedication.
[161] See *Twelfth Night*, 5.1.26, *King John*, 3.1.237 and *Henry VIII*, 1.2.124.

said, it is interesting to note that the Quarto, Benson and *Eromena* all agree that 'monument' in the opening line should be singular: 'Not marble, nor the gilded Monument,/ Of Princes ...' and this might give twenty-first-century editors pause when they reach for the plural 'monuments' just because it would rhyme better with 'contents'. The omission of the second quatrain, 'When wasteful war shall statues overturn ... [and] burn/ The living record of your memory' (5–8), we can probably ascribe to Chamberlayne himself. Its negative attitude towards war was presumably offensive to one who had fought among the king's troops and who prided himself on his acquaintance with Royalist martyrs.

By whatever means Sonnet 55 came to appear in this form, it seems clear that towards the end of the century, when Shakespeare's Sonnets are supposed to be entering a period of oblivion, they have loyal supporters still, and that they retain a certain Royalist flavour. Perhaps, then, the eighteenth century will prove to be less of an abyss than has previously been thought?

CHAPTER 3

One Thing to My Purpose Nothing, 1709–1816

In the eighteenth century, Shakespeare emerges as the preeminent English dramatist, and the ultimate literary icon. How this happened has been the subject of a recent explosion of critical work, but the Sonnets have figured very little in this history.[1] In *Shakespeare in the Eighteenth Century*, Fiona Ritchie and Peter Sabor account for Shakespeare's new cultural authority in the late 1730s as follows:

> The price war between publishers Jacob Tonson and Robert Walker made cheap editions of individual Shakespeare playtexts readily available, increasing the public's access to his works. And access to Shakespeare in the theatre was unwittingly augmented by the 1737 Licensing Act which mandated that all new plays be approved by the Lord Chamberlain before performance. Theatre managers therefore began to rely on classic plays already well established in the repertoire ... Shakespeare also benefitted from the vigorous advocacy of women, who were active in promoting his works in the theatre before the age of Garrick ... Women remained crucial to the development of eighteenth century Shakespeare: actresses interpreted his plays in performance, influencing their reception by spectators; female playgoers made up a substantial part of the theatre audience and thus helped determine which of Shakespeare's works were seen in the playhouses; and women increasingly entered the literary sphere, contributing to the burgeoning genre of critical commentary on Shakespeare.[2]

The Sonnets would have very little to contribute in any of these categories. Although available in a greater number of texts than ever before in the eighteenth century, they remained marginal to Shakespeare-in-print, as suggested by their lack of reprints and their tendency to drop out of the

---

[1] Key works include Michael Dobson's seminal *The Making of the National Poet*, Michael Caines, *Shakespeare and the Eighteenth Century*, Fiona Ritchie, *Women and Shakespeare in the Eighteenth Century*, and Kate Rumbold, *Shakespeare and the Eighteenth-Century Novel*. Most recently, Emma Depledge and Peter Kirwan, *Canonising Shakespeare*, has made an important contribution to the rethinking of the Sonnets' afterlife in this period, with individual essays referenced below.
[2] Ritchie and Sabor, *Shakespeare in the Eighteenth Century*, p. 6.

'Works'. Of course, they could not benefit directly from the dominance of Shakespeare in the theatrical repertoire (although there is a record of Garrick performing the Sonnets). More surprising is the fact that the Shakespeare Ladies Club did not get behind them,[3] and that female critics would often ignore or denigrate the Sonnets. In a letter of 19 October 1798, Anna Seward complained of the 'stiff infelicity of expression ... the quaintness ... quibbling ... and utter want of harmonious flow' in all poetry between Chaucer and Spenser, finding that 'the detached poems of our immortal Shakespear are strongly tinctured with them'.[4] It is also true that, as Seward's terminology implies, 'Shakespeare's Sonnets' do not technically exist for most of the period. This is not only because both the word 'Sonnet' and the poetical form were generally out of favour, with writers preferring 'Poem' or 'Epigram' to define the fourteen-line lyric, but because copies of *Shake-speares Sonnets* were extremely rare, and the Quarto's existence largely forgotten. Readers encountered the poems not in a sequence but in a miscellany, such as *The Passionate Pilgrim* (1599) or Benson's *Poems* (which included *The Passionate Pilgrim* (1612)).

But if the absence of the Quarto is regrettable, it would be inaccurate to claim that *The Passionate Pilgrim*/Benson's *Poems* were 'responsible for an almost complete absence of critical writing and creative appropriation' or that 'the low evaluation of the Sonnets resulting from Benson's corruptions' hindered the Sonnets' appreciation.[5] I have found no evidence that the poems falsely attributed to Shakespeare impacted negatively on the Sonnets' reputation – on the contrary, lyrics such as 'Come live with me and be my love' and 'If music and sweet poetry agree' were consistently admired and anthologised, thereby elevating Shakespeare's status as a poet. It was an edition of Benson's poems edited by Charles Gildon that prompted the first serious critical discussion of the plays and poetry together.[6] Nor did Benson's collection totally dominate the market – the Quarto was reprinted in 1711 and 1766 – it was just that readers preferred Benson.[7] Had his edition not existed, the Sonnets would arguably have

---

[3] Ritchie found no evidence of women promoting the Sonnets in *Women and Shakespeare in the Eighteenth Century*.

[4] Seward, *Letters of Anna Seward*, Letter 24, vol. 5, p. 159.

[5] Edmondson and Wells, *Shakespeare's Sonnets*, p. 120.

[6] Gildon's critical work is described by Peter Holland as 'an extremely important and hugely undervalued commentary on Shakespeare' in his 'Introduction' to *The Works of Mr. William Shakespeare: in six volumes*, p. xxvi.

[7] Generalisations such as that 'it was only in this form, until Malone, that Shakespeare's sonnets appeared in eighteenth century editions' (de Grazia, *Shakespeare Verbatim*, p. 153), or that 'Until 1780 no edition of the collected poems ... contained the genuine *Sonnets* in their original form' (Dawson,

failed to make any incursion into the great eighteenth-century collections of Shakespeare, as they did successfully (if temporarily) in 1714 and 1728.

There is no question that the Sonnets' creative influence in the eighteenth century was significantly less than that of the plays. By exploring some of the places where we might expect to find them but do not – in anthologies, the eighteenth-century novel, and the sentimental sonnet – we gain a sense of what the Sonnets were perceived to lack, which is an important part of their reception history. That said, there is more to the Sonnets' cultural influence in the eighteenth century than has previously been allowed, and one final misconception this chapter seeks to address is that their history was a blank until they were 'discovered' by Edmond Malone in 1780. In fact, the Sonnets had long troubled the idea of what a 'complete' Shakespearean canon might be, as the history of eighteenth-century editions of the Sonnets implies. It is also misleading to view Malone as the 'saviour' of the Sonnets in any unambiguous sense. Certainly, he made it easier to read the Quarto sequence, and his interpretation of the Sonnets – as confessional, autobiographical material by which one might know Shakespeare better – gave late eighteenth-century readers a new reason to seek the Sonnets out. Nevertheless, Malone arguably did lasting damage to how the Sonnets would be read as individual lyrics.

Works, Supplements, Miscellanies: The Sonnets in Print 1709–1779

By comparison with the years 1640–99, which produced only one edition of the Sonnets, the early eighteenth century was a period of reinvestment and renewal. Between 1709 and 1711 alone, three editions of Sonnets were published, each with a different textual origin. This interest was sparked by the poetry's perceived omission from the *Works*, but unlike the previous century, when it took nearly twenty years for a publisher to respond, here the reaction was immediate and dynamic.

Nicholas Rowe's *The Works of Mr William Shakespear; in six volumes* (1709), published by Jacob Tonson, replaced the unwieldy bulk of the folios with octavos.[8] It offered partially modernised texts of the plays, with

---

Four Centuries of Shakespeare Publication, p. 9) are unhelpful. For an important re-evaluation of the Sonnets at this time, see Alexander, 'Province of Pirates'.

[8] These were not, in fact, cheaper than the Folio, but cost 50 per cent more at 30 shillings. See Dugas and Hume, 'The Dissemination of Shakespeare's Plays', 270. The extent to which they expanded the readership of Shakespeare's plays is therefore fairly modest. See Hume's further discussion in 'Before the Bard'.

engravings which recalled key moments in performance, and *dramatis personae* to help orientate the reader.[9] It nevertheless followed its copy-text F4's lead in including the six apocryphal plays, but omitting the narrative poems and Sonnets. At the end of his biographical essay, 'Some Account of the Life &c. of Mr. *William Shakespear*', Rowe acknowledged: 'There is a Book of Poems, publish'd in 1640, under the Name of Mr. *William Shakespear*, but as I have but lately seen it, without an Opportunity of making any Judgement upon it, I won't pretend to determine, whether it be his or no.'[10] Rowe's dismissive tone may have been defensive, reflecting the fact that Benson's *Poems* had genuinely come to his notice too late (though this omission was not atoned for in the second and third editions).[11] More likely, his choice of verb ('I won't *pretend*') attests to a deeper suspicion of the lyrics' authenticity. Nevertheless, the opportunity to supplement the great *Works* with a 'Book of Poems' was one that more enterprising printers would embrace.

First came Bernard Lintott's *A Collection of Poems, viz. I. Venus and Adonis, II. The Rape of Lucrece, III. The Passionate Pilgrim, IV. Sonnets to Sundry Notes of Musick. By Mr. William Shakespear* (1709). Lintott confessed in the 'Advertisement' that the subscription of gentlemen to Rowe's *Works* 'makes me hope, that this little Book will not be unacceptable to the Publick'.[12] The volume was clearly put together in a hurry, and with the minimum of effort. Its only engagement in debate about the Sonnets was the *non sequitur* that, given *The Passionate Pilgrim* was published in 1599, 'it appears plainly they were published by himself'.[13] Nevertheless, the value Lintott placed on returning to the earliest texts of Shakespeare was radical in the face of contemporary editorial practice, which was to assume the superiority of the recent text – Rowe's *Works* being based on the 1685 rather than the 1623 Folio.

Following quickly on the *Collection*'s heels was Charles Gildon's *The Works of Mr. William Shakespear. Volume Seventh. Containing Venus & Adonis. Tarquin & Lucrece And His Miscellany Poems*, for Edmund Curll, dated 1710 though published the previous year. This included the entirety of Benson's *Poems* – 146 Sonnets and the complete 1612 *Passionate Pilgrim*. Given its title, and the fact that it replicated the size, print and binding of

9 For further discussion, see Murphy, *Shakespeare in Print*, pp. 60–2.
10 Shakespeare, *The Works of Mr. William Shakespeare: in six volumes*, ed. Rowe, p. xl.
11 These are the recently discovered second 1709 edition, and the first 1714 edition.
12 Shakespeare, *A Collection of Poems*, ed. Lintott, A2r.
13 Ibid.

the six-volume *Works*,[14] this edition was clearly intended as a supplement to Rowe. Yet it existed in a defiant relationship to the *Works*, as it struggled to make a case for its own legitimacy. In one of the three critical essays Gildon wrote for the volume, he observed:

> Tho' the Works of SHAKESPEAR have been lately publish'd without the Poems, which now visit the World in a *Seventh* Volume by themselves; yet the Reader must not imagine, that the *Bookseller* of those, rejected these as spurious, or doubtful, or as unwilling to shelter under his Name, what was not genuine; for by re-printing those Plays, in this Edition, which carry no Mark of this celebrated Author, and which were only added to former Impressions, according to the laudable Custom of the Trade, to swell the Volume and the Price (Mr. *Betterton* having more, than once assur'd me, that the first Folio Edition by the Players, contain'd all those, which were truly his) 'tis plain that no such nice Scruple gave him any disturbance: But out of a good natur'd Principle, agreeable to the Man; he thought it not impolitic to lessen the Towns Expectation of these Poems, because he had no Hand in their Publication.[15]

Gildon makes a connection between the Sonnets and the apocryphal plays that would be inescapable for the rest of the eighteenth century – even Malone prints them in the same two-volume set.[16] Here, however, he emphasises their distinction, arguing that Rowe's inclusion of plays 'which carry no Mark of this celebrated Author' disqualifies him from judging Shakespeare's poems, of which 'There is not one … that doth not carry its Author's Mark, and Stamp upon it'.[17] This was a wholly untenable position, given Benson's inclusion of a section entitled 'An Addition of some Excellent Poems … by other Gentlemen', elegies for Shakespeare, and at least one lyric known to be by Marlowe,[18] but Gildon was willing to

---

[14] It was offered in *The Tatler* no. 57 (1709) as intending 'to compleat sets', quoted by Lynch, *Jacob Tonson, Kit-Cat Publisher*, p. 131.

[15] 'An Essay on the Art, Rise and Progress of the Stage in *Greece*, *Rome* and *England*', in Shakespeare, *The Works of Mr. William Shakespear. Volume the Seventh. Containing Venus & Adonis. Tarquin & Lucrece And His Miscellany Poems*, ed. Gildon, pp. i–ii.

[16] For further discussion of the apocryphal plays in the eighteenth century, see Kirwan, *Shakespeare and the Idea of Apocrypha*.

[17] 'Remarks on the Poems of Shakespear', in Shakespeare, *The Works of Mr. William Shakespear. Volume the Seventh. Containing Venus & Adonis. Tarquin & Lucrece And His Miscellany Poems*, ed. Gildon, p. 445.

[18] The attribution to Marlowe of 'Come live with me' had been made in print as early as 1600. Gildon argues that its incorporation into *The Merry Wives of Windsor* 'gives us a strong proof of its being Shakespear's', but then quickly backtracks: 'This at least proves it a known and celebrated Song when *Shakespear* wrote that play, which was Years before his death', p. 448. Gildon would make a similar argument for 'Take O take', a lyric whose presence in *Measure for Measure* suggests to him that it is Shakespeare's, although its occurrence in Fletcher's *Rollo, Duke of Normandy* had already led to its being reassigned to Fletcher. For a detailed discussion of this song as a posthumous addition to *Measure*, see Taylor and Jowett, *Shakespeare Reshaped*, pp. 123–40.

overlook such details. In countering the objection that 'if these Poems had been Genuine, they had been publish'd in the Life time of the Author', Gildon reminds his readers that 'after all there were more in Proportion of these Poems of this Volume, printed in his Lifetime, than of his Plays, as is plain from his *Venus* and *Adonis*, his *Tarquin* and *Lucrece*, and several *Epigrams* and *Sonnets*'.[19] Since Gildon shows no knowledge of the 1609 Quarto,[20] he seems to be referring to *The Passionate Pilgrim* and the *Sonnets to Sundry Notes of Musick* (which Lintott had separated out) as the '*Epigrams* and *Sonnets*' reprinted in Shakespeare's lifetime. Unfortunately, Gildon's familiarity with Benson's *Poems* makes it impossible for him to appreciate the original text of *The Passionate Pilgrim*:

> There is a Book lately publish'd [Lintott's 1709 *Collection*] containing only some few of his Poems confusedly put together; for what is there call'd *The Passionate Pilgrim* is no more than a medly [*sic*] of *Shakespear's* thrown into a Heap without any Distinction, tho' they are on several and different Subjects … The first *Stanza*, in these Poems, is call'd *The false Relief*. The next *Stanza* is call'd *The Temptation* and on quite another Subject tho' incorporated into one under that general Title of the *Passionate Pilgrim*. The next *Stanza* is call'd *Fast and Loose* and still of another Subject; the next *Stanza* tho' join'd as the Rest as Part of the same Poem is on a Subject vastly different from that of the former *Stanza* and is call'd the *Sweet Provocation*, the same holds good of the next which is call'd *The Constant Vow* …[21]

Gildon is baffled to encounter the original *Passionate Pilgrim* lyrics without Benson's distinctive titles (see Figure 3.1). Moreover, Lintott's failure to preserve Jaggard's original spacing of one poem per recto, creates the impression of a single narrative poem, called 'The Passionate Pilgrim', out of what Gildon knows to be miscellaneous poems.[22]

In his criticism, Gildon does not identify a body of lyrics which we would recognise as 'the Sonnets'. He begins a conversation about the literary merit of Shakespeare's 'Poems', offering extracts from *Venus and*

---

[19] 'Remarks', in Shakespeare, *The Works of Mr. William Shakespear. Volume the Seventh. Containing Venus & Adonis. Tarquin & Lucrece And His Miscellany Poems*, ed. Gildon, pp. 447–8.

[20] It is unfortunate that he did not later record his responses to Lintott's 1711 edition. When this essay was reprinted in 1714, the above quoted passage about *The Passionate Pilgrim* was simply removed, rather than being replaced with anything on the Quarto.

[21] Ibid.

[22] This concurs with the argument made in Chapter 1 that Jaggard was trying to market this miscellany as Shakespeare's third narrative poem. The running order of Benson's *Poems* in this section is PP1, PP2, PP3, Sonnet 21, Sonnet 23, Sonnet 22, PP4 and PP5. It is interesting that Benson does not object to the 'absence' of the Sonnets from *The Passionate Pilgrim*, perhaps suggesting he naturally valued the PP lyrics more.

(a)　　　　　　　　　　　　　　　　　(b)

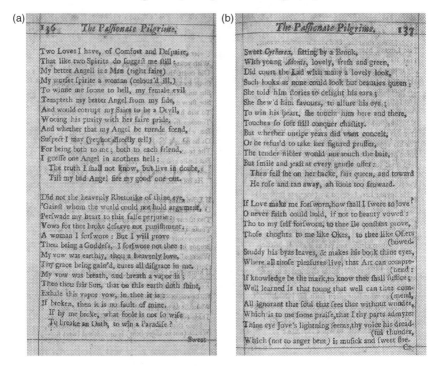

Figure 3.1　Bernard Lintott, *A Collection of Poems* (1709), pp. 136–7
© The British Library Board, 1163.b.42

Lucrece as demonstrating 'many good Lines, some very good Topics'.[23] He also takes an example from 'A Lover's Complaint' to prove their Shakespearean style. Perhaps most relevant to the Sonnets is his discussion of the Poems' artificiality:

> Tho' Love and its Effects are often happily enough touch'd in many of these Poems, yet I must confess that it is but too visible, that *Petrarch* had a little infected his way of thinking on that Subject, yet who ever can admire Mr *Cowley's* Mistress,[24] has a thousand Times more Cause of Admiration of our *Shakespear* in his Love Verses, because he has sometimes such touches of Nature as will make Amends for those Points, those *Epigrammatic Acumina*,

---

[23]　Ibid., p. 456.

[24]　Cowley's collection entitled *The Mistress* was originally published in 1647 but included in *The Works of Abraham Cowley* published by Tonson in 1707 and 1710. Cowley was a Royalist exile in Paris with the Queen, and his identification with Shakespeare here may extend that association discussed in the previous chapter between the Sonnets and the Royalist cause.

which are not or ever can be the Product of a Soul truly touch'd with the Passion of Love.[25]

'Points' here suggests a 'witticism' or 'ingenious remark' (OED 25b), although its other meaning of 'conclusion' might allude to the Sonnet's closing couplet. Later, in his *Complete Art of Poetry* (1718), Gildon would expand on what he saw as the stylistic flaws of the epigram, in terms which might equally apply to Shakespeare's Sonnets:

> For my Part, though I have no manner of Relish of [the epigram], I am yet for retaining it as a separate Body; that the Lovers of pert Turns, quaint Thoughts, and Point may have some way of venting themselves, so as not to corrupt the other Parts of Poetry with it, to the prejudice of Nature, and all Poetic Excellence.[26]

When Gildon praises Shakespeare's Sonnets it is on the basis that they transcend their inevitable formal deficiencies.

In a transparent effort to trump Gildon, Lintott finally published an edition which included for the first time since 1609 a copy of the Sonnets in their Quarto arrangement. It was entitled *A Collection of Poems in Two Volumes, being all the Miscellanies of Mr William Shakespear, which were Publish'd by himself in the Year 1609, and now correctly Printed from those Editions. The First Volume contains, I. Venus and Adonis. II. The Rape of Lucrece. III. The Passionate Pilgrim. IV. Some Sonnets set to Sundry Notes of Musick. The Second Volume contains One Hundred and Fifty Four Sonnets, all of them in Praise of his Mistress. II. A Lover's Complaint of his Angry Mistress* (London, 1711). This second volume containing the *Sonnets* was originally advertised singly, but Lintott seems almost immediately to have lost confidence in its appeal and so bound it with the 1709 volume.[27] The provenance of Lintott's copy of the Quarto suggests how scarce this book had become by 1711. In an advertisement printed in the *Post Boy* (1–3 March), Lintott describes how 'Some of these Miscellanies were printed from an Old Edition, which Mr Congreve oblig'd me with; others from an ingenious Gentleman of the Middle-Temple, who is pleas'd to leave his old Copy with me to shew any Person that has a mind to gratify this Curiosity therewith'.[28] Since Congreve is later identified as having supplied *The Passionate Pilgrim* (and thus *Sonnets to Sundry Notes of Musick*), the

---

[25] 'Remarks', in Shakespeare, *The Works of Mr. William Shakespear. Volume the Seventh. Containing Venus & Adonis. Tarquin & Lucrece And His Miscellany Poems*, ed. Gildon, p. 450.
[26] Gildon, *Complete Art of Poetry*, vol. 1, p. 149.
[27] I am indebted here to Paul Cannan's 'The 1709/11 Editions of Shakespeare's Poems', p. 179.
[28] Quoted in ibid., p. 180.

Quarto Sonnets must have come from the 'ingenious Gentleman'. This nicely fits Shakespeare's connection with the Middle Temple during his lifetime, and the evidence of literary manuscripts containing Sonnets issuing from thence in the mid-seventeenth century.[29] Lintott's devotion to authenticity, and to recovering poetic texts printed in Shakespeare's lifetime, was somewhat paradoxically expressed by his forging new title-pages for the narrative poems and *The Passionate Pilgrim*, so that they all read 1609,[30] thereby implying that Shakespeare had constructed his own Complete Poems.

In 1714, these poems had apparently proven desirable enough to merit the attentions of the Tonson house. An edition of the Gildon text, intended as a supplement to Rowe's 1714 *Works*, was incorporated into the third issue, requiring a new title-page: *The Works of Mr. William Shakespeare: in Nine Volumes; with his Life, by N. Rowe … Printed for J. Tonson, E. Curll, J. Pemberton, and K. Sanger*. It is usually argued that the Tonsons' lack of copyright over the poems meant that they were forced to collaborate with Curll and Sanger on this volume.[31] However, Paul D. Cannan has recently argued that it was Edmund Curll who bought up copies of the eight-volume edition, appended his ninth volume, and sold them with a new title-page, whilst the Tonson house continued to advertise their eight-volume edition.[32] This would certainly explain why subsequent Tonson *Works* still did not include the Sonnets.

But apart from Curll's collaboration with Gildon, there were other reasons why his Benson-based edition of the Sonnets might have been preferred over the Quarto. Lintott seems not to have read the Quarto Sonnets before he published them. He makes no acknowledgement of the fact that his composite volume prints Sonnets 138 and 144 in two different versions, nor does he attempt to weigh up the merits of *The Passionate Pilgrim* against either the Quarto or Gildon's *Miscellany Poems*. There is no introduction and no annotation. His title *One Hundred and Fifty Four Sonnets, all of them in Praise of his Mistress* might have been a deliberate tactic to obscure their unorthodoxy,[33] but it is more likely to reflect his total ignorance of what they contained, just as he would describe 'A Lover's Complaint' as voiced

[29] See Lamb, ' "Love is not love" ', on Elias Ashmole who was admitted to the Middle Temple in 1657–8 and owned a manuscript containing a copy of Shakespeare's Sonnet 116 (see Chapter 1).

[30] Neither *Venus* nor *Lucrece* had been reprinted in this year. Alexander suggests that the editions used were actually 1593 for *Venus* and 1616 for *Lucrece*, 'Province of Pirates', p. 347.

[31] See Burrow, 'Life and Work in Shakespeare's Poems', p. 19.

[32] Cannan, 'The 1709/11 Editions of Shakespeare's Poems', p. 182.

[33] See Smith, 'Shakespeare's Sonnets', p. 15.

by a male against 'his Angry Mistress'.[34] By contrast, Gildon's volume had made some attempt to render the poems more accessible through critical discussion and a glossary of difficult words. It acknowledged the obstacles that contemporary readers might face in understanding them, whilst also advertising their merits: 'much of the Beauty and Sweetness of Expression ... is lost by the Injury of Time and the great Change of our Language since his Time; and yet there is a wonderful Smoothness in many of them, that makes the Blood dance to its Numbers'.[35]

Even so, the Sonnets' claim to incorporation within the Works remained a fragile one. In 1725, Pope's edition was once again entirely given over to the plays, requiring George Sewell to produce a further supplementary volume, *The Poems of Shakespear* (London, 1725), based on Gildon's text. Sewell's preface makes a potentially interesting contribution to understanding of the Sonnets, though we are hampered once again by the editor's vagueness in defining which part of the poetic canon he means. Excluding *Venus* and *Lucrece*, he observes that 'the Occasional ones will appear to be the first of his Work', given that 'A young Muse must have a Mistress to play off the beginnings of Fancy, nothing being so apt to raise and elevate the Soul to a pitch of Poetry, as the Passion of Love'.[36] Also important is his emphasis on Shakespeare's indebtedness (and inferiority) to Spenser:

> I conjecture, that SHAKESPEAR took fire on reading our admirable *Spenser*, who went but just before him in the Line of Life, and was in all probability the Poet most in Vogue at that time. To make this Argument the stronger, *Spenser* is taken notice of in one of these little Pieces as a Favourite of our Author's. He alludes certainly to the *Fairy Queen*, when he mentions his *Deep Conceit*, that Poem being entirely Allegorical ...[37]

This represents one of the earliest recorded attempts to read the lyric poems as autobiography – though, once again, a lyric wrongly attributed to Shakespeare stands in place of an 'authentic' Sonnet. Sewell refers here to *The Passionate Pilgrim* no. 8 ('If music and sweet poetry agree')[38] which

---

[34] The importance of a mistress may have come from Gildon who conjectured that 'these Poems being most to [Shakespeare's] Mistress it is not at all unlikely, that she kept them by her till they fell into her Executors Hands or some Friend, who would not let them be any longer conceal'd', 'Remarks', in Shakespeare, *The Works of Mr. William Shakespear. Volume the Seventh. Containing Venus & Adonis. Tarquin & Lucrece And His Miscellany Poems*, ed. Gildon, p. 447.

[35] Ibid., p. 463.

[36] Shakespeare, *The Poems of Shakespear*, ed. Sewell, p. v.

[37] Ibid.

[38] This Sonnet was reproduced by Benson under the title 'Friendly concord' (no. 25).

describes the speaker's preference for Spenser, 'whose deep conceit is such/ As, passing all conceit, needs no defence' (ll 7–8).

Sewell's edition made a sufficiently good impression that it was incorporated into the second edition of 1728, reissued as *The Works of Mr. William Shakespear. In Ten Volumes. Publish'd by Mr Pope and Dr Sewell*, but the effect was temporary. The Sonnets would be excluded from subsequent Works, including Theobald (1733), Hanmer (1744), Warburton (1747), Johnson (1765), Capell (1767–8), the posthumous second edition of Hanmer (1771), and Johnson and Steevens (1773). A desire to include the Sonnets was occasionally acted upon by these editors. In 1733, Theobald revealed: 'I have been importun'd, and am prepar'd, to give a correct Edition of our Author's POEMS',[39] and the volume was advertised as for sale in June 1734, but never reached print. Similarly, Edward Capell was working on a text of Lintott's Quarto, which he suggested would follow as a supplement to his own *Works*, but for reasons unknown it remained in manuscript.[40]

By the 1760s, there seems to be increasing pressure to afford the Sonnets canonical status, but this comes with an intensified awareness of what is at stake for 'Shakespeare' if one does. Years before he became Malone's antagonist in the *Supplement*, George Steevens published *Twenty of the Plays of Shakespeare, Being the Whole Number Printed in Quarto During his Lifetime ...* (1766). Having justified reprinting the old *King Leir* play, on the basis of its serving as a source for Shakespeare's play, and as 'a curiosity worthy the notice of the public', Steevens admits: 'I have likewise reprinted SHAKESPEARE'S SONNETS from a copy published in 1609, by G. ELD, one of the printers of his plays; which added to the consideration that they made their appearance with his name, and in his life-time, seems to be no slender proof of their authenticity.'[41] Steevens goes on to link the Sonnets with the apocryphal plays, whose authenticity might be demonstrated on similar textual evidence, but this leads him to consider what damage might be done to Shakespeare's reputation by this expansion of the canon. He asks specifically 'whether we are to send into the world all his works without distinction, or arbitrarily to leave out what may be thought a disgrace to him', and although he appears still to be referring

[39] Shakespeare, *The Works of Shakespeare: In Seven Volumes*, ed. Theobald, vol. 1, p. xliv.
[40] Shakespeare, *Mr William Shakespeare His Comedies, Histories and Tragedies*, ed. Capell, vol. 1, p. 10. Capell's MS can be found in the Trinity College library, Cambridge.
[41] Shakespeare, *Twenty of the Plays of Shakespeare*, ed. Steevens, pp. 16–17.

to the apocryphal plays, his ensuing comments strongly suggest that he is thinking of the Sonnets:

> Life does not often receive good unmixed with evil. The benefits of the art of printing are depraved by the facility with which scandal may be diffused, and secrets revealed; and by the temptation by which traffic solicits avarice to betray the weaknesses of passion, or the confidence of friendships.[42]

Notwithstanding this admonishment of those whose 'avarice' would lead them to betray Shakespeare's secrets, further editions of the Sonnets were produced, although none of them reverted to the Quarto. Thomas Ewing's 1771 Dublin edition reprints 'the Poems, which are unquestionably Shakespear's, and which have very unreasonably been omitted in almost all the editions of his Works', but chooses Benson's collection;[43] so does Francis Gentleman's *Poems written by Shakespear* (1774),[44] and Thomas Evans' *Poems written by Mr William Shakespeare* (1775).[45] But even though he is dealing with a different collection, Gentleman echoes Steevens' scruples, suggesting that apprehensions about 'the Sonnets' now exceed any particular textual edition. He explains the editors' 'desire of gratifying the admirers of our Author with an *entire* edition of his works', but ventures the opinion that 'If *Shakespeare's* merit, as a poet, a philosopher, or a man, was to be estimated from his Poems, though they possess many instances of powerful genius, he would, in every point of view, sink beneath himself, in these characters'.[46]

Gentleman's complaints that the Sonnets' subject matter is 'trifling, [and their] versification mostly laboured and quibbling, with too great a degree of licentiousness', represent standard eighteenth-century objections, but the reason why the Sonnets failed to be incorporated permanently into the Works before 1780 may have more to do with their publishing history – who edited them and for whom – than their style or subject matter. Catherine Alexander contrasts laurel-bound Nicholas Rowe with libellous Edmund Curll, and concludes that 'Shakespeare's poems were tainted by the reputation and unscrupulous practices of their

---

[42] Ibid., pp. 18–19.
[43] Shakespeare, *The Plays of Shakespeare from the text of Dr S Johnson*, ed. Ewing, vol. 1. Advertisement, no. 6.
[44] This appeared as volume 9 in *Bell's Edition of Shakespeare's Plays* (1773–4).
[45] Evans reproduced Gildon's edition of Benson, as reprinted by Sewell in 1728. In the Advertisement, Evans repeated verbatim Gildon's claims about the poems bearing the 'author's mark'. It has been suggested that this volume was designed to supplement the Capell *Works*, and may even have been edited by Capell, but Alexander argues that this is unlikely. See 'Province of Pirates'.
[46] Shakespeare, *Poems written by Shakespear*, ed. Gentleman, 'Introduction', n.p.

early editors who, despite their hard-selling techniques, contributed to the outsider status of the verse'.[47] This argument is supported by R. S., who averred in 1725 that the volume of poems he had recently purchased (presumably Sewell's) 'has not … been look'd upon with equal Favour, because this Edition of it was not midwif'd into the World, by the *great Names* that have condescended, for the *Emolument* of the *Publick*, to shine in the Title Page of the First Six Volumes [Pope's edition]'.[48] This lack of patronage did more than affect the poems' social standing. Gary Taylor observes that

> for over a century the finest practitioners of the English language from Dryden to Pope to Johnson, contributed to the public remodelling and transmission of Shakespeare's plays; while he in turn contributed inevitably to the stylistic development of each, immersed as they were for years in working over the minutiae of his texts, adapting or editing them. By the end of the eighteenth century, Shakespeare had been, by such means, insinuated into the network of English literature; he could not be extracted without uprooting a century and a half of the national canon.[49]

The same, unfortunately, could not be said for the Sonnets. Although his editorial work between the 1709 and 1714 editions identifies Gildon as 'the one important predecessor of Malone in the making of the text of Shakespeare's Sonnets',[50] the Sonnets did not experience the extensive modernisation which early editors visited upon the plays. Nor, for all Gildon's tussles with Lintott, did they benefit from the spirit of competitiveness which came to define those editions; for example, the faultiness of Rowe's edition being used to justify Pope's; Pope's errors inspiring Theobald's *Shakespeare Restor'd* (1726) and then his own edition, and so on.[51] This lack of celebrity mud-slinging probably impacted upon the Sonnets' failure to make an impact through literary reviews. Alexander notes that

> Johnson's 1765 edition … was considered in *Monthly Review*, *Critical Review*, *Gentleman's Magazine*, and the *Annual Register*. Shakespeare's poems, however, in the form of Evans's edition of 1775, were only reviewed twice … the absence of the poems from this important new development

---

[47] Alexander, 'Province of Pirates', p. 357.

[48] Letter to the *Plain Dealer*, 3rd May 1725, reprinted in Aaron Hill, *The Plain Dealer*, vol. 2, no. 116, pp. 483–92, 484. It is notable that R. S. does not quote anything from the Sonnets, preferring *Lucrece*, specifically the speeches to Opportunity and Time, and the comparison with the Troy painting.

[49] Taylor, *Reinventing Shakespeare*, p. 71.

[50] Alden, 'The 1640 Text of Shakespeare's Sonnets', 274.

[51] For further discussion of this competitive editing, see Murphy, *Shakespeare in Print*, pp. 64–79.

in eighteenth-century life increased their invisibility and compounded their questionable status.[52]

But perhaps most detrimental to the Sonnets' wider cultural influence, beyond Shakespearean editors and antiquarians, was their absence from eighteenth-century anthologies and quotation books.[53]

Two of the most influential eighteenth-century anthologies were Edward Bysshe's *Art of English Poetry* (1702) and William Dodd's *The Beauties of Shakespear* (1752). Bysshe's anthology was reprinted nine times until 1762. In its most voluminous form, it included 118 quotations from Shakespeare, but was limited to the plays.[54] In this respect, Bysshe departed from his main source, Josua Poole's *English Parnassus* (1657), which did quote from the Sonnets, though in a dense, fragmented and unattributed form (see Chapter 2). As a consequence, Bysshe borrowers would overlook the Sonnets – even Gildon, who was personally invested in the reputation of Shakespeare's poetry, ignored them when selecting passages for his *Complete Art of Poetry* (1718).[55] William Dodd, whose anthology was reprinted five times in the eighteenth century, and thirty-nine in the nineteenth,[56] was circumscribed by his source: Pope had indicated 'shining passages' by the use of asterisks in his 1725 *Works*, but given that this edition did not include the narrative poems or Sonnets, he could offer them no such assistance. Even a collection that specifically aimed to address the absence of sixteenth- and seventeenth-century non-dramatic poetry from anthologies, John Hayward's *The British Muse* (1738),[57] could be hampered by a source text, in this case Theobald (1733), which did not include the poetry. Hence, Hayward borrows extracts from Daniel, Spenser, Drayton and Donne, including sonnets, but represents Shakespeare only through his plays.

My own search of the Digital Miscellanies Index (DMI), which covers approximately 1,400 eighteenth-century anthologies, reveals not a single Sonnet, implying that all those lyrics whose influence and/or transmission

52   Alexander, 'Province of Pirates', p. 362. See also the Sonnets' absence from Stone, Jr., 'Shakespeare in the Periodicals 1700–1740'.
53   Kate Rumbold makes a similar case for the narrative poems in the eighteenth century. See 'Shakespeare's Poems in Pieces'.
54   See Culler, 'Edward Bysshe and the Poet's Handbook', 868, and Anne Isherwood's Appendix 12 in 'Cut out "into little stars"', pp. 345–56.
55   Shakespeare appears in a discrete section, the *Shakespeariana* (vol. 1), and in 'A Collection of the most beautiful Descriptions ...' (vol. 2) but is only represented by his dramatic works. On Gildon's debt to Bysshe, see Culler, 'Edward Bysshe', 868.
56   Isherwood, 'Cut out "into little stars"', p. 126.
57   See Hayward's Preface, *The British Muse*, p. iv.

we were able to trace in the previous chapters – 138, 144, 116, 128, 2 and 106 – had been forgotten. This cannot be true, and I have found a number of Sonnets anthologised after 1780 which do not appear in the database.[58] Nevertheless, the putative absence of Sonnets in the DMI is revealing in comparison with the modest showing made by the narrative poems,[59] and, more importantly, five *Passionate Pilgrim* lyrics: PP19, 'Come live with me ...'; PP12, 'Crabbed age and youth'; PP13, 'Beauty is but a vain ...'; PP6, 'Scarce had the sun'; and PP20, 'As it fell upon a day'.[60] As we saw in Chapter 1, lyrics from *The Passionate Pilgrim* were anthologised almost as soon as that text was published in 1599, and they remained accessible through original copies of Jaggard and Benson, and those eighteenth-century editions which included the 1612 *Passionate Pilgrim*. This made them more deeply embedded in English literary culture and, ironically, more Shakespearean than the Sonnets.

Further evidence for this assertion can be found in the hugely popular anthology, *Reliques of Ancient English Poetry* (London, 1765), in which Thomas Percy explains that PP12, which he reprints under the title 'Youth and Age', derives from

> the little collection of Shakespeare's Sonnets, intitled the PASSIONATE PILGRIM, the greatest part of which seems to relate to the amours of Venus and Adonis, being little effusions of fancy, probably written, while he was composing his larger Poem on that subject.[61]

Percy shows no awareness of the Quarto's existence, but he does have access to Lintott's 1709 *Collection*, and so for him 'Shakespeare's Sonnets' and 'Shakespeare's Book of Sonnets'[62] refers to *The Passionate Pilgrim/ Sonnets to Sundry Notes of Musick*. Moreover, 'Youth and Age' is printed in a volume dedicated to 'Ballads that illustrate Shakespeare', by which Percy means texts quoted by, or acting as a source for, Shakespeare's plays.

---

[58] These include Sonnet 57 ('Being your slave, what should I do but tend') which appears in George Ellis' *Specimens of the Early English Poets* (1790), p. 35, and the eighteen Sonnets included in George Kearsley's *The Beauties of Shakespeare*. These are Sonnets 39, 98, 73, 2, 27, 153, 138, 18, 15, 116, 94, 64, 65, 12, 9, 70, 19 and 123, appearing under titles such as 'Age', 'Beauty Perpetuated', 'Fame', 'Inconstancy', 'Mortality', 'Old Age' and 'Time'.

[59] *Lucrece* provides three extracts ('O opportunity ...', 'Her lily hand ...', 'From the besieged Ardea') and *Venus* one ('Even as the sun ...').

[60] None of the entries for 'Come live with me' finally attributes that poem to Shakespeare, though many mention that it was once considered his. Of the rest, however, 'Crabbed age and youth', 'As it fell' and one version of 'Beauty' are still believed to be by Shakespeare. The poem 'Take O take', which Benson's *Poems* defined as a Shakespeare lyric, also recurs in anthologies with this attribution.

[61] Percy, *Reliques*, vol. 1, p. 186.

[62] Ibid., p. 170.

We might now make such a case for the Sonnets – Paul Edmondson and Stanley Wells have described them as 'Shakespeare's Sketchbook ... a collection of fourteen-line monologues, compressed character studies which, in the plays, are given fuller dramatic treatment',[63] and the repetition of the couplet 'Lilies that fester ...' in both Sonnet 94 and *Edward III* is well known. Yet, with the exception of Charles Gildon, very few critics in the eighteenth century thought about the Sonnets in this way, though it was an approach that served *The Passionate Pilgrim* well. The Venus and Adonis theme acknowledged by Percy made the miscellany an easier fit with the narrative poems and reinforced the *Pilgrim*'s authenticity (as Jaggard had anticipated 150 years before). Finally, Percy's aesthetic judgement is clearly at work in the selection of lyrics. He includes PP19, 'The Passionate Shepherd to his Love', partly on the basis that it reappears in *The Merry Wives of Windsor*, but also because he admires 'This beautiful Sonnet', which he only grudgingly concedes not to have been written by Shakespeare.[64]

The failure of the Sonnets to become part of Shakespeare's cultural capital had an obvious effect on their literary reach. According to David Fairer, 'we cannot speak of the "Shakespearean" verse of this period, as we can of the "Spenserian" or "Miltonic"',[65] and Shakespeare's poetry was not included in the English poetic canon, as defined by Alexander Pope and Thomas Gray.[66] Where allusions to Shakespeare can be detected in eighteenth-century poetry, they are most often to the supernatural elements of *A Midsummer Night's Dream*, *The Tempest* or *Macbeth*.[67] A richer hunting-ground for Sonnet influence ought to be the novel, which demonstrates how the appreciation of Shakespeare was increasing exponentially in the mid-eighteenth century.[68] And yet, even the most detailed recent studies

---

[63] Edmondson and Wells, *Shakespeare's Sonnets*, p. 101.

[64] Percy, *Reliques*, p. 199. There are many more examples of this inclusion of *Passionate Pilgrim* lyrics under Shakespeare's name, even though the anthologist 'knows' they are not his. In 1877, F. J. Furnivall reprinted Barnfield's lyric, 'If music and sweet poetry agree' in *The Leopold Shakspere*, acknowledging its true authorship but admitting: 'I wish the Sonnet, with its love of Spenser, had been Shakspere's'. See Cannan, 'Edmond Malone', 155.

[65] Fairer, 'Shakespeare in Poetry', p. 99.

[66] Ibid., pp. 99, 100.

[67] Fairer cites Joseph Addison who claimed in *The Spectator* in 1712 that Shakespeare 'incomparably excelled all others ... in the Faerie way of writing ... There is something so wild and yet so solemn in the Speeches of his Ghosts, Fairies, Witches, and the like Imaginary Persons, that we cannot forbear thinking them natural', 'Shakespeare in Poetry', p. 107.

[68] Michael Dobson has observed the phenomenon by which 'Shakespeare and his characters begin to migrate independently into the novel in the 1750s and 1760s', in *The Making of the National Poet*, pp. 213, 214.

have failed to find any indebtedness to the Sonnets.[69] A single exception would seem to be Samuel Richardson's *Clarissa, or the History of a Young Lady* (1747–8), and it is worth pausing here to offer a more detailed consideration of the evidence than it has yet received. Have we assumed too easily that the Sonnets have no influence upon the eighteenth-century novel?

'Were the Sonnett Worthy of the Subject': Samuel Richardson and Thomas Edwards

Although Richardson is often mentioned in the same breath as David Garrick for making Shakespeare 'a central resource for the emergent genre [of the novel]',[70] the question of how directly and how deeply he engaged with Shakespeare remains a matter of debate. Michael Connaughton accuses Richardson of ' "pretend[ing]" to read most of the writers he quotes',[71] due in part to his substantial reliance on Bysshe's *Art of Poetry* which is evident in 'at least three [quotations] in *Pamela*, five in *Sir Charles Grandison*, and forty-three in *Clarissa*'.[72] Misquotations, misattributions, and a sense of inappropriateness when the quote is understood in its original context, suggest that Richardson was not a perceptive reader of Shakespeare. Only *Clarissa* promises to redeem this reputation through its juxtaposition of 'banal' Shakespeare with a more personal response.[73] According to this theory, Richardson has Lovelace borrow from Bysshe 'to characterise him as a self-dramatising rake with a morally alarming taste for hyperbole and excess'.[74] Clarissa digs deeper, 'handl[ing] Shakespeare as a source of apothegmatic wisdom, the stuff of commonplace books'.[75] In the case of the Sonnets, however, neither frame of reference is apposite: they lack the literary cachet that would render them desirable to Lovelace, and they are absent from the commonplace tradition which shapes Clarissa's reading. Connaughton observes that where Richardson eschews Bysshe and consults Shakespeare directly, as he seems to have done with *The Tempest*, 'he shows greater awareness of the importance of context, avoids ironic parallels in situation, and even uses context in a positive

---

[69] See Rumbold's admirable *Shakespeare and the Eighteenth-Century Novel*, whose index contains no entry for the Sonnets.

[70] Keymer, 'Shakespeare in the Novel', p. 123.

[71] Connaughton, 'Richardson's Familiar Quotations', 183.

[72] Culler, 'Edward Bysshe', 870. Connaughton finds at least thirty more in 'Richardson's Familiar Quotations'.

[73] See Rumbold, ' "So Common-Hackneyed in the Eyes of Men" '.

[74] Keymer, 'Shakespeare in the Novel', p. 124.

[75] Rumbold, ' "Alas, Poor YORICK" ', 8.

fashion'.[76] To discover allusions to the Sonnets in *Clarissa* would thence not only demonstrate their effect upon the eighteenth-century novel, but would support the idea of Richardson as a serious reader of Shakespeare.

Two possible echoes have been found. Both occur after Clarissa's rape and invoke the recurrent theme of beauty's corruption. In a letter to Belford, Lovelace refers to his various schemes to degrade Clarissa: 'Yet [she] from step to step, from distress to distress, to maintain her superiority; and, like the sun, to break out upon me with the greater refulgence for the clouds that I had contrived to cast about her – And now to escape me thus!'[77] Jocelyn Harris likens this to Sonnet 33, specifically the lines: 'Anon permit the basest clouds to ride/ With ugly rack on his celestial face,/ And from the forlorn world his visage hide,/ Stealing unseen to west, with his disgrace./ Even so my sun one early morn did shine/ With all-triumphant splendour on my brow.'[78] But if Richardson was thinking of this Sonnet, he read it against the grain, for it does not emphasise the beloved's ability to emerge from 'the basest clouds' untainted, but rather his inevitable corruption. The final couplet offers the bitter consolation that 'Sons of the world may stain when heaven's sun staineth', 'stain' meaning to 'lose colour and luster, sustain a mortal blot, suffer dishonour'.[79] Given Lovelace's intention to celebrate Clarissa's purity, it seems more likely that Richardson was thinking of Prince Hal:

> Yet herein will I imitate the sun,
> Who doth permit the base contagious clouds
> To smother up his beauty from the world,
> That, when he please again to be himself,
> Being wanted, he may be more wondered at
> By breaking through the foul and ugly mist
> Of vapors that did seem to strangle him.[80]

The kind of company that obscures Hal – namely thieves and prostitutes – is not dissimilar to that which Clarissa is forced to keep. The fact that this passage was anthologised, unlike the Sonnet, also makes this attribution more likely.[81]

---

[76] Connaughton, 'Richardson's Familiar Quotations', 189.

[77] Richardson, *Clarissa*, p. 1344.

[78] See Harris, *Samuel Richardson*, p. 114.

[79] Booth, *Shakespeare's Sonnets*, p. 187.

[80] *1 Henry IV*, 1.2.167–73.

[81] It does not appear in Bysshe, but the whole of 1.2 was included in 'Scenes from Shakspeare's Plays' in the later editions of *Beauties of Shakespeare* (3rd edition, 1784, onwards), suggesting that it was one of the speeches Richardson might have known.

The second possible allusion occurs in Paper VII, where 'echoes of *Twelfth Night* and the Sonnets' have been found in Clarissa's expostulation against Lovelace: 'Thou eating canker-worm that preyest upon the opening bud, and turnest the damask rose into yellow lividness!'[82] The likeness to Viola's 'sister' who 'never told her love/ But let concealment, like a worm i'th'bud,/ Feed on her damask cheek' is initially compelling,[83] not least because this was a passage Richardson would cite later in *Sir Charles Grandison* (1753–4), where Clementina takes affront at having the lines read to her, and repeats them defiantly in her own accent.[84] But where this is consistent with Clementina's character and situation, the same cannot be said for Clarissa. The destruction of Viola's imagined sister by her own passion runs counter to Clarissa's angry indictment of Lovelace. The Sonnets are much more relevant. At least five poems include the image of the canker-ruined flower, and Sonnet 95 is particularly apt, beginning 'How sweet and lovely dost thou make the shame/ Which, like a canker in the fragrant rose,/ Doth spot the beauty of thy budding name'. The Sonnets direct this imagery against the male beloved, first describing his beauty and perfections and then condoling (and condemning) their decay. In a similar fashion, Clarissa bears witness to Lovelace's initial attractions: 'At first I saw something in your air and person that displeased me not. Your birth and fortunes were no small advantages to you.'[85] The Shakespearean analogy enables Clarissa to deflect attention away from herself towards Lovelace as both canker and despoiled rose. She arguably does something similar in her borrowing from *Hamlet* in Paper X. Composed wholly of abstracts from Bysshe, reproduced on the page in a disorderly fashion – both features suggesting the destruction of Clarissa's sense of self – this paper has been used to demonstrate Richardson's lack of regard for context.[86] However, Clarissa appropriates Hamlet's condemnation of female sexual appetite in order to direct it at Lovelace: 'Oh! You have done an act/ That blots the face and blush of modesty.'[87] The female victim, though blighted, remains fundamentally 'an innocent love'.

---

[82] Richardson, *Clarissa*, p. 892. This identification is made by Scofield, 'Shakespeare and *Clarissa*', 35.

[83] *Twelfth Night*, 2.5.110–12. Keymer describes it as 'the single most hackneyed Shakespeare tag in currency by the end of the century', 'Shakespeare in the Novel', p. 119.

[84] Richardson, *The History of Sir Charles Grandison*, p. 153.

[85] Richardson, *Clarissa*, Paper VIII, p. 892.

[86] See Connaughton, 'Richardson's Familiar Quotations', 188. See also James Smith's compelling argument that Clarissa uses these quotations as fantasies that allow her to 'wrestl[e] some … trace of agency for herself', *Samuel Richardson and the Theory of Tragedy*, p. 74. See also his discussion of the *Hamlet* quotation, pp. 78–81.

[87] Richardson, *Clarissa*, p. 893.

It is certainly appealing to think of Richardson reading and engaging with the Sonnets, not least because of their similarities with the epistolary form. Shakespeare's speaker often refers to them as missives, intended to communicate directly with the addressee, and they have something of the same erotic materiality as letters in Richardson's fiction. The 'small room' of the sonnet in which the writer explores his private obsession also speaks to the function of the closet in Richardson's work as a space in which the heroine explores her own conflicted feelings.[88] And yet, perhaps the most compelling evidence that Richardson did *not* know the Sonnets can be found in his conversation with a man who clearly did, Thomas Edwards.

Edwards was the author of *A Supplement to Mr Warburton's Edition of Shakespear* (1748), later known by its subtitle *The Canons of Criticism*, which was reprinted more than any other piece of Shakespeare criticism in the eighteenth century.[89] It described in considerable detail how Warburton's 1747 *Works* had misrepresented Shakespeare's plays and abused the powers of an editor, many of which were defined here for the first time. The third edition (1750) was prefaced by a sonnet of Edwards' own composition, excoriating Warburton as a 'Tongue-doughty Pedant, whose ambitious mind/Prompts thee beyond thy native pitch to soar',[90] and it was as a sonneteer that Edwards would also become renowned. He published thirteen sonnets in Robert Dodsley's *A Collection of Poems in Three Volumes by Several Hands* (1748), followed by a larger selection in the posthumous seventh edition of *Canons* (1765), and has been described as 'the real father of the eighteenth-century sonnet, "the only begetter" whom his contemporaries knew as such'.[91]

It was Edwards' admiration for *Clarissa* that initially prompted him to write to Richardson, but they corresponded thereafter between 1748 and 1756, sending each other volumes of epistolary novels and sonnets respectively. In Edwards' letter of 28 December 1749, he apologises for the enclosed poem, 'To the Author of *Clarissa*':

> Were the Sonnett worthy of the Subject, it would be the best I ever wrote; Such as it is, it comes from the heart, & the productions of that I know you prefer to those merely of the head.[92]

[88] For further discussion, see Fisher, ' "Closet-Work" '.

[89] Marder, *His Exits and his Entrances*, pp. 102–3. See also Dussinger, 'Edwards, Thomas (*d*. 1757)'.

[90] Edwards, *Canons of Criticism*, p. 14.

[91] Havens, *The Influence of Milton on English Poetry*, p. 492. See also Rinaker, 'Thomas Edwards and the Sonnet Revival', 272.

[92] Richardson, *The Cambridge Edition of the Correspondence of Samuel Richardson*, pp. 183–4.

The sonnet apparently pleased Richardson so much that he had it prefixed to the third and fourth editions of *Clarissa*, though without the poet's name, much to Edwards' chagrin. In the ensuing years, Edwards makes frequent reference to sonnets accompanying his letters, but the most explicit discussion of his sonneteering is in the letter of 18 July 1754, wherein he reviews his poetic career:

> But for my Sonnets – whether I shall ever transgress in that way again I cannot tell; at present I have no impulse to it; and therefore I must beg leave to vindicate or at least excuse myself in prose. The reading of Spenser's Sonnets was the first occasion of my writing that species of little poems, and my first six were written in the same sort of stanza as all his and Shakespeare's are. But after that Mr Wray brought me acquainted with the Italian authors, who were the originals of that sort of poetry, and whose measures have more variety and harmony in them – ever since, I wrote in that stanza; drawing from the same fountains as Milton drew from; – so that I was complimented with having well imitated Milton when I was not acquainted with his Sonnets. I hope I shall never be ashamed of imitating such great originals as Shakespeare, Spenser and Milton, whom to imitate with any degree of success is no small praise.[93]

This effusive confession was met with almost total silence from Richardson, as is consistent with the rest of their correspondence that relates to sonnets. Richardson offers thanks for those he receives and has copies of the *Clarissa* eulogy printed up and sent to Edwards; he urges him to publish a collection of sonnets alongside his literary criticism; but he never offers a critical response or discusses the relative merits of Shakespeare, Spenser and Milton. In a letter to Lady Bradshaigh dated 1753 Richardson admitted that he had not read all the Shakespeare he might have, and 'hope[d] to live to read the rest of Thee, the far greater Part'.[94] This seems likely to have included the Sonnets.

By contrast, Edwards was more influenced than he might have wished by those lyrics. His debts to Spenser in terms of structure and vocabulary were sufficiently extensive that he was implored by Susanna Highmore to unchain his Muse 'with ancient Rules opprest'.[95] His debt to Milton is apparent in sonnets to both admired contemporaries and scorned literary critics, the latter particularly recalling Milton's urgent, vitriolic style. Nevertheless, Shakespeare's preoccupation with time is strongly, if

---

[93] Ibid., p. 336.
[94] Letter dated 8 December 1753, quoted in Duncan-Eaves and Kimpel, *Samuel Richardson*, p. 573.
[95] See her poem included in a letter from Richardson to Edwards on 12 June 1754, Richardson, *The Cambridge Edition of the Correspondence of Samuel Richardson*, pp. 331–3.

subversively, felt in many of Edwards' poems. In anticipation of his own death, Edwards addressed sonnets to the doctors who treated him (*Canons* no. 27, 29), and to the sexton who would bury him (no. 44), and his allusions to quitting this 'mortal coil' and to the 'cowslip, violet or the pale primrose' that will 'deck' his grave carry subdued echoes of *Hamlet*. Richardson was uncharacteristically moved to comment on these sonnets when he received them, observing that 'The melancholy Turn becomes the Muse you have chosen; But I hope has not taken Possession of the good Heart, which dictated them to a Head equally good'.[96] In Sonnet 3 ('To Francis Knollys Esq.'), Edwards struggles with grief by coming up with a trite (and distinctly un-Shakespearean) consolation:

> Did the sharp pang we feel for friends deceas'd
> Unbated last, we must with anguish die;
> But Nature bids it's [*sic*] rigour should be eas'd
> By lenient Time, and strong Necessity;
> These calm the passions, and subdue the mind,
> To bear th'appointed lot of human kind.[97]

But elsewhere, the more anarchic Shakespearean Time will not be subdued, as in Sonnet 5, 'On a Family-Picture', in which Edwards meditates on the death of all his siblings, leaving himself the barren heir to his father's name. The sonnet begins from an act of contemplation which is both Shakespearean and Miltonic:

> When pensive on that Portraiture I gaze,
> Where my four Brothers round about me stand,
> And four fair Sisters smile with graces bland,
> The goodly monument of happier days;
>
> And think how soon insatiate Death, who preys
> On all, has cropp'd the rest with ruthless hand,
> While only I survive of all that band,
> Which one chaste bed did to my Father raise;
>
> It seems that like a Column left alone
> The tottering remnant of some splendid Fane,
> Scaped from the fury of the barbarous Gaul,
> And wasting Time, which has the rest o'er thrown;
> Amidst our House's ruins I remain,
> Single, unpropp'd, and nodding to my fall.[98]

---

[96] Ibid., p. 318.
[97] Edwards, *Canons of Criticism*, p. 309.
[98] Ibid., p. 311.

Far from 'lenient Time', this sonnet calls upon a set of aggressively Shakespearean personifications: 'insatiate Death', whose 'ruthless hand' recalls 'Time's fell hand' in Sonnet 64; and 'wasting Time', which we might remember from the variant 106 'When in the annals of all wasting Time'. Edwards' lack of descendants had been alluded to by Richardson in a letter urging him to secure his reputation through literary/editorial endeavours: 'Be a Work of this Nature … (if you will not make some happy Woman continue to [use] your Name).'[99] The echo of the procreation sonnets (specifically Sonnet 3) is probably unintentional on Richardson's part, but for Edwards Shakespeare's Sonnets lingered in the memory, an un-Christian whispering to his secret fears of extinction.

In the next stage of the eighteenth-century revival of the sonnet, in the 1780s,[100] Shakespeare's influence as a sonneteer becomes increasingly remote. Foremost among these poets was Charlotte Turner Smith, whose much-admired *Elegiac Sonnets* (1784) often deployed the Shakespearean form. Yet, as a reviewer in *The Gentleman's Magazine* 56 (April, 1786) put it, 'a very trifling compliment is paid to Mrs Smith, when it is observed how much her Sonnets exceed those of *Shakespeare* and *Milton*. She has undoubtedly conferred honour on a species of poetry which most of her predecessors in this country have disgraced'.[101] Smith took inspiration from the sympathetic landscapes and suffering characters of Shakespeare's plays, particularly the bereaved mother Constance in *King John* and the anguished King Lear. As Joy Currie observes: 'Through allusions and quotations, she creates moments of shared emotion between her speakers, Shakespeare and herself; appropriates his language and metaphors; claims authority for her expression of political views; and develops extended analogies between Shakespeare's themes and characters and her own.'[102] However, Smith seems to have done none of this through the Sonnets, raising doubts that she had read them.

A more striking example of the Sonnets' obsolescence is *Sonnets from Shakespeare: By Albert* (1791), originally printed in contemporary newspapers. Their author, John Armstrong, acknowledges the existence of Shakespeare's lyrics, reminding his readers 'that the sonnet was a form of writing adopted by the great Bard himself',[103] but he does not encourage readers to seek them out. Rather, Armstrong derives sonnets

[99] Richardson, *The Cambridge Edition of the Correspondence of Samuel Richardson*, p. 206.
[100] For further discussion, see Feldman and Robinson, *A Century of Sonnets*, pp. 9–11.
[101] *The Gentleman's Magazine* 56 (April 1786), p. 334.
[102] Currie, '"Mature Poets Steal"', p. 100.
[103] Armstrong, *Sonnets from Shakespeare*, p. vi.

from Shakespeare's plays. *Romeo and Juliet*, for example, 'seemed, from the tenderness of the sentiments, and the pathos of the situations, to afford materials peculiarly adapted to the nature of the sonnet',[104] and Armstrong hopes that 'from the perusal of these little verses, [readers will] find part of that pleasure restored, which it afforded them on the stage, in the closet, and, if we may so express it, the image of their own minds again reflected'.[105] The way in which he adapts passages into sonnets is revealing. Finding the language of *Romeo and Juliet* too compressed, he draws a nineteen-line speech out into two sonnets and dispenses with the puns: 'To preserve the sentiment, and separate it from the quibble, has been the object of these sonnets.'[106] A new moralising strain also suggests the different social mores at work in 1790 than 1590, as when Juliet's speech at 2.1.132ff is transformed in sonnet 8:

> Ah! If thou lovest me, Romeo, don't deceive;
> Why should I ask? I know thou'lt answer ay;
> And I, *weak maid*, I fondly will believe –
> Jove laughs at lovers perjuries, they say.
>
> Yet, why should I so soon my passion tell?
> But ah! Think not that I'm too quickly won,
> *Nor let it be my crime to love too well –*
> *If you are false, my Romeo, I'm undone!*
>
> Tho' soon I gave away *my virgin heart,*
> Yet deem me not, sweet youth, too flighty grown,
> More true I'll prove that they that have more art,
> Yet would the heart I gave were still my own:
>
> Ask'st thou, why Juliet breaths a wish so vain?
> But to be frank, my Love, and give it thee again.
>
> (Italics mine)

It is notable that when Armstrong's *Sonnets from Shakespeare* was first published, Edmund Malone's text of *Shake-speares Sonnets* was already available, in both the 1780 and 1790 editions. Perhaps Armstrong's decision to publish represents his awareness of a new interest in the Sonnets; perhaps it implies a desire to keep his distance, offering an alternative to fill the Sonnet-shaped gap in the Shakespearean canon. Certainly, the nature of Armstrong's adaptations hints at the potential difficulties of *Shake-speares*

---

[104] Ibid., p. 49. Armstrong shows no awareness that *Romeo* contains at least one complete sonnet in the palmer's kiss dialogue between the protagonists.

[105] *Gazetteer*, 25 September 1790, p. 2.

[106] Armstrong, *Sonnets from Shakespeare*, p. 58.

Sonnets for an eighteenth-century audience: their elaborate wordplay, their 'unromantic' and indelicate emotions of bitterness and rage, their lack of narrative and of dramatic persona (Armstrong prints the character's name above each sonnet). These were not difficulties that a late eighteenth-century editor would easily overcome, but to identify Shakespeare as the amorous protagonist of his own Sonnets would certainly help.

Edmond Malone: Re-Reading *Shake-speares Sonnets*

Edmond Malone's editorial work on the Sonnets has been rightly praised for its radical intervention in the history of their neglect. But to claim that he was the first 'to publish, annotate and canonize the 1609 Sonnets' is to take him too much at his own estimation.[107] The choice of the Quarto as copy-text for his *Supplement to the edition of Shakspeare's Plays published in 1778 by Samuel Johnson and George Steevens* (1780) was surprising – as recently as 1775, Thomas Evans had reprinted Benson – but it was not unprecedented. Malone had consulted Capell's manuscript, which was based on Lintott's 1711 edition of the Quarto, and he must also have been aware of Steevens' reprinting of the Quarto in *Twenty of the Plays of Shakespeare* (1766), discussed above. In terms of canonisation, whilst his inclusion of the Quarto Sonnets within *The Plays and Poems of William Shakspeare* (1790) was hugely significant, it was not until the posthumous edition of 1821 that the Sonnets' position in the *Works* looked secure, Malone having failed to persuade Steevens to include them in his 1793 edition.[108] Nor, for all his influence in authenticating the Quarto Sonnets, did Malone purge his own poetic canon of imposters in the way that he would have had his readers believe. Despite his contempt for editors who had failed to 'separate [Shakespeare's] genuine poetical compositions from the spurious performances with which they have so long been intermixed', he reprinted the 1599 *Passionate Pilgrim*, immediately after the Sonnets and before 'A Lover's Complaint', and accepted its Venus and Adonis poems as 'essays of the author when he first conceived the idea of writing a poem on the subject'.[109]

---

[107] De Grazia, *Shakespeare Verbatim*, p. 2. Malone stated in the Preface that 'Shortly after [Shakespeare's] death, a very incorrect impression of his poems was issued out, which in every subsequent edition has been implicitly followed. They are now all faithfully printed from the original copies', p. iv.

[108] The appeal of Benson's *Poems* also lingered on, producing the strange hybrid that is *Poems by William Shakespeare*, in which Benson's text of the Sonnets is accompanied by Malone's notes.

[109] Shakespeare, *Supplement*, ed. Malone, pp. iv, 710. This argument had also been made by Thomas Percy in 1765, cited above. Malone expanded the number of Venus sonnets, including 'Sweet rose, fair flower' (PP10) and 'Crabbed age' (PP12), p. 751.

Perhaps most surprisingly, given his reverence for original texts,[110] Malone mangled the 1599 *Passionate Pilgrim*, omitting Sonnets 138 and 144, and Marlowe's 'Come live with me', and putting in their place 'Take O take those lips away' and 'Let the bird of loudest lay' ('The Phoenix and the Turtle'), both of which had been reprinted by Benson. His distortion of *The Passionate Pilgrim* in the 1790 *Works* was even more extreme. Having identified that 'If music and sweet poetry', and 'As it fell upon a day' were by Barnfield, Malone dropped them, but then gathered all the remaining Venus and Adonis poems at the beginning.[111] As Cannan has shown, Malone's editing of *The Passionate Pilgrim* had significant consequences for Shakespeare's poetic canon until the end of the nineteenth century:

> [he] encouraged editors, scholars, and readers after him to radically re-present and reimagine Jaggard's collection, transforming an antiquarian curiosity of questionable authenticity into an invaluable source about Shakespeare's artistry and life, and, in particular, an indispensable showcase for 'his' very best poems.[112]

Malone's unique achievement is arguably not the publication or canonisation of the Quarto text, but his annotation of individual Sonnets, which provided his audience not only with the tools to read these lyrics but with a reason for doing so. Given the almost total blankness which had previously surrounded the Sonnets, his proliferation of glosses, alternative readings, and parallel passages from the plays was a revelation, and by including Steevens' notes, Malone implied that Shakespeareans felt it worth engaging in lengthy dialogue about the Sonnets – that they mattered and could expect to have a readership.[113] Malone also worked hard to render the lyrics accessible in a way they had never been before, explaining in the notes to Sonnet 2, for example, that 'tatter'd weed' is a 'torn garment', 'unear'd' means 'untilled' and 'Fond, in old language, is foolish'.[114] That said, this annotation did little to elucidate the most difficult poems. As Hilton Landry observes:

---

[110] See de Grazia's argument that 'Malone's overwhelming preoccupation with objectivity marks a significant shift in the focus of Shakespeare studies from what might be termed the discursively acceptable to the factually verifiable', *Shakespeare Verbatim*, p. 5.

[111] For further discussion, see Oya, 'Authenticating the Inauthentic'.

[112] Cannan, 'Edmond Malone', p. 144.

[113] What Burrow says of the apparatus for the 1790 edition is also true of the *Supplement*, namely that it 'presents that text as a suitable subject for argument between competent authorities, and encourages readers to participate in those arguments', 'Editing the Sonnets', p. 151.

[114] Shakespeare, *Supplement*, ed. Malone, p. 583.

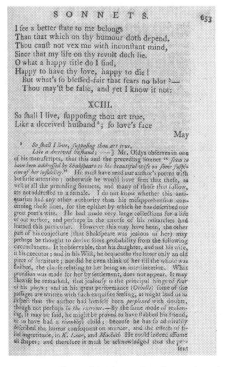

Figure 3.2 Sonnet 93 in Edmond Malone, *Supplement* (1780), vol. 1, p. 653
© The British Library Board, 686, f. 17

Malone fails to provide even one critical comment on the notoriously difficult Sonnet 94, 'They that have powere to hurt'; he ignores the problems in
the first six lines of Sonnet 121, ''Tis better to be vile then vile esteemed'; he
gives only one interpretive note on Sonnet 124. 'Yf my deare love were but
the childe of state', perhaps the most difficult of all the Sonnets; and only
two on Sonnet 125, 'Wer't ought to me I bore the canopy'.[115]

By contrast, Sonnet 93 ('So shall I live, supposing thou art true/ Like a
deceived husband …'), despite receiving little attention in twenty-first century editions, generates the longest set of notes, extending over five pages
(see Figure 3.2).

This is because it provides Malone with an opportunity to explore the
two major preoccupations of his reading of the Sonnets: firstly, their value
as historical documents which might (as Boswell later put it) 'eke out

---

[115] Landry, 'Malone as Editor of Shakespeare's Sonnets', 441.

the scanty memorials, which have come down to us, of the incidents of [Shakespeare's] life',[116] and, second, the division of the sequence at Sonnet 126 between lyrics addressed to a man and a woman – a critical intervention so monumental that criticism has only just begun to tear it down.[117]

The process of discovering Shakespeare and dividing the Sonnets begins not with a poem but with Thorpe's dedication to 'Mr W. H.'. Malone disagrees with Richard Farmer's supposition that this is William Harte, the poet's nephew, for he would have been no more than twelve years old, and 'many of [the Sonnets] are written to show the propriety of marriage; and therefore cannot well be supposed to be addressed to a school-boy'.[118] Thomas Tyrwhitt's discovery of a pun on 'Hews' (W. Hughes) in Sonnet 20 seems more likely, and so 'To this person, whoever he was, one hundred and twenty [six] of the following poems are addressed; the remaining twenty-eight are addressed to a lady'.[119] Malone's revelation may be expressed in neutral tones, but it was an extraordinary observation to make, given that until this moment editors and anthologists had happily assigned most, if not all, of the Sonnets to a mistress (see Gildon, Lintott and Sewell). Nor, for all his commitment to historical research, could Malone offer a precedent for two addressees. He proposes Samuel Daniel's sonnets as 'the model that Shakspeare followed',[120] and observes that Barnfield's *The Affectionate Shepherd* features amorous language addressed to a male,[121] but these discrete collections could not explain a 'sequence' which suddenly changes beloved.

Malone seems to have been driven partly by the desire to elevate himself above his fellow scholars:

> Mr Oldys observes in one of his manuscripts that this and the preceding Sonnet [92 and 93] '*seem to have been addressed by Shakspeare to his beautiful wife on some suspicion of her infidelity*'. He must have read our author's poems with but little attention; otherwise he would have seen that these, as well as all the preceding Sonnets, and many of those that follow, are not addressed to a female.[122]

Yet, as this negative ('not addressed to') implies, Malone was not fully enamoured of his own revelation, showing a marked reluctance to develop many of the narrative hints provided by his 'sequence'. He

---

[116] Shakespeare, *The Plays and Poems of William Shakespeare*, ed. Boswell, p. 219.
[117] See Dubrow, ' "Incertainties now crown themselves assur'd" ', and Wells, ' "My Name is Will" '.
[118] Shakespeare, *Supplement*, ed. Malone, p. 529.
[119] Ibid.
[120] Ibid., p. 581.
[121] Shakespeare, *The Plays and Poems*, ed. Malone, p. 220.
[122] Shakespeare, *Supplement*, ed. Malone, p. 653.

does not acknowledge the adulterous relationship that emerges between the speaker, the male friend and the lady (here synonymous with Shakespeare's wife), and the allusions to some particular vice or blemish in the male addressee go without comment. His biographical readings of individual Sonnets tend to focus on Shakespeare's career; for example, Sonnet 111, with its regret that Fortune 'did not better for my life pro-vide/ Than public means which public manners breeds', prompts the response: 'The author seems here to lament his being reduced to the necessity of appearing on the stage, or writing for the theatre.'[123] The reference to 'my pupil pen' in Sonnet 16 offers 'a slight proof that the poems before us were our author's earliest compositions', and Sonnet 80 implies that the 'better spirit' before whom Shakespeare's genius falters was Spenser: 'these Sonnets being probably written when [Shakespeare's] name was but little known and at a time when Spenser was in the zenith of his reputation'.[124] But having identified Shakespeare's most amorous lyrics as being addressed to a male, Malone could not wholly avoid explaining *how* Shakespeare loved him.

The *Supplement* offers at least three strategies for dealing with this crux: disgust by reading literally, exoneration by reading historically, and denial by avoiding the subject altogether. The first two approaches are indicated by the comments provoked by Sonnet 20 ('A woman's face with nature's own hand painted'). This lyric appears to have caused no distress and to have merited no attention until 1780, when Steevens suddenly breaks out: 'It is impossible to read this fulsome panegyrick, addressed to a male object, without an equal mixture of disgust and indignation.'[125] In the *Supplement*, Malone simply lets this observation stand, but in the 1790 text he counters:

> Some part of this indignation might perhaps have been abated, if it had been considered that such addresses to men, however indelicate, were cus-tomary in our author's time, and neither imported criminality, nor were esteemed indecorous … [And besides] *Master-mistress* does not perhaps mean *man*-mistress, but *sovereign* Mistress …[126]

---

[123] Ibid., p. 670. The notion that Shakespeare was ashamed of his profession would be exploited by Charles Lamb. Citing Sonnets 23 and 111, he describes the 'jealous self-watchfulness of our sweet Shakespeare' as what necessarily distinguishes him from the 'envy and jealousy' of a vicious player. See 'On the Tragedies of Shakespeare', p. 120. It will subsequently become important to Charles Dickens, as explored in Chapter 4.

[124] Shakespeare, *Supplement*, ed. Malone, pp. 594, 645.

[125] Ibid., p. 597.

[126] Shakespeare, *The Plays and Poems*, ed. Malone, vol. 11, p. 207.

More detail is given in the annotation to Sonnet 32, which explains Shakespeare's description of himself as 'deceased lover' to a man:

> The numerous expressions of this kind that occur in these Sonnets, as well as the general tenour of the greater part of them, cannot but appear strange to a modern reader. In justice therefore to our author, it is proper to observe, that such addresses to men were common in Shakspeare's time, and were not thought indecorous.[127] That age seems to have been very indelicate and gross in many other particulars beside this, but they certainly did not think themselves so. Nothing can prove more strongly the different notions which they entertained on subjects of decorum than those which prevail at present, than the eulogiums which were pronounced on Fletcher's plays for the *chastity* of their language; those very plays which are now banished from the stage for their *licentiousness* and *obscenity*.[128]

But if Shakespeare's desires cannot be projected onto a rival such as Fletcher (whose collaboration with Beaumont had long raised questions over his sexuality),[129] Malone has other means to straighten them out. In the notes on Sonnet 93, he upbraids Oldys for mistaking the male addressee for Shakespeare's wife, but then becomes locked in a debate over what Shakespeare's relations with that wife must have been like, ending with the question of whether or not Shakespeare resembled Othello in being particularly prone to jealousy[130] – his jealousy over a *male* beloved quietly set aside.

A further manoeuvre is to pull back and reflect upon the formal 'vices' which are fundamental to the sonnet per se and to Shakespeare's Sonnets in particular. This is most obviously seen in the act of *legerdemain* by which Steevens moves from addressing the gender of the addressee to a deprecation of the Sonnets' style which casually heterosexualises them:

> Of the Sonnets before us, one hundred and twenty-six are inscribed (as Mr. Malone observes) to a friend: the remaining twenty-eight (a small proportion out of so many) are devoted to a mistress. Yet if our author's Ferdinand or Romeo had not expressed themselves in terms more familiar to human

---

[127] Both editions include the following examples: 'B. Jonson concludes one of his letters to Dr. Donne by telling him that he is his "ever true *lover*"; and Drayton, in a letter to Mr. Drummond of Hawthornden, informs him, that Mr. Joseph Davis is *in love* with him' (Shakespeare, *Supplement*, ed. Malone, p. 664, Shakespeare, *The Plays and Poems*, ed. Malone, p. 220).

[128] Shakespeare, *The Plays and Poems*, ed. Malone, pp. 219–20. This note is transposed and expanded from the note to Sonnet 102 in the 1780 edition.

[129] See McMullan, *The Politics of Unease in the Plays of John Fletcher*, pp. 139–40, and Masten, *Textual Intercourse*, pp. 113–55.

[130] Shakespeare, *Supplement*, ed. Malone, p. 653. This passage would prove influential much later in the fictional biography of Shakespeare, beginning with James Joyce, but furthered by Anthony Burgess and William Boyd, in which Shakespeare's cuckoldry inspires him to play an Othello-like role.

understanding, I believe few readers would have rejoiced in the happiness of the one, or sympathized with the sorrows of the other. Perhaps, indeed, quaintness, obscurity, and tautology, are to be regarded as the constituent parts of this exotick species of composition. But, in whatever the excellence of it may consist, I protest I am one of those who should have wished it to have expired in the country where it was born ...[131]

In Malone's defence of the Sonnets, he effectively repeats Steevens' rhetorical strategy: burying the problem of their sexuality in a secondary clause, before turning his attention to their stylistic features:

When they are described as a mass of affectation, pedantry, circumlocution, and nonsense, the picture appears to me over-charged. Their great defects seem to be a want of variety, *and the majority of them not being directed to a female*, to whom alone such ardent expressions of esteem could with propriety be addressed ... [And yet] I do not perceive that the versification of these pieces is less smooth and harmonious than that of Shakespeare's other compositions. Though many of them are not so simple and clear as they ought to be, yet some of them are written with perspicacity and energy. A few have been already pointed out as deserving this character; and many beautiful lines, scattered through these poems will, it is supposed, strike every reader who is not determined to allow no praise to any species of poetry except blank verse or heroic couplets ...[132]

Even some of Malone's early critics adopted this strategy of engaging with issues of style over substance. The *Monthly Review* (October, 1780) acknowledges 'This very *curious* Supplement', and anticipates that 'admirers of Shakespeare will esteem themselves indebted to Mr Malone for the pains he hath taken to gratify their *curiosity*'.[133] The repeated term enfolds within itself allusions to the Sonnets' artfulness and complexity (OED7a), their novelty or strangeness (16a), and their appeal to a connoisseur audience (6). As the reviewers focus on the 'species of poetry adopted by Shakspeare in his Sonnets', and the different values placed on it by Steevens and Malone, they once again occlude the real contention over how one should regard a collection of amorous poems addressed to a man: 'The Reader, if he will see how the dispute begins, and how it is carried on, must consult the work itself.'[134] The implications of Malone's bipartite division start to be felt more explicitly towards the end of the century, however, when they are addressed by two different respondents: the antiquarian and political

[131] Ibid., p. 683.
[132] Shakespeare, *Supplement*, ed. Malone, pp. 684–5, italics mine.
[133] *The Monthly Review*, p. 249, italics mine.
[134] Ibid., p. 257.

writer, George Chalmers, and the poet and critic, Samuel Taylor Coleridge. Both return with ill-concealed anxiety to Sonnet 20.

That '[Im]possible Object of Desire': Sonnet 20 After Malone

In 1795, George Chalmers was one of many who thronged to the house of Samuel Ireland in Norfolk Street to inspect a cache of original Shakespeare documents recently discovered by his son, William-Henry Ireland. Now recognised as 'wish fulfilments, late-eighteenth century bardolatrous versions of what the poet "should" have been like',[135] these forgeries testified to Shakespeare's staunch Protestant faith, his heterosexuality, and his successful patronage by Elizabeth I. Nevertheless, it would take someone with more detailed knowledge of Shakespeare's biography, and of early modern orthography, than Chalmers to disprove them. This was Edmond Malone, who destroyed the legitimacy of the documents, and the credibility of both William-Henry and Samuel Ireland, in *An Inquiry into the Authenticity of Certain Papers and Instruments ... attributed to Shakspeare, Queen Elizabeth and Henry, Earl of Southampton* (London, 1796). But although Chalmers had to admit that he had been fooled, he refused to accept that he was wrong in principle, and he called upon Shakespeare's lyrical verse as evidence.

William-Henry produced two forgeries relating to the Shakespearean poetic canon. The first was a letter by Elizabeth I to Shakespeare, which mentions that 'Wee didde receive youre prettye Verses goode Masterre William through the hands off oure Lorde Chambelayne ande wee doe Complemente thee onne theyre great excellence',[136] although the poems themselves were not included.[137] This would have been an opportunity for William-Henry to produce either his own fake sonnet, or a fake manuscript version of a Sonnet (as he had done with *King Lear*) but he did neither. In his later confession, Ireland averred that the 'Verses' 'certainly never had existence, to the best of my knowledge'.[138] Perhaps William-Henry

---

[135] Keevak, 'Shakespeare's *Queer* Sonnets', 168. For a detailed account of Ireland's career, see Schoenbaum, *Shakespeare's Lives*, pp. 135–56.

[136] 'Queen Elizabeth's Letter' in Ireland, *Miscellaneous Papers and Legal Instruments under the Hand and Seal of William Shakespeare*, Ar.

[137] Malone would use this as an argument to undermine the forgery's claim: 'it is remarkable the poet should here take such care that this gracious Epistle should be "kepte with all care possible", and yet should not have preserved the pretty verses that gave occasion to it', Malone, *An Inquiry into the Authenticity of Certain Papers and Instruments ... attributed to Shakspeare, Queen Elizabeth and Henry, Earl of Southampton*, p. 97.

[138] Ireland, *The Confessions of William Henry Ireland*, p. 76.

did not know the Sonnets, or he suspected that they were not sufficiently familiar to his readers to be worth faking, or he feared that their ambiguities, in light of Malone's bipartite division, would work against his image of Shakespeare as a faithful husband. The poem that he did invent was a twenty-line lyric, directed by Shakespeare to Anne Hathaway, beginning 'Is there inne heavenne aught more rare/ Thanne thou sweete Nymphe of Avon fayre … Is there onne Earthe a Manne more trewe/ Thanne Willy Shakspeare is toe you'.[139]

When Chalmers came to defend his own gullibility in *An Apology for the Believers in the Shakspeare-Papers* (1797), he argued that it was perfectly reasonable to think Elizabeth would condescend to write to Shakespeare, 'whose *prettye verses* were, no doubt, written with his best pen, in his gayest fancy, on the encomiastic topics of love, and marriage, with "twenty odd conceited true-love knots"'.[140] He proceeds to castigate Malone for failing to believe in the existence of such verses, just because he has not seen them:

> Mr Secretary Cecil's songs on Queen Bess's frolick, though they were once sung, are now sung no more.[141] And the sonnets of Shakspeare, which inflamed the desire, and roused the gratitude of Elizabeth, may possibly exist in the same casket with Cecil's *dittays*, though none of our Cottons or Harleys, have preserved them, and none of our Waldrons, or Malones, have found them.[142]

Chalmers seems to wish that these verses *did* exist, and that they might displace Shakespeare's Sonnets, whose homoerotic undertones would thence be happily replaced by the theme of marriage and true-love knots. Almost immediately, however, he changes tactic and proposes that these '*prettye verses*' have, in fact, been under Malone's nose the whole time, and they are 'the Sonnets', which were all written for Elizabeth '[who] was often addressed as a man'.[143] Chalmers is incredulous at Malone's notion 'that Shakespeare, a husband, a father, a moral man, addressed a hundred and twenty, nay, a hundred and twenty-six *Amourous* Sonnets to a *male* object!'.[144]

The need to repudiate Malone's male addressee involves Chalmers in an increasingly elaborate (obfuscatory) interpretation of individual Sonnets.

[139] 'Verses to Anna Hatherrawaye', in Ireland, *Miscellaneous Papers*, n.p.
[140] Chalmers, *An Apology for the Believers*, p. 39.
[141] Chalmers had earlier quoted a letter from William Browne to the Earl of Shaftesbury over a flirtation between Elizabeth and Cecil, ibid., pp. 36–7.
[142] Ibid., p. 39.
[143] Ibid., p. 51.
[144] Chalmers, *A Supplementary Apology for the Believers in the Shakspeare-Papers*, p. 55.

He identifies 'feminine' endearments in Sonnets 1–126, asking whether Shakespeare could really have meant 'to apply to *his man*, the feminine *Epithet*, *"tender churl"*, in the first Sonnet, and the womanish epithets "unthrifty *loveliness*" and "*beauteous* niggard" in the fourth sonnet'?[145] Equally unlikely is that the male pronouns are really directed at a man, with Chalmers concluding that 'he and his, him and she, are grievously intermixed by Shakespeare', and that '*his* was, in those days, not only used in a neutral sense, but in a feminine sense; as by Spenser, in his Aeclogue of April: "And, now ye dainty Damsels may depart/ Each one *his* way"'.[146] None of the following Sonnets then is really addressed to a man: Sonnet 67 ('Ah, wherefore with infection should he live'); Sonnet 63 ('His beauty shall in these black lines be seen'); or Sonnet 3 ('Look in thy glass, and tell the face thou viewest'), in which Chalmers is put to remarkable contortions to explain the lines 'For where is she so fair, whose unear'd womb/Disdains the tillage of thy husbandry'.[147] The crucial poem for Chalmers, however, is Sonnet 20, given that this is the cornerstone of Malone's male-addressee theory, and the origin of Steevens' shocking disgust:

> A woman's face with Nature's own hand painted
> Hast thou, the master-mistress of my passion;
> A woman's gentle heart, but not acquainted
> With shifting change, as is false women's fashion;
> An eye more bright than theirs, less false in rolling,
> Gilding the object whereupon it gazeth;
> A man in hue, all hues in his controlling,
> That steals men's eyes and women's souls amazeth.
> And for a woman wert thou first created;
> Till Nature, as she wrought thee, fell a-doting,
> And by addition me of thee defeated,
> By adding one thing to my purpose nothing.
> > But since she prick'd thee out for women's pleasure,
> > Mine be thy love and thy love's use their treasure.

Chalmers begins by suggesting that, just as the entire sequence is modelled on Spenser's *Amoretti*, which he takes to be directed to the Queen, so Sonnet 20 is indebted to *Amoretti* 17, with its conceit of a female beauty that defies mortal representation. He then goes through each potentially offensive word or phrase to make it conform to this reading:

---

[145] Ibid., p. 53.
[146] Ibid., pp. 68–9.
[147] Ibid., pp. 69, 71.

The *master mistress*, which has given such offence and raised such prejudices, only means, *Chiefest* ... *Hew*, as I have already shown, was the appropriate word for *mien*, in that age ... In the *Princely Pleasures of Kenelworth Castle*, it is said:

> 'But tydings of our English Queene,
> Whom heaven hath deck'd with hewes.'

... To *prick* is often used by Shakspeare for to *mark*, as indeed the word is used sometimes at present ... what *additional* circumstance was it, which nature, in her *doting*, superadded, and which defeated the poet from possessing his *master-mistress* [?] ... the divine origin, or high birth, of his master mistress.[148]

Chalmers' wilful deafness to the puns on 'prick' and 'thing' is offered as evidence of his own virtue: 'It is for impure minds only, to be continually finding something obscene in objects, that convey nothing obscene, or offensive, to the chastest hearts.'[149] For Coleridge, however, it would prove much harder to repress his understanding of Sonnet 20's 'obscene' meanings, and this clearly caused him considerable anxiety, not simply about Shakespeare's virtue, but about his own.

Although Coleridge wrote extensively on *Venus and Adonis* and *The Rape of Lucrece*, he paid little public attention to the Sonnets.[150] Henry Crabbe Robinson wrote of his disappointment on attending Coleridge's fourth Shakespeare lecture on 28 November 1811: 'He certainly might, with a little exertion, have collected matter enough for *one* lecture at least out of the poems of Shakespeare. But he utterly passed over the *Sonnets*, and made no remark on the reception the poems have met with from modern critics.'[151] The reasons for this become rapidly apparent from the two extended discussions that do remain.

On 2 November 1803, Coleridge responded to a critique of the Sonnets inscribed by Wordsworth in a copy of Robert Anderson's *British Poets* (1792–5, repr. 1804):

> These sonnets <beginning at 127,> to his Mistress, are worse than ~~a game at~~ a puzzle peg. They <are> abominably harsh obscure & worthless. The others are for the most part much better, have many fine lines very fine lines & passages. They are also in many places warm with passion. Their chief

---

[148] Ibid., pp. 59–61.

[149] Ibid., p. 63.

[150] For a more detailed discussion of Coleridge's critical response to the Sonnets, see Pointner, 'Bardolatry and Biography', pp. 122–36.

[151] Quoted by Rollins, *Variorum*, vol. 2, p. 349.

faults, and heavy ones they are, are sameness, tediousness, ~~laboriousness,~~ quaintness, & elaborate obscurity.[152]

Wordsworth's opprobrium is directed against the 'Dark Lady' sonnets; he takes in his stride the fact that 'the others' (the supposed male-directed Sonnets) are 'in many places warm with passion'. Coleridge, however, launches into an impassioned defence of Shakespeare's love, which may or may not reflect on his own feelings for Wordsworth.[153] He prepares his imagined addressee, his seven year-old son, Hartley, to be on the side of the angels, by urging him to read the death of the Theban brothers 'each with his shield over his friend', in 'Potter's *Antiquities*', and to condemn those 'whose base, fleshly, and most calumnious fancies had suspected their love of desires against nature'.[154] Hartley must trust to the innocence of Theban love, and recognise it in the Sonnets:

> This pure love Shakespeare appears to have felt – to have been in no way ashamed of it – or even to have suspected that others could have suspected it. Yet at the same time he knew that so strong a love would have been made more completely a thing of permanence and reality, and have been more blessed by nature and taken under her more especial protection, if this object of his love had been at the same time a possible object of desire – for nature is not soul only. In this feeling he must have written the twentieth sonnet; but its possibility seems never to have entered even his imagination. It is noticeable that not even an allusion to that very worst of all possible vices (for it is wise to think of the disposition, as a *vice*, not of the absurd and despicable act, as a *crime*) not even any allusion to it [occurs] in all his plays – whereas Jonson, Beaumont and Fletcher, and Massinger are full of them. O my son! I pray fervently that thou may'st know inwardly how impossible it was for a Shakespeare not to have been in his heart's heart chaste.[155]

If Shakespeare's imagination was so limited as not to imagine these desires, and his innocence so impregnable as to render him immune to shame, Coleridge imagines and is ashamed for them both. His denial of any allusions to homoerotic desire in the dramatic canon echoes Malone's

---

[152] Transcribed by George Whalley in Coleridge, *Marginalia*, vol. i, p. 41.

[153] Peter Stallybrass observes that 'Coleridge seems to forget that Wordsworth is writing about the later poems, as if what names his relation to Wordsworth were the name that Steevens silently attributes to the earlier sonnets and to the relationship between Shakespeare and the young man [i.e. sodomy]' in 'Editing as Cultural Formation', pp. 98–9.

[154] T. M. Raysor notes that Coleridge has rendered the defence more emphatic. The original phrase in Potter reads: 'Let them perish, who suspect that these Men either did, or suffer'd anything base', Coleridge, *Coleridge's Miscellaneous Criticism*, fn. 2, p. 455.

[155] Ibid., p. 455.

deflection of criticism from Shakespeare to Fletcher (cited above), but is unfortunately undercut by Steevens' note to Sonnet 20 in which he avers that Shakespeare *did* know the correct moral attitude towards a 'master-mistress' ('Let me be just, however, to our author, who has made a proper use of the term "male varlet" in *Troilus and Cressida*').[156] We should also acknowledge Coleridge's repetition of the disturbing term 'thing' as an unconscious echo of Sonnet 20. In the Sonnet, the 'thing' added by nature is to his purpose 'nothing'.[157] Coleridge argues that Shakespeare's love lacks what would make it 'a thing of permanence and reality' – what would allow Shakespeare to fully experience his love. Hence, even as Coleridge tries to deny the Sonnet's phallic provocations, he draws attention to his own critical act of castration.

Thirty years later, on 14 May 1833, Coleridge would venture an alternative reading of the Sonnets, beginning once again with the idealisation of male–male love, and with Malone's argument that this 'passion' needs to be understood historically:

> I believe it possible that a man may, under certain states of the moral feeling, entertain something that deserves the name of Love towards a male object – an affection beyond Friendship and wholly aloof from Appetite. In Elizabeth's and James's time it seems to have been almost fashionable – and perhaps we may account in some measure for it by considering how very inferior the women of that age were, taken generally, in education and accomplishment of mind to the men.[158]

But even as he endorses the sense of female inferiority which underpins Sonnet 20, Coleridge deploys the figure of the mistress to extricate Shakespeare from homoerotic desire. Acknowledging the recent theory that Pembroke was the Sonnets' addressee,[159] Coleridge demurs on the basis that Shakespeare's moral innocence in an age when such expressions were fashionable, would not have required such subterfuge:

> I do not think Shakespeare, merely because he was an actor, would have thought it necessary to veil his emotions towards Herbert under a disguise, though he might if the real object had been a Laura or a Leonora. It seems

---

[156] Shakespeare, *Supplement*, ed. Malone, p. 597.
[157] Pointner explores the pronunciation of this word as 'noting' so that it would read 'my purpose noting', thereby contradicting a denial of 'homosexual' interest. See 'Bardolatry and Biography', p. 134.
[158] Coleridge, *Table Talk*, vol. i, pp. 376–8.
[159] This was first published by James Boaden in *On the Sonnets of Shakespeare identifying the Person to whom they are Addressed*, but had been mooted before.

to me that the sonnets could only have come from a man deeply in love, and in love with a woman – and there is one Sonnet, which from its incongruity of tone I take to be a purposed blind.[160]

Peter Stallybrass points out the absurdity of Shakespeare 'disguis[ing] himself as a pederast to avoid detection as a man "deeply in love" with a woman'.[161] In the process, however, Coleridge tacitly acknowledges the homoerotic bawdy of Sonnet 20 – though to state that there is only 'one Sonnet' which represents this 'incongruity of tone' is a further misrepresentation. Coleridge's repetition of the term 'purpose' once again suggests how Sonnet 20 lingers in his mind, betraying his will to displace Shakespeare's darker 'purpose' in the lyric, with an adulterous but heterosexual intent in his exegesis.

Perhaps unsurprisingly, Coleridge's defence of Sonnet 20 did not meet with credulity on all sides. Henry Hallam, for one, found it 'absolutely untenable'.[162] Nevertheless, in the thirty years between Coleridge's analyses, it had become possible to discuss the Sonnets without dwelling torturously on this subtext, if only through the expedient of omitting Sonnet 20 from the number of Shakespeare Sonnets that it was advisable to read. In his 'Essay, Supplementary to the Preface' of *Poems* (1815), Wordsworth ignores both the stylistic and the erotic basis for Steevens' hostility to the Sonnets, attributing it to his 'exult[ation] over a supposed fall into the mire of a genius whom he had been compelled to regard with admiration'.[163] Steevens' notorious defence of his decision not to include the Sonnets in his 1793 edition had obvious sodomitical undertones; he insisted that 'the strongest act of parliament that could be framed would fail to compel readers into their service'.[164] But this concerns Wordsworth only as evidence of the ignorance of late eighteenth-century readers regarding the 'treasures' the Sonnets contain.[165] To rectify this ignorance, he lists twenty-seven Sonnets to be admired for 'exquisite feelings, felicitously expressed' (the list does not include Sonnet 20).[166] From thence, the epithet 'exquisite' starts to replace 'curious' in defining the Sonnets. Its aptness lies not only in the way it allows the Sonnets to participate in

[160] Coleridge, *Table Talk*, vol. 1, pp. 376–8.
[161] Stallybrass, 'Editing as Cultural Formation', p. 99.
[162] Hallam, *Introduction to the Literature of Europe*, p. 264. This is discussed further in Chapter 4.
[163] Wordsworth, 'Essay, Supplementary to the Preface', p. 69.
[164] Shakespeare, *The Plays of William Shakspeare: in fifteen volumes*, ed. Steevens, p. vii.
[165] Ibid.
[166] For further details, see Chapter 4.

Romantic sensibility – 'exquisite' as 'acutely susceptible of pain, pleasure; delicate, finely tuned' (OED 7a), but from the Latin origins of the word, '*exquisitus*', 'sought out' or 'aptly chosen' (OED 1b). Engaging with individual Sonnets and not a 'sequence', selecting choice images and phrases rather than the whole, would be crucial to the Romantic poets' rediscovery of the Sonnets.

CHAPTER 4

As With Your Shadow I With These Did Play, 1817–1900

On 22 November 1817, John Keats wrote in a letter to J. H. Reynolds:

> One of the three Books I have with me is Shakespear's Poems: I ne'er found so many beauties in the sonnets – they seem to be full of fine things said unintentionally – in the intensity of working out conceits – Is this to be borne? Hark ye!

> > When lofty trees I see barren of leaves
> > Which from heat did canopy the herd,
> > And Summer's green all girded up in sheaves,
> > Borne on the bier with white and bristly beard. (Sonnet 12)

> … He overwhelms a genuine Lover of Poesy with all manner of abuse, talking about –

> a poets rage

> And stretched metre of an antique song – (Sonnet 17)
> Which by the by will be a capital Motto for my Poem – won't it? – He speaks too of 'Time's antique pen' [Sonnet 19] – and 'aprils first born flowers' [Sonnet 21] – and 'deaths eternal cold' (Sonnet 13).[1]

Keats' approach to the Sonnets marks a significant break with the critical perspectives of the previous century and ushers in a new, more receptive age. After decades of regret at the Sonnets' quibbles and elaborate conceits, Keats ventures his own pun on 'borne', and by identifying in the Sonnets 'things said unintentionally', he aligns them not only with his own method of working,[2] but with the Wordsworthian ideal of poetry as 'the spontaneous overflow of powerful feelings',[3] thus making them look suddenly

---

[1] Keats, *The Letters of John Keats 1814–1821*, vol. 1, p. 189.
[2] Richard Woodhouse recorded *c.* July 1820 that Keats 'has said, that he has often not been aware of the beauty of some thought until after he has composed and written it down – It has then struck him with astonishment', as quoted by Miriam Allott in Keats, *The Poems of John Keats*, p. 297.
[3] Wordsworth and Coleridge, *Lyrical Ballads*, p. 22.

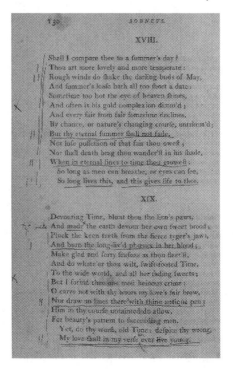

Figure 4.1 Keats' annotations to Sonnet 18 in *The Poetical Works of William Shakespeare* (1806). Image courtesy of Keats House, City of London

contemporary. As D. L. Richardson would aver in 1835, 'the merit of these little poems does not consist in unity, point and finish, but in the freshness, force, beauty and abundance of the thoughts and images'.[4] It was an abundance Keats was happy to plunder. He did indeed use the above extract from Sonnet 17 as his epigraph for *Endymion*,[5] and his copy of *The Poetical Works of Shakespeare* (1806) shows numerous enthusiastic markings, particularly around Sonnets 18 and 19 (see Figure 4.1).

Moreover, Keats *revisits* the Sonnets with sensations of pleasure and surprise ('I ne'er found so many beauties …'). Coleridge had recently claimed that 'essential poetry' could be defined as 'that to which we return with the

---

[4] 'On Shakspeare's Sonnets, their poetical merits, and on the question to whom they are addressed', *Gentleman's Magazine* (July 1835), pp. 250–6, 254.
[5] We will consider Keats' creative debt to the Sonnets briefly later, but for a useful discussion of how his own sonnets came more closely to resemble those of Shakespeare, see Bate, *The Stylistic Development of Keats*, pp. 120–5.

greatest pleasure',[6] and the experience of re-reading is a recurrent theme with Victorian admirers, not least George Eliot who confessed: 'I love the Sonnets better & better whenever I return to them.'[7]

This chapter begins with the years 1815–18, when the Sonnets' neglect suddenly seems to reflect badly on English critics, and on English literature in general.[8] The increasing value placed on the Sonnets as Shakespearean biography is central to their growing status, but although we might now regret this approach,[9] it does not at this time inhibit aesthetic appreciation. What begins as a biographical interest often becomes a poetic one, and crucial to the appeal and adaptability of the Sonnets in the early nineteenth century is their readers' refusal to be limited by the Quarto sequence. As Thomas Campbell observed in 1829: 'There is no necessity ... for our making a toil of a pleasure in reading the sonnets of either Shakespeare or Petrarch, for the character of *taedium* belongs not to those pieces individually, any more than the pressure of a crowd belongs to the presence of a single person.'[10] Wordsworth's listing of his favourite Sonnets in print leads to other Romantic poets and critics (including Keats) making their own selections, with 64, 98 and 116 emerging as particular favourites. By the second phase of the nineteenth century up to the 1870s,[11] these Sonnets, along with 29, 30, 73 and 111, are regularly included in selections of the best English poets and in Shakespeare anthologies.

This dissemination of the Sonnets would have a profound impact on their creative influence. Victorian poets and novelists could presume their readers had enough familiarity with the Sonnets to make conscious allusion worthwhile. At the same time, the ideal of Shakespeare the author now included his identity as a sonneteer. One pressing question in the 1850s and 1860s was not whom Shakespeare loved, but *how* – was his love nobly constant, or excessive and effeminising? Alfred Tennyson, Elizabeth Barrett Browning and George Eliot all invoke particular Shakespeare Sonnets as a means of defining love, and their work would be discussed by comparison with the *Sonnets*. But perhaps the most notorious Shakespeare-lover of the late Victorian period is Oscar Wilde, whose 'The Portrait of Master W. H.' (1889) represents a decisive moment in the Sonnets' queer history, but

---

[6] Coleridge, *Biographia Literaria*, ch. 1, vol. 1, p. 14.

[7] Eliot, *Middlemarch Notebooks*, p. 213.

[8] I place this key moment in the Sonnets' revised reputation slightly later than George Sanderlin, who argues for 1813/14 in 'The Repute of Shakespeare's Sonnets in the Early Nineteenth Century'.

[9] I am sympathetic to Jonathan Bate's observation that 'We still have not escaped from wrong-headed biographical readings of the sonnets', *Shakespeare and the English Romantic Imagination*, p. 85.

[10] *New Monthly Magazine* 26, 577 (1829), p. 355.

[11] See Poole, *Shakespeare and the Victorians*, pp. 3–4.

also makes the creative interpretation of individual lyrics subordinate to the scandal of the Sonnets as a sequence. The Sonnets become notorious, and for a while at least individual lyrics lose their unique polyvocality and mean 'one thing'.

Nathan Drake and 'The Beauties of these Calumniated Poems'

In 1817, the physician and fellow of the Royal Society of Literature, Nathan Drake, produced an extensive defence of the Sonnets in his 1,400-page work, *Shakspeare and His Times*. He indicted 'the unaccountable prejudices of Mr. Steevens', holding the dead critic up to scorn as many later apostates would do, and promised to 'unfold, at length, the beauties of these calumniated poems, and to refute the sweeping censure which they have so unworthily incurred'.[12] This was more surprising given that, nearly twenty years earlier, in *Literary Hours: or Sketches Critical, Narrative and Poetical* (1798), Drake had objected to the Sonnets' 'obscurity and quaintness', and congratulated Steevens for refusing to reprint them: 'Mr. Malone has once more given them to the press: but his last Editor has, I think, acted with greater judgment, in forbearing to obtrude such crude efforts upon the public eye: for where is the utility of propagating compositions which no one can endure to read?'[13]

Drake's change of heart partly reflects a change in the reputation of the sonnet per se.[14] Wordsworth's success in the form required admirers of poetry to reconsider its possibilities and encouraged imitation. In 1807, he published *Poems in Two Volumes*, containing two collections, 'Miscellaneous Sonnets' and 'Sonnets Dedicated to Liberty'. This was prefaced by a sonnet, which defended the form's limitations:

> Nuns fret not at their Convent's narrow room;
> And Hermits are contented with their Cells …
> In truth, the prison unto which we doom
> Ourselves, no prison is: and hence to me,
> In sundry moods, 'twas pastime to be bound
> Within the Sonnet's scanty plot of ground.
>
> (1–2, 8–11)[15]

[12] Drake, *Shakspeare and His Times*, vol. 2, p. 86.
[13] Drake, *Literary Hours*, vol. 1, p. 108.
[14] For further discussion, see O'Neill, 'The Romantic Sonnet', pp. 185–203, and Curran, *Poetic Form and British Romanticism*, pp. 29–55.
[15] For an illuminating discussion of the contradictions represented by this sonnet, see Phelan, *The Nineteenth-Century Sonnet*, pp. 14–18.

This poetic form also spoke to the Romantic 'attraction to vivid person-ality … both the poetic voice speaking within the poem and also the bio-graphical, historical self of the actual poet. In effect, these two voices were most admired when they seemed most one'.[16] Charlotte Smith's *Elegiac Sonnets*, written when she was in debtors' prison, had deplored 'the rugged path, I'm doomed to tread', and reviewers responded concernedly to the author's plight. Wordsworth emphasised the intimate and confessional nature of his 'Miscellaneous Sonnets', which he described as 'Transcripts of the private heart',[17] and he famously extended this to Shakespeare's Sonnets, claiming that 'with this key,/ Shakespeare unlocked his heart'.[18] From 1815, the biographical reading of, and thus the renewed interest in, Shakespeare's Sonnets gained momentum. That year saw the publication of Wordsworth's 'Essay, Supplementary to the Preface' in which he described the Sonnets as 'Poems in which Shakespeare expresses his own feelings in his own Person'.[19] It also saw the translation into English of August Wilhelm von Schlegel's lectures, in which he upbraided English critics for not having made more use of the Sonnets, given that they 'paint most unequivocally the actual situation and sentiments of the poet; they make us acquainted with the passions of the man; they even contain remarkable confessions of his youthful errors'.[20]

Two years later, in *Shakspeare and His Times* (1817), Drake would acknow-ledge his debt to Schlegel and turn to the Sonnets for new facts about Shakespeare's life. Drake argued, for the first time in print,[21] that Mr W. H. was Henry Wriothesley, Earl of Southampton, on the basis of similarities of address between Sonnets 26 ('Lord of my love, to whom in vassalage') and 110 ('Alas, 'tis true, I have gone here and there'), and the dedication to *The Rape of Lucrece*. The fact that this public eulogy used the same kind of amatory language as the Sonnets arguably cleared them from imputations of untoward desire – Sonnet 20 being conveniently overlooked in Drake's analysis. This chastening effect extended to Sonnet 101 ('O truant Muse,

---

[16] Foster, *Bloom's Shakespeare Through the Ages*, p. 61. See also Schoenbaum, *Shakespeare's Lives*, pp. 251–2.

[17] For further discussion see Phelan, *The Nineteenth-Century Sonnet*, ch. 2.

[18] 'Scorn not the sonnet', published in his *Poetical Works* (1827). See also Charles Armitage Brown's variation: 'With this key … every difficulty is unlocked, and we have nothing but pure uninter-rupted biography' in *Shakespeare's Autobiographical Poems*.

[19] Wordsworth, 'Essay, Supplementary to the Preface', p. 69.

[20] Schlegel blames certain 'wild excesses' in Shakespeare's early life to his being part of a company of players. He finds evidence for Shakespeare's sense of 'degradation' in Sonnet 111 and 'vulgar scandal' in Sonnet 112. See *A Course of Lectures on Dramatic Art and Literature*, Lecture 22, p. 352.

[21] In the 1821 *Works*, James Boswell notes that the connection with Southampton had been made by Capell. See Shakespeare, *The Plays and Poems*, ed. Boswell, vol. 20, p. 249.

what shall be thy amends'), whose allusion to a male figure as 'my love' was explained by references to 'depend[ence]', performing one's 'office' and being 'dignified': 'To whom can this sonnet … apply, if not to Lord Southampton, the bosom-friend, the munificent patron of Shakspeare, the noble, the elegant, the brave, the protector of literature and the theme of many a song'.[22] The Sonnets' female addressee – that 'false plague', 'worser spirit', 'female evil' – posed significantly more of a threat, to the extent that Drake refused to seek out her identity. Rather than allow the possibility of Shakespeare's adultery to challenge 'the general moral beauty of his character', Drake concluded that this mistress must be a fiction. The 'Dark Lady' sequence was 'intended to express, aloof from all individual application, the contrarieties, the inconsistencies, and the miseries of illicit love'.[23]

Drake now has the dubious honour of being considered 'the first biographer to take [the Sonnets] seriously as a source of personal revelation',[24] and yet it would be wrong to assume that his approach inhibited their aesthetic appreciation. After twelve pages of sleuthing, the next twelve pages of *Shakspeare and His Times* defend the literary reputation of the Sonnets through a judicious selection of passages and whole poems. The discussion of Sonnet 54 ('O how much more doth beauty beauteous seem') makes clear how late eighteenth-century prejudices are being challenged. Drake concedes the 'slight blemish, arising from the pharmaceutical allusion in the last line ["my verse *distils* your truth"]'. He also acknowledges the 'trifling inaccuracy' in the assertion: 'The canker blooms have full as deep a dye/ As the perfumed tincture of the roses.' Yet he takes issue with Steevens' 'splenetic interrogation' of the Sonnet on this basis, declaring it 'somewhat strange that the beauties of the poem could not disarm the prejudices of the critic'.[25] Drake's own criteria are pictorial, rhythmic and affective. He

---

[22] Drake, *Shakspeare and His Times*, vol. 2, p. 69. Drake explains that an imagined vow of chastity by Southampton, after he was refused permission to marry Elizabeth Vernon, prompted the procreation sonnets (*c.* 1594–8). Elizabeth's hostility to the match and imprisonment of the couple in 1599 further explains why Jaggard did not include any of these sonnets in the *Passionate Pilgrim*, and why Shakespeare could not publish the Sonnets himself until after the queen's death, ibid., p. 65.

[23] Drake, *Shakspeare and His Times*, vol. 2, pp. 72, 73. In fact, Drake disputes that all final twenty-eight Sonnets are addressed to a mistress, noting that 129 and 146 have no gender signifiers and casting doubt on another four. He therefore identifies only twenty-two Sonnets as suggesting a female addressee.

[24] Schoenbaum, *Shakespeare's Lives*, p. 273.

[25] Drake, *Shakspeare and His Times*, vol. 2, p. 81. In the notes to Sonnet 54, published in the 1780 *Supplement* and 1790 *Works*, Steevens objects: 'Shakspeare had not yet begun to observe the productions of nature with accuracy, or his eyes would have convinced him that the *cynorhoden* is by no means of as deep a colour as the *rose*. But what has truth or nature to do with Sonnets?', Shakespeare, *Supplement*, ed. Malone, pp. 624–5.

finds the description of the sun in Sonnet 7 ('Lo, in the Orient when the gracious light') to be 'enlivened by imagery peculiarly vivid and rich', with lines 7–8 praised as 'contain[ing] a picture of great beauty'.[26] Of Sonnet 71 ('No longer mourn for me when I am dead'), he remarks that 'Simplicity of style, and tenderness of sentiment, form the sole features of this sonnet'. On the basis of its 'elegance', 'the skill and texture of its modulation', and the 'dignified and highly poetical close of the third quatrain', he finds Sonnet 29 ('When in disgrace with Fortune and men's eyes') to be most excellent.[27]

Having created a commonplace book of favourite extracts, with Sonnets 71, 116, 54 and 29 reproduced in full, Drake makes an illuminating comparison with other miscellanies:

> That many more [than these four Sonnets] might be brought forward, of equal value with those which we have selected, will be allowed perhaps when we state that in the *Specimens* of Mr. Ellis, the *Petrarca* of Mr. Henderson, and the *Laura* of Mr. Lofft, eleven have been chosen, of which we find upon reference, only one among the four just now adduced.[28]

Drake attests to the fact that the critical rejuvenation of the Sonnets had still to make itself felt through anthologies. Most of those published in the first decade of the nineteenth century containing Shakespeare were reprints from the 1780s and 1790s which had habitually excluded the Sonnets – the most obvious example being William Dodd's *Beauties*.[29] A notable exception was George Kearsley's *The Beauties of Shakespeare, Selected from his Plays and Poems* (1783) which included eighteen Sonnets. However, from the third edition of 1784 onwards, the separate section at the end dedicated to 'The Beauties of Shakspeare's Poems' was replaced by 'A Selection of the most Interesting Scenes in Shakspeare's Plays'.

One effect of Drake's work was not only to encourage a re-evaluation of the Sonnets, but to stimulate the process of selection. Drake's reviewer

---

[26] Drake, *Shakspeare and His Times*, p. 77.

[27] Ibid., pp. 81–2.

[28] Ibid., p. 82. The one Sonnet that Drake reprints which also features in these anthologies is 116. George Ellis's *Specimens of the Early English Poets* (1790, repr. 1801, 1803 and 1811) features only Sonnet 57 ('Being your slave'). George Henderson's *Petrarca: A Selection of Sonnets from Various Authors* (1803) includes 64 and 73. Capel Lofft's *Laura* (1814) reprints Sonnets 116, 64, 52, 145, 73, 79, 78 and 25.

[29] For more on the *Beauties*, see Chapter 3. Vicesimus Knox's *Elegant Extracts* (1789, repr. 1801, 1803, 1807) limits itself to extracts from the plays, plus the song 'Under the Greenwood Tree'. A later incarnation, *The Poetical Epitome* (1809, 1816), adds 'Beauty is but a vain' from *The Passionate Pilgrim* (Bk 4, p. 392). William Enfield's *The Speaker* (1774), frequently reprinted in the early nineteenth century (1800, 1801, 1803, 1805, 1806, 1808, etc.), included only passages from the plays.

in *Blackwood's Edinburgh Magazine* (August, 1818) begins by re-examining the Sonnets from a biographical perspective but ends up by compiling his own list of 'beauties':

> It is true as remarked by Wordsworth and Frederick Schlegel, that these sonnets are invaluable, beyond anything else of Shakespeare's poetry, because they give us little notices, and occasional glimpses of his own kindred feelings, and of some of the most interesting events and situations of his life. They are, however, admirable compositions in themselves; and Wordsworth, in one of those philosophical notes to the collected edition of his poems, in which he frequently embodies so much obvious, but at the same time so little understood truth, mentions those which he thinks truly Shakespearean. The readers of poetry may wish to know what Sonnets are Wordsworth's prime favourites, – they are 27, 29, 30, 32, 33, 54, 64, 66, 68, 73, 76, 86, 91, 92, 93, 97, 98, 105, 108, 109, 111, 113, 114, 116, 117, 129. Of these we shall quote five that seem to us exquisitely beautiful … [29 ('When in disgrace'), 30 ('When in the sessions'), 54 ('O how much more doth beauty'), 64 ('When I have seen by Time's fell hand'), 98 ('From you have I been absent in the spring')].[30]

It is worth pausing over the phrase 'those which he thinks truly Shakespearean', for here we may detect a significant shift from the eighteenth-century debate about the authenticity of the Sonnets to the nineteenth-century assumption that they are by Shakespeare, but may not all be properly 'Shakespearean'.

Between 1798 and 1819, a set of not just Wordsworthian but 'Romantic' favourites begins to emerge. This includes not only those Sonnets anthologised in collections of sonnets and/or British verse, and those singled out for praise in critical discussions of Shakespeare, but also those Sonnet echoes and allusions which appear in Romantic poetry, particularly that of Wordsworth, Coleridge and Keats. The possible influence of these borrowings in terms of making the Sonnets more 'popular' varies considerably – Wordsworth's use of quotation marks in the *Prelude* might encourage a reader to chase up the allusion to Sonnet 64; Keats' borrowings are more deeply embedded in poems which remained largely unpublished during his lifetime. Nevertheless, the question of which Sonnets predominate remains one worth posing. My study of Sonnet anthologisation/allusion between 1798 and 1819 suggests that six Sonnets were gaining prominence: 29, 54, 64, 73, 98 and 116.[31] Of these, three speak particularly to the concerns of Romantic poetry, and merit more sustained attention.

---

[30] *Blackwood's Edinburgh Magazine* (August 1818), pp. 586–7.
[31] These findings are based on a study of the following anthologies: Ellis's *Specimens*, Henderson's *Petrarca*, Lofft's *Laura* and Campbell's *Specimens of the British Poets*; as well as the critical discussions

Shakespeare's 'Romantic' Sonnets: 64, 98, 116

Sonnet 64 has hitherto won scant attention from readers, but it finds a new audience at the beginning of the nineteenth century.

> When I have seen by time's fell hand defaced,
> The rich proud cost of outworn buried age;
> When sometime lofty towers I see down razed,
> And brass eternal slave to mortal rage;
> When I have seen the hungry ocean gain
> Advantage on the kingdom of the shore,
> And the firm soil win of the wat'ry main,
> Increasing store with loss and loss with store;
> When I have seen such interchange of state,
> Or state itself confounded, to decay,
> Ruin hath taught me thus to ruminate:
> That time will come and take my love away
> > This thought is as a death which cannot choose
> > But weep to have that which it fears to lose.

This Sonnet's new visibility is partly explained by its lachrymose conclusion, which appealed to tastes developed at the end of the eighteenth century, when 'Sonnets of sensibility flooded forth like tears'.[32] In *Petrarca: A Selection of Sonnets from Various Authors* (1803), George Henderson praised the sonnet's power 'to give expression to tender or melancholy sensations' with the final couplet 'not unfitly adapted to give a stronger and more feeling utterance to a pathetic thought'.[33] Sonnet 64 is one of only two Shakespeare Sonnets included in Henderson's collection, perhaps because it fulfils this requirement.

Equally significant is the Sonnet's theme. Although Shakespeare had ruminated elsewhere on the fallibility of 'gilded monuments' (Sonnet 55) and 'tombs of brass' (Sonnet 107), he had not dwelt so long on a spectacle of ruins. Indeed, the word 'ruin' appears nowhere else in the Sonnets.[34] The authors of 'Tintern Abbey', 'The Ruined Cottage', 'Kubla Kahn' and 'Ozymandias'[35] might naturally have sympathised with Sonnet 64's

---

in Hazlitt's *Characters of Shakespear's Plays*, Coleridge's *Biographia Literaria*, Drake's *Shakspeare* and its subsequent reviews 1817–18; and on the poetry, letters and annotated *Sonnets* of Wordsworth, Coleridge, Shelley and Keats.

[32] Curran, *Poetic Form and British Romanticism*, p. 30.

[33] Henderson, *Petrarca*, p. xxxiv.

[34] 'Ruin'd' appears in Sonnets 73 and 119.

[35] Although there are no obvious echoes of Sonnet 64 in Shelley's poem, they share the revelation that it is the artefact (the sculpture/the sonnet) rather than the subject of the artwork (Ozymandias, the Fair Youth) which endures. For further discussion of Shelley's knowledge of the Sonnets, see Clark,

evocation of decay, although they ignored its romantic ending in favour of something more 'Romantic'. At the beginning of Book 5 of *The Prelude* (1805), for example, Wordsworth contemplates the works of the sovereign Intellect, and laments:

> Thou also, Man, hast wrought
> For commerce of thy nature with itself,
> Things worthy of unconquerable life;
> And yet we feel, we *cannot chuse* but feel
> That these must perish. Tremblings of the heart
> It gives, to think that the immortal being
> No more shall need such garments; and yet Man,
> As long as he shall be the Child of Earth,
> Might almost *'weep to have'* what he may lose.
>
> (17–25, italics mine)

Book 5 of *The Prelude* is marked by numerous references to death, used primarily 'to give meaning to other forms of loss over which the poet does grieve'. As Evelyn Shakir has argued, 'This reduction of human death to a vehicle of another tenor seems to devaluate human existence and to be the reverse of the more normal process'.[36] I would argue that the echoes of Sonnet 64 are part of this effect. They invite comparison with man's predicament in Shakespeare's poem, but where the Sonnet speaker weeps to contemplate the beloved's death, Wordsworth mourns the loss of man's works.[37] Rejecting the Horatian truism of books as monuments stronger than brass, he deplores that writings should be 'lodge[d] in shrines so frail' (48), and specifically that Milton and Shakespeare should depend upon 'poor earthly casket[s] of immortal Verse' (164). Shakespeare's Sonnet is arguably also 'about' the loss of poetic immortality. It adopts the same detached, meditative stance on mortal decay as Sonnets 15 and 55, but it defeats the expectation created by those Sonnets that poetry will intervene. Rather than promise 'So long lives this and this gives life to thee', the speaker is powerless. Indeed, he throws these other Sonnets into an ironic light, as Anne Ferry remarks, 'seem[ing] to mock himself for the detachment with which he felt free to "ruminate" at a privileged distance

'Shelley and Shakespeare'. On Wordsworth's distress at ruined dwellings, see Kerrigan, 'Wordsworth and the Sonnet'.

[36] Shakir, 'Books, Death and Immortality', 157.

[37] David Perkins suggests that Wordsworth's perspective on the immortality of man's creative achievements was considerably more pessimistic than that of other Romantic and mid-twentieth-century poets: 'Only the "living Presence" of nature can be regarded as permanent and undying'. See *The Quest for Permanence*, p. 35.

from time's destructiveness'.[38] We know that Wordsworth read the Sonnets in the Quarto sequence at least once. If he appropriated Sonnet 64's language of mourning 'inappropriately', by redirecting it to literary fame, he also acknowledges the shocking absence of the immortality trope within that Sonnet.

Writing for posterity was arguably one of the defining conditions of Romanticism, and a discourse in which Shakespeare's Sonnets played an important, though ambiguous, role. Andrew Bennett has traced the importance of the writer's 'textual afterlife' to the eighteenth century, when posterity 'begins to be figured as a determining force in cultural production', but locates its fuller development and theorisation in the early nineteenth century:

> For the Romantics … posterity is not so much what comes after poetry as its necessary prerequisite – the judgement of future generations becomes the necessary condition of the act of writing itself. While the poetry of the Renaissance may be said to be obsessed with the question of immortality and while Enlightenment poetics figure the test of time as the necessary arbiter of poetic value, Romanticism reinvents posterity as the very condition of the possibility of poetry itself: to be neglected in one's lifetime, and *not to care*, is the necessary (though not of course sufficient) condition of genius.[39]

Shakespeare had long been a touchstone in discussions of literary fame, having become immortal 'in his own despight',[40] given that half of his dramatic canon had gone unpublished during his lifetime, and his poetic canon had been infiltrated by 'spurious' works. At the beginning of the nineteenth century, this carelessness was examined with greater urgency through interpretation of the Sonnets. In the essay 'On Posthumous Fame, – Whether Shakspeare was influenced by a love of it?' (1814), William Hazlitt argues that Shakespeare expressed no satisfaction at the prospect of fame in his writings, 'nor any appearance of anxiety for their fate, or of a desire to perfect them or make them worthy of that immortality to which they were destined'.[41] He accounts for this by Shakespeare's paying little heed to the works of his predecessors (admiration of whom might naturally kindle the desire for fame), and by his lack of egotism: 'To feel a strong desire that others should think highly of us, it is, in general,

---

[38] Ferry, *All in War with Time*, p. 27.
[39] Bennett, *Romantic Poets and the Culture of Posterity*, p. 4.
[40] Pope, *The First Epistle of the Second Book of Horace Imitated* (*c.* 1736, pub. 1737), line 72.
[41] Hazlitt, *The Collected Works of William Hazlitt*, vol. 1, p. 23.

necessary that we should think highly of ourselves ... and there is no author who was so little tinctured with [this] as Shakspeare.'[42] Hazlitt cites in evidence the poet's shameful profession and degraded reputation, as described in Sonnet III ('O, for my sake do you with Fortune chide'), whilst in Sonnet 29, he finds him ' "desiring this man's art, and that man's scope": so little was Shakspeare, as far as we can learn, enamoured of himself'.[43] For Coleridge, a sense of self-worth is not incompatible with hopes of posterity. In the *Biographia Literaria*, he advances his theory that 'men of the greatest genius' have possessed a 'calm and tranquil temper in all that related to themselves':[44]

> In the inward assurance of permanent fame, they seem to have been either indifferent or resigned with regard to immediate reputation. Shakespeare's evenness and sweetness of temper were almost proverbial in his own age. That this did not arise from ignorance of his own comparative greatness, we have abundant proof in his Sonnets.[45]

Sonnet 81 ('Or I shall live, your epitaph to make') expresses Shakespeare's belief that his works will endure after his own death: 'Your name from hence immortal life shall have,/Tho' I once gone to all the world must die'. Sonnet 86 ('Was it the proud full sail of his great verse') demonstrates Shakespeare's 'confidence of his own equality with those whom he deemed most worthy of his praise'.[46] These readings are certainly strained. Sonnet 86 was already famous through Milton as an expression of creative block. Sonnet 81 exalts the immortality of the beloved at the expense of Shakespeare, who is imagined lying in a 'common grave'. Coleridge seems to share the general assumption that the Sonnets are concerned with the poet's fame rather than that of the addressee: 'just as they misread Milton as neglected, the Romantics misread Shakespeare's sonnets as appeals to posterity over the heads of a neglectful contemporary audience'.[47] Yet if this conception of Shakespeare had a liberating effect, freeing Romantic poets from the necessity of being popular in their own time, it also erected criteria for genius which they would find it depressingly difficult to reach. In a curious echo of the psychological double bind represented by Calvinism, whereby to doubt that one was saved probably meant that one was not,

---

[42] Ibid., pp. 23–4.
[43] Ibid., p. 24.
[44] On the likelihood that this was a dig aimed at Wordsworth, see Raimonda Modiano, 'Coleridge as Literary Critic'.
[45] Coleridge, *Biographia Literaria*, vol. 1, p. 21.
[46] Bennett, *Romantic Poets and the Culture of Posterity*, pp. 22–3.
[47] Ibid., p. 29.

to worry about one's posterity might imply that one did not deserve to be remembered, or as Bennett puts it: 'the narcissistic concern to survive in the future might itself be the cause of one's inevitable neglect in that future'.[48]

One poet who repeatedly examined himself for signs of future fame was John Keats.[49] In a letter of 14 October 1818 to George and Georgiana Keats, following negative reviews for *Endymion*, he insisted that 'This is a mere matter of the moment – I think I shall be among the English poets after my death'. In a subsequent letter to Sarah Jeffrey (9 June 1819), he describes himself as having 'been very idle lately, very averse to writing; both from the overpowering idea of our dead poets and from abatement of my love of fame'.[50] It is perhaps unsurprising that Sonnet 64 should have caught Keats' attention, not so much for its doubts about the possibility of literary fame (which fascinated Wordsworth) as for the fact that Shakespeare seems not to care. In Hazlitt's essay, there is a faint but intriguing echo of Sonnet 64 when he describes why the poet might have been dismissive of fame:

> Shakspeare had looked too much into the world, and his views of things were of too universal and comprehensive a cast, not to have taught him to estimate the importance of posthumous fame according to its true value and relative proportions.[51]

'Taught me thus to ruminate' seems to resonate in 'taught him to estimate', since both relate to the broader life experience that diminishes the pleasures of fame. Keats derived much of his thinking about Shakespeare as a poet from Hazlitt,[52] but his response to Sonnet 64 is subtly different.

Jonathan Bate has described Keats' sonnet 'When I have fears' (1818) as a major turning-point in English lyric poetry: 'the Shakespearean sonnet is actively revived both formally and tonally, by a major English poet, for the first time in two hundred years'.[53] Whilst it bears traces of Sonnets 12 and 107,[54] its debt to 64 seems to me to go much deeper:

[48] Ibid., p. 35.

[49] For further discussion of Keats' reliance on Hazlitt in the formulation of his thinking about Shakespeare, see Bate, *Shakespeare and the English Romantic Imagination*, pp. 161–5.

[50] Keats, *The Letters of John Keats*, vol. 1, p. 394, vol. 2, p. 116.

[51] 'On Posthumous Fame', in Hazlitt, *The Collected Works of William Hazlitt*, vol. 1, p. 24.

[52] See Bate, *Shakespeare and the English Romantic Imagination*, pp. 161–5.

[53] Ibid., p. 183.

[54] Ibid., pp. 182–3, and Flesch, 'The Ambivalence of Generosity', 18. I would add that the phrase 'fair creature of an hour' owes something to Sonnet 33 in which Shakespeare's speaker laments 'he was but one hour mine'.

When I have fears that I may cease to be
Before my pen has gleaned my teeming brain,
Before high-pilèd books, in charactery,
Hold like rich garners the full ripened grain;
When I behold, upon the night's starred face,
Huge cloudy symbols of a high romance,
And think that I may never live to trace
Their shadows with the magic hand of chance;
And when I feel, fair creature of an hour,
That I shall never look upon thee more,
Never have relish in the fairy power
Of unreflecting love; – then on the shore
Of the wide world I stand alone, and think
Till love and fame to nothingness do sink.

Shakespeare's repetition of the phrase 'When I have seen' at the beginning
of lines 1, 5 and 9, is echoed at the same points in Keats' sonnet but with
a significant shift of tense and mood. In Sonnet 64, everything has been
created and experienced already, so all that remains is for Time to destroy
it. This relates to visions of ruin, 'When I have seen by time's fell hand',
but also to the experience of love, 'And weep to have' i.e. 'weep while
in possession of'. In Keats' sonnet, by contrast, the young poet finds in
the world a hundred invitations to invent and to create, and his fleeting
experience of love is yet to be fulfilled: 'weep to have' now signifying 'weep
with desire to possess'.[55] Sonnet 64 has the luxury of being a mature man's
sonnet, itself a spectacle of 'the rich proud cost of outworn buried age'.
The youthful 'When I have fears' appropriates it aggressively, and insists
that it is far harder to contemplate extinction when the actions by which
one might live into posterity have yet to be performed. It is all very well
for Shakespeare to contemplate oblivion when his legacy is assured, when
his books are indeed 'high-piled'. Nevertheless, both sonnets end with a
similar conclusion. Just as the thought of the beloved's loss 'is as a death'
which annihilates the older poet's creativity, so in Keats' sonnet to stand
on the shore and 'think' ensures that 'love and fame to nothingness do
sink'.[56] Without these spurs to ambition, and these sources of inspiration,
he writes no more. And yet, there is also an implicit heroism in these lines
as the poet 'stand[s] alone' at the edge of the world, no longer troubled by
the mortal ambitions for love and fame. It is arguably in this state that he

[55] Shakespeare, *Shakespeare's Sonnets*, ed. Duncan-Jones, p. 238.
[56] The lines 'When I have seen the hungry Ocean gain/ Advantage on the Kingdom of the shore' are
especially marked in Keats' copy of the Sonnets. See Spurgeon, *Keats' Shakespeare*, p. 40.

discovers in himself the marks of posterity, and that he becomes another Shakespeare.

Appealing to a quite different set of Romantic assumptions is Sonnet 98:

> From you have I been absent in the spring,
> When proud pied April, dressed in all his trim,
> Hath put a spirit of youth in everything,
> That heavy Saturn laughed, and leaped with him.
> Yet nor the lays of birds, nor the sweet smell
> Of different flowers in odour and in hue,
> Could make me any summer's story tell,
> Or from their proud lap pluck them where they grew;
> Nor did I wonder at the lily's white,
> Nor praise the deep vermilion in the rose;
> They were but sweet, but figures of delight,
> Drawn after you, you pattern of all those.
>> Yet seemed it winter still, and, you away,
>> As with your shadow I with these did play.

This Sonnet anticipates the Romantic enthusiasm for the close observation of nature. As Sara Lodge notes, 'in the new era of botany and ornithology', the sonnet form found a new function, 'as a "microscope" that in the hands of the naturalist "discloses many beautiful things which, if embedded in some greater mass, might have been but faintly visible and incoherent"'.[57] John Clare's belief that 'there is happiness in examining minutely into the wild flowers' resonates with the temptation in Shakespeare's Sonnet 98: 'Nor did I wonder at the lily's white,/ Nor praise the deep vermilion in the rose.'[58] Clare wrote in his journal for 13 September 1824 that he had 'read some of the Sonnets of shaksper which are great favourites of mine',[59] though sadly he does not tell us which ones.[60] Nevertheless, Sonnet 98 left an indelible trace on some of his fellow nature poets.

I would suggest that the line 'Nor praise the deep vermilion in the rose' occurred to Wordsworth when he was composing 'The Thorn' (1798), wherein the contrast between the withered thorn and the bank

---

[57] Lodge quotes William Sharp, *Sonnets of this Century* (1886), p. xxviii, in her article 'Contested Bounds', 545.

[58] 'Taste' in Clare, *John Clare: The Oxford Authors*, p. 479.

[59] Clare, *The Natural History Prose Writings of John Clare*, p. 177.

[60] There are some likely echoes of Sonnets 2 and 12 in Clare's sonnet 'The Ragwort' which celebrates the beauty of the weed. Mina Gorji observes that 'Thinking about the beauty of a wild, uncultivated landscape, it is perhaps not entirely surprising that Clare should remember lines from Shakespeare, who had a reputation at the time for wildness and irregularity', *John Clare and the Place of Poetry*, pp. 55–6.

that covers the infant's grave includes 'cups, the darlings of the eye,/ So deep is their vermillion dye' (43–4). For Coleridge more generally, Shakespeare would be found to possess 'all the requisites of a Poet', which included 'the affectionate Love of Nature, and Natural Objects, without which no man could have observed so steadily, or painted so truly & passionately the <very> minutest beauties of the external world'.[61] He offers Sonnet 98 as evidence of such detailed observation, but also as showing how the poetic use of natural imagery is elevated 'when it moulds and colours itself to the circumstances, passion, or character, present and foremost in the mind'.[62] The Sonnet's secular pantheism, whereby nature reflects the earthly beloved, chimed with the ways in which Romantic poets tended to approach nature, though it might also expose contradictions. Shakespeare's description of Spring, in all its youthful vigour and proud beauty, is merely a foil to the speaker's unhappiness: 'Yet seemed it winter still'. As Graham Davidson has observed, such an approach was to 'undermine an essential aspect of [Coleridge's] proclaimed thought – that everything in nature has a life of its own, and that we are all one life':

> The forms of nature either are co-existent with the products of self-reflection, or they are not, and if not, they cannot be adequate objects of knowledge, however much stamped upon, and therefore may not be employed as such in poetry ... Poetry pursued according to this prescription of Coleridge's will quickly degenerate into a series of pathetic fallacies, and everything in nature, far from having a life of its own, will become a dreary phantom, substanceless and without reality, except for that which it borrows temporarily from the mind.[63]

It was partly for this reason that John Ruskin consigned Wordsworth, Coleridge and Keats to the second rank of poets in his essay 'Of the Pathetic Fallacy' (1856), whilst Dante and Shakespeare remained in the first rank.[64] And yet, if the much-admired line 'As with your shadow I with these did play' – doubly underlined in Keats' edition of the Sonnets[65] – represents the abuse of Nature, it is also a more self-conscious expression of monomania. In 'Time's sea', Keats describes how the beloved's memory can alter one's relationship to the natural world:

[61] Coleridge, *The Notebooks of Samuel Taylor Coleridge*, vol. 3, p. 3290.
[62] Coleridge, *Biographia Literaria*, vol. 2, p. 18.
[63] Davidson, *Coleridge's Career*, p. 205.
[64] For further discussion see Bate, *Shakespeare and the English Romantic Imagination*, p. 73.
[65] Spurgeon, *Keats' Shakespeare*, p. 40.

> I cannot look upon the rose's dye,
> But to thy cheek my soul doth take its flight;
> I cannot look on any budding flower,
> But my fond ear, in fancy at thy lips,
> And hearkening for a love-sound, doth devour
> Its sweets in the wrong sense: – Thou dost eclipse
> Every delight with sweet remembering,
> And grief unto my darling joys dost bring.
>
> (7–14)

This final line makes exemplary use of Shakespearean antithesis, and the proximity in which it places 'remembering' and 'bring' recalls Sonnet 29: 'For thy sweet love remembered such wealth brings/ That then I scorn to change my state with kings.'[66] But the contrast only serves to sharpen this speaker's 'grief'. Coleridge would also remember Sonnet 98 in a more anguished sense, applying it to his experience of betrayal by Sara Hutchinson, Wordsworth's future sister-in-law, whom Coleridge loved despite being married to someone else:

> What have you done in *deceiving* him who for *10* years did so love you as never woman was beloved; in body, in soul, in brain, in heart, in hope, in fear, in prospect, in retrospect!/ Not he alone in the vulgar meaning of *he*, but every living atom that composed him was wedded & faithful to you/ Every single thought, every image, every perception, was no sooner itself, than it became *you* by some wish that you saw it & felt it or had – or by some recollection that it suggested – some way or other it always became a symbol of *you* – I played with them, as with *your shadow* – as Shakespeare has so profoundly expressed it in his Sonnet.[67]

The innocent pantheism of Sonnet 98 has become erotic obsession.

Finally, we should note the enduring appeal of Sonnet 116 in the early nineteenth century. This was annotated by Wordsworth as 'The best sonnet, I think' some time before 1803, and its final couplet reverberates in *The Prelude*:

> If this be error, and another faith
> Find easier access to the pious mind,
> Yet were I grossly destitute of all
> Those human sentiments which make this earth
> So dear, if I should fail, with grateful voice
> To speak of you, Ye Mountains and Ye Lakes,
> And sounding Cataracts![68]

---

[66] See Keats, *The Poems of John Keats*, p. 307.
[67] Coleridge, *The Notebooks of Samuel Taylor Coleridge*, vol. 3, p. 3303.
[68] Wordsworth, *The Prelude*, 2.435–41.

Critics have been openly condescending about this borrowing of Sonnet 116. W. B. J. Owen states that 'There is no connection, even by contrast or absurd association, between the two poems'.[69] Jonathan Bate agrees that it 'does no more than give a vague rhetorical authority' to the poem, 'since the tonal and contextual weight of the precursor text is not brought into play, the allusion is hollow'.[70] I am not so sure that contextual weight *is* lacking, given that Wordsworth goes on to thank Nature for enabling him to remain steadfast: 'if in this time/ Of dereliction and dismay, I yet/ Despair not of our nature; but retain/ A more than Roman confidence, a faith/That fails not …' (456–60). As we have seen, Sonnet 116's praise of constancy was a key aspect of its appeal from the early seventeenth century onwards. Where it resonates more precisely with Romantic interests is in its fixation on the star, as evident in Keats' poem 'Bright Star'. In the *Excursion*, Wordsworth praises the 'polar star' which acts as 'guide/ And guardian' of the Chaldean shepherds, and which 'never closed/ His steadfast eye' (4.697–9),[71] and it was probably this that most immediately influenced Keats' poem. Nevertheless, Keats' decision to inscribe 'Bright star' 'upon a blank page in Shakespeare's Poems' (October–November 1819) suggests an allusion to the Shakespearean constellation of Sonnet 116:

> Bright star! Would I were steadfast as thou art –
> Not in lone splendour hung aloft the night
> And watching, with eternal lids apart,
> Like nature's patient, sleepless eremite,
> The moving waters at their priestlike task
> Of pure ablution round earth's human shores,
> Or gazing on the new soft-fallen mask
> Of snow upon the mountains and the moors;
> No – yet still steadfast, still unchangeable,
> Pillowed upon my fair love's ripening breast,
> To feel for ever its soft fall and swell,
> Awake for ever in a sweet unrest,
> Still, still, to hear her tender-taken breath,
> And so live ever – or else swoon to death.

Sonnet 116's popularity by the early nineteenth century was largely conservative – it exemplified the moral value of steadfastness and the timelessness

---

[69] Owen, *Understanding the Prelude*, p. 61.
[70] Bate, *Shakespeare and the English Romantic Imagination*, pp. 107–8.
[71] See Bate, *John Keats*, p. 539 and Keats, *The Poems of John Keats*, pp. 737–8 on the star image in Keats' work.

of the natural world. Keats, however, has little patience with the vertical imagery which preserves amorous frustration and cold chastity. Rather than be the 'wandering bark' bobbing on the sea, Keats prefers to set his steadfast cheek against the 'soft fall and swell' of the beloved's breast. He uses Sonnet 116 romantically, but also oppositionally to define a reciprocal desire.

The Romantic poets' advocacy of Shakespeare's Sonnets, critically and creatively, profoundly influenced encounters with those poems in the Victorian period; Tennyson, for example, responds with surprising sensuality to Sonnet 116.[72] Larger pressures were being brought to bear by the mid-nineteenth century, however, for Shakespeare was required to fulfil a more 'public-facing and nationally prominent role ... treated as a publicly acknowledged inspiration and figurehead'.[73] At the same time, the desire to imagine Shakespeare in private life had never been greater and this led to the increasing status of the Sonnets. As one critic wrote in the *Westminster Review* in 1857: 'The dramas are as it were his monument which we gaze at from afar: these sonnets the miniature which we can hang around our necks, and wear close to our bosom.'[74] As we will see, the experience of loving Shakespeare, and of loving like Shakespeare, were inextricably related in the mid-Victorian period, but there were some very obvious discrepancies between the kind of Shakespeare Victorian readers might wish to find in the Sonnets – the loving husband and father, 'so full of self-respect, domestic prudence, practical sagacity, wise reserve'[75] – and the lust-benighted adulterer and 'homosexual' that it was equally possible to detect. Adrian Poole describes the dilemma of the Victorian reader of the Sonnets: 'to retain belief in the sincerity of the emotions expressed, while staving off the anxiety that the passions involved might be dangerous or even positively illegitimate'.[76] The process of bringing Shakespeare's Sonnets to a wider audience, particularly the working classes and young people, would require a series of checks and measures to keep the private Shakespeare consistent with what he was required to be in public.

[72] On Tennyson's reading of Keats, see James Najarian, *Victorian Keats*, pp. 53–71, although this makes no specific reference to Sonnet 116.

[73] Shaw and Marshall, 'Shakespeare and Poetry', p. 121.

[74] 'The Sonnets of Shakspere', *The Westminster Review* 12 (July–October 1857), pp. 116–37, 128.

[75] Gerald Massey qtd by Murphy, *Shakespeare for the People*, p. 120.

[76] Poole, *Shakespeare and the Victorians*, p. 164.

'They All Sell': Sonnet Editions and Anthologies, 1837–1869

Victorian bardolatry was built on an unprecedented number of Shakespeare works in the marketplace.[77] As one commentator wrote in *The Daily News* (26 April 1864):

> Every year sees now three or four fresh impressions of his works. They are of all sorts and sizes and prices, with notes and without notes, with illustrations and without illustrations, reproductions of old and scarce copies for the luxurious student, penny a week issues for the apprentice or artisan. And they all sell. No book that ever was printed – save one – has had a circulation so enormous, so increasing, so real.[78]

As we have seen, what is true for Shakespeare's plays is rarely true for the Sonnets, and yet the nineteenth century produced 150 editions of Shakespeare's poetry,[79] and the Sonnets were also included in some of the 800 or so 'Works' produced in this period. These include editions by Charles Knight (1842–4), Alexander Dyce (1857),[80] John Payne Collier (1843, 1858) and James Orchard Halliwell (1853–65), the nine-volume *Works* edited by William George Clark, John Glover and William Aldis Wright for Macmillan (1863–6), and the single volume *Globe Shakespeare* (1866), which described itself as 'an edition of Shakespeare which every Englishman of the tolerably educated classes, from the intelligent mechanic to the peer of the realm, might gladly possess'.[81] Cheaper still were John Dicks' and Frederick Warne's shilling Shakespeares, in the 1860s, both of which reprinted the Quarto *Sonnets* at the end. As a result, the Sonnets became accessible to the working classes, and we find mention of them in the memoirs of several young men, born into poverty in the mid-nineteenth century, who made up for a lack of formal education by reading 'classic' literature including the Sonnets.[82]

---

[77] See Murphy, *Shakespeare in Print*, pp. 168–9.

[78] Qtd by Murphy, *Shakespeare for the People*, p. 3.

[79] Decker, 'Shakespeare Editions', p. 30.

[80] Dyce had published an extensive selection of thirty-eight Sonnets in *Specimens of English Sonnets* (1833). These are 7, 12, 19, 27, 29, 30, 32, 33, 52, 54, 55, 57, 60, 64, 66, 68, 71, 73, 76, 90, 91, 92, 93, 95, 97, 98, 102, 105, 106, 107, 108, 109, 111, 113, 114, 116, 117, 129.

[81] Qtd by Murphy, *Shakespeare in Print*, p. 176.

[82] Robert Smillie is one such example. Born in 1857 into a poor labouring family, he rose to become a Labour MP. In his memoirs, published in 1924, he recalled how little formal schooling he had: at the age of twelve he was working full-time in a mill. Nevertheless, he and his brother pursued their pleasure in reading, through potboilers such as *Dick Turpin* and *Three-Fingered Jack*, but also 'We managed to borrow, or pick up from a bookstall, at a small price, two or three of the Waverley novels, and one or two of the novels of Charles Dickens. At the age of fourteen I knew something of Burns, and had read several of Shakespeare's plays and some of his sonnets'. See *My Life for Labour*,

The responsibility of reproducing the full Quarto text and defending its position within the canon weighed heavily on editors' shoulders, however, and some of these *Works* offer surprisingly radical, recognisably modern strategies for distancing the Sonnets from Shakespearean biography (and, specifically, from Malone's male-addressee theory). In *The Works of William Shakespeare* (1865), James Orchard Halliwell rejects the assumption that

> the history of much of the great Poet's life is revealed in these obscure and remarkable compositions; as if a man of Shakespeare's practical wisdom, if we can believe that his passions so far outbalanced his judgement as to invest the history in the Sonnets with a truthful personal application, would have had the incredible folly to record the story of his indiscretions.[83]

Halliwell may well be alluding to Schlegel here, who had embraced the Sonnets on the assumption that they expressed Shakespeare's 'youthful errors' (see above). As a general rule, Victorian editors were uncomfortable with the notion of a Shakespeare so publicly flawed being recommended to youthful readers. Halliwell's solution is to reject the arrangement of the Quarto (and thus the implied Malonean division between a man and a woman), and to allow for the possibility that not all of these poems are by Shakespeare. He reminds his readers that it was usual in Shakespeare's time to keep 'poetical albums in which were collected in manuscript short poems obtained from similar volumes in private hands and from printed books, accompanied when practicable with original pieces written by friends':

> These circumstances, taken in connexion with the testimony of Meres, lead to the conclusion that the Sonnets of Shakespeare, at the close of the six-teenth century, were scattered amongst the numerous manuscript poetical miscellanies of the time, and were thus preserved in fragmentary portions. Some few perhaps may have been originally written continuously as a single poem and so preserved together, but the majority were no doubt composed separately on different occasions, and it is extremely unlikely that the whole were transcribed at that time anywhere in the form in which they were collectively published. So, when one Mr W. H. about the year 1608, commenced making a collection of Shakespeare's sonnets, he would have recourse to the poetical albums of the poet's friends, of whom he may him-self have been one, obtaining copies of as many of the sonnets as he could procure, which were probably, notwithstanding his efforts, not a complete collection. He contrived, however, to obtain no fewer than one hundred

---

pp. 15–16. For more on the labouring class and its experience of 'classic' literature, see Rose, *The Intellectual Life of the British Working Classes*.

[83] Shakespeare, *The Works of William Shakespeare*, ed. Halliwell-Phillips, p. 369.

and fifty-four, a number sufficient to make a saleable volume, which he delivered to the care of one Thomas Thorpe, a London publisher.[84]

Although he does not make it explicit, Halliwell's scenario allows for the possibility that Mr W. H. might have made a mistake and that not all of the Quarto Sonnets are by Shakespeare or, indeed, that not all of the 'genuine' Shakespeare Sonnets got into the Quarto. These are notions which are still strongly resisted in the early twenty-first century, but which ought perhaps to be given more serious consideration in the light of other work on Shakespeare's apocryphal and collaborative plays.

Also propounded by Victorian editors is the theory that Shakespeare wrote the Sonnets in other voices. In *The Poems of Shakespeare* (1832, 1866), Alexander Dyce declared: 'I have long felt convinced, after repeated perusals of the *Sonnets*, that the greater number of them was composed in an assumed character, on different subjects, and at different times, for the amusement, and probably at the suggestion, of the author's intimate associates.'[85] This idea was taken up by John Payne Collier in both *The Works of William Shakespeare* (1843) and *Shakespeare's Comedies, Histories, Tragedies and Poems* (1858). Collier quotes from Sir John Harington's 1591 *Epigrams* to prove that there were sonneteers for hire: 'Verses are grown such merchantable ware/ That now for Sonnets sellers are and buyers.' He concludes that 'if Shakespeare had now and then condescended in this way to supply the wants of his "private friends", who thus became possessed of his "sugred sonnets," as Meres calls them, it would, at all events, not have been without precedent'.[86]

Even a critic apparently devoted to the biographical narrative of the Sonnets could do much to undermine it by challenging the integrity of the Quarto. In the mid-1860s, Gerald Massey, the Chartist poet and one of the first working-class scholars of Shakespeare, published 'Shakspeare and his Sonnets' (*Quarterly Review* no. 115, April, 1864), and then a five-hundred page book, *Shakespeare's Sonnets Never Before Interpreted: His Private Friends Identified* (1866). Here, Massey argued that the Quarto consisted of lyrics written by Shakespeare for the Earl of Southampton to give to Elizabeth Vernon, and for William Herbert to give to Lady Penelope Rich. Just as Arthur F. Marotti has found evidence of a possible Pembroke lyric intertwined with a Shakespeare Sonnet in manuscript (see Chapter 2), so Massey argues that four Shakespeare Sonnets were actually

---

[84] Ibid., pp. 367–8.
[85] Shakespeare, *The Poems of Shakespeare*, ed. Dyce, pp. lxxvi–vii.
[86] Shakespeare, *Works*, ed. Collier, vol. 8, pp. 475–6.

written by Herbert, including, most surprisingly, Sonnet 130 ('My mistress' eyes are nothing like the sun') which lacks Shakespeare's 'certainty of touch'.[87] Massey goes on to argue that the Cupid Sonnets (153 and 154) demonstrate that 'the Poet had nothing to do with making up the collection for the Press ... They, together with the "Lover's Lament" [A Lover's Complaint] also prove that extraneous things were gathered into Thorpe's Book, by William Herbert'.[88]

The attraction for a Victorian readership of this disintegrationist approach is obvious: not only does it facilitate consistency between Shakespeare the dramatist and Shakespeare the poet, it also avoids the slurs upon Shakespeare's reputation which the speaker's desire for a man, and adultery with a mistress, had called forth. Collier described his ventriloquist theory 'as a mode merely of removing some of the difficulties attending this portion of the works of Shakespeare'.[89] But whilst editors reprinted the 1609 sequence and then paratextually undid it by describing the Sonnets' miscellaneous origins, Victorian anthologists recreated those origins, inscribing the Sonnets within the annals of British poetry,[90] whilst at the same time liberating them from the constraints of a biographical reading.

The 1860s were a dynamic decade for lyric anthologies, offering a variety of platforms for the Sonnets, including selections of the best English poets, Shakespeare anthologies, treasuries of children's verse and sonnet collections. With a few exceptions, it was still the norm for anthologies such as *Beauties of Shakespeare* or *Choice Thoughts from Shakespeare* (both 1861) to ignore the Sonnets in favour of extracts from the plays. Treasuries of verse for children, such as Coventry Patmore's *The Children's Garland from the Best Poets* (1861, rev. 1862, 1866, 1871 etc.), preferred the dramatic songs. Nevertheless, the Sonnets made some important cultural advances in this decade, as evident if we compare three significantly different types of anthology which helped to define a 'Victorian' Sonnet canon. These are: Francis Palgrave's *The Golden Treasury of the Best Songs and Lyrical Poems in the English Language* (1861), *Laurie's Graduated Series of Reading Lesson Books* (1866) and Leigh Hunt and Samuel Adams Lee's *The Book of the Sonnet* (1867).

---

[87] Massey, *Shakespeare's Sonnets Never Before Interpreted*, p. 359.
[88] Ibid., p. 569.
[89] Shakespeare, *Works*, ed. Collier, vol. 8, p. 475.
[90] On the importance of anthologies for the canon-building of the nineteenth century, see Houston, 'Anthologies and the Making of the Poetic Canon'.

Palgrave was initially unsure about the inclusion of sonnets into the *Golden Treasury*. On 30 October 1860, he wrote to Tennyson, the volume's literary consultant and dedicatee:

> I hesitate whether Elegies such as Gray's, and Sonnets should properly be included. They are lyrical in structure, and sonnets have always ranked as lyrical; but their didactic tone appears to me not decisively lyrical in a whatever strictness of sense so vague a word can bear. What do you think? The Greeks classified elegies as non-lyrical, and they had no sonnets.[91]

Tennyson was a passionate admirer of Shakespeare's Sonnets,[92] and his enthusiasm seems to have produced in Palgrave a significant change of heart. The anthology would be arranged in four historical periods, dominated by one poet: Shakespeare, Milton, Gray and Wordsworth. The Shakespeare section would include twenty Sonnets, ten songs and two *Passionate Pilgrim* lyrics still attributed to Shakespeare,[93] unlike its recent predecessor, William Allingham's *Nightingale Valley* (1860), which contained four sonnets (98, 57, 52, 29) and eight songs.[94] The lyrics within each book were arranged loosely, thematically, 'symphonic[ally]', with each book moving 'from nature, through the various phases of love – infatuation, passion and disappointment, – to mutability and death'.[95] This meant that the emphasis fell on particular lyrics rather than on the poet who produced them, and Palgrave dispensed with any biographical preamble. Moreover, the disruption of the Quarto arrangement – as well as some judicious titling, reminiscent of Benson – meant that it became impossible to read any Fair Youth/Dark Lady narrative into the Sonnets. They developed discrete musical and thematic relationships with other Sonnets, or with the work of other early modern poets.

Within six months *The Golden Treasury* had sold 10,000 copies, making it a bestseller, and by Palgrave's death in 1897, it had been reprinted thirty-five times, being republished after 1900 in single volumes by Macmillan

---

[91] Palgrave, *Francis Turner Palgrave*, p. 64.

[92] As Palgrave himself noted: 'Between Shakespeare's sonnets [Tennyson] hardly liked to decide, all were so powerful'. See 'Personal Recollections by F. T. Palgrave (including some criticism by Tennyson)' in Tennyson, *Alfred Lord Tennyson*, vol. 2, p. 500.

[93] These are 64, 65, 57, 97, 29, 109, 104, 18, 106, 116, 73, 30, 60, 87, 94, 148, 32, 71, 146 and 66. The *Passionate Pilgrim* lyrics are 'Crabbed age' and 'On a day'; the other two in the collection are attributed to Marlowe and Barnfield.

[94] On Palgrave's indebtedness to and rivalry with *Nightingale Valley*, see Spevack, '*The Golden Treasury*', pp. 3, 9–10.

[95] Nelson, 'Frances Turner Palgrave and *The Golden Treasury*', pp. 22–3. For further discussion of the volume's careful arrangement, see Ferry, 'Palgrave's "Symphony"'.

for use in schools.[96] Palgrave's daughter averred: 'There is no doubt that this little book has taught many – in all ranks of life – to know and love much of our best lyrical poetry which might otherwise have always remained untrodden ground.'[97] In terms of which Shakespeare Sonnets were chosen, Palgrave's selection made good its claim to offer what was 'already known and valued', by including the Romantic favourites identified earlier, specifically 29, 64, 73 and 116, and foregrounding the themes of 'Time and Love', beginning with 64: 'When I have seen by Time's fell hand defaced ...' and 65: 'Since brass, nor stone, nor earth, nor boundless sea ...'. Perhaps not surprisingly, Palgrave avoided more than a glancing encounter with Shakespearean lust, and almost entirely excluded male–male desire,[98] omitting homoerotic lyrics such as 20 ('A woman's face') and 126 ('O thou my lovely Boy') and downplaying the pun on 'your Will/will' in Sonnet 57 by the removal of Q's capitalisation. His selection seems to have been circumscribed by external factors, rather than reflecting his own taste. Megan Nelson records that:

> Not himself prudish, Palgrave personally regretted his emasculation of the English love lyric tradition, apologising in a letter to Macmillan for his '"Golden Treasury" prudery', and he excused his bowdlerisations by arguing that he was not putting together an anthology for his sophisticated friends, who included the collector of pornography Richard Monckton Milnes, but for an audience primarily composed of children and newly literate adults.[99]

That said, *The Golden Treasury* expanded the canon of Sonnets in some influential ways. Sonnet 18 ('Shall I compare thee to a summer's day') had almost disappeared since its absence from Benson's *Poems* in 1640: it was not anthologised in late eighteenth-century collections, and Wordsworth made no mention of it in his 'Essay, Supplementary'. However, Palgrave reclaimed it for Victorian readers under the title 'To his Love', implying

---

[96] On its status as a bestseller, see Spevack, '*The Golden Treasury*', p. 11, and Palgrave, *The Golden Treasury*, ed. Ricks, p. 444. On the number of reprints, considerably higher than Ricks' estimate, see Nelson, 'Frances Turner Palgrave and *The Golden Treasury*', p. 152.

[97] Palgrave, *Francis Turner Palgrave*, p. 65.

[98] There is one intriguing exception, which is the title for Sonnet 116. In the first three printings of *The Golden Treasury* in July, October and November 1861, this was given as 'Man's Love' – Palgrave's invention, but apparently approved by Tennyson who indicated 'Print' in the MS (Palgrave, *The Golden Treasury*, ed. Ricks, p. 474). Whilst this was probably intended to be a shorthand for 'the epitome of human' love, the Sonnet was succeeded by Sidney's lyric, 'My true love hath my heart and I have his', now released from the context of the *Arcadia*, in which it was sung by a shepherdess. The two lyrics combined create a temporary, homoerotic *aporia* – until the edition of December 1861 in which Sonnet 116 is quietly re-titled 'True Love' (p. 15).

[99] Macmillan Papers, 8 November 1870, quoted by Nelson in 'Francis Turner Palgrave and *The Golden Treasury*', p. 130.

a biographical connection with Shakespeare that would cause no consternation. Sonnet 94 ('They that have power to hurt') is another Sonnet that had been overlooked by Wordsworth and early nineteenth-century anthologists, but would start to engage Victorian readers, most notably George Eliot. Finally, we should acknowledge Palgrave's unusual venture into the 'Dark Lady' collection, although his choice of Sonnet 146 ('Poor soul, the centre of my sinful earth') represents perhaps 'Shakespeare's only explicitly religious poem',[100] one that would be reprinted seven years later by Richard Chevenix Trench, Archbishop of Dublin, in *A Household Book of English Poetry* (1868).

What *The Golden Treasury* did for the Sonnets' literary canonicity, *Laurie's Graduated Series of Reading Lesson Books: Cheap and Abridged Edition for Elementary Schools* (1866) did for their pedagogical status. Following the Revised Code of 1862, which linked financial assistance to schools' examination results, a single Shakespeare Sonnet became required reading when it was included in the sixth and final volume of *Laurie's … Reading Lesson Books*:

> That time of year thou mayst in me behold,
> When yellow leaves, or none, or few do hang
> Upon those boughs which shake against the cold,
> Bare ruined choirs where late the sweet birds sang.
>
> (Sonnet 73)

As early as 1822, Reverend J. R. Pitman had chosen this Sonnet for *The School-Shakespeare: or, Plays and Scenes from Shakspeare, illustrated for the use of Schools*,[101] but its status as a Romantic favourite also influenced its appearance in the Laurie anthology. The sixth and final volume exhorts its young readers to meditate on their own mortality through Coleridge's poem, 'Youth and Age', which laments: 'What strange disguise is now put on,/ To make believe that thou art gone!/ I see these locks in silvery slips,/ This drooping gait, this altered size'.[102] This is followed immediately by Sonnet 73, whose line 'That on the ashes of his youth doth lie' extends Coleridge's theme. Further evidence that Shakespeare's Sonnets on time and mortality, reflecting 'the sober sadness of that early autumn of his age',[103] were judged suitable for the young is provided by John Bellew's

---

[100] Shakespeare, *Shakespeare's Sonnets*, ed. Duncan-Jones, p. 408. Palgrave's other 'Dark Lady' sonnet is 148 ('O me what eyes hath love put in my head') which becomes generically misogynist when printed alongside lyrics such as 'The Unfaithful Shepherdess' (Anon), and the Earl of Oxford's 'A Renunciation'.

[101] Pitman includes twelve Sonnets: 18, 25, 27, 29, 38, 71, 73, 90, 91, 98, 99, 102.

[102] *Laurie's Graduated Series*, p. 11.

[103] Massey, 'Shakspeare and his Sonnets', Part 1, n.p.

Poets' Corner: A Manual for Students in English Poetry (1868). Questions of morality and age appropriateness weigh heavily on Bellew's mind. He omits poets 'whose compositions are so greatly tainted with licentiousness, that it cannot be desirable to reproduce them',[104] and is particularly concerned to defend Shakespeare against 'the vulgar and gossiping stories which have been commonly introduced into the biographies of the greatest of all men ... fabrications which would be ludicrous, if they were not wicked and offensive'.[105] His resulting selection emphasises the Sonnets' *ubi sunt* rather than their *carpe diem* themes, though he prefers Sonnet 60 to Sonnet 73: 'Like as the waves make towards the pebbled shore,/So do our minutes hasten to their end.'[106]

Finally, Leigh Hunt and S. Adams Lee's anthology *The Book of the Sonnet* (1867) passionately defends the aesthetic value of certain Shakespeare Sonnets,[107] whilst emphasising their biographical interest. The poet, journalist and theatre critic Hunt was a close friend of Keats, Shelley and Charles Armitage Brown, and his selection owes much to Brown's assumption that readers will want to use the Sonnets to 'see [Shakespeare] face to face, hear him speak, be in his companionship, live with him altogether'.[108] Thus, Sonnet 128 ('How oft when thou, my music, music play'st'), which had fallen out of favour since the early seventeenth century, is included on the basis that 'the reader might like to see [Shakespeare] in a lady's company while she was playing on the musical instrument that was the prototype of the wooden piano-forte. To find him thus situated seems like the next thing to having him with us to *tea*'.[109] Sonnet 111 is also included, not because it is among Shakespeare's best ('though it has one admirable passage – about the dyer's hand'[110]) but because 'Shakespeare is here "unlocking his heart"'.[111] This Sonnet was usually understood as expressing Shakespeare's shame at his theatrical profession, though it was also used to imply that the plays were better read than performed:[112]

---

[104] Bellew, *Poets' Corner*, p. iv.
[105] Ibid., pp. 171–2.
[106] Bellew chooses Sonnets 12, 19, 30, 60, 71 and 91, as well as PP 12, 13 and 17.
[107] Hunt and Adams Lee choose the now-familiar Sonnets 111, 29, 128, 98, 116, 33, 73 and 71. 'Obscure and perplexing as some of them are', Hunt writes, 'others contain passages of as exquisite poetry as any he wrote, and the best of them are veritable jewels', *The Book of the Sonnet*, p. 77.
[108] Brown, *Shakespeare's Autobiographical Poems*, p. 3.
[109] Hunt and Lee, *The Book of the Sonnet*, p. 157.
[110] Hunt singles out the phrase '[nature] subdued/ To what it works in, like the dyer's hand', describing it as 'true Shakespearean writing', ibid., p. 155.
[111] Ibid., p. 154.
[112] See Malone in the 1780 *Supplement* and Lamb's 1811 essay, discussed in Chapter 3.

> O for my sake do you with Fortune chide,
> The guilty goddess of my harmful deeds,
> That did not better for my life provide
> Than public means which public manners breeds.
> Thence comes it that my name receives a brand,
> And almost thence my nature is subdued
> To what it works in, like the dyer's hand …

But in light of the increasing popularity of Shakespeare on stage in the mid-Victorian period, Sonnet 111 required more explanation. Rather than accept that Shakespeare condemns the theatrical profession per se, Hunt concludes that 'all his sonnets appear to have been written after he had entered upon a line of life for which he and others had not yet procured its just social consideration'.[113]

One of Leigh Hunt's friends who would have been very much in agreement with this sentiment is Charles Dickens.[114] In 'The Amusements of the People' (1850), Dickens defended the lower class's passion for 'dramatic entertainment', exemplified by 'Joe Whelks' who has 'no great store of books' but whose imagination is captured by plays. Dickens refuses to blame the quality of these plays on either the theatre manager or the actors:

> It is not the Manager's province to hold the Mirror up to Nature, but to Mr Whelks – the only person who acknowledges him. If, in like manner, the actor's nature, like the dyer's hand, becomes subdued to what it works in, the actor can hardly be blamed for it. He grinds hard at his vocation, is often steeped in direful poverty, and lives, at the best, in a little world of mockeries. It is bad enough to give away a great estate six nights-a-week, and want a shilling; to preside at imaginary banquets, hungry for a mutton chop; to smack the lips over a tankard of toast and water, and declaim about the mellow produce of the sunny vineyard on the banks of the Rhine; to be a rattling young lover, with the measles at home; and to paint sorrow over, with burnt cork and rouge; without being called upon to despise his vocation too. If he can utter the trash to which he is condemned, with any relish, so much the better for him, Heaven knows; and peace be with him!'[115]

Here, Dickens shows an awareness of Sonnet 111 in its critical tradition – as an indictment of the theatre by Romantic critics – and in the process defends the nobility of the actor's profession from Shakespearean

---

[113] Hunt and Lee, *The Book of the Sonnet*, pp. 154–5.
[114] Valerie Gager finds echoes of this Sonnet in a private letter, the article in *Household Words*, and three novels: *Bleak House*, *Our Mutual Friend* and *The Mystery of Edwin Drood*. She also discusses the influence of Sonnet 144 ('Two loves I have') on Dickens' work. See *Shakespeare and Dickens*, pp. 362–3.
[115] *Household Words* (30 March 1850), pp. 13–15, p. 13.

snobbery.[116] Elsewhere, Dickens would identify the phrase with the world of honourable labour, when in *Our Mutual Friend* (1865) he has the feckless Eugene Wrayburn lament of Mortimer: 'Observe the mind! ... Observe the dyer's hand, assimilating itself to what it works in, – or would work in, if anybody would give it anything to do'.[117] But this image also carries negative connotations in Dickens' work – presumably because of the way in which it resonates with his formative experience as a twelve-year-old working in Warren's blacking factory, pasting labels onto the pots of boot-blacking. Peter Ackroyd describes a man for whom Sonnet 111 might carry memories of repressed trauma:

> He always retained throughout his life a morbid susceptibility to any form of slight – his 'shrinking sensitiveness', as he called it – and we see in his huge appetite for success, his huge will for what he himself called 'power', the need to remove the taint of poverty and social disgrace. This latent fear of social degradation and his memory of the past clearly led him to overwork as well (how easy, after all, it was to 'go under'!), just as it was his childhood association with the soiled life of the blacking factory which made him as a man so extraordinarily neat and so particularly clean. (How hard it must have been to remove the blacking from his nails and hands!)[118]

Whilst Dickens had escaped this childhood purgatory relatively unscathed, his fictional creations would not always fare so well, and this is particularly the case for those involved in the court of Chancery. The Preface to *Bleak House* (1853) begins with an anecdote in which a Chancery judge defends that institution to Dickens, acknowledging only 'a trivial blemish or so in its rate of progress'. This opinion, Dickens tells us, he would gladly have given to Conversation Kenge or Mr Vholes:

> In such mouths I might have coupled it with an apt quotation from one of SHAKESPEARE'S Sonnets.
>
> > My nature is subdued
> > To what it works in, like the dyer's hand:
> > Pity me then, and wish I were renew'd![119]

It is significant that where the Sonnet allows for hope, '*almost thence* my nature is subdued', Dickens has removed the qualifier to make the effect more permanent, and this is played out in the novel through the tragedy

[116] For further discussion of Dickens's defence of popular theatre in the face of a Romantic, anti-theatrical Shakespeare, see Juliet John, 'Dickens and Hamlet'.

[117] Dickens, *Our Mutual Friend*, Book 3, ch. 10, p. 541.

[118] Ackroyd, *Dickens*, p. 105.

[119] Dickens, *Bleak House*, p. 3.

of Richard Carstone. In Chapter xxxvii, 'Jarndyce and Jarndyce', Esther and Richard agree about the effects of the case – how it 'taints everybody' – before Richard's refusal to accept her advice brings on a more specific allusion:

> 'It's impossible that I can [accept advice] on this subject, my dear girl. On any other, readily!'
> As if there were any other in his life! As if his whole career and character were not being dyed one colour!¹²⁰

It may not be a coincidence that *Bleak House* contains a caricature of Leigh Hunt in the character of Harold Skimpole,¹²¹ who hangs around Richard Carstone and abets his contamination. Part of Dickens' satire of his 'friend' may well have been this repeated allusion to one of their favourite Sonnets.¹²²

But if Dickens took a pessimistic view, Hunt's reading of the Sonnets focused on the capacity of Shakespearean love to transcend degradation. Two of the most frequently anthologised Sonnets in the 1860s are 30 ('When to the sessions of sweet silent thought') and 29 ('When in disgrace with Fortune and men's eyes').¹²³ The appeal of Sonnet 30 potentially lies in the final couplet, which counters a long list of the poet's remembered sorrows with the consolation: 'But if the while I think on thee, dear friend,/ All losses are restored and sorrows end.' The emphasis on friendship rather than any more complicated passion seems to have pleased Victorian anthologists. It may also account for the recurrence of Sonnet 29, which

¹²⁰ Ibid., p. 465.

¹²¹ Dickens denied it in print, but admitted in a private letter of 21 September 1853 that Skimpole was 'the most exact portrait that ever was painted in words ... It is an absolute reproduction of a real man' (*The Letters of Charles Dickens*, 7.154). Hunt had been dead for eight years by the time *The Book of the Sonnet* was published but we might speculate when he had first prepared his selection, and whether he shared this with Dickens.

¹²² Gager also lists an allusion to Sonnet 73, 'Upon those boughs which shake against the cold,/ Bare ruined choirs where late the sweet birds sang', in Chapter VI of *Bleak House*: 'Harold Skimpole loves to see the sun shine; loves to hear the wind blow; loves to watch the changing lights and shadows; loves to hear the birds, those choristers in Nature's great cathedral', *Shakespeare and Dickens*, p. 362.

¹²³ This is based on a survey of ten anthologies including Shakespeare's Sonnets published 1860–9, not including their subsequent reprints: William Allingham's *Nightingale Valley* (1860), Palgrave's *The Golden Treasury* (1861), *Shakespeare's Songs and Sonnets* illustrated by John Gilbert (1865), *Chambers' Readings in English Poetry* (1865), James Stuart Laurie, *Laurie's Graduated Series of Reading Lesson Books* (1867), Charles Mackay, *A Thousand and One Gems of English Poetry* (1867), Leigh Hunt and S. Adams Lee, *The Book of the Sonnet* (1867), J. C. M. Bellew, *Poets' Corner: A Manual for Students in English Poetry* (1868), Richard Chevenix Trench, *A Household Book of English Poetry* (1868), and Charles Anderson Dana, *The Household Book of Poetry* (1859, repr. 1868). These anthologies reproduce forty-seven different Sonnets in total. Sonnet 30 appears six times out of ten, Sonnets 29 and 98 five times, and Sonnets 71, 116 and 33 four.

not only offers an attractive image of Shakespeare's humility,[124] but sees him restored by an ennobling affection. As Hunt puts it, 'The gladdening influences of a lover's thoughts, the cheering light of a true affection, were never depicted with truer feeling than in this sonnet'.[125] But if the selectivity of an anthology made possible the idealisation of Shakespearean love, this would be much harder to maintain if one were reprinting the Quarto in full. This idealisation would also require some defence in a critical field which had begun to explore the implications of loving like Shakespeare in terms of both gender and sexuality.

How Did Shakespeare Love? Francis Palgrave, Henry Hallam and Tennyson's *In Memoriam*

When in 1865, Palgrave was commissioned by Macmillan to re-produce the full Quarto sequence, he discretely removed four Sonnets. These were Sonnet 20 ('A woman's face'), whose homoeroticism he could not ignore, and three Cupid poems – 151 ('Love is too young'), 153 ('Cupid laid by his brand') and 154 ('The little love-god') which he believed to be efflorescences of the narrative poems, and 'marked, like them, by a warmth of colouring unsuited for the world at large'.[126] This is a surprisingly restrained act of expurgation on Palgrave's part,[127] perhaps because he felt he had defended the rest of the collection sufficiently in the preface. And yet, he admits here that most readers will find themselves profoundly alienated from Shakespeare-in-love:

> we can hardly understand, we cannot enter into the strange series of feelings which [the Sonnets] paint; we cannot understand how our great and gentle Shakespeare could have submitted himself to such passions; we have hardly courage to think that he really endured them. Such excess, however, as it must appear in the light of common day, is perhaps rarely wanting among the great gifts of genius. The poet's nature differs in degree so much from other men's, that we might almost speak of it as a difference in kind. This,

---

[124] Hunt may have been recalling his friend Charles Lamb's praise of this Sonnet in 1811 (see Chapter 3).

[125] Hunt notes that 'The modesty evinced in the wishes for the features and faculties of other persons has, in such a man especially, been deservedly admired', Hunt and Lee, *The Book of the Sonnet*, p. 156.

[126] Shakespeare, *Songs and Sonnets by William Shakespeare*, p. 236.

[127] Christopher Decker has noted of the plays that 'Though expurgated editions were popular in the nineteenth century, the number of unexpurgated editions far exceeded them. It is consequently an oversimplification to characterise expurgated editions as embodying "Victorian values", as though the vast majority of unexpurgated texts in print throughout the century were somehow less typical than the minority of expurgated ones', 'Shakespeare Editions', p. 20.

in the sublime language of the *Phaedrus*, is that 'possession and ecstasy with which the Muses seize on a plastic and pure soul, awakening it and hurrying it forth like a Bacchanal in the ways of song'. A sensitiveness unexperienced by lesser men exalts every feeling to a range beyond ordinary sympathies. Friendship blazes into passion. The furnace of love is seven times heated … We cannot bring ourselves to wish that 'Shakespeare had never written them', or that the world should have wanted perhaps the most singular, utterances of passion which Poetry has yet supplied. But there is pleasure also in the belief, that this phase of feeling was transient, and that the sanity which, not less than ecstasy, is an especial attribute of the great poet, returned to the Shakespeare whom, with Jonson, we 'love and honour, on this side idolatry, as much as any'.[128]

Here Palgrave confronts the strangeness not only of the feelings the Sonnets record, but of Shakespeare himself. He identifies with a tradition of reading the Sonnets for what they reveal of Shakespeare's experience of love, but instead of universal truths, he finds an alienating 'singular[ity]'. This kind of passion will not be understood by the common man, let alone experienced by him, and it was not even suffered by Shakespeare for very long. In his deliberate avoidance of male pronouns, and his emphasis on the Platonic soul rather than the desiring body (although the *Phaedrus* was the text in which Socrates discussed the ideal pederastic relationship), Palgrave acknowledges the ways in which Shakespeare's loving had become newly controversial in the Victorian period. To do so, he quotes the foremost agitator of this controversy, Henry Hallam.

If George Steevens' hostility to the Sonnets had channelled the apprehensions of the late eighteenth century, it was Henry Hallam's opinion, particularly his wish that 'Shakespeare had never written them', which haunted admirers in the mid-nineteenth.[129] In *An Introduction to the Literature of Europe* (1839, repr. 1842), Hallam averred that 'no one can doubt that [the Sonnets] express not only real but intense emotions of the heart', and required that they be read biographically:

> We find them relate to one definite, though obscure, period of the poet's life; in which an attachment to some female, which seems to have touched neither his heart nor his fancy very sensibly, was overpowered, without entirely ceasing, by one to a friend; and this last is of such an enthusiastic character, and so extravagant in the phrase that the author uses, as to have thrown an unaccountable mystery over the whole work. It is true that in

---

[128] Shakespeare, *Songs and Sonnets by William Shakespeare*, pp. 241–3.
[129] Among those who refuted Hallam's views explicitly are Charles Knight, Tennyson, Massey and Oscar Wilde.

the poetry as well as in the fictions of early ages, we find a more ardent tone of affection in the language of friendship than has since been usual; and yet no instance has been adduced of such rapturous devotedness, such idolatry of admiring love, as the greatest being whom nature ever produced in the human form pours forth to some unknown youth in the majority of these sonnets … Notwithstanding the frequent beauties of these sonnets, the pleasure of their perusal is greatly diminished by these circumstances; and it is impossible not to wish that Shakespeare had never written them. There is a weakness and folly in all excessive and mis-placed affection, which is not redeemed by the touches of nobler sentiments that abound in this long series of sonnets.[130]

Hallam's critique was particularly painful for Shakespeare's mid-nineteenth-century admirers because he rejected the mystifications of Malone and Coleridge i.e. that this was the standard rhetoric of male friendship, or that the Sonnets were really addressed to a woman. Moreover, Hallam's Shakespeare is effeminate – an identity which 'does not yet depend on the criterion of sexuality', but focuses on a classical ideal of 'civic masculinity': 'the *vir* must perform as a husband who fulfils his role as procreator … the *effeminatus* or effeminate man … acts like a woman, lacking self-control'.[131] Much of Hallam's concern about the Sonnets relates to their emotional excess: 'There is a weakness and folly in all excessive and mis-placed affection.' 'Rapturous devotedness' and 'idolatry of admiring love' imply a loss of self-control that renders Shakespeare as helpless as a woman. Perhaps equally disturbing is Shakespeare's abjectness, so that Hallam welcomes the identification of Mr W. H. as the Earl of Pembroke:

Something of the strangeness, as it appears to us, of Shakespeare's humiliation in addressing him as a being before whose feet he crouched, whose frown he feared, whose injuries, and those of the most insulting kind, the seduction of the mistress to whom we have alluded, he felt and bewailed without resenting; something, I say, of the strangeness of this humiliation, and at best it is but little, may be lightened and in a certain sense rendered intelligible.[132]

And yet, Hallam's accusation also glances at Shakespeare's sexuality when it deploys the language already in use for contemporary male–male desire. As Richard Dellamora has suggested, the description of Shakespeare's attachment as being of 'such an enthusiastic character' may have invoked

---

[130] Hallam, *An Introduction to the Literature of Europe*, pp. 501, 502, 504.
[131] Morgan, 'Victorian Effeminacies', pp. 109, 112. For further discussion of the changing interpretation of effeminacy, see Sinfield, *The Wilde Century*.
[132] Hallam, *An Introduction to the Literature of Europe*, p. 503.

the use of 'enthusiast' to mean 'a male committed to sexual and emotional relations with other males'.[133] Moreover, despite attempting to limit these emotions to 'one definite, though obscure, period' of Shakespeare's life, as Palgrave would do, Hallam implies that Shakespeare's loving was not a temporary aberration but something deeper, something essential, anticipating Foucault's definition of homosexuality, as it emerged in the later nineteenth century, as 'less a type of sexual relations than … a certain quality of sexual sensibility, a certain way of inverting the masculine and the feminine in oneself'.[134] Hallam also hints at a possible danger for the male reader – a danger which would find its most daring expression in Oscar Wilde's 'The Portrait of Mr W. H.' – when he observes: 'Perhaps there is now a tendency, especially among young men of poetical tempers, to exaggerate the beauties of these remarkable productions', and proceeds to disabuse them of this opinion. Hallam may have been remembering his son, Arthur, and his friend Alfred Tennyson as such admirers of the Sonnets,[135] and Tennyson's *In Memoriam* ironically brings together the poet, the critic and the reader in an extended debate about what it means to love the Sonnets, and to love like Shakespeare.

That Tennyson's grief, following the death of Arthur Hallam on 15 September 1833, affected his aesthetic judgement is attested to by Benjamin Jowett. He describes Tennyson's tendency to 'think Shakespeare greater in his sonnets than in his plays' as a grief-inflected delusion. He also testifies to the dangers of the Sonnets, which encourage the admirer into effeminacy, and sympathy with (if not performance of) homosexuality:

> he soon returned to the thought which is indeed the thought of all the world. He would have seemed to me to be reverting for a moment to the great sorrow of his own mind. *It would not have been manly or natural to have lived in it always.* But in that peculiar phase of mind he found the sonnets a deeper expression of the never to be forgotten love which he felt more than any of the many moods of many minds which appear among his dramas. *The love of the sonnets which he so strikingly expressed was a sort of sympathy with Hellenism.* (Italics mine)[136]

---

[133] Dellamora, *Masculine Desire*, p. 27.

[134] See Foucault, *The History of Sexuality*, 1.43. Foucault traced the emergence of this concept to 1870, but subsequent critics have evidenced it considerably earlier in the century. Those who have disputed this late date include Dellamora, *Masculine Desire*, and Sinfield, *The Wilde Century*.

[135] Arthur had admired the Sonnets in his essay, 'The Influence of Italian upon English Literature', printed at Cambridge in 1832. His suggestion that they were a homage to Dante avoids any acknowledgement of their male addressee. See *The Writings of Arthur Hallam*, p. 229.

[136] Quoted by Christopher Ricks in Tennyson, *The Poems of Tennyson*, p. 860. Both sentences in italics would be excised by Hallam Tennyson in *Alfred Lord Tennyson*.

Tennyson's early poetry had been criticised for its indebtedness to the Sonnets.[137] *In Memoriam* (1839–50, pub. 1850), whose loose narrative structure resembles that of a sonnet sequence, seemed to evidence a deeper engagement,[138] as well as a more superficial similarity which was repeatedly commented on by its critics. Again and again, they invoke Shakespeare's Sonnets either to celebrate the superiority of Tennyson's poem or to cast it in a more dubious light. In *The Examiner* (8 June 1850), for example, John Forster places *In Memoriam* within the 'annals of manly and enduring friendship', inviting comparison with the 'extraordinary friendship, love, and grief' of Shakespeare's Sonnets, though Tennyson's poem exceeds its predecessor in 'the heavenward tone of its thoughts, soaring upward from the earlier and more intense expressions of palsy-stricken grief'.[139] By contrast, in his review for *The Times* (28 November 1851), Manley Hopkins blamed the effeminacy of Tennyson's style on 'floating remembrances of Shakspeare's Sonnets'. Quoting Elegy LXXIV, 5–12, he observes:

> Very sweet and plaintive these verses are; but who would not give them a feminine application? Shakspeare may be considered the founder of this style in English. In classical and Oriental poetry it is unpleasantly familiar. His mysterious sonnets present the startling peculiarity of transferring every epithet of womanly endearment to a masculine friend – his master-mistress, as he calls him by a compound epithet, harsh as it is disagreeable. We should never expect to hear a young lawyer calling a member of the same inn 'his rose' except in the Middle Temple of Ispahan, with Hafiz for a laureate. Equally objectionable are the following lines in the 42nd sonnet: –
>
> > If I could write the beauty of your eyes,
> > And in fresh numbers number all your graces,
> > The age to come would say this poet lies;
> > Such heavenly touches ne'er touched earthly faces …[140]

Whilst Hopkins insists that the Sonnets are stylistically (and thus superficially) aberrant, he acknowledges their innate queerness by referring to Sonnet 20 through the phrase 'master-mistress', and by likening the use of

---

[137] See Decker, 'Shakespeare and the Death of Tennyson', p. 134.
[138] Ricks identifies allusions to eight different poems: Sonnets 1, 26, 31, 33, 43, 59, 77, 144, suggesting Tennyson's connoisseur taste for these Sonnets were rarely anthologised. Elegy I, for example, includes the lines 'Or reach a hand through time to catch/ The far-off interest of tears' (7–8), which recall Sonnet 31's 'holy and obsequious tear … as interest of the dead'. In his own extensive knowledge of the Sonnets, Ricks overlooks the obvious debt to Sonnet 116.
[139] *The Examiner*, p. 356.
[140] Manley Hopkins, 'The Poetry of Sorrow', *The Times* (28 November 1851), p. 8.

'my love' from Sonnet 109 to the work of the fourteenth-century Iranian poet, Hafiz i-Shirazi, whose ghazals celebrated a beautiful boy.[141]

Tennyson had, of course, actively encouraged critics to read *In Memoriam* through the lens of Shakespeare's Sonnets, when the speaker implores Hallam's spirit:

> Yet turn thee to the doubtful shore,
> Where thy first form was made a man;
> I loved thee, Spirit, and love, nor can
> The soul of Shakspeare love thee more.
>
> (LXI, 9–12)

As we have seen, this love might be read in a variety of ways. The *Blackwood's Magazine* article of 1818 had found Shakespeare to possess 'a heart overflowing with tenderness, purity and love. His feelings are intense, profound, acute, even to selfishness'.[142] And yet, the more transgressive possibilities of loving like Shakespeare had also been invoked by Shelley in the manuscript of *Epipsychidion* (*c.* 1822): 'If any should be curious to discover/ Whether to you I am a friend or lover,/ Let them read Shakespeare's sonnets, taking thence/ A whetstone for their dull intelligence/ That tears and will not cut.'[143] These lines were omitted from the printed text, perhaps because they alluded too directly to Shelley's own 'master-mistress'.[144] Given this ambiguity, it is difficult to judge how risky was Tennyson's strategy in aligning himself with Shakespeare-the-lover. According to Gregory Woods,

> This moment of identification relies on the critical mass which had been established to rescue Shakespeare's sonnets from the potential 'taint' of accusations of physical passion. Tennyson hopes to capitalise on patriotic defences of Shakespeare, thereby ensuring that his own poem will be read as befitting the emotional requirements of English manliness.[145]

Alternatively, Jeff Nunokawa has argued that Tennyson invokes the Sonnets 'as an exemplary figuration of male homoerotic passion' in order that he may leave it behind:

> In keeping with the construction of the homoerotic as an early point on the developmental agenda of male desire, a stage which *precedes* and is

---

[141] On this commonplace theme in Persian lyric poetry, see the *Encyclopedia Iranica*, www .iranicaonline.org/articles/homosexuality-iii, accessed 18 April 2019.
[142] *Blackwood's Magazine*, p. 587.
[143] Shelley, *The Complete Poetical Works of Percy Bysshe Shelley*, p. 428, ll 97–101.
[144] See Lauritsen, 'Homoeroticism in Epipsychidion', in *The Shelley-Byron Men*.
[145] Woods, *A History of Gay Literature*, p. 119.

terminated by matrimony, Tennyson's poem draws marriage away from the form of devotion that Victorians attributed to the Sonnets and situates it at a height where that form has been transcended.[146]

More specifically, this transcendence is achieved by invoking and negating Sonnet 116, as paraphrased in Elegy LXII:

> Tho' if an eye that's downward cast
> Could make thee somewhat blench or fail,
> Then be my love an idle tale,
> And fading legend of the past;
>
> And thou, as one that once declined,
> When he was little more than boy,
> On some unworthy heart with joy,
> But lives to wed an equal mind.
>
> (1–8)

The concluding line, 'But lives to wed an equal mind' recalls Sonnet 116's 'marriage of true minds', ostensibly supporting the movement from a youthful, homosocial passion to a lasting heterosexual union.[147] And yet, I would argue this does not necessarily cancel out the speaker's enduring passion. The couplet 'If this be error and upon me proved/ I never writ nor no man ever loved', which resonates in lines 3–4, works in the Sonnet to uphold the speaker's claim that true love is constancy: it would be as truthful to aver that he never wrote nor loved as to deny this definition of love. By incorporating this into a dismissal of his passion as an 'idle tale/ And fading legend of the past', Tennyson undermines his own efforts. He also exposes their abjectness and insincerity. His concern that the beloved neither 'blench nor fail' at the memory recalls Sonnet 71: 'I love you so,/ That I in your sweet thoughts would be forgot,/ If thinking on me then should make you woe' (6–8). Although this Sonnet was much admired by Hunt, as 'deeply and affectingly beautiful',[148] there is reason to doubt the sincerity of both Shakespeare's speaker and Tennyson's in the act of repression. Their self-abnegation is a paradoxically self-aggrandising expression of enduring love.

Rather than use Sonnet 116 to cancel out homoerotic desire, Tennyson uses the lyric to romanticise it. By the 1830s, this had become one of the most respectable of the Sonnets, singled out by Nathan Drake for its 'chastity of diction', and 'noble and appropriate imagery'.[149] The vertical tension

---

[146] Nunokawa, '*In Memoriam* and the Extinction of the Homosexual', 432.
[147] Dellamora, *Masculine Desire*, p. 32.
[148] Hunt and Lee, *The Book of the Sonnet*, p. 77.
[149] Drake, *Shakspeare and His Times*, p. 81.

between star and wandering bark precluded amorous/sexual fulfilment, invoking the Petrarchan conventions of a devoted but unconsummated love. The poem's sense of distance, inequality and abjection may even have given it a personal resonance for Tennyson. Alan Sinfield has remarked on the tone of condescension in at least one of Hallam's letters, and concludes that although 'their admiration may indeed have been mutual ... Tennyson may have felt, even so, that he was dependent on the attention of his sophisticated, charismatic and popular friend'. *In Memoriam* becomes a way to express this disparity:

> Death rendered Arthur remote, lost, beyond communication, and made it possible for that to be considered openly – through the discourse of death and heaven. But for Tennyson there had always been the sense that their commitment was not quite equal.[150]

Where Sonnet 116 becomes transgressive, in a way that Tennyson may not have been able to control, is its assertion of the persistence of homoerotic desire, outside of social convention, outside of time. In Elegy xxx the poet testifies of the dead, 'They do not die/ Nor lose their mortal sympathy,/ Nor change to us, although they change' (22–4) which loosely recalls 'nor bend with the remover to remove'. Moreover, Elegy LIX calls upon Sorrow to live with the speaker 'as a wife', combining elements of 116 with the final line of Sonnet 98:

> My centred passion cannot move,
> Nor will it lessen from to-day;
> But I'll have leave at times to play,
> As with the creature of my love.
> (9–12)

Here, Nunokawa's substitution of wife for dead male lover is arguably reversed, as Tennyson emphasises how false and unsatisfying is this substitution – again invoking the context of the original Sonnet: 'Yet seem'd it winter still, and you away,/ As with your shadow I with these [flowers/ mistresses] did play.' Moreover, the stubborn fixity of Sonnet 116's passion disrupts the poem's efforts to move forward. As Christopher Craft puts it,

> Whatever bliss or agony the poem owns, it owes to its interminable desire for Hallam; nor can the dispersions of that 'vaster passion' displace Hallam as the affective center of *In Memoriam*'s world of desire. In this sense, *In Memoriam* refuses to complete its work of mourning; refuses, that is, the work of normal (and normalizing) substitution. Thus, in the sheer ferocity

[150] Sinfield, *Alfred Tennyson*, pp. 148–9.

of its personal loss, as in the extreme extensiveness of its reparational hungering, Tennyson's elegy manages to counterspeak its own submission to its culture's heterosexualising conventions.[151]

Surprisingly enough, for all that it was identified with marriage and the sealing of heterosexual bonds,[152] Sonnet 116 becomes part of this counter-speech.

'The Human Heart's Large Seasons': Elizabeth Barrett Browning and George Eliot

If the perceived effeminacy of the Sonnets was problematic for a male writer, but also potentially creative – part of the 'continual effort to fashion better ways of being-masculine in the world'[153] – it offered similarly ambiguous possibilities for women. Always ignoring the 'Dark Lady' sequence, commentators had begun to add the Sonnets to the Shakespearean works which held up an image of the ideal Victorian woman.[154] In *The Book of the Sonnet*, Hunt identifies the speaker of Sonnet 116 with the primarily female values of constancy and patient suffering:

> We at once recognise in it the abstraction of that conception which has found a dwelling and a name in the familiar forms of Desdemona, Juliet, Imogen, Cordelia, of Romeo, and of Othello too, if that character be correctly understood. If this sonnet was written before his dramas, then it was the pregnant thought from which were destined to spring those inimitable creations of female character that have been loved, as if they were living beings, by thousands.[155]

Twenty years later in her essay, 'Shakespeare as the Girl's Friend' (1887), Mary Cowden Clark would encourage female readers to see themselves in Shakespeare: 'Witness his sonnets, – where tenderness, patience, devotion, and constancy worthy of gentlest womanhood are conspicuous

---

[151] Craft, '"Descend and Touch and Enter"', 98.

[152] Massey argues that Shakespeare wrote the Sonnet to celebrate the wedding of Southampton and Elizabeth Vernon in *Shakespeare's Sonnets*, pp. 201–2. His reviewer, Robert Bell, disagrees: 'Mr. Massey could hardly have been more unfortunate had he picked out as an epithalamium one of the Sonnets on Death. The witness he has called into court answers in an opposite direction. There is absolutely nothing relating to marriage, or remotely suggestive of marriage, in the sonnet from beginning to end, except the word "marriage" in the first line, and there it is used in a figurative sense', *Fortnightly Review* 5 (August 1866). This is a contention that still rages about Sonnet 116.

[153] Dellamora, *Masculine Desire*, p. 2.

[154] The classic account is John Ruskin's praise of Shakespeare's perfect women in *Sesame and Lilies* (1865).

[155] Hunt and Lee, *The Book of the Sonnet*, pp. 160–1.

in combination with a strength of passion and fervour of attachment belonging to manliest manhood.'[156] But if the Sonnets praised women at the expense of confining them to this role of patient constancy, they also provoked reactions which revealed how limited and contingent this understanding of the female heart was.

Gail Marshall's study, *Shakespeare and Victorian Women*, demonstrates 'the enormous variety of ways in which Victorian women read, quoted, responded to, argued with and countered Shakespeare', creating 'a space in Victorian's women's culture … characterised by discursive, interrogative energy'.[157] Two of the authors Marshall goes on to discuss, Elizabeth Barrett Browning and George Eliot, recur here, but I will focus specifically on their engagements with the Sonnets. For both women, identification with Shakespeare as a sonneteer facilitates their self-definition as authors and their acceptance into the literary canon.[158] At the same time, their personal readings of the Sonnets reveal a sense that to love like Shakespeare is not everything: the Sonnets give only a partial account of the love experienced by women which no male author, even Shakespeare, can fully express.

Elizabeth Barrett Browning's early sonnets were largely indebted to those of Wordsworth, with their characteristic themes of freedom and limitation.[159] *Sonnets from the Portuguese* (1850), however, is more Shakespearean. The sequence includes trochaic inversion ('Shall I compare thee'/'How do I love thee?') and a pleasure in chiasmus ('and love so wrought/May be unwrought') which are both familiar from the Sonnets. There are also particular debts, including allusions to those two Romantic staples, 64 and 116.[160] The latter concentrates its influence in Sonnet 11 through the simple verb 'bend' ('Or bends with the remover to remove'), when the speaker offers a more contingent expression of loving constancy; if only God were willing, 'Men could not part us with their worldly jars,/ Nor the seas change us, nor the tempests, bend' (2.10–11). Sonnet XXII takes the despair of Sonnet 64, in the encroaching of the 'hungry ocean' upon the shore, and transforms it into something more like Lear's prison:

---

[156] Quoted by Thompson and Roberts in *Women Reading Shakespeare 1660–1900*, p. 102.

[157] Marshall, *Shakespeare and Victorian Women*, p. 4.

[158] Other women writers who incorporated allusions to the Sonnets in their work are Emily Brontë, who borrows from Sonnets 27 and 29 in 'To Imagination' (1844), and Christina Rossetti who borrows from Sonnet 71 in 'Remember me' (1872). For further discussion, see Edmondson and Wells, *Shakespeare's Sonnets*, pp. 147–51.

[159] See Phelan, *Nineteenth-Century Sonnet*, pp. 49–52.

[160] I am indebted here to Josie Billington's revisionary work, *Elizabeth Barrett Browning and Shakespeare*, pp. 68–81. As well as 64 and 116, she detects traces of Sonnets 36, 47, 53, 56 and 71, to which I would add 20 ('Which steals men's eyes') in Sonnet XII.

> Let us stay
> Rather on earth, Beloved – where the unfit
> Contrarious moods of men recoil away
> And isolate pure spirits, and permit
> A place to stand and love in for a day,
> With darkness and the death-hour rounding it.
>
> (9–14)

But perhaps the most intriguing means by which Shakespeare's Sonnets support Barrett Browning's work is through their speaker's abjection.

Angela Leighton notes a 'language of self-abasement that is paradoxically proud' in *Sonnets from the Portuguese*. The poet 'clings with proud tenacity to the role of loving rather than of being loved', but '[this] newfound right to love was also a right to claim the object of that love for her poetry'.[161] I would suggest that Barrett Browning was influenced here by Shakespeare's Sonnets, whose abject poetic persona sets a precedent for the Victorian female poet who nevertheless asserts her claims to posterity.[162] In Sonnet 32, the speaker stresses his poetic and personal unworthiness but defends his affection: 'And though [my poems] be outstripped by every pen,/ Reserve them for my love, not for their rhyme' (7). In Sonnet x, Barrett Browning's speaker similarly distinguishes her personal unworthiness from the value of her love:

> Yet, love, mere love, is beautiful indeed
> And worthy of acceptation …
> And what I *feel*, across the inferior features
> Of what I *am*, doth flash itself, and show
> How that great work of Love enhances Nature's.
>
> (1–2, 12–13)

It seems a small step from this appropriation of the Sonnets to an identification with Shakespearean loving, and this occurs through the figure of Aurora Leigh, who asserts:

> … God has made me – I've a heart
> That's capable of worship, love, and loss;
> We say the same of Shakespeare's. I'll be meek
> And learn to reverence, even this poor myself.
>
> (*Aurora Leigh* (1856), 7.734–7)[163]

---

[161] Ibid., pp. 94–5.

[162] Tricia Lootens argues that Barrett Browning's career 'could be read as one long succession of attempts to accommodate – and to alter – the shape of feminine literary canonicity' in *Lost Saints*, p. 121.

[163] Ruskin praised *Aurora Leigh* (1856) in a letter to Robert Browning as 'the greatest poem in the English language: unsurpassed by anything but Shakespeare – not surpassed by Shakespeare[']s

David Morse notes the 'subtle yet powerful irony' here, given that 'for the Victorians meekness in a woman meant submission to her husband, and most emphatically not any subservient desire to reverence herself'.[164] Aurora's capacity to love like Shakespeare supports her ambition to write like him.

For later critics, Barrett Browning's kind of loving would enable her to equal and even to triumph over Shakespeare. G. B. Smith, writing for the *Cornhill Magazine* 29 (January–June 1874), notes that 'The same large-heartedness which pertained to the great dramatist is shown by the later poet', and he singles out Sonnet 11 as 'a description of love, whose power nothing can conquer, and which man is helpless to destroy'.[165] By 1894, and on the eve of the Oscar Wilde trials, Edmund Gosse would praise Barrett Browning's Sonnets at the expense of Shakespeare's:

> her sympathy with a universal passion, the freshness and poignancy with which she treats a mood that is not rare and almost sickly, not foreign to the common experience of mankind, but eminently normal, direct, and obvious, give her a curious advantage. It is probable that the sonnets written by Shakespeare to his friend contain lovelier poetry and a style more perennially admirable, but those addressed by Elizabeth Barrett to her lover are hardly less exquisite to any of us, and to many of us are more wholesome and more intelligible.[166]

Yet if Gosse tacitly alludes to the queerness of the Sonnets here, he requires those same Sonnets to express the heterosexual norm. As he celebrates the nuptial conclusion of Barrett Browning's sequence, he observes that 'We may pursue no further, save in the divine words of the sonnets themselves, the record of this noble and exquisite "marriage of true minds"'.[167] There is a poignant irony in the fact that the state depicted by Barrett Browning is not summarised in her 'divine words', but rather those of Sonnet 116. Nevertheless, Gosse's quotation reminds us that individual Sonnets (and perhaps this one in particular) could transcend the suspicion and/or moral distaste that might linger around Shakespeare's *Sonnets* as a collection.

---

sonnets – & therefore the greatest poem in the language'. Letter of 27 November 1856, reproduced and transcribed at http://digitalcollections.baylor.edu/cdm/ref/collection/ab-letters/id/30203, accessed 15 March 2017. Jane Wood finds an echo of Sonnet 130 in Aurora's description of Marian Erle's unconventional beauty (3.808–25) in 'Elizabeth Barrett Browning and Shakespeare's Sonnet 130', 79. For discussion of Aurora Leigh's engagement with Shakespeare more generally, see Marshall, *Shakespeare and Victorian Women*, pp. 49–52, 54–5.

[164] Morse, *High Victorian Culture*, p. 27.
[165] *Cornhill Magazine*, pp. 475, 486.
[166] 'The Sonnets from the Portuguese' (1894), reprinted in Gosse, *Critical Kit-Kats*, pp. 1–17, 10.
[167] Ibid., p. 16.

More generally, Barrett Browning's superiority to Shakespeare would be built on her poetic expression of a love that the poet could never know, namely maternal love.[168] Aurora Leigh had expressed her ambition to 'speak my poems' in tune

> With the human heart's large seasons, when it hopes
> And fears, joys, grieves, and loves? – with all that strain
> Of sexual passion, which devours the flesh
> In a sacrament of souls? With mother's breasts
> Which, around the new-made creatures hanging there,
> Throb luminous and harmonious like pure spheres?
> With multitudinous life …
>
> (5.13–19)

In 1865, the critic Hannah Lawrance – who had written elsewhere of the neglect of motherhood in history and in literature[169] – praised this aspect of Barrett Browning's poetry, in particular 'The Virgin Mary to the Child Jesus', to the implied detriment of Shakespeare. She writes:

> Looking back to other poetry, we are surprised to find how little we have really seen of the female heart. Many, like Byron, care only to set before us a lovely ideal beauty, flashing like a meteor across the eye of youth – the source of a moment's wild delirious joy, and fading then unnoticed, or leaving behind the blackness of a fierce and moody despair. Or we are told of woman's tenderness or her fickleness. We see her now worshipped as an angel, and now cursed as if almost a fiend.[170]

Lawrance makes no reference to the Sonnets here – she refers only to Shakespeare's depiction of women in his plays, which she finds praiseworthy but limited by the demands of dramatic representation.[171] Nevertheless, the stereotyping of woman as either angel or fiend recalls Sonnet 144, 'And whether that my angel be turned fiend', though there the fickle mistress threatens to make a fiend out of the angelic male.[172] If this echo is merely coincidental, it is a salutary reminder of how little the Dark Lady Sonnets were read until the early twentieth century. But if Lawrance did not, as

---

[168] See Lootens' discussion of Barrett Browning's maternalism as an essential part of her canonisation, *Lost Saints*, pp. 141–2.

[169] See Wilkes, *Women Reviewing Women*, p. 63.

[170] *British Quarterly Review* 42 (October 1865), pp. 359–84, 359–60.

[171] Ibid., p. 360.

[172] Ibid. Sonnet 144 is the other Sonnet to which Dickens referred numerous times, most particularly in *David Copperfield* (1850) where it defines the relationship between David, Steerforth and Little Emily, and between David, Steerforth and Agnes. Gager suggests that this allusion adds another layer to David's professed love for Steerforth: 'No one can have loved him better, no one can hold him in dearer remembrance than I', *Shakespeare and Dickens*, p. 363.

yet, know the Sonnets, she implies that Barrett Browning would have surpassed Shakespeare if he had attempted to represent woman's emotional life in lyric form:

> There is much in woman that is incapable of outward dramatic display – feelings which lie concealed in the inmost depths of the heart, and which none but a woman and a genius can express. Who else can tell what passes in her thought while she nurses the world of the future in her arms?[173]

In the following year, Lawrance would engage directly with Shakespeare's Sonnets and try to find there, if not maternal feeling, then at least an image of maternal beauty.

In an article entitled 'Shakespeare in Domestic Life', which is ostensibly a review of Massey's book on the Sonnets, Lawrance strives to present a Shakespeare more in line with Victorian ideals of familial love. She argues that Shakespeare left Stratford for London, not because of any disgrace, but to provide for his young family:

> On his first arrival, Shakespeare was doubtless alone and amidst all the stir and excitement of London scenes, would not his thoughts often dwell upon the pleasant cottage at Shottery, and Anne with the twins on her knee, and little Susanna nestling close beside her? And then, might not that loveliest of his sonnets have been poured forth in unpremeditated sweetness?
>
> > When in disgrace with Fortune, and men's eyes,
> > I all alone beweep my outcast state …[174]

Lawrance's sense that there is something missing – not only in Shakespeare's affective capacity (she is forced to explain why, unlike Ben Jonson, he wrote no sonnets for his dead son), but in his poetic canon – produces this reading of Sonnet 29. But her sense that the Sonnets were lacking in this way would be taken up by another Victorian writer, who was also often praised for her kinship with Shakespeare: George Eliot.

Eliot's diary tells us that she 'read through all Shakspeare's sonnets' on 31 July 1869, the same day that she completed her sonnet sequence, 'Brother and Sister'.[175] In fact, she had become acquainted with at least 'some of the *Sonnets*' and *The Passionate Pilgrim* as early as March 1855.[176] Reflecting back on the achievement of 'Brother and Sister' in a letter to her publisher,

[173] *British Quarterly Review*, p. 360.
[174] Lawrance, 'Mrs Browning's Poetry', 81–109, 99.
[175] Eliot, *The Journals of George Eliot*, p. 137. See also Eliot, *The Complete Shorter Poetry*, pp. 1–2.
[176] See the entry for 16 March 1855 in Eliot, *The Journals of George Eliot*, p. 54.

John Blackwood, of 2 April 1874, she seems to justify her preference for the topic of sibling love over Shakespearean *eros*:

> That picnic of the young ones to Strathtyrum was very pretty, and a good enough subject for a poem. I hope that the brother and sister love each other very dearly: life might be so enriched if that relation were made the most of, as one of the highest forms of friendship. A good while ago I made a poem, in the form of eleven sonnets after the Shakspeare type, on the childhood of a brother and a sister—little descriptive bits on the mutual influences in their small lives. This was always one of my best loved subjects.[177]

Eliot's resistance to the Sonnets' kind of loving may be detected in the first two lyrics of 'Brother and Sister' in which the former's conceits are transplanted into new soil. The opening line of Sonnet 1, for example, reads 'I cannot choose but think upon the time/ When our two lives grew like two buds that kiss'. Eliot's nostalgia for sibling love gains some of its melancholy from the echo of Sonnet 64, 'This thought is as a death which cannot choose/ But weep to have that which it fears to lose', though in this case their estrangement is partly the natural process of growing up. Sonnet 11 begins with another possible allusion, 'Long years have left their writing on my brow' recalling Sonnet 19, in which the lover pleads with Time: 'O, carve not with thy hours my love's fair brow.' But rather than focus on fleeting personal beauty, Eliot emphasises the eternal beauty of Nature which transports the subject back in time: 'The bunched cowslip's pale transparency/ Carries that sunshine of sweet memories,/ And wild-rose branches take their finest scent/ From those blest hours of infantine content.' Where Shakespeare, and Romantic admirers such as Keats, had used the natural landscape to reflect the beloved's beauty (for example, in Sonnet 98), Eliot rejects adult vanity in favour of a more innocent, mutual passion.

If 'Brother and Sister' was in some ways a reaction against Shakespeare's Sonnets, so too was *Middlemarch* (1871–2). Eliot began the novel, or at least 'The Vincy and Featherstone parts', on 2 August 1869, two days after having 'read through all Shakespeare's Sonnets',[178] and in the Notebook entries for 1869–72, which cover the composition of *Middlemarch* through to its publication, we find a wide-ranging discussion of the Sonnets with reference to no less than forty-six poems.[179] This reading manifests itself in

---

[177] Eliot, *The George Eliot Letters*, vol. 5, p. 403.
[178] Eliot, *The Journals of George Eliot*, p. 137.
[179] These are 2, 5, 18, 19, 22, 23, 27–30, 32–4, 43, 50, 54, 55, 57–9, 62, 64, 66, 68, 71–3, 76, 79, 81, 86, 87, 90, 91, 93, 94, 96–8, 102, 104, 106, 107, 109, 116, 128. Like Wordsworth and nineteenth-century anthologists, Eliot shows no interest in the Dark Lady sonnets, although she notes the unusual stress on 'envy' in Sonnet 128. Eliot, *Middlemarch Notebooks*, p. 210.

Middlemarch in the use of chapter epigraphs taken from Sonnets 34, 93 and 50,[180] and extends to subtler allusions embedded in the text. Yet although in the Notebooks Eliot praises some individual lines and discrete lyrics – Sonnet 22 ('My glass shall not persuade me I am old') is 'an exquisite utterance of love'; Sonnet 23 ('As an unperfect actor on the stage') has a 'fine ending'[181] – her prevailing emotional response is one of irritation. Only twenty-four Sonnets are really worth reading, '& some of these one lingers over rather for the music of a few verses in them than for their value as wholes'.[182] The rest are 'artificial products', imitations of Italian poets, whose current standing is attributable to 'the imaginations of writers who set out with the notion that Shakespeare was in all things exceptional, & so never think of comparison with contemporaries even when the occasion is thrust upon them'.[183] Structurally, she finds a number of defects; for example, 'The final couplet, which in this form of sonnet should be the satisfactory completion of the climax, is often feeble'.[184] Moreover, unlike Barrett Browning, Eliot is openly offended by the effeminate posture of the speaker. She dislikes Sonnets 58 and 57 for being 'painfully abject … adopt[ing] language which might be taken to describe the miserable slavery of oppressed wives'.[185]

Eliot's relationship to Shakespeare's plays has been characterised as 'at times … fundamentally cautious, even suspicious and rebarbative', 'divided between admiration and suspicion',[186] and her response to the Sonnets shares this ambivalence. More specifically, she identifies points of difference between herself and Shakespeare on affairs of the heart. *Middlemarch* is famously critical of the early modern style of loving which produced the sonnet,[187] and although Shakespeare is not named as an offending poet (unlike Samuel Daniel), there are hints that Eliot had him in mind. 'The

---

[180] On the use of epigraphs in Eliot's work generally, see Ginsburg, 'Pseudonym, Epigraphs and Narrative Voice', and Higdon, 'George Eliot and the Art of the Epigraph'.

[181] Eliot, *Middlemarch Notebooks*, p. 212. On the quotation of this sonnet in *Middlemarch* and *Felix Holt*, chapter 27, see Novy, *Engaging with Shakespeare*, p. 84, and Marshall, *Shakespeare and Victorian Women*, pp. 115–16.

[182] Eliot, *Middlemarch Notebooks*, p. 213.

[183] Ibid., p. 213.

[184] Ibid., p. 212.

[185] Ibid., p. 211.

[186] Marshall, *Shakespeare and Victorian Women*, p. 100; Poole, *Shakespeare and the Victorians*, pp. 132, 133.

[187] For further discussion, see Knoepflmacher, 'Fusing Fact and Myth', and Sircy, ' "The Fashion of Sentiment" ', who observes that 'the sonnets are not a product of an aesthetic [Eliot] trusts, nor are they reflections of a reality with which she can sympathize', 225.

sonneteers of the sixteenth century' are blamed for Casaubon's belief that by marriage

> he should receive family pleasures and leave behind him that copy of himself which seemed so urgently required of a man ... Times had altered since then, and no sonneteer had insisted on Mr Casaubon's leaving a copy of himself; moreover, he had not yet succeeded in issuing copies of his mythological key.[188]

To a well-trained ear like that of Eliot, 'copy' and 'issue' probably recalled both Sonnet 11, in which Nature intends 'Thou shouldst print more, not let that copy die', and Sonnet 13, which insists that 'your sweet issue your sweet form should bear'. Moreover, the repeated praise of the beloved in the procreation sonnets – described by Eliot as 'that wearisome series'[189] – sharpens the irony of Casaubon's identification with Shakespeare's Fair Youth, given that he has no beauty to be distilled.

Where Eliot's invocation of the Sonnets starts to sound more critical of those poems is in the discussion of Peter Featherstone, who *has* managed to make a copy of himself. In acknowledging the objections of Middlemarch society that 'low people' reproduce, the narrator observes:

> It would be well, certainly, if we could help to reduce their number, and something might perhaps be done by not lightly giving occasion to their existence. Socially speaking, Joshua Rigg, would have been generally pronounced a superfluity. But those who like Peter Featherstone never had a copy of themselves demanded, are the very last to wait for such a request either in prose or verse.[190]

The absurdity of the old man's being placed in the role of Sonnet beloved reaffirms the irrelevance of sonnets to the modern world. However, there may also be a comment on the snobbery that underpins Shakespeare's sequence in particular, for example, Sonnet 1 begins 'From fairest creatures we desire increase ...'; Sonnet 11 proposes: 'Let those whom nature hath not made for store,/ Harsh, featureless, and rude, barrenly perish.'

Eliot's explicit critique of the Sonnets in *Middlemarch* centres on their false idea of beauty, which is in turn related to their narrow conception of love.[191] Chapter 58, which details Lydgate's revelation to Rosamond of their

---

[188] Eliot, *Middlemarch*, p. 293.
[189] Eliot, *Middlemarch Notebooks*, p. 212.
[190] Eliot, *Middlemarch*, p. 436.
[191] For an alternative reading of *Middlemarch*'s use of the Sonnets, which examines the possibilities for erotic fulfilment and self-expression available in the Sonnets but denied to women in the novel, see Siegel, ' "This thing I like my sister may not do" '. I would disagree with the reading of the Sonnets that partly underpins this interpretation, most notably Siegel's assertion that 'The first 126 sonnets offer an ideal model for a woman who wants to love without losing power, because the

serious financial difficulties, and her response, begins with the following extract from Sonnet 93:

> For there can live no hatred in thine eye,
> Therefore in that I cannot know thy change:
> In many's looks the false heart's history
> Is writ in moods and frowns and wrinkles strange;
> But Heaven in thy creation did decree
> That in thy face sweet love should ever dwell;
> Whate'er thy thoughts or thy heart's workings be,
> Thy looks should nothing thence but sweetness tell.[192]

Where Shakespeare's speaker seems on the brink of seeing behind the mask but shrinks from the truth, Eliot forces Lydgate through a devastating epiphany as he discovers how cold, intransigent and selfish Rosamond is. Yet her beauty continues to disguise her rebellion against and even hatred of her husband: 'Rosamond was arranging her hair before dinner and the reflection of her head in the glass showed no change in its loveliness except a little turning aside of the long neck'; '[she] was silent and did not smile again, but the lovely curves of her face looked good tempered enough without smiling'.[193] We might be reminded here of Sonnet 94, 'They that have pow'r to hurt and will do none', which Eliot had singled out in her Notebooks. Its bitterly ambivalent praise of those who 'moving others are themselves as stone', 'the lords and owners of their faces', stands as a further judgement on Rosamond's proud, unruffled surface.

By contrast, true beauty in Eliot's novels is defined by kindness and sympathy,[194] qualities which are specifically linked to maternal love. In *Adam Bede* (1859), the narrator observes that

> it is more than a woman's love that moves us in a woman's eyes – it seems to be a far-off mighty love that has come near to us … The rounded neck, the dimpled arm, move us by something more than their prettiness – by their close kinship with all we have known of tenderness and peace.[195]

The implication that female beauty takes us back to our first infant experience of love is explored further by Judith Mitchell who finds a distinction

---

love between men portrayed in the sonnets takes place in a sort of emotional meritocracy where the lover with the most passion and artistry in its expression can prevail', 49. Nevertheless, the analogies she draws between Will Ladislaw and Shakespeare's Fair Youth are intriguing.

[192] Eliot, *Middlemarch*, p. 614.

[193] Ibid., pp. 618, 616.

[194] For a useful introduction to the importance of sympathy in Eliot's work, see Anger, 'George Eliot and Philosophy'.

[195] Eliot, *Adam Bede*, p. 400.

in Eliot's novels between true and false female beauty, the former combining 'reluctant sexual receptivity and "the mother's yearning, that completest type of the life in another life which is the essence of real human love" '.[196] Women like Dinah and Dorothea are those 'whose beauty signifies what it is supposed to signify, a sort of maternal loving-kindness'.[197]

As stated above, Eliot began the Vincy portions of *Middlemarch* immediately after reading Shakespeare's Sonnets, and another chapter epigraph taken from Sonnet 34 relates to Fred.[198] These beautiful but flawed siblings seem to be connected in Eliot's mind with Shakespeare's beautiful but flawed addressee, and just as Sonnet 2 was easily redirected to a woman in the seventeenth century, so Eliot is able to adapt the Sonnets to either sibling. Where identification of female beauty with maternal love comes to the fore is in Eliot's description of Mrs Vincy. At the beginning of the novel, she instructs a servant to tell her indolent son that 'it has struck half-past ten':

> This was said without any change in the radiant good-humour of Mrs Vincy's face, in which forty-five years had delved neither angles nor parallels; and pushing back her pink cap-strings, she let her work rest on her lap, while she looked admiringly at her daughter.[199]

Where Sonnets 2 and 60 had imagined the sad degradation of beauty ('When forty winters shall besiege thy brow,/ And dig deep trenches ...'; '[Time] ... delves the parallels in beauty's brow'), Mrs Vincy seems proof of the contrary, and the preservation of her beauty is implicitly attributed to maternal love. This is not the self-love of the Sonnets, in which to produce a child is to secure one's own immortality, but a loving nurturance, which continues to shape the child in adulthood. Mrs Vincy's sensitivity to Fred's needs in his illness produces another Sonnet allusion:

> No word pressed his lips; but 'to hear with eyes belongs to love's rare wit', and the mother in the fullness of her heart not only divined Fred's longing, but felt ready for any sacrifice in order to satisfy him. 'If I can only see my boy strong again', she said, in her loving folly.[200]

Shakespeare's Sonnet distinguishes between the inadequate verbal performance of love and its written articulation, imploring the beloved 'to

[196] Mitchell, 'George Eliot and the Problematic of Female Beauty', 19.
[197] Ibid., 21.
[198] Eliot's use of this Sonnet is discussed further in my article, 'The Failure of Shame in Shakespeare's Sonnets'.
[199] Eliot, *Middlemarch*, p. 99.
[200] Ibid., p. 279.

hear with eyes' by reading the poem. Eliot moves beyond the limits of the 'reading eye', using the novel to explore how 'the eyes become a channel that can both hear and speak, that can even surpass the limitations of language, and certainly the formal limits of the sonnet'.[201] But if this quotation implies a *paragone* between sonnet and novel, it also rebukes the narrowness of that love with which the Sonnets are absorbed. Kate Flint has shown how 'the figure of the mother is a key one in George Eliot's writing … She invested the role of motherhood with sacredness, representing the highest form of duty of which most women were capable'.[202] This idealisation seems to have intensified in 1869, when Eliot wrote that 'in proportion as I profoundly rejoice that I never brought a child into a world, I am conscious of having an unused stock of motherly tenderness which sometimes overflows'.[203] This maternal feeling arguably does spill out into Eliot's reading of the Sonnets in *Middlemarch*, even as it is produced by their worship of false – because unsympathetic – beauty. It is no surprise perhaps that the other Sonnet Eliot commends in the Notebooks, no. 22, is one in which the speaker promises to 'bear … thy heart so chary,/ As tender nurse her babe from faring ill'.

What George Eliot notably avoids in her reading of the Sonnets, as both critic and novelist, is a biographical approach. In a letter of 1879 she would aver: 'Biographies generally are a disease of English literature',[204] and she turned down the opportunity to write one for Shakespeare.[205] This seems to have left her free to judge the way in which love is represented in the Sonnets without requiring that it be consistent with an icon of Shakespeare to which she was herself emotionally attached. In stark contrast was Oscar Wilde, whose exploration of the way in which Shakespeare loved would become personally disastrous, as the rest of this chapter will consider.

Oscar Wilde and Shakespeare's Secret Love

Most people are other people. Their thoughts are someone else's opinions, their life a mimicry, their passions a quotation … Out of Shakespeare's

---

[201] Marshall, *Shakespeare and Victorian Women*, p. 116.
[202] Flint, 'George Eliot and Gender', p. 165.
[203] Eliot, *Letters*, vol. 5, p. 52, quoted by Zimmerman, 'The Mother's History', p. 86. For further discussion of Eliot's appropriation of maternal imagery to describe her writing career, and of her later reinvention as a non-biological mother, see Williams, *George Eliot, Poetess*, pp. 107–34, and Bodenheimer, *The Real Life of Mary Ann Evans*, pp. 161–88.
[204] Eliot, *Letters*, vol. 7, p. 230.
[205] See Marshall, *Shakespeare and Victorian Women*, p. 110.

sonnets, they draw, to their own hurt it may be, the secret of his love and make it their own.[206]

Apprehensive of such damage, Wilde would sometimes find it necessary to pretend there was only a superficial, stylistic resemblance between his work and Shakespeare's Sonnets. At the libel trial of 1895, Edward Carson read aloud a passage from *The Picture of Dorian Gray* (1890) in which Basil Hallward admits to having 'adored' Dorian 'madly, extravagantly, absurdly'. When Carson asked Wilde if he had ever 'had that feeling that you depict there?', Wilde replied: 'No, it was borrowed from Shakespeare I regret to say ... from Shakespeare's sonnets.'[207] But more consistent with Wilde was the belief that Shakespeare's Sonnets could speak for him.[208] In a letter written to Lord Alfred Douglas in July 1894, Wilde implored him: 'Write me a line and take all my love – now and for ever. Always, and with devotion – but I have no words for how I love you. Oscar.'[209] Having no words, Wilde relies on the opening of Sonnet 40, 'Take all my loves, my love, yea take them all' – an ominous precedent for his relationship with Bosie, given the poem's conclusion: 'Lascivious grace, in whom all ill well shows,/ Kill me with spites; yet we must not be foes.' As in the case of Arthur Hallam and Tennyson, the language of the Sonnets may have been part of the dialogue between Wilde and Douglas. The latter's allegorical poem, 'Two Loves', published in the Oxford magazine *The Chameleon* the same year, implies a connection with Sonnet 144 ('Two loves I have of comfort and despair'), and its citation in the libel trial required that Wilde defend his own identification with the loving of Shakespeare's Sonnets:

> 'The love that dare not speak its name' in this century is such a great affection of an elder for a younger man as there was between David and Jonathan, such as Plato made the very basis of his philosophy, and such as you find in the sonnets of Michelangelo and Shakespeare. It is that deep, spiritual affection that is as pure as it is perfect. It dictates and pervades great works of art like those of Shakespeare and Michelangelo, and those two letters of mine, such as they are ... It is beautiful, it is fine, it is the noblest form of affection. There is nothing unnatural about it. It is intellectual, and it repeatedly exists between an elder and a younger man, when the elder man has intellect, and the younger man has all the joy, hope, and glamour of life before him.[210]

---

[206] Wilde, *De Profundis* (1897), in *The Collins Complete Works*, pp. 1030–1.
[207] Holland, *Irish Peacock & Scarlet Marquess*, pp. 87–92.
[208] Kate Chedgzoy has argued that 'Throughout his career ... Wilde invoked Shakespeare to legitimise the existence and representation of love between men', *Shakespeare's Queer Children*, p. 137.
[209] Wilde, *The Complete Letters of Oscar Wilde*, p. 594.
[210] Hyde, *Famous Trials 7: Oscar Wilde*, p. 201.

Ironically, it was Wilde's own earlier interrogation of the Sonnets, 'The Portrait of Mr W. H.', first published in *Blackwood's Edinburgh Magazine* in July 1889, that had made this kind of defence necessary.

'The Portrait of Mr W. H.' presents the theory of the 'very fascinating … very foolish … very heartless' Cyril Graham, who tries to persuade his older friend, Erskine, that the famous Mr W. H. was Willie Hughes, a boy-player with whom Shakespeare was infatuated and who inspired his play-writing. Having failed to find archival proof of Hughes' existence, Cyril commissions a painting which he passes off as original. When Erskine discovers the fraud, he is appalled and rejects the theory entirely, at which point Cyril commits suicide. The unnamed narrator who hears Erskine's tale now takes over the research and becomes increasingly convinced by Willie Hughes. He manages to persuade Erskine, only to lose all belief himself, at which point Erskine fakes his own suicide (he has really died of consumption) in a further martyrdom for the Willie Hughes cause.

Wilde's fiction was initially viewed merely as the vehicle for a critical theory. He proposed it for publication in *Blackwood's* because he had read 'some interesting articles on Shakespeare's Sonnets' in that journal, and because his story offered 'an entirely new view on the subject of the identity of the young man to whom the sonnets are addressed'.[211] 'Mr W. H.' would go on to be praised by contemporary reviewers, who 'discussed it not from the point of view of morality, or rather immorality, but in the first place from the point of view of Shakespearean criticism'.[212] But just as the reputation of the story subsequently darkened – Frank Harris would describe it as giving 'his enemies for the first time the very weapon they had been wanting'[213] – so within the story the narrator's initial enthusiasm ('I love theories about the Sonnets')[214] gives way to a sense of danger.

The implications of Shakespeare's passion for a poor player are approached with trepidation, whilst deploying the reassurance of the Wordsworthian metaphor:

> Who was that young man of Shakespeare's day who, without being of noble birth or even of noble nature, was addressed by him in terms of such passionate adoration that we can but wonder at the strange worship, and are almost afraid to turn the key that unlocks the mystery of the poet's heart?[215]

[211] Quoted by Schroeder, *Oscar Wilde*, p. 8. On Wilde's familiarity with scholarship on the Sonnets, see Jackson, 'Oscar Wilde and Shakespeare's Secrets', pp. 302–3.

[212] Schroeder, *Oscar Wilde*, pp. 12, 14–16.

[213] Harris, *Oscar Wilde*, pp. 80–1.

[214] Wilde, 'The Portrait of Mr. W. H.', p. 141.

[215] Ibid., p. 146.

These prospective fears are largely assuaged by the fiction that follows. The narrator repeatedly defines Hughes as a Muse: the boy's beauty is 'the very corner-stone of Shakespeare's art; the very source of Shakespeare's inspiration; the very incarnation of Shakespeare's dreams'.[216] Not only does the story refuse to reveal whether or not this love was sexually consummated, but the readings of individual Sonnets often obscure the moral and/or sexual sins alluded to in favour of aesthetic theory. Sonnet 54, for example, which arguably warns the addressee against betrayal ('O how much more doth beauty beauteous seem/ By that sweet ornament which truth doth give') is reinterpreted as 'Shakespeare invit[ing] us to notice how the truth of acting, the truth of visible presentation on the stage, adds to the wonder of poetry, giving life to its loveliness, and actual reality to its ideal form'.[217] Such re-readings reflect the novella's subordination of the Sonnets to Shakespeare's plays:

> To look upon [Mr W. H.] as simply the object of certain love-poems is to miss the whole meaning of the poems; for the art of which Shakespeare talks in the Sonnets is not the art of the Sonnets themselves, which indeed were to him but slight and secret things – it is the art of the dramatist to which he is always alluding.[218]

This does not mean that the narrator's theatrical allegorising is always positive, but it does consistently distract from the personal relationship between Shakespeare and Willie Hughes. In Sonnet 67 ('Ah, wherefore with infection should he live'), for example, there is some acknowledgement of the addressee's contamination, but as a condition of theatrical life: 'Shakespeare calls upon Willie Hughes to abandon the stage with its artificiality, its false mimic life of painted face and unreal costume, its immoral influences and suggestions, its remoteness from the true world of noble action and sincere utterance.'[219] Perhaps most innovative is Wilde's re-reading of Sonnet 94 as a general indictment of the actor:

> How well ... had Shakespeare drawn the temperament of the stage-player! Willie Hughes was one of those:
>
> > 'That do not do the thing they most do show,
> > Who, moving others, are themselves as stone.'

---

[216] Ibid., p. 146.

[217] Ibid., pp. 154–5. This reading only works if one ignores the next two lines which prioritise inner truth over external show: 'The rose looks fair, but fairer we it deem/ For that sweet odour which doth in it live.'

[218] Ibid., p. 146.

[219] Ibid., p. 155.

> He could act love, but could not feel it, could mimic passion without realising it.[220]

By focusing on Willie Hughes' heartlessness as an actor, the story is also able to suggest the impossibility of Shakespeare's fulfilment. He becomes the victim of a same-sex passion understood in reassuringly familiar, Petrarchan terms. But if the desire produced in Shakespeare by the figure of Willie Hughes is carefully circumscribed, the desire produced in the reader by Shakespeare's Sonnets is more threatening.

The story hints at the Sonnets' dubious reputation on at least two occasions, most notably when Erskine describes Cyril's endeavours:

> He went through all the Sonnets carefully, and showed, or fancied that he showed, that, according to his new explanation of their meaning, things that had seemed obscure or evil, or exaggerated, became clear and rational, and of high artistic import, illustrating Shakespeare's conception of the true relations between the art of the actor and the art of the dramatist.[221]

Obscurity was a familiar enough criticism of the Sonnets, but 'evil'? The term is quickly hurried over, but the possibility of one's being corrupted by the Sonnets persists, particularly through the novella's compulsive recurrence to Sonnet 20. This had been understood from the late eighteenth century onwards as one of the most potentially sinful of the Sonnets, inspiring in George Steevens both 'disgust and indignation'. In 'The Portrait of Mr W. H.', it provides the pun on 'Hews/Hughes',[222] and the phrase 'master-mistress' to describe the boy player,[223] but it clearly has a more extensive (repressed) influence on the story.[224] The Sonnet's description of 'A woman's face with nature's own hand painted' echoes in the portrait of Willie Hughes, which depicts a young man 'of quite extraordinary personal beauty, though evidently somewhat effeminate. Indeed, had it not been for the dress and the closely cropped hair, one would have said that the face, with its dreamy wistful eyes, and its delicate scarlet lips, was the face of a girl'.[225] The fact that Wilde would write another painting-centred,

---

[220] Ibid., p. 161.
[221] Ibid., p. 147.
[222] Ibid., p. 148.
[223] Ibid., p. 159.
[224] It may be significant that this is a Sonnet to which Douglas gave particular attention when he was trying to proclaim his innocence in the wake of the scandal. In his *Autobiography* (1919), he describes the ending of Sonnet 20 as a definitive and unconscious denial of any sexual interest in the youth: 'Obviously it never occurred to [Shakespeare] that anyone would put a bad interpretation on his love and adoration for "Master W. H."' (pp. 61–2). The perversity lies with those who misconstrue Shakespeare and Wilde.
[225] Wilde, 'The Portrait of Mr. W. H.', p. 140.

homoerotic fiction almost immediately after this in *The Picture of Dorian Gray* has perhaps understandably obscured Sonnet 20's influence on the short story. However, its first line, 'A woman's face with nature's own hand painted', which in Shakespeare's time would have referred to cosmetics and the statue created by Pygmalion, was widely misunderstood as referring to portraiture in the nineteenth century. In the 1850s, David Masson's unpublished *Autobiography of Shakespeare from his Thirty-fourth to his Thirty-ninth Year, Derived from his Sonnets* imagined just such a painting on the basis of Sonnet 20:

> Reclining on a chair, tearing his spaniel's neck with his ringed & ruffled hand from which he has just dropped a volume, is a youth in the first bloom of years, his forehead fair as a girls' [*sic*], although with manlier locks clustering round it, his eye-lids downcast so that their orbs are fringed, & the soft peach of his cheek first dimpling where it curls towards the small proud lip, & then rounding itself away in the white chin & throat.[226]

Not simply the evidence that supports a theory, the portrait comes to represent an intensified expression of the Sonnets itself, or more specifically their power to produce homoerotic desire; as the narrator remarks: 'I thought of the wonderful boy-actor, and saw his face in every line.'[227] It is perhaps unsurprising that Wilde gave so much attention to the cover design, commissioning from the artist Charles Ricketts (a possible model for Basil Hayward) a portrait of Willie Hughes as if by Clouet, which he subsequently pretended to find authentic.[228] For all that Coleridge had described Sonnet 20 as a 'purposed blind', which Wilde translates into a forged painting, there is nothing inauthentic about the desire it produces.

The 'danger' of the Sonnets is not only their production and dissemination of an idealised male beauty, but the bonds that they forge between men. 'The Portrait of Mr W. H.' had been partly generated by Wilde's romantic and sexual relationship with Robert Ross: 'the story is half yours, and but for you it would not have been written'.[229] Traces of these origins arguably persist in the textual intercourse between Cyril Graham, Erskine and the narrator. The furtiveness and secrecy with which they read and re-read the Sonnets, passionately avowing their devotion to an ideal that eludes them, might well have resonated in the homosexual subculture to which Wilde belonged. Kate Chedgzoy notes the way in which the Sonnets'

---

[226] Quoted by Schoenbaum, *Shakespeare's Lives*, p. 315.
[227] Wilde, 'The Portrait of Mr. W. H.', p. 154.
[228] Ellmann, *Oscar Wilde*, p. 281.
[229] Ibid.

private circulation is reconstructed 'in the image of the homosexual coterie publications with which Wilde was himself involved – magazines such as *The Spirit Lamp* and *The Chameleon*, and the collectively written work of homosexual pornography, *Teleny*'.[230] Moreover, the punishment meted out to both Cyril Graham and Erskine is suggestive. As Bruce R. Smith observes: 'The deaths of Cyril and Erskine imply that the fantasy of homosexual love could not be tolerated in Victorian society. "I believe there is something fatal about the idea", Erskine confesses to the narrator.'[231] But if the Sonnets are the medium for this homoerotic encounter, they are hardly innocent, producing endless, elusive images of Willie Hughes for the reader to 'break his heart over',[232] and creating a sexually charged intimacy with even Shakespeare himself: 'I felt as if I had my hand upon Shakespeare's heart, and was counting each separate throb and pulse of passion.'[233]

Thus, Wilde's own work had made it untenable to use the Sonnets as an alibi. Despite his impassioned defence of the love of Plato, Michelangelo and Shakespeare in court, Carson countered with 'The Portrait of Mr. W. H.', which he described as 'an article pointing out that Shakespeare's sonnets were practically sodomitical'.[234] When Wilde was found guilty of gross indecency and sentenced to two years' hard labour, the Sonnets were found guilty with him. But they may always have spoken to Wilde about his secret love. In the expanded version of 'Mr W. H.' (*c.* 1889, pub. 1921), the narrator wonders that 'A book of Sonnets, published nearly three hundred years ago, written by a dead hand and in honour of a dead youth, had suddenly explained to me the whole story of my soul's romance'.[235] Wilde's mistake was to think that they might any longer redeem it publicly – that they would not 'do the thing they most do show'.

[230] Chedgzoy, *Shakespeare's Queer Children*, p. 144.
[231] Smith, 'Shakespeare's Sonnets', pp. 21–2.
[232] Wilde, 'The Portrait of Mr. W. H.', p. 152.
[233] Ibid., p. 154.
[234] Holland, *Irish Peacock & Scarlet Marquess*, p. 93.
[235] Wilde, 'The Portrait of Mr. W. H', expanded edition, in *The Collins Complete Works*, p. 344.

CHAPTER 5

A Waste of Shame, 1901–1997

in a waste of shame (1) in a shameful waste, in a waste that is shameful (suggesting both that to waste spirit is a shame on general principles and that this particular action is shameful; the phrase charges both lack of economy and positive misbehaviour); (2) an action that isn't worth the shame it entails (note 'the act of shame' in *Oth* V.ii.214). Ingram and Redpath hesitantly suggest 'the possibility of an image of vital energy squandered in a desert of shame'; they cite *Ham* v. ii.198, 'In the dead waste and middle of the night,' as a possible Shakespearian use of 'waste' to mean 'wasteland'. Kokeritz (p.152) found a pun here on 'in a waist', which may be less farfetched than one's knowledge of anatomy would suggest; he cites Marston, *The Malcontent* II.v.89: ''Tis now about the immodest waist of night'; 'waist' suggests the region of the hips and crotch to Shakespeare in *Ham* II.II.231–35: – 'Then you live about her [Fortune's] waist, or in the middle of her favours? – Faith, her privates, we.' – 'In the secret parts of Fortune? O, most true; she is a strumpet.'[1]

The hermeneutic abundance generated by just half of the opening line of Sonnet 129 ('Th'expense of spirit in a waste of shame') serves as an appropriate prologue to this final chapter on the twentieth century, because it would be inconceivable without the critical/creative innovations of that century. Laura Riding's and Robert Graves' work on Sonnet 129 in *A Survey of Modernist Poetry* (1927), influenced William Empson, and the development of New Criticism, both of which inform Stephen Booth's work in 1977.[2] The new century's Freudian interpretation of Shakespeare's sexual

---

[1] Booth, *Shakespeare's Sonnets*, p. 443.

[2] Booth's description of the movement backwards and forwards when reading is particularly Empsonian: 'a word or phrase can (and in the sonnets regularly does) have one meaning as a reader comes on it, another as its sentence concludes, and a third when considered from the vantage point of a summary statement in the couplet. The notes to this edition attempt to indicate not only what words mean but when they mean it; the notes try actively to discourage analyses that treat syntax as if it existed in a static state', p. x. For further discussion of Booth's extension of Empson's method, see Engle, 'William Empson and the Sonnets'.

desire and its relation to his creativity also presupposes that this Sonnet will require a substantial gloss.[3] In 1868, Rev. Richard Trench had anthologised Sonnet 129 as embodying Shakespeare's experience of 'the bitter delusion of all sinful pleasures, [and] the reaction of a swift remorse'.[4] By the second decade of the twentieth century, Shakespeare's repressed sexuality was becoming the mainspring of his literary work through the critical fictions of Frank Harris and James Joyce, and by 2005 'A Waste of Shame' stands for Shakespeare's life in its entirety.[5] Finally, Booth's overlaying of 'waste' and 'waist' reminds us of the infamous Dark Lady who potentially lingers behind this Sonnet and emerges more explicitly in 127–52. The early twentieth century sees the first sustained attention given to this sequence, so that for the first time in this book, two of the defining Sonnets of the period, 129 and 130 ('My mistress' eyes are nothing like the sun'), come from the Dark Lady sequence.

This chapter cannot attempt a comprehensive overview of the twentieth century's engagement with the Sonnets, given the huge editorial, critical and creative attention they have received. It can only offer a series of significant moments, and of individual acts of recollection and adaptation by some of the key writers of the twentieth century. It illuminates for the first time Wilfred Owen's hostility to the Sonnets as shaped by the experience of the First World War; the Sonnets' reinvention as essentially modernist by Laura Riding and Virginia Woolf; the fragmentation of the Quarto facilitated by William Empson and W. H. Auden; and Anthony Burgess' re-imagining of the Dark Lady as black, which anticipates the critical revision of the Sonnets' colour politics at the end of the century.

One of the most notable changes effected during this period is the stabilisation of the Sonnet canon: *The Passionate Pilgrim* lyrics no longer offer serious rivalry, and a proliferation of parodies and 'fakes' testifies to the authority and familiarity of individual Sonnets. The story that the Sonnets tell – the love-triangle between Shakespeare, a Fair Youth and a Dark Lady – is fleshed out in increasingly elaborate and ingenious ways by a novel tradition that produces not only Shakespeare novels, but 'Sonnet novels'. At the same time, a critical reaction against the biographical interpretation of the *Sonnets* underpins a more forensic approach to individual

---

[3] On the emergence of a psychosexual reading of Shakespeare's creativity at the beginning of the twentieth century, which anticipated the findings of Freud but was then extended by them, see DiPietro, *Shakespeare and Modernism*, ch. 2. On the denial of Shakespeare's sexuality until well into the eighteenth century, see Dobson, 'Bowdler and Britannia'.

[4] Trench, *A Household Book of English Poetry*, p. 392.

[5] See William Boyd's TV screenplay for the BBC4 *Shakespea(Re)Told* series.

Sonnets, which have become intricate devices producing a range of linguistic and emotional effects. But if by the end of the twentieth century, it is the Sonnets, rather than the plays, that seem to embody Shakespeare at his 'most romantic', this was an unlikely prospect in 1901, the year after Oscar Wilde's death, and this chapter begins with attempts to manage the aftermath of the Sonnets' notoriety through the newly conceived figure of the Dark Lady.

After Wilde: *Enter the* DARK LADY

One of Wilde's justifications for expanding 'The Portrait of Mr W. H.' was his consciousness of having 'not yet tackled the problem of the "dark woman"'.[6] Nevertheless, the revised text would depict this infatuation as an interlude rather than a climax: 'like a shadow or a thing of evil omen [she] came across Shakespeare's great romance, and for a season stood between him and Willie Hughes'.[7] Re-ordering the sequence, so that Sonnets 127–52 came between 33 and 40, Wilde imagined Shakespeare leaving London, and then returning to find that the Dark Lady's power had ebbed: 'Willie Hughes seems to have grown tired of the woman who for a little time had fascinated him. Her name is never mentioned again in the Sonnets, nor is there any allusion made to her.'[8] The sequence ends not with the Dark Lady or Cupid poems but with Sonnet 126 ('O thou my lovely boy'), whose abbreviated, twelve-line stanza symbolises 'the triumph of Beauty over Time, and of Death over Beauty'.[9]

In the years after Wilde's death, his friends continued to write about the Sonnets, as though continuing the debate at the heart of the 'Portrait'. But if this was a kind of memorialisation—the Sonnets acting as 'a medium through which his friends kept thinking about and talking to the fallen angel'[10] – it was also a form of censorship, displacing Wilde's homoerotic reading with one of extreme, yet still apparently normative, heterosexuality. Between 1909 and 1914, Wilde's friend and editor, Frank Harris, and his fellow dramatist and acquaintance, George Bernard Shaw, published a series of works which extended Wilde's challenge to the idealising tendencies of nineteenth-century literary biography through their attention to Shakespeare's sex life, whilst attempting to save him from scandal.

---

[6] Quoted by Schroeder, *Oscar Wilde*, p. 22.
[7] Wilde, 'The Portrait of Mr. W. H.' (1921), in *The Collins Complete Works*, p. 334.
[8] Ibid., p. 337.
[9] Ibid., p. 340.
[10] See Oya, 'Talk to Him', 23.

In his critical-biographical work, *The Man Shakespeare and His Tragic Life Story* (1909), Harris locates frustrated heterosexual desire at the heart of the Sonnets, which are at their most sincere in the Dark Lady sequence: 'when the deepest depth of us is stirred we cannot feign, or depict ourselves from the outside dispassionately; we can only cry our passion, our pain and our despair … that is the subject of the sonnets'.[11] The woman who produced this tragic effect Shakespeare 'picture[d] … to the life; strong, proud, with dark eyes and hair, [and] pale complexion', and her image recurs throughout the canon.[12] By contrast, Harris finds little trace of the Fair Youth:

> what is [he] like? – the 'master-mistress' of his passion, to give him the title which seems to have convinced the witless of Shakespeare's guilt. Not one word of description is to be found anywhere; no painting epithet – nothing. Where is the cry of this terrible, shameless, outrageous passion that mastered Shakespeare's conscience and enslaved his will? Hardly a phrase that goes beyond affection – such affection as Shakespeare at thirty-four might well feel for a gifted, handsome aristocrat like Lord Herbert, who had youth, beauty, wealth, wit to recommend him.[13]

Harris' dismissal of Sonnet 20's 'master-mistress', and his denial of any 'painting epithet', effect a particularly brutal rejection of Wilde's 'Portrait'.

When it comes to dramatising his theory in a play, Harris imagines the Dark Lady and Fair Youth in equally substantial terms, yet the singular object of desire indicated by his title, *Shakespeare and His Love* (c. 1903, pub. 1910), is the Dark Lady. The play follows the erotic structure of the supposed Sonnet narrative by triangulating desire, but this is initially between Shakespeare and two women – Violet Vernon and Mary Fitton – so that 'The dark lady … has her rival in the fair maid'.[14] As the Shakespeare-Fitton-Herbert liaison takes shape, its homoerotic potential is carefully negotiated by Shakespeare himself. In a reclamation of Sonnet 144 – queered by Lord Alfred Douglas' poem, 'Two Loves', and cited at Wilde's trial – Shakespeare tells Herbert: 'I had two idolatries – my friendship for you; I loved your youth and bravery! – And my passion for her, the queen and pearl of women.'[15] When questioned on his deathbed, Shakespeare admits that since he lost Mary 'it was always ill with me here about my heart', but the loss of Herbert 'didn't touch [me] so nearly'.[16]

---

[11] Harris, *The Man Shakespeare and His Tragic Life Story*, pp. 203–4.
[12] Ibid., pp. 236, 253.
[13] Ibid., pp. 236–7.
[14] Harris, *Shakespeare and His Love*, p. 78.
[15] Ibid., pp. 130–1.
[16] Ibid., pp. 172–3.

If Harris' plot rigorously polices the desire which the Sonnets depict, it also carefully restricts the desire that the Sonnets produce as a text in circulation among readers. In Wilde's narrative, the male love object inspires the Sonnets, which then generate erotic tension and textual intercourse between their male interpreters. By contrast, Harris' play insists that Shakespeare only writes love poetry for Mary, and the table book which contains his verse can only have found its way into Herbert's keeping as a mark of her betrayal.[17] This gift-exchange plot derives from the opening of Sonnet 122 ('Thy gift, thy tables, are within my brain …'), but Harris rejects the implied narrative of the poet receiving a gift (from his male patron?) which he then passed on (to a woman?) and once again straightens it out. The Sonnets have no business being in a man's bedchamber.

George Bernard Shaw would perform some similar manoeuvres in his comic skit, *The Dark Lady of the Sonnets*, performed at the Haymarket theatre, London, on 24 November 1910, and published in 1914. Here, Herbert is mentioned as the Dark Lady's lover and a writer of sonnets, but he never appears on stage. Rather, in a further substitution of female for male love object, Shaw brings in Queen Elizabeth as the mysterious lady Shakespeare stumbles upon in the dark. Whilst it was obviously more appropriate to a play written to support the case for a national theatre to have Shakespeare address a royal patron, the encounter with Elizabeth was already a kind of shorthand for the normalisation of Shakespeare's sexuality.[18] Although briefly distressed at the discovery of the Dark Lady's liaisons with Herbert, Shakespeare soon rallies, and his robust heterosexuality is affirmed by his flirtatious behaviour with Elizabeth: 'It is no fault of mine that you are a virgin, madam, albeit 'tis my misfortune.'[19] Furthermore, by emphasising her own transgressions against female chastity and her noble birth, the Dark Lady deflects attention away from Shakespeare's homosexual 'shame':

> THE DARK LADY: He hath swore to me ten times over that the day shall come in England when black women,[20] for all their foulness, shall be more thought on than fair ones … Oh, he is compact of lies and scorns. I am tired of being tossed up to heaven and dragged down to hell at every whim that takes him. I am ashamed to my very soul that I have abased myself to love

---

[17] Ibid., p. 125.

[18] See George Chalmers' theory discussed in the previous chapter, and also Hackett, *Shakespeare and Elizabeth*, pp. 15–16.

[19] Shaw, *The Dark Lady of the Sonnets*, p. 142.

[20] For an intriguing discussion of what happens if we take Shaw's 'black' here as a racial epithet, see Hunt, 'Be Dark but Not Too Dark', pp. 375–7, as discussed at the end of the chapter.

one that my father would not have deemed fit to hold my stirrup – one that will talk to all the world about me – that will put my love and my shame into his plays and make me blush for myself there – that will write sonnets about me that no man of gentle strain would put his hand to. I am all disordered: I know not what I am saying to your Majesty: I am of all ladies most deject and wretched.[21]

The Dark Lady's identification with Ophelia testifies to the ease with which the Sonnets play the understudy to *Hamlet* as Shakespeare's most auto-biographical work.[22] However, the Dark Lady's appeal to our sympathies is comparatively new and represents a significant intervention in Sonnet criticism. Although there is no mention of it in the play, the Sonnet most resonant to Shaw in developing this approach was 130:

> My mistress's eyes are nothing like the sun;
> Coral is far more red than her lips' red;
> If snow be white, why then her breasts are dun;
> If hairs be wires, black wires grow on her head;
> I have seen roses damasked red and white,
> But no such roses see I in her cheeks;
> And in some perfumes is there more delight
> Than in the breath that from my mistress reeks.
> I love to hear her speak, yet well I know
> That music hath a far more pleasing sound;
> I grant I never saw a goddess go;
> My mistress when she walks treads on the ground.
>> And yet, by heaven, I think my love as rare
>> As any she belied with false compare.

Harris had invoked this Sonnet in *The Man Shakespeare* as evidence of Shakespeare's romantic infatuation with the Dark Lady, such that 'he finds a method new to literature to describe her. He will have no poetic exagger-ation; snow is whiter than her breasts; violets sweeter than her breath: "And yet, by heaven, I think my love as rare/ As any she belied with false com-pare"'.[23] Shaw, however, uses it to demonstrate Shakespeare's irony:

> Mr Harris writes as if Shakespear did all the suffering and the Dark Lady all the cruelty. But why does he not put himself in the Dark Lady's place for a moment as he has put himself so successfully in Shakespear's? Imagine her reading the hundred and thirtieth sonnet! [quoted in full] Take this as a sample of the sort of compliment from which she was never for a

[21] Ibid., p. 143.
[22] See DiPietro, *Shakespeare and Modernism*, pp. 54–5.
[23] Harris, *The Man Shakespeare*, p. 236.

moment safe with Shakespear. Bear in mind that she was not a comedian; that the Elizabethan fashion of treating brunettes as ugly women must have made her rather sore on the subject of her complexion; that no human being, male or female, can conceivably enjoy being chaffed on that point in the fourth couplet about the perfumes ['the breath that from my mistress reeks']; that Shakespear's revulsions, as the sonnet immediately preceding shews ['Th'expense of spirit'], were as violent as his ardors, and were expressed with the realistic power and horror that makes Hamlet say that the heavens got sick when they saw the queen's conduct; and then ask Mr Harris whether any woman could have stood it for long, or have thought the 'sugred' compliment worth the cruel wounds, the cleaving of the heart in twain.[24]

But Shaw's plea to his readers to take the Dark Lady's part seems to have been ignored. Her next most influential critic would be James Joyce's Stephen Dedalus, whose extempore lecture on Shakespeare in the National Library of Dublin on 16 July 1904, takes up Shaw's idea of Shakespeare's sexual revulsion, but blames the woman.

The 'Scylla and Charybdis' scene of *Ulysses* (*c.* 1917, serialised 1918–20, pub. 1922) is explicitly indebted to the work of Wilde, Harris and Shaw, who are all name-checked in the debate.[25] More specifically, Stephen develops Harris' notion of an originary sexual wound, inflicted by the Dark Lady, which drives his creativity:

> The passion for [her] was the passion of Shakespeare's whole life. The adoration of her, and the insane desire of her, can be seen in every play he wrote from 1597 to 1608. After he lost her, he went back to her; but the wound of her frailty cankered and took on proud flesh in him, and tortured him to nervous breakdown and to madness.[26]

Where Harris preferred Mary Fitton, Stephen's Dark Lady is Anne Hathaway. She is the cause of Shakespeare's sexual self-doubt, first by seducing him as a young man (as recorded in *Venus and Adonis*), and then by cuckolding him with two of his brothers (see *Hamlet* and *Richard III*). Stephen uses the Sonnets to support this thesis by combining the Hathaway/'hate away' pun in Sonnet 145, with Sonnet 135's 'Whoever hath her wish, thou hast thy Will' to produce the line: 'If others have their

---

[24] Shaw, *The Dark Lady of the Sonnets*, Preface, pp. 118–19.
[25] See Joyce, *Ulysses*, pp. 251, 254.
[26] Harris, *The Man Shakespeare*, p. 253. Harris also identified Anne Hathaway as having a profound effect on Shakespeare's psychic development: 'His marriage is perhaps the first serious mistake that Shakespeare made, and it certainly influenced his whole life', pp. 361–2.

will Ann hath a way'.[27] Sonnet 152 ('In loving thee thou know'st I am for-sworn') supports his argument that the Dark Lady must be Anne rather than the 'court wanton', Mary Fitton, because only the former had broken a 'bed-vow'.[28] By this means, Stephen performs a similar sleight of hand to that of Harris and Shaw. He divides Shakespeare's desire between two (or more) women, thereby marginalising the homoerotic desire between two Wills. When Lyster invokes the Herbert-Fitton-Shakespeare theory, suggesting that 'if the poet must be rejected, such a rejection would seem more in harmony with – what shall I say? – our notions of what ought not to have been',[29] Stephen swerves away from this homoerotic theme,[30] to a question that had troubled Harris, namely why Shakespeare sent Herbert to woo for him:

> Why does he send to one who is a *buonaroba*, a bay where all men ride,[31] a maid of honour with a scandalous girlhood, a lordling to woo for him? He was himself a lord of language and had made himself a coistrel gentleman and had written *Romeo and Juliet*. Why? Belief in himself has been untimely killed. He was overborne in a cornfield first (ryefield I should say) and he will never be a victor in his own eyes after … No later undoing will undo the first undoing.[32]

Sexuality itself is the affliction created in Shakespeare by the Dark Lady, and so whatever other kind of desire the Sonnets might encode is subor-dinate to her crime.

This is not to say that the influence of the Sonnets in *Ulysses* is limited to the 'Scylla and Charybdis' episode. The love-triangle plot potentially underpins the relationship between Leopold, Molly Bloom and Blazes Boylan, as the former's meditation on this 'dark lady and fair man' implies.[33] But in general, the function of the Sonnets as plot material for Harris, Shaw and Joyce detracts from their being read as poetry. Harris has

---

[27] Joyce, *Ulysses*, p. 244. William Schutte adds Sonnet 143 as a possible source for the pun but acknow-ledges that it had appeared as early as 1792, in Charles Dibdin's 'A Love Dittie', in his novel *Hannah Hewit, or The Female Crusoe*, in *Joyce and Shakespeare*, p. 62.

[28] Joyce, *Ulysses*, p. 259.

[29] Ibid., p. 251.

[30] Stephen's reluctance here is consistent with his attitude throughout the novel: '[he] knows about homosexuality but wishes that he did not, reverting to the topic in his thoughts yet refusing to speak of it'. For further analysis of Stephen's *non sequiturs* and evasions in the discussion of Shakespeare's sexuality, see Lamos, *Deviant Modernism*, pp. 126, 142–50.

[31] This quotation from Sonnet 137 also appears in Harris's *The Man Shakespeare*, which Joyce had clearly consulted.

[32] Ibid., p. 251.

[33] See Michelle Burnham's suggestive essay, ' "Dark Lady and Fair Man" '.

Shakespeare recite some of the Sonnets' most familiar lines, declaring that 'in a true marriage the mind, I think, is more than the body' (Sonnet 116), and deploring his own decay: 'My summer is past! The leaves shake against the cold' (Sonnet 73).[34] But if the audience was supposed to recognise these as quotations, Shakespeare himself never writes a Sonnet or crafts a line.[35] Shaw's Shakespeare hastily scribbles down phrases from *Hamlet* and *Macbeth*, which the other characters throw out to him, but he is the only one who quotes the Sonnets, in a context that emphasises his solipsism and conceit: 'I have said that "not marble nor the gilded monuments of princes shall outlive" the words with which I make the world glorious or foolish at my will.'[36] In *Ulysses*, Stephen incorporates a few snatches from the Sonnets to support his biographical narrative, including the Quarto Dedication ('From only begetter to only begotten'), and Sonnets 2 and 3 ('youth's proud livery', 'uneared wombs'), but these merge into the ninety or so quotations from Shakespeare that make up his lecture.[37] And yet, if the emergence of the Dark Lady in the early twentieth century took the Sonnets down a biographical dead-end, the ongoing attractions of the Fair Youth (and Mr W. H. specifically) had the opposite effect.

After Wilde: *Manet* the FAIR YOUTH

Despite the efforts of Harris, Shaw and Joyce, the identification of male readers with the homoerotic desire generated within the Sonnets for Mr W. H. ensured that they continued to be read creatively decades after Wilde's disgrace. One such reader was Charles Scott Moncrieff, the translator of Proust's *A La Recherche du Temps Perdu* (1922), whose English title he would borrow, somewhat misleadingly, from Sonnet 30: 'When to the sessions of sweet silent thought/ I summon up remembrance of things past …' Moncrieff was a member of the literary circle in London dominated by Wilde's former lover, and the inspiration for Mr W. H., Robbie Ross. Into

---

[34] Most accurate is the borrowing from Sonnet 128 when Shakespeare tells Mary: 'How I envy even the dead things about you; the dress your body warms, the bracelets that clip your wrists; even the jacks that leap to kiss the tender inward of your hand', p. 74.

[35] The only lyric referred to as having been written in this book by Shakespeare is not a Sonnet, but Hamlet's love lyric to Ophelia: 'Doubt thou the stars are fire/ Doubt that the sun doth move …'.

[36] Shaw, *The Dark Lady of the Sonnets*, pp. 143–4. In Shaw's Preface, this quotation from Sonnet 55 is coupled with Sonnet 107: '[this] being only one out of a dozen passages in which he … proclaimed his place and power in "the wide world dreaming on things to come"', p. 120.

[37] See Schutte, *Joyce and Shakespeare*, p. 66.

this group in the summer of 1917 came Wilfred Owen. As his biographer, Dominic Hibberd, notes:

> The importance of Owen's friendship with Ross has not been generally understood. It was not only that 'Owen, the poet' was introduced to a number of talented literary people … but also that in getting to know Ross he came as near as was possible to knowing Wilde himself … As might be expected among Wilde's followers, there was much lively conversation about art and literature, and an assumption that the outside world was ignorant and wilfully 'deaf to truth'.[38]

It seems likely that Shakespeare's Sonnets were part of this 'lively conversation', for Moncrieff would subsequently write a number of Shakespearean-style sonnets to Owen, whom he described in a dedication as 'Mr W. O.'.[39] The first of these Sonnets was dated 19 March 1918, and begins:

> Remembering rather all my waste of days
> Ere I had learned the wonders thou hast shewn
> Blame not my tongue that did not speak thy praise
> Having no language equal to thine own.

This opening recalls Sonnet 106 ('When in the chronicle of wasted time') in its emphasis on a period before the beloved was known, and its acknowledgement of wonders that the poet has 'no language' to express: 'For we which now behold these present days/ Have eyes to wonder, but lack tongues to praise.' Perhaps Moncrieff, the translator of the *Chanson de Roland*, was attracted to Sonnet 106 as Shakespeare's most chivalric and deliberately archaic Sonnet (it is the only one which uses the term 'wight'). In a letter to Owen, dated 26 May 1918, Moncrieff identifies himself as continuing Wilde's legacy in reading the Sonnets biographically, hints at their potential to express his own homoerotic desire, and offers us a handy anthology of Sonnet quotations familiar in 1918:

> No sealing up of the fount of passion is indicated by the cessation of the flow of sonnets – but simply an inflow of work here which will keep me busy till this damnable pamphlet leaves the printers … As to the sonnets – you mustn't take them too seriously. It's vivisection really – of both you and me – I want very much to add to the Shakespearean controversy a conclusive word based on experience. I feel pretty sure that Shakespeare selected some wight to whom he sent 'From Fairest Creatures' in a letter.

---

[38] Hibberd, *Owen the Poet*, p. 153. For further discussion of Wilde's influence on Owen, see Campbell, *Oscar Wilde, Wilfred Owen and Male Desire*.
[39] See the manuscript copy of *Song of Roland*, reprinted by Hibberd in *Wilfred Owen: The Last Year*, p. 117.

He then went on with them – bringing in a few passing events and current relations (the dark lady ... the other poet, etc.) and making use of the amazing fine lines which as simple lines were always coming into his head. The fact of his having set himself to write against time accounts for the frequent obscurities – dulnesses – paddings – and for the general incoherence and weariness of the whole thing. Then sudden [*sic*] you come upon Bare ruined choirs where late the sweet birds sang [73], Rough winds do shake the darling buds of May [18] etc etc. Lines which had obviously come first like raisins on the kitchen table before the mince pies are mixed.[40]

Moncrieff's sense that the beauty of individual lines inspired Shakespeare's Sonnets is a refreshing alternative to biographical readings in which the Sonnet is simply a verbal container for lived experience. Unfortunately for Moncrieff, his passion for the Sonnets and for Owen does not seem to have produced any reciprocal response. Although Owen was flattered enough to keep, and to date, the sonnet he received, no answering poems survive.

Nevertheless, Owen had already written at least one sonnet which invokes a Wildean-Shakespearean desire, reinforcing the idea that Ross's circle nurtured a particular identification with the Sonnets.[41] The lyric 'How do I love thee?' (*c.* May 1917) foregrounds its debt to Elizabeth Barrett Browning, and the reference to 'husbandhood' in line 6 overtly locates it within the terms of heterosexual courtship. Yet its allusion to loving like Shakespeare (and therefore Tennyson), plus the tragic, thwarted nature of its desire, with the repetition of 'pain' in the couplet,[42] strongly suggest that it was really aimed at a male addressee:

> But I do love thee even as Shakespeare loved,
> Most gently wild, and desperately for ever,
> Full-hearted, grave, and manfully in vain,
> With thought, high pain, and ever vaster pain.[43]

The lyrics Owen wrote which address his experience as a soldier are coloured by this Wildean encounter, even as they reflect the other meanings which Shakespeare's Sonnets accrued during the First World War.

---

[40] See the Owen Collection, English Faculty Library, University of Oxford, Owen OEF 461. I am grateful to Oliver House and the staff of the Bodleian for providing this transcription for me.

[41] On Owen's homosexuality, see Hibberd, *Wilfred Owen: A New Biography*, pp. 275–6, 301–2. His most explicit poem is probably 'The Shadwell Stair' which suggests familiarity with gay slang terms such as 'ghost' and 'haunting' and strongly implies Owen's own sexual hunting in the East End.

[42] See Stuart Sillars' discussion of this poem in *Structure and Dissolution in English Writing*, p. 80.

[43] Owen, *Wilfred Owen: The Complete Poems and Fragments*, vol. 1, p. 86, ll 11–14.

'Beauty's Summer Dead': Shakespeare's Sonnets in the Trenches

In *The Great War and Modern Memory*, Paul Fussell describes how belief in 'the educative powers of classical and English literature' and 'the appeal of popular education and "self-improvement"' reached a peak at the moment of the Great War, to produce soldiers who were 'not merely literate but vigorously literary'.[44] Private John Ball, for example, carried a copy of the *Oxford Book of English Verse* in his haversack, and held a conversation with his fellow soldiers about 'the poetry of Rupert Brooke' during a lull in the Battle of the Somme: 'Ball and his friends have no feeling that literature is not very near the centre of normal experience, no sense that it belongs to intellectuals or aesthetes or teachers or critics.'[45] Shakespeare's Sonnets receive no specific mention in the extant letters and diaries of the lower ranks of soldier, though many of these lyrics were available to those who carried anthologies like the *Oxford Book of English Verse* or *Palgrave's Golden Treasury*.[46] Among the higher ranks, however, we find allusions to the possession and reading of Shakespeare's Sonnets, and given how many of these officers were themselves engaged in the act of writing sonnets,[47] we inevitably find appropriation. The range of functions served by the Complete Works of Shakespeare during the Great War was wide and varied. Those in combat and those left at home used Shakespeare 'analytically, liturgically, expressively, politically, in commemoration and celebration'.[48] For First World War soldiers, I would argue, the unique function of Shakespeare's Sonnets seems to have been to provoke nostalgia and contempt, often simultaneously.

Among the possessions of Edward Thomas listed at his death at the Battle of Arras in April 1917 was *The Plays and Poems of William Shakespeare* (London: William Pickering, 1825), the final (eleventh) volume of which contains the Sonnets. Nevertheless, Thomas' diary entry for 19 January

---

[44] Fussell, *The Great War and Modern Memory*, p. 157.

[45] Ibid., pp. 157–8.

[46] Edmund G. C. King notes that the *Golden Treasury* was carried by Second Lieutenant Arthur Preston White of the Northamptonshire Regiment along with a complete Shakespeare. See '"A Priceless Book to Have Out Here"', 234.

[47] The popularity of this traditional form has been attributed to the protection it offered against the unspeakable horrors of the war. As Santanu Das observes, 'Trench lyric stubbornly inhabits the formal, in spite of or perhaps because of the all-surrounding threat of the formless'. See 'Reframing First World War Poetry', p. 13. See also Howarth, 'Poetic Form and the First World War', p. 53.

[48] Lee, 'Shakespeare and the Great War', p. 151.

1917, whilst he was stationed at Codford before embarkation, records a further source:

> Letters from Mother, Helen, Miss Coltman, [W. H.] Hudson. Letters to Mother, Helen, M. Freeman, Lady Newbolt, Oscar [Thomas, Edward's fourth brother]. Morning orderly officer – latrines etc. – lectured on maps – paid Battery. Afternoon learnt to ride motor cycle. Mild and drizzly. Guns are due to arrive. A cake from Mother. Shakespeare's Sonnets from Helen. Capt. Fenner talks of having to take sick leave.[49]

Here, a copy of Shakespeare's Sonnets is potentially a love token, sent by Thomas' wife, a kind of sustenance (the equivalent of Mother's cake), and a nostalgic reminder of a former life,[50] for in November 1915, when Thomas was still in England teaching officers map-reading, he had begun a poem with the opening line from Sonnet 130:

> There's nothing like the sun as the year dies,
> Kind as it can be, this world being made so,
> To stones and men and beasts and birds and flies,
> To all things that it touches except snow,
> Whether on mountain side or street of town.
> The south wall warms me: November has begun,
> Yet never shone the sun as fair as now
> While the sweet last-left damsons from the bough
> With spangles of the morning's storm drop down
> Because the starling shakes it, whistling what
> Once swallows sang. But I have not forgot
> That there is nothing, too, like March's sun,
> Like April's, or July's, or June's, or May's,
> Or January's, or February's, great days:
> And August, September, October, and December
> Have equal days, all different from November.
> No day of the month but I have said –
> Or, if I could live long enough, should say –
> 'There's nothing like the sun that shines today'.
> There's nothing like the sun till we are dead.[51]

---

[49] The diary is reprinted in *The Collected Poems of Edward Thomas*, pp. 460–82, 464.

[50] See King's discussion of how soldiers 'used books as access routes to an earlier, altogether less fraught phase of life, one which could be relived nostalgically through the act of re-reading ... Books read and re-read during wartime were not only sources of "patriotic" motivation; they could also be tokens of identity, reminders both of the past and of the lives soldiers hoped to resume after the war', '"A Priceless Book to Have Out Here"', 234, 237.

[51] Thomas, *The Collected Poems of Edward Thomas*, p. 249.

This poem rejects the amorous subject matter of Sonnet 130, in favour of a celebration of nature which is altogether more generous and inclusive. Rather than critique the deficiencies of November, it sees the pleasures of that month. It also gives a more cheerful twist to Sonnet 73's famous line, 'Bare ruined choirs where late the sweet birds sang', in 'the starling ... whistling what/Once swallows sang'. And yet, the possibility that the poet may not 'live long enough' daily to recite his altered line, 'There's nothing like the sun that shines today', suggests a trace of antagonism with the Shakespearean original. Not only did Shakespeare not appreciate the important things in life, but he had the opportunity to have his voice echo into posterity which may be denied to the present speaker.

Wilfred Owen's allusions to Shakespeare's Sonnets, including the one he inscribed into a notebook he carried with him in the trenches, suggest a similar tension between nostalgia and resentment. This notebook contains a copy of Sonnet 104 ('To me, fair friend, you never can be old'), in Owen's handwriting, as well as his own Shakespearean sonnet 'With an identity disc'. This has led critics to assume that the latter poem 'shows the influence of Sonnet 104',[52] though they do not usually investigate what or how. I would argue that this connection is more interesting and less straightforward than the poems' physical proximity suggests, and opens up broader questions about how Owen read Shakespeare's Sonnets.

> To me, fair friend, you never can be old;
> For as you were when first your eye I eyed,
> Such seems your beauty still: three winters cold
> Have from the forest shook three summers' pride;
> Three beauteous springs to yellow autumn turned
> In process of the seasons have I seen;
> Three April perfumes in three hot Junes burned,
> Since first I saw you fresh, which yet art green.
> Ah, yet doth beauty, like a dial hand,
> Steal from his figure, and no pace perceived;
> So your sweet hue, which methinks still doth stand,
> Hath motion, and mine eye may be deceived;
>   For fear of which, hear this, thou age unbred,
>   Ere you were born was beauty's summer dead.

The notebook version of Sonnet 104 suggests that Owen wrote it down from memory and then consulted a printed text, perhaps *Palgrave's Golden*

---

[52] See Owen, *Wilfred Owen: The Complete Poems and Fragments*, p. 96.

Treasury which he also carried with him.[53] But why this Sonnet? Even before the war, Owen seems to have been aware of the brevity of mortal life; as his brother, Harold, put it: 'His obsession with time was extraordinary … he was shaken with panic and fear that he would not have time, time, TIME.'[54] It was a preoccupation Owen shared with his early idol, Keats, and the latter's sonnet 'When I have fears' (discussed in Chapter 4) is also transcribed into the notebook. Owen's experience as a soldier fighting in the First World War can only have intensified this 'panic and fear', and perhaps drew him more compulsively towards the Sonnets. As John Lee points out, the title 'Anthem for Doomed Youth' 'reads like a compressed paraphrase of the subject of the sonnets to the young man, and gains pathos by doing so'.[55] Read in the context of Owen's military service, Sonnet 104's warning to future ages, 'Ere you were born was beauty's summer dead', figures the destruction of an entire generation, rather than that of one beloved friend whose beauty yet is green. At the same time, Owen's choice of this Sonnet looks like an act of self-consolation. Although directed to a 'fair friend', it holds out the possibility that Owen's own youth may not wear away too fast, despite the 'three beauteous springs' which have passed since the outbreak of the First World War in 1914.

Yet this does not mean that 'With an identity disc' – the sonnet Owen composed in the same notebook – has any simple derivation from 104, despite their physical closeness. Owen described his sonnet as a return to past preoccupations. Knocked unconscious after falling into a crater, he was taken to hospital and it was from there that he wrote to his brother, Colin, on 24 March: 'Perhaps you will think me clean mad and translated by my knock on the head. How shall I prove that my old form of madness has in no way changed? I will send you my last Sonnet, which I started yesterday.'[56] There follows a more polished version of the notebook draft:

SONNET … with an Identity Disc

If ever I had dreamed of my dead name
High in the heart of London; unsurpassed
By Time forever; and the fugitive, Fame,
There taking a long sanctuary at last,

---

[53] This is the Dent Everyman edition of 1906, as noted by Sillars, *Structure and Dissolution*, p. 78. The manuscript can be seen at the British Library, Manuscript collections, ADD 43721: Poems of Wilfred Owen f.157, 'To me fair friend, you never can be old'.
[54] Owen, *Journey from Obscurity*, vol. 2, p. 263.
[55] Lee, 'Shakespeare and the Great War', p. 137.
[56] Stallworthy, *Wilfred Owen: A Biography*, p. 174.

> – I'll better that! Yea, now I think with shame
> How once I wished it hidd'n from its defeats
> Under those holy cypresses, the same
> That mourn around the quiet place of Keats.
>
> Now rather let's be thankful there's no risk
> Of gravers ~~notching~~ scoring it with hideous screed,
> For let my gravestone be this body-disc
> Which was my yoke. Inscribe no date nor deed.
>
> But let thy heart-beat kiss it night & day,
> Until the name grow vague and wear away.[57]

Critics who describe the Shakespearean-ness of this sonnet are usually referring to the version revised at Craiglockhart in August–September 1917, under the influence of Siegfried Sassoon, whose third quatrain reads:

> Now rather thank I God there is no risk
> Of gravers scoring it with florid screed.
> Let my inscription be this soldier's disc.
> Wear it, sweet friend. Inscribe no date nor deed.

The allusion to 'sweet friend' in the revised text aligns it with other Shakespeare Sonnets, including 104, addressed to a 'fair friend'.[58] However, I would argue that the original version, written in hospital following Owen's traumatic experience on the front, is unsurprisingly more ragged, aggressive and even anti-Shakespeare. It describes the body-disc as 'my yoke', a burden emphasised by the caesura, which makes his insistence upon 'no date, nor deed' seem more dismissive of military service and acts of heroism. The impossibility of being memorialised also sounds sarcastic, if not openly bitter: 'Now rather let's be thankful …'. This is in contrast to the revision, 'Now rather thank I God …' which relates more directly to the poetic presumption from which he now distances himself. Many of Shakespeare's Sonnets are characterised by a casual rejection of tombs – 'Not marble nor the monuments of princes/ Shall outlive this powerful rhyme' – which must have been hard to reconcile with Owen's horrifying experience of the unburied dead, not least his sharing that crater with the dismembered corpse of a friend. Similarly, the kind of 'decay' Shakespeare imagines in, for example, Sonnet 71, which is a slow decomposition in the

---

[57] 'Letter To Colin Owen / With an Identity Disc', *First World War Poetry Digital Archive*, http://ww1lit.nsms.ox.ac.uk/ww1lit/items/show/8200, accessed 31 July 2018.
[58] Edmondson and Wells usefully suggest some of the various echoes the lyric invokes in *Shakespeare's Sonnets*, pp. 151–2.

earth, matched with a gradual fading of the memory, bears no resemblance to the annihilation that Owen witnessed, writing in January 1917 of 'the sentries over the dugout [being] blown to nothing'.[59] Finally, we might note Owen's use of the term 'hideous' in the phrase 'scoring it with hideous screed'. Shakespeare only uses this word in the Sonnets to describe Time's destructive power: 'For never-resting time leads summer on/ To hideous winter and confounds him there' (5.5–6); 'When I do count the clock that tells the time,/ And see the brave day sunk in hideous night' (12.1–2). Owen's 'hideous' invokes Shakespeare's warning against the ruin of youth by Time, whilst also exposing as fraudulent his promise of immortality, particularly for the soldier in no-man's-land.

Their glibness about being forgotten is not the only aspect of the Sonnets that Owen apparently struggled with. During his convalescence at Craiglockhart, he came into possession of a copy of Shakespeare's Sonnets, and may have re-read them.[60] Around the same time, he was engrossed in Siegfried Sassoon's 'sketches on trench life' and observed that: 'Shakespere reads vapid after these. Not of course because Sassoon is a greater artist, but because of the subjects, I mean.'[61] As we have seen, Owen identified with the homosexuality of Shakespeare's Sonnets, but he was also dismissive of their celebration of heterosexual desire. The inferiority of the latter when compared with the friendship between soldiers was already a familiar trope of First World War poetry.[62] Owen owned a copy of Robert Nichols' *Ardours and Endurances* (1917), which includes a lyric called 'Fulfilment' whose opening and concluding stanzas read:

> Was there love once? I have forgotten her.
> Was there grief once? Grief yet is mine.
> Other loves I have, men rough, but men who stir
> More grief, more joy, than love of thee and thine …
>
> Was there love once? I have forgotten her.
> Was there grief once? Grief yet is mine.
> O loved, living, dying, heroic soldier,
> All, all, my joy, my grief, my love, are thine!

---

[59] Stallworthy, *Wilfred Owen: A Biography*, p. 156.

[60] This was *Sonnets and Poems, with Notes* by Henry N. Hudson (1910?), inscribed 'WEO/ EDINBURGH/JULY/1917'. See Appendix C in Stallworthy, *Wilfred Owen: A Biography*, p. 320.

[61] Ibid., p. 204.

[62] For further discussion of this trope, see Cole, *Modernism, Male Friendship and the First World War*, p. 161.

Two of Owen's 'most misogynist' lyrics which also explore this theme are 'Apologia Pro Poemate Meo' (November–December 1917) and 'Greater Love' (September 1917, rev. May 1918).[63] The extent to which these also imply a rejection of Shakespeare's Sonnets has not been acknowledged, however 'Apologia' invokes the famous maxim from Sonnet 116:

> I have made fellowships –
> Untold of happy lovers in old song,
> *For love is not* the binding of fair lips
> With the soft silk of eyes that look and long,
>
> By Joy, whose ribbon slips, –
> But wound with war's hard wire whose stakes are strong;
> Bound with the bandage of the arm that drips;
> Knit in the webbing of the rifle-thong … (Italics mine)[64]

Owen turns 'love is not love' against heterosexuality by transforming the romantic metaphors of silk and ribbon into the horrific but strangely seductive ties of barbed wire and bloody bandage; Shakespeare's 'ever-fixed' love is 'Knit' through bearing arms. More daringly, 'Greater Love' looks to me like a rewriting of Sonnet 130. The title invokes the oft-cited biblical dictum, 'Greater love hath no man than this, that a man lay down his life for his friends' (John 15:13). For a secular source, critics usually turn to A. C. Swinburne's lyric, 'Before the Mirror/(Verses written under a Picture)/ Inscribed to J. A. Whistler',[65] which describes Whistler's mistress in a white dress, staring into the mirror: 'White rose in red rose-garden/ Is not so white …'. Yet I would argue that Owen's focus on a red which is not so red more obviously recalls Sonnet 130, whose blazon of lips, eyes and voice Owen adapts to harrowing effect:

> Red lips are not so red
> As the stained stones kissed by the English dead.
> Kindness of wooed and wooer
> Seems shame to their love pure.
> O Love, your eyes lose lure
> When I behold eyes blinded in my stead!
>
> Your slender attitude
> Trembles not exquisite like limbs knife-skewed,
> Rolling and rolling there
> Where God seems not to care;

---

[63] See Campbell, '"For you may touch them not"', 833.

[64] Owen, *Wilfred Owen: The Complete Poems and Fragments*, p. 124.

[65] Ibid., p. 166.

Till the fierce love they bear
Cramps them in death's extreme decrepitude.

Your voice sings not so soft, –
Though even as wind murmuring through raftered loft, –
Your dear voice is not dear,
Gentle, and evening clear,
As theirs whom none now hear,
Now earth has stopped their piteous mouths that coughed.

Heart, you were never hot
Nor large, nor full like hearts made great with shot;
And though your hand be pale,
Paler are all which trail
Your cross through flame and hail:
Weep, you may weep, for you may touch them not.[66]

Owen takes the theme of false comparison in the Shakespeare Sonnet, and expands it into a devastating exposure of the irrelevance of Shakespeare, amorous poetry and heterosexual love, at the same time as he condemns the insensitivity and inhumanity of those for whom this sacrifice is performed. His poem is arguably the most political use of a Shakespeare Sonnet we have seen in this study since the Interregnum. And yet, there is also something disturbingly sexy about Owen's combination of violence and arousal, an *eros* that the Shakespeare Sonnet notably lacks. As Santanu Das has aptly shown, 'A visceral thrill as well as an acute physical empathy constitute the body in pain in Owen's poetry'.[67]

If Shakespeare's Sonnets are approached by soldier-poets in the First World War with both nostalgia and hostility, the fact that they were part of First World War poetry and poetry-reading potentially left them on the wrong side of history as post-war Europe recovered from the seismic impact on political, cultural and literary traditions effected by the Great War. One of the literary movements that emerged in the aftermath (though its roots stretch back into the nineteenth century) was modernism, and Vincent Sherry usefully explores the appropriateness of this term:

> To the experience of being chronologically modern, the suffix adds a sense of self-consciousness about the experience of being 'modern'. Most accurately, then, the word conveys a feeling of belonging to a particular moment of history, a specified Now, a *special* present, which is made more intense by virtue of some self-conscious difference from what went before ...

[66] Ibid., p. 166.
[67] Das, *Touch and Intimacy in First World War Literature*, p. 141.

[the] Great War inscribed a manifold line of divide between centuries new and old.[68]

Whilst the Sonnets would retain an air of wistful nostalgia for some post-war writers, they would also be appropriated as examples of high modernism, as emphatically 'now'. In 1927 both Virginia Woolf's *To the Lighthouse* and Laura Riding and Robert Graves' *A Survey of Modernist Poetry* were published. In both texts, the notion of the Sonnets as romanticised relics from the past is countered by an equally pressing sense of their immediacy and relevance to the present.

1927: *To the Lighthouse* and *A Survey of Modernist Poetry*

Virginia Woolf was well versed in Shakespeare from childhood, and her work reveals an enduring but ambivalent appreciation: she found his dramatic characterisation unconvincing, but admired his lyricism; she was intimidated by and resentful of his reputation, but claimed him for the cause of women writers; she found the Sonnets 'difficult', but their 'tremendous phrases' stuck in her mind.[69] Whilst quotations from Sonnets 116 and 66 appear in *The Waves* and *Between the Acts* respectively,[70] most prominent and richly allusive is Sonnet 98 ('From you have I been absent in the spring'), as read by Mrs Ramsay in *To The Lighthouse*. Before we try to account for this particular choice, we need to consider Woolf's approach to the Sonnets more generally, as revealed by the holograph manuscript of *To the Lighthouse* (*c.* 1925–7).

In the scene after dinner, where her husband is absorbed in Scott's *The Antiquary*, Mrs Ramsay's choice of reading material is described thus:

> – she ~~took~~ looked over her knitting at the books on the little table, & took one, an anthology of poems, & opened it ~~anywhere~~, laying it on her knee, ~~And~~ Never reading at all, except in this way, ~~she turned leaves~~, turning leaves, climbing from this to that, she had not any ~~sense of~~ security whatever, or any knowledge even, but of names, but only ~~how the that the lines about the sonnets of Shakespeare~~ felt it a great relief; & ~~at the same time had~~

---

[68] Sherry, 'The Great War and Literary Modernism in England', p. 194.

[69] Quoted by Alice Fox in *Virginia Woolf and the Literature of the English Renaissance*, p. 75. For a fuller discussion of Woolf's engagement with Shakespeare, see Froula, 'Virginia Woolf as Shakespeare's Sister', pp. 123–42, and Briggs, 'Virginia Woolf Reads Shakespeare or, Her Silence on Master William'.

[70] 'Let me not to the marriage of true minds' is one of the snippets of Shakespeare that Bernard recalls in *The Waves*. In *Between the Acts*, one of the actors borrows a line from Sonnet 66 'and maiden virtue rudely strumpeted'. For further discussion see Fox, *Virginia Woolf and the Literature of the English Renaissance*, pp. 94–158.

for she loved ~~to get at~~ the repose of the words; & ~~its~~ [the] counterbalancing [the soft flowers] ~~of this one that she did feel, more & more.~~[71]

There is a diagonal line from 'Shakespeare' up to 'how the', suggesting that Woolf wanted this phrase to read 'but only how the sonnets of Shakespeare' but could not think how to end and so crossed it out. She may have decided that such a conjecture was out of character – where Mr Ramsay reads Scott to reassure himself of his own literary posterity, Mrs Ramsay takes up an 'anthology of poems' among which she pleasurably wanders without caring what has been written by whom. Nevertheless, Woolf's insistence that she read the Sonnets is signalled again subsequently, and is here allowed to stand:

> Mrs Ramsay raised her head, but like a person in a light sleep, seemed to ~~ask~~ say that if he wanted her to wake she would, otherwise she was sleeping. She was rocking; she was [stretched] ~~sa brooding; on the rhythm, in the~~ mesh ~~stretched tight~~ of Shakespeare's sonnets.[72]

The 'mesh' of Shakespeare's Sonnets suggests the standard fourteen lines, connected by a formal rhyme scheme, but interwoven with internal echoes. It also anticipates Mrs Ramsay's language of reliance upon the male intellect in the published text: 'she let it uphold her and sustain her, this admirable fabric of the masculine intelligence, which ran up and down, crossed this way and that, like iron girders spanning the swaying fabric, upholding the world'.[73]

In the final version of the novel, Woolf is much more reticent about associating Mrs Ramsay with Shakespeare and this 'masculine intelligence'. Although she includes lines from Sonnet 98 (which may have been anticipated by the allusion to 'soft flowers' in the holograph), she excises Shakespeare's name and suggests that the first poem Mrs Ramsay reads is the (untitled, unattributed) 'Sirens' Song' by the minor seventeenth-century poet, William Browne. That Mrs Ramsay reads this poem and Sonnet 98 in the same anthology might identify it as the *Oxford Book of English Verse* edited by Arthur Quiller-Couch (1900, repr. 1917) which, as we saw in our discussion of First World War poetry, was a popular reading choice in the trenches. Indeed, Fussell argues that this anthology 'presides over the Great War in a way that has never been sufficiently appreciated'.[74] The suggestion of this specific anthology prepares the ground for a

---

[71] Woolf, *To the Lighthouse*, 145, p. 194.
[72] Ibid., 146, p. 195.
[73] Ibid., p. 98.
[74] Ibid., pp. 159–60.

nostalgic view of the Sonnets. At the same time, the fact that Mrs Ramsay reads the Sonnets in an anthology rather than a *Sonnets* edition or volume of Shakespeare implies the sacrifice of male authorial ego, at the expense of female readerly pleasure:

> She opened the book and began reading here and there at random, and as she did so she felt that she was climbing backwards, upwards, shoving her way up under petals that curved over her, so that she only knew this is white, or this is red. She did not know at first what the words meant at all.
>
> Steer, hither steer your winged pines, all beaten Mariners.
>
> She read and turned the page, swinging herself, zigzagging this way and that, from one line to another as from one branch to another, from one red and white flower to another.[75]

It is Mrs Ramsay's intoxicating experience of reading which seems to prompt the selection of Sonnet 98 with its heady promise of losing oneself in the depths of the rose:

> [She] raised her head and like a person in a light sleep seemed to say that if he wanted her to wake she would, she really would, but otherwise, might she go on sleeping, just a little longer, just a little longer? She was climbing up those branches, this way and that, laying hands on one flower and another.
>
> Nor praise the deep vermilion in the rose,
>
> she read, and so reading she was ascending, she felt, on the top, on to the summit. How satisfying! How restful! All the odds and ends of the day stuck to this magnet; her mind felt swept, felt clean. And then there it was, suddenly entire shaped in her hands, beautiful and reasonable, clear and complete, the essence sucked out of life and held rounded here – the sonnet.[76]

This account of Mrs Ramsay's reading needs to be set against that of her husband – not only the latter's narcissistic reading of Scott, but his implied reading of the Sonnets. Imagining himself the doomed leader of a polar expedition, Mr Ramsay wonders how long his fame will last, and comes up with the figure of 'two thousand years':

---

[75] Ibid., pp. 110–11.
[76] Ibid., p. 112. Woolf seems here to be recalling Wordsworth's praise of the sonnet, with its 'pervading sense of intense Unity', which he likened to 'an orbicular body – a sphere – or a dew-drop'. See the letter of 1833, Wordsworth, *The Letters of William and Dorothy Wordsworth*, vol. 2, pp. 604–5.

And what are two thousand years? (asked Mr Ramsay ironically, staring at
the hedge). What, indeed, if you look from a mountain-top down the long
wastes of the ages? The very stone one kicks with one's boot will outlast
Shakespeare.[77]

The phrase 'Wastes of the ages' or 'waste of ages' recurs twice more on this
page, and seems particularly to recall Sonnet 12: 'Then of thy beauty do
I question make/ That thou among the wastes of time must go.'[78] But where
the Sonnets produce no aesthetic response in Mr Ramsay, only a fretful
questioning of posterity, Mrs Ramsay's openness to Sonnet 98 resembles a
kind of 'rapture', producing 'an erotic, almost orgasmic experience'.[79] And
where for Mr Ramsay the Shakespearean Sonnet is essentially inhibitive,
for his wife it encapsulates her creative achievement of the dinner party –
'And then there it was … the essence sucked out of life and held rounded
here' – and recalls the other kinds of microcosm that women create in the
novel, such as Lily's painting or Rose's arrangement of fruit. At the heart
of Woolf's own creative engagement with the Sonnets in this novel is the
refusal to consider them as an edition or a collection or a narrative:[80] the
single lyric allows the expression of a female experience that 'Shakespeare's
Sonnets' would potentially overwhelm and destroy.

The choice of Sonnet 98 resonates with various aspects of Mrs Ramsay's
characterisation. Most obviously, it reinforces her identification with
Spring and rebirth.[81] We might remember Charles Tansley's image of her
'with stars in her eyes and veils in her hair, with cyclamen and wild violets
… Stepping through fields of flowers and taking to her breast buds that
had broken and lambs that had fallen'.[82] The Sonnet's secular pantheism, in
which the natural world is imbued with the beauties of the beloved, is also
a repeated motif: 'it was odd, [Mrs Ramsay] thought, how if one was alone,
one leant to inanimate things: trees, streams, flowers; felt they expressed
one; felt they became one; felt they knew one'.[83] At the same time, Sonnet

---

[77] Woolf, *To the Lighthouse*, p. 33.

[78] There is also something of Shakespeare's Sonnet 64, filtered through Keats, in the image of Mr
Ramsay 'on his little ledge facing the dark of human ignorance, how we know nothing and the sea
eats away the ground we stand on', p. 41.

[79] In *Art & Anger*, Jane Marcus likens Mrs Ramsay's experience to Woolf's own professed rapture and
'dissolution of the ego' when she read, pp. 224, 242.

[80] In a passage from *Orlando* (1928), deleted at the proof stage, Woolf's narrator claims to have
destroyed 'Shakespeare's own account of his sonnets' in which he described his relationship with Mr
W. H. and the Dark Lady. See Scott, 'Tantalising Fragments', 299.

[81] See Maria DiBattista's discussion of Mrs Ramsay as 'at the centre of a circle of life which encloses a
green world of gardens and marriage', *Virginia Woolf's Major Novels*, p. 83.

[82] Woolf, *To the Lighthouse*, p. 13.

[83] Ibid., p. 59.

98's association with Coleridge, and its popularity in Victorian anthologies, makes it a markedly nostalgic, pre-war Sonnet, which belongs in the first part of the novel, 'The Window', set in 1909, but also looks further back to the late nineteenth-century idyll in which Woolf imagined her mother, Julia Stephen:

> [She] comes out of the window wearing that striped silk dress buttoned at the throat with a flowing skirt that appears in the photograph. She is of course a 'vision' as they used to say; and there she stands, silent, with her plate of strawberries and cream … The sound of music also comes from those long low rooms where the great Watts pictures hang; Joachim playing the violin; also the sound of a voice reading poetry.[84]

Sonnet 98 might well feel at home in such a setting. But if the nostalgia for this pre-war world is already felt in 'The Window', it is reinforced by the way in which the First World War emerges as a destructive force in 'Time Passes' (1909–19) – during which we learn that Mrs Ramsay, Andrew and Prue have died – and 'The Lighthouse' (1919), in which the family tries to adjust to its losses.[85] Viewed retrospectively, Mrs Ramsay's immersion in Sonnet 98 represents a kind of avoidance of reality similar to that practised technically by Woolf and other post-war writers; as Randall Stevenson notes, 'Modernist fiction's transcriptions of inner consciousness did not necessarily offer unalloyed happiness. Yet they distanced some of the distresses of "objective reality"'.[86] But although it may be tempting to consign the Sonnets to the old world, they are also part of the 'integration' of modern and Victorian which Steve Ellis finds in the novel, part of the 'complex of desire and rejection, preservation and challenge the writing constantly shows towards the "old order"'.[87]

At the end of 'The Window', Mrs Ramsay sets down her book to attend to her husband, murmuring 'As with your shadow I with these did play'. The line's immediate relevance is to the Sonnet's themes of absence and substitution: 'What had happened she wondered, as she took up her knitting, since she had last seen him alone?'[88] But for Lily Briscoe, this line has a different power which only fully emerges after Mrs Ramsay's death. For Lily, cultural pursuits, such as reading or painting, are not substitutes for or distractions from personal relationships, as they are for Mrs Ramsay, but

[84] 'Reminiscences' (1908), qtd by Hermione Lee, *Virginia Woolf*, p. 86.
[85] For further discussion of *To the Lighthouse* as a war novel, see Levenback, *Virginia Woolf and the Great War*, ch. 3, and Poole, '"We all put up with you Virginia"', pp. 79–100.
[86] Stevenson, 'Woolf and Modernity', p. 154.
[87] Ellis, *Virginia Woolf and the Victorians*, p. 80.
[88] Woolf, *To the Lighthouse*, p. 113.

the thing itself. She reduces Mrs Ramsay and James to a 'purple shadow',[89] and berates herself for 'playing at painting, playing at the one thing one did not play at'.[90] But where the line gains an unexpected emotional depth is in the process by which it stops representing absence and starts to talk about grief. In 'The Lighthouse', Lily has felt herself somewhat detached from the fact of Mrs Ramsay's death: 'Oh the dead! she murmured, one pitied them, one brushed them aside, one had even a little contempt for them.'[91] But then the memory of Mrs Ramsay, comes back with a vengeance through Sonnet 98, whose closing line no longer seems so trite:

> It had seemed so safe, thinking of her. Ghost, air, nothingness, a thing you could play with easily and safely at any time of day or night, she had been that, and then suddenly she put her hand out and wrung the heart thus.[92]

Moreover, the pantheistic fantasy of Sonnet 98 takes on a more affective, elegiac tone when it again recreates Mrs Ramsay before Lily's eyes: 'It was strange how clearly she saw her, stepping with her usual quickness across the fields among whose folds, purplish and soft, among whose flowers, hyacinths or lilies, she vanished.'[93] In this manner, Woolf registers the strange and enduring tangibility of the Shakespeare Sonnet itself.

In the year after its publication, *To the Lighthouse* would be attacked in print by Laura Riding on the basis of a language 'strained, supersensitized, loaded with comparisons, suggestive images, emotional analogies: used, that is, in a poetic way to write something that is not poetry'.[94] For Riding, poetry is by definition 'unreal', as Lisa Samuels summarises: 'The true poetic word is an unreal thing, made by an unreal individual, serving no tradition of reality. And poetry is a realm for engaging with unknowables, not an historical accumulation of individual points of view.'[95] From this perspective it is surprising to find Riding defending a Shakespeare Sonnet, by any standards a kind of lyric 'loaded with comparisons' and operating within a 'tradition of reality'. Yet, Riding appears to concur with Woolf on

---

[89] Ibid., p. 49.
[90] Ibid., p. 143.
[91] Ibid., p. 166.
[92] Ibid., p. 170. I am indebted to Fox for identifying the Sonnet allusion in this line, though I read its effect rather differently than she does, *Virginia Woolf and the Literature of the English Renaissance*, p. 77.
[93] Woolf, *To the Lighthouse*, p. 172. For further discussion of the novel as elegy, a term which Woolf herself used of it, see Peter Knox-Shaw, '*To the Lighthouse*'.
[94] Riding, *Anarchism is Not Enough*, p. 47.
[95] 'Introduction', in ibid., p. xix.

the essential 'modernism' of Shakespeare's Sonnets, and to direct hostility rather to the traditional apparatus that has obscured their unknowability.

Riding's authorship of the critical method enshrined in the essay, 'William Shakespeare and e. e. cummings: A Study in Original Spelling and Punctuation', would be threatened by the profoundly sexist assumption that only a man, i.e. Robert Graves, could have come up with it. It was also undermined by the fantasy that this reading of the Sonnets must have originated in the First World War, among the soldier-poets. In a letter dated 29 January 1934, Robert Graves wrote to Aubrey Attwater, with whom he had served in the Welch Fusiliers, to deny the story that he had carried a copy of the Sonnets with him in his pocket whilst in the trenches – Graves insisted that he had not even read them. He also tried to correct the mistake about the essay's authorship: 'it is simply untrue that I ever made any such analysis of any particular sonnet. I could not have done so, because it was Laura Riding who originated this exegetic method ... We worked the whole thing out together at great labour and in pursuance of LR's idea in the Spring of 1926'.[96]

Within the essay, Riding and Graves expose the damage that the wartime-anthology, Quiller-Couch's *Oxford Book of English Verse*, has done both to Shakespeare's Sonnets and to modernist poetry: 'because the reading public has been so undertrained on a simplified Shakespeare and on anthology verse generally ... modernist poetry seems as difficult as Shakespeare really ought to seem'.[97] In this sense, the epitome of modernist poetry is not e. e. cummings, whose difficulty is really only superficial, but Shakespeare's Sonnets. The choice of 129 is an effect of its being singled out by 'popular anthologies from all the others as being particularly easy to understand'.[98] There would also be some prestige in reinventing this Sonnet, given its status at the end of the nineteenth century. Theodore Watts' assertion that this was 'the greatest sonnet ever written' was repeated by William Sharp in *The Songs, Poems and Sonnets of William Shakespeare* (1885), and by Oscar Wilde in his expanded 'Portrait of Mr W. H.'.[99]

Through a comparison of the Quarto version with that of Quiller-Couch, Riding and Graves explore the ways in which modern punctuation

---

[96] This unpublished letter is quoted by Mark Jacobs in his important discussion of how Laura Riding's authorship of the Sonnet analysis was misrepresented by William Empson and other critics and reviewers, including most recently Empson's biographer, John Haffenden. See Jacobs' essay, 'Contemporary Misogyny', 230.

[97] Riding and Graves, *A Survey of Modernist Poetry*, p. 38.

[98] Ibid., p. 31.

[99] See Shakespeare, *The Songs, Poems and Sonnets of William Shakespeare*, p. 34, and Wilde, *The Collins Complete Works of Oscar Wilde*, p. 335.

closes off potential meaning. In the modern edition, for example, lines 6–8 read:

> Past reason hunted; and, no sooner had,
> Past reason hated, as a swallow'd bait
> On purpose laid to make the taker mad.

Riding and Graves object to the addition of a comma after 'no sooner had', 'for this confines the phrase to a special meaning i.e. "lust no sooner had is hated past reason", whereas it also means "lust no sooner had *past reason* is hated past reason" '.[100] They also prefer what look like obvious errors in the Quarto's version of lines 9–11:

Mad in pursuit, and in possession so;	Made In pursut and in possession so,
Had, having and in quest to have, extreme;	Had, hauing, and in quest, to have extreame,
A bliss in proof, and proved, a very woe; (Quiller-Couch)	A blisse in proofe and proud and very wo, (1609 Quarto)

The Quarto's 'Made' serves as a logical progression from 'make the taker mad' in the previous line and opens up what 'so' might mean. The placement of the comma after 'quest' emphasises 'that lust comprises all the stages of lust: the after-lust period (*Had*), the actual experience of lust (*having*), and the anticipation of lust (*in quest*); and that the extremes of lust are felt in all these stages (*to have extreame, i.e.* to have extremes, to have in extreme degrees)'.[101] The retention of 'and' in line 11 serves the same function:

> To fulfil the paradox implied in *extreame* it should mean that lust is a bliss during the proof and after the proof, and also *very wo* (real woe) during and after the proof. The altered line only means that lust is a bliss during the proof but a woe after the proof, denying what Shakespeare has been at pains to show all along, that lust is all things at all times.[102]

These moments of ambiguity linger on in modern editions of Sonnet 129. John Kerrigan notes that placing the comma after 'quest', 'points up a secondary identification of *lust in action* with the desire to posess (an) *extreme*, to capture an extremity of passion (the *bliss* of line 11, but also the *woe*)'.[103] But what did Riding and Graves do for the Sonnets as a whole? Many

---

[100] Riding and Graves, *A Survey of Modernist Poetry*, p. 33.
[101] Ibid., pp. 33–4.
[102] Ibid., p. 34.
[103] Shakespeare, *The Sonnets and A Lover's Complaint*, ed. Kerrigan, p. 358.

of the premises of their essay have since been discredited: the assumption that the Quarto represents Shakespeare's desired punctuation, for example, or that his spelling encodes pronunciation. However, Riding and Graves encouraged readers to challenge the intervention of editors and promoted engagement with the 'original' text. They also offered a brief reception history of the Sonnets to demonstrate their critical neglect, whilst acknowledging that without Malone's interventions 'the plain man of today would undoubtedly be unaware of the existence of the *Sonnets*'.[104] At the same time, Riding and Graves argue strongly that the Sonnets should not belong to 'the plain man' but rather to admirers of modernist poetry: 'The failure of imagination and knowledge in Shakespeare's emendators has reduced Shakespeare to the indignity of being easy for everybody.'[105] Their legacy, then, remains double-edged: by actively promoting the Sonnets' obscurity – 'if we must choose any one meaning, then we owe it to Shakespeare to choose at least one he intended and one embracing as many meanings as possible, that is, the most difficult'[106] – Riding and Graves transformed one of the Sonnets' most derided features into evidence of their genius. But in so doing, they also reversed the late nineteenth century insistence that the Sonnets were suitable for all social classes to read. The Sonnets become once again difficult and obscure, and thence prestigious.[107]

In dispensing with the 'plain man of today' as implied reader, Riding and Graves also disposed of the biographical reading which had made the Sonnets accessible and titillating. The essay shows no interest whatever in interpreting the individual lyric through the narrative sequence, and their focus on the poem, as replete in itself, would exert a major influence on the development of New Criticism.[108] It would also resonate with two contemporary poets and critics, William Empson and W. H. Auden, although both men would struggle to leave the biographical narrative alone entirely. Empson's reading of Sonnet 83 ('I never saw that you did painting need'), for example, was shaped by its position in the sequence: '(Shakespeare seems to have been taunted for his inferiority, and is being abandoned for the rival poet).'[109] Empson may have turned to the Sonnets in the

---

[104] Riding and Graves, *A Survey of Modernist Poetry*, p. 37.

[105] Ibid., pp. 37 and 39.

[106] Ibid., p. 36.

[107] See also Carey, *The Intellectuals and the Masses*.

[108] Jacobs notes that 'the Sonnet examination in *A Survey of Modernist Poetry* … has become increasingly accepted by critics as the starting place … of much of what came to be known as the "New Criticism"'. See his 'Contemporary Misogyny', 223.

[109] Empson, *Seven Types of Ambiguity* (2004), pp. 2, 134.

first place because they were so 'biographically suggestive', enabling him
to discover 'how to join ... extremely close textual analysis with specu-
lative authorial biography'.[110] By contrast, Auden would be much more
outspoken in his denunciation, averring that 'no amount of research into
[the lives of Catullus and Lesbia] can tell us why Catullus wrote the actual
poems he did, instead of an infinite number of similar poems he might
have written instead, why, indeed, he wrote any, or why those he did are
good'.[111] Yet this did not stop Auden from offering his own biographical
(and autobiographical) reading of the Sonnets, which tell 'the story of an
agonized struggle by Shakespeare to preserve the glory of the vision he had
been granted in a relationship, lasting at least three years, with a person
who seemed intent by his actions upon covering the vision with dirt'.[112]
Even as they perpetuated a biographical reading, however, Empson's and
Auden's close attention to the individual lyric, in terms of its ambiguity
and its lyrical power, would be their more enduring contribution.

'Consider the Sonnets Themselves': William Empson and W. H. Auden

Empson read Riding and Graves' essay as an undergraduate at Cambridge,
and it profoundly influenced *Seven Types of Ambiguity* (1930), as both his
tutor, I. A. Richards,[113] and Empson himself acknowledged. Indeed, the
dedication to the first edition reads: 'I derive the method I am using from
Mr Robert Graves' analysis of a Shakespeare Sonnet, "The expense of spirit
in a waste of shame" in *A Survey of Modernist Poetry*.'[114] Empson would
later attach an erratum slip to include the name of Laura Riding, before
dropping the acknowledgement altogether. But if he would later become
distressingly amnesiac about his debt to both Riding and Sonnet 129,[115]

---

[110] See Engle, 'William Empson and the Sonnets', p. 169.
[111] Auden, 'Introduction', p. xix.
[112] Ibid., p. xxxiiii.
[113] I. A. Richards recalled their tutorials at Cambridge: 'At about his third visit he brought up the
games of interpretation which Laura Riding and Robert Graves had been playing with the unpunc-
tuated form of "The expense of spirit in a waste of shame". Taking the sonnet as a conjuror takes his
hat, he produced an endless swarm of lively rabbits from it and ended by "You could do that with
any poetry, couldn't you?"'. Two weeks later, he returned 'with a thick wad of very illegible type-
script under his arm – the central 30,000 words or so of the book', quoted by Haffenden, *William
Empson*, p. 207.
[114] Empson, *Seven Types of Ambiguity* (1930), dedication.
[115] For a full discussion of the way in which Riding's contribution to the essay has been obscured, by
the efforts of Graves himself, Empson and most recently Haffenden, see Jacobs, 'Contemporary
Misogyny'.

Empson's reliance on Shakespeare's Sonnets to explain his methodology was undeniable. The first type of ambiguity – 'when a detail is effective in several ways at once'[116] – is introduced by means of Sonnet 73, specifically its most famous line, 'Bare ruined choirs, where late the sweet birds sang'. This description of tree branches in Autumn demonstrates ambiguity:

> Because ruined monastery choirs are places in which to sing, because they involve sitting in a row, because they are made of wood, are carved into knots and so forth, because they used to be surrounded by a sheltering building crystallised out of the likeness of a forest, and coloured with stained glass and painting like flowers and leaves, because they are now abandoned by all but the grey walls coloured like the skies of winter, because the cold and Narcissistic charm suggested by the choir-boys suits well with Shakespeare's feeling for the object of the Sonnets, and for various sociological and histor-ical reasons (the protestant destruction of monasteries; fear of puritanism) which it would be hard now to trace out in their proportions.[117]

Whilst Empson finds these meanings combined to produce the line's beauty, he claims that there is 'a sort of ambiguity in not knowing which of them to hold most clearly in mind. Clearly this is involved in all such richness and heightening of effect, and the machinations of ambiguity are among the very roots of poetry'.[118] By this means, Empson reinforces the Sonnets' position not only at the forefront of his own exegesis, but those of poetry itself. Elsewhere in the book, Empson ranges across the Sonnets to furnish examples of other kinds of ambiguity.[119] His treatment of the grammatical type, closely modelled on Riding's method, assumes its function to give 'an interpenetrating, and as it were, fluid unity, in which phrases will go either with the sentence before or after and there is no break in the movement of the thought'. In Sonnet 16 ('But wherefore do not you a mightier way'), explored in a stand-alone article published before the book,[120] Empson finds a range of meanings for 'So should the lines of life that life repaire', depending on whether 'lines of life' or 'that life' is the subject of 'repaire'.[121]

Empson's most significant impact on the interpretation of Shakespeare's Sonnets came through his analysis of Sonnet 94 in *Some Versions of Pastoral* (1935). Here, his unfolding of the Sonnet's ambiguity is driven by the question of what kind of irony the text is producing, and against

---

[116] Empson, *Seven Types of Ambiguity* (2004), p. 2.
[117] Ibid., pp. 2–3.
[118] Ibid., p. 2.
[119] He quotes Sonnets 93, 95, 32, 42, 13, 31, 74, 81, 18, 16 and 83.
[120] See his 'Ambiguity in Shakespeare: Sonnet XVI', *Experiment* (February 1929).
[121] Ibid., p. 55.

whom: 'It is agreed that *They that have power to hurt and will do none* is a piece of grave irony, but there the matter is generally left; you can work through all the notes in the Variorum without finding out whether flower, lily, "owner", and person addressed are alike or opposed.'[122] Empson analyses the Sonnet in the original punctuation of the Quarto, as Riding and Graves had advised, noting the flexibility allowed by the lack of any but a concluding period:

> They that have powre to hurt, and will doe none,
> That doe not do the thing, they most do showe,
> Who moving others, are themselves as stone,
> Unmoved, could, and to temptation slow:
> They rightly do inherit heavens graces,
> And husband natures ritches from expence,
> They are the Lords and owners of their faces,
> Others, but stewards of their excellence:
> The sommers flowre is to the sommer sweet,
> Though to it selfe, it onely live and die,
> But if that flowre with base infection meete,
> The basest weed out-braves his dignity:
>> For sweetest things turns sowrest by their deedes,
>> Lilies that fester, smell far worse than weeds.

Whilst the Sonnet proves to be a knotty source of ambiguity, it is also a dazzling vehicle for Empson's theory of pastoral. For a start, it demonstrates the translation of the 'complex into the simple'[123] in the transition from octave to sestet – 'turning oddly from *pow'r* to *flow'r*' as Vendler puts it.[124] The vexed question of what WH (as Empson calls him) should do and be is translated into the supposedly simpler example of 'The sommers flower' which remains sweet, 'though to it selfe, it onely live and die'. Perhaps, Empson argues, WH is like the flower 'in its beauty, vulnerability, tendency to excite thoughts about the shortness of life, self-centredness, and power in spite of it to give pleasure, not in its innocence and fertility', or perhaps not.[125] To what extent should the flower be blamed? 'It may do good to others though not by effort or may simply be a good end in itself (or combining these, may only be able to do good by concentrating on itself as an end); a preparatory evasion of the central issue about egotism.'[126]

[122] Empson, *Some Versions of Pastoral*, p. 89.
[123] Ibid., p. 23. See Paul J. Alpers' helpful consolidation and analysis of his theory in 'Empson on Pastoral'.
[124] Vendler, *The Art of Shakespeare's Sonnets*, p. 403.
[125] Empson, *Some Versions of Pastoral*, p. 91.
[126] Ibid., p. 96.

At the same time, Sonnet 94 fits Empson's other definition of pastoral as a mediation between the social classes. The chapter is entitled 'They That Have Power: Twist of Heroic-Pastoral Ideas into an Ironical Acceptance of Aristocracy', and one of the cruxes which Empson explores most fruitfully is the conclusion that 'Lords ... rightly do inherit heavens graces,/ And husband natures ritches from expence'. Whilst this seems to defend the status quo, it also generates irony through its echo of the procreation sonnets in which 'Rightly to husband nature's riches ... was to accept the fact that one is only steward of them'.[127] Empson's sense of the poet struggling to deal with WH on a personal level also fulfils his notion of literature as 'a social process, and also an attempt to reconcile the conflicts of an individual in whom those of society will be mirrored'. The tension between the mutuality desirable in love, and the asymmetrical relationship of master and servant in the Sonnets, broadens into a larger question, as rephrased by Vendler: 'An aristocrat takes, but does not give. Should we resent this?'[128]

Empson's demonstration of Sonnet 94's difficulty (he claimed to find in it '4096 possible movements of thought')[129] placed it at the pinnacle of Shakespeare's achievement and contributed to its being 'the most discussed in the collection',[130] at least by academics. He also offered a view of the Sonnets as both more politically engaged than previously thought, and as 'anti-Christian' and even anti-puritan. Having detected in Sonnet 94 the generalisation that 'all men do most good to others by fulfilling their own natures', he finds the Sonnets in general 'stat[ing] the opposite to the idea of self-sacrifice'.[131] This reading of 94 would be developed further by L. C. Knights in 1946: 'If nothing else "Lilies that fester" (an image suggesting less the excesses of sensuality than "the distortions of ingrown virginity") might cast some doubts on this simple [unironic] interpretation.'[132] The more general identification of the Sonnets with 'fear of puritanism' was likely prompted by Empson's own sense of betrayal on being expelled from Cambridge for 'sexual misconduct', specifically his possession of contraceptives.[133] He had failed to act like the 'Lords and owners of their faces' to hide his sexual appetites. But Empson was not alone in the 1920s and 1930s in responding to the Sonnets' claims for self-fulfilment.

---

[127] Ibid., p. 95.
[128] Vendler, *The Art of Shakespeare's Sonnets*, p. 404.
[129] Empson, *Some Versions of Pastoral*, p. 89.
[130] Shakespeare, *The Sonnets and A Lover's Complaint*, ed. Kerrigan, p. 290.
[131] Empson, *Some Versions of Pastoral*, p. 98.
[132] Knights, 'Shakespeare's Sonnets', p. 287.
[133] For more detailed discussion, see Haffenden, *William Empson*, pp. 243–58.

W. H. Auden's relationship with the Sonnets as a reader began in his late teens and early twenties. They appear to have offered comfort as he embarked on a series of unreciprocated or unbalanced relationships with young men.[134] He carried a copy of the Sonnets with him to Hamburg with Gerhart Meyer in 1929, for example, and the situation he describes in his diary, where he found himself alone, unable to sleep, in a hotel room whilst Meyer pursued other men and Auden read the Sonnets,[135] resonates strongly with 57 ('Being your slave, what should I do but tend') or the conclusion of 58: 'I am to wait, though waiting so be hell/ Not blame your pleasure be it ill or well.' Auden's feelings on the end of the affair are also familiar:

> When someone begins to lose the glamour they had for us on our first meeting, we tell ourselves that we have been deceived, that our phantasy cast a halo over them which they are unworthy to bear. It is always possible however that the reverse is the case: that our disappointment is due to a failure of our own sensibility which lacks the strength to maintain itself at the acuteness with which it began. People may really be what we first thought them, and what we subsequently think of as the disappointing reality, the person obscured by the staleness of our senses.[136]

We might be reminded of Sonnet 56 in which Shakespeare's speaker pleads 'Sweet love, renew thy force; be it not said/ Thy edge should blunter be than appetite'.

In his poetry, Auden explored the potential of the sonnet, and of the sequence, in the twelve love sonnets he sent to Christopher Isherwood in 1934, and the short sequence 'In Time of War' (1938).[137] But there is one Shakespearean Sonnet to which Auden returned more often than any other in his creative and critical work, and this is 121:

> 'Tis better to be vile than vile esteemed,
> When not to be, receives reproach of being,
> And the just pleasure lost, which is so deemed
> Not by our feeling, but by others' seeing.
> For why should others' false adulterate eyes
> Give salutation to my sportive blood?

[134] Richard Davenport-Hines suggests that Auden read the Sonnets as an undergraduate in 1926, when he was in love with Bill McElwee, who returned his affection but denied any sexual advances. See *Auden*, pp. 192, 69.

[135] See the diary entry quoted by Luke, 'Gerhart Meyer and the Vision of Eros', p. 106.

[136] Ibid., p. 107.

[137] For further discussion of Auden's interest in the Sonnet form, see Regan, 'Auden and Shakespeare', p. 267.

Or on my frailties why are frailer spies,
Which in their wills count bad what I think good?
No, I am that I am, and they that level
At my abuses, reckon up their own.
I may be straight, though they themselves be bevel;
By their rank thoughts my deeds must not be shown,
       Unless this general evil they maintain:
       All men are bad, and in their badness reign.

This is a fascinating choice of Sonnet because it is significantly out of kilter with the speaker's sentimental and moral position in the rest of the collection. He sounds more like an Iago or Richard III, who solipsistically, blasphemously, adapts God's assertion to Moses: 'I am that I am' (Exodus 3:14), than the abject and unworthy lover we encounter elsewhere. Stephen Regan identifies the appeal of Sonnet 121 for Auden thus:

> In its forthright disclosure of private dilemmas in the face of public admonishment, and in its acutely sensitive weighing of self-worth against social reputation, the sonnet encapsulates a concern with self-realization and self-representation that was to preoccupy Auden profoundly in both his critical and creative writings.[138]

More specifically, it represents a kind of defiance Auden aspired to, but couldn't reach. In his autobiographical poem, 'Letter to Lord Byron' (1936), he uses Shakespeare to defend himself against criticism of his 'immaturity', which is perhaps also a coded allusion to his homosexuality:

> 'No, I am that I am, and those that level
> At my abuses reckon up their own.
> I may be straight though they, themselves, be bevel.'
> So Shakespeare said, but Shakespeare must have known.
> I daren't say that except when I'm alone,
> Must hear in silence till I turn my toes up,
> 'It's such a pity Wystan never grows up.'[139]

The notion that 'Shakespeare must have known ...' resonates with Neil Corcoran's larger assertion that 'Auden identifies with Shakespeare not in his mastery but in his vulnerability'.[140]

---

[138] Ibid., p. 266. There are other allusions to 121 in Auden's essay 'Writing', published in Naomi Mitchison's *An Outline for Boys and Girls and their Parents* (1932), and in *The Sea and the Mirror* (1944), where it is identified with both Prospero and Antonio. For further discussion, see Garrington, 'Early Auden', p. 3, and Noel-Tod, 'W. H. Auden', pp. 135–8.

[139] Auden, *Letters from Iceland*.

[140] Corcoran, *Shakespeare and the Modern Poet*, p. 144.

Equally revealing is the use Auden makes of Sonnet 121 in his critical essay, 'The Prince's Dog', printed in *The Dyer's Hand and Other Essays* (1963).[141] Here Auden examines the way in which Falstaff stands apart from the other characters in *Henry IV*, whose speech is a product of 'the external situation with its questions, answers, and commands, and the inner need of each character to disclose himself to others':

> But Falstaff's speech has only one cause, his absolute insistence, at every moment and at all costs, upon disclosing himself. Half his lines could be moved from one speech to another without our noticing, for nearly everything he says is a variant upon one theme – 'I am that I am'.[142]

Whilst this makes Falstaff a natural performer, it also makes him more genuine than the types of the wicked and the worldly man, Iago and Hal respectively, who only ever say what is politic. Their deceptions are contrasted with his self-disclosure: 'Falstaff is perfectly willing to tell the world: "I am that I am, a drunken old failure".[143] But if Sonnet 121 represents a kind of self-assertion that Auden admires, Sonnet 94 stands as a warning against such openness. With more than a little autobiographical projection, Auden describes Falstaff's tragic 'absolute devotion' to a younger man:

> [Hal] finds Falstaff amusing but no more. If we could warn Falstaff of what he is too blind to see, we might well say: 'Beware, before it is too late, of becoming involved with one of those mortals
>
> > That do not do the thing they most do show,
> > Who, moving others, are themselves as stone' ...[144]

Auden may have been following his own advice when he wrote his notorious 'Introduction' to the Signet Classics edition of the *Sonnets* (1964).

In this essay, Auden distanced himself from 'The homosexual reader ... determined to secure our Top-Bard as a patron saint of the Homintern',[145] and preferred a reading based on Neo-Platonic 'mystery' rather than homosexual 'aberration':

> men and women whose sexual tastes are perfectly normal, but who enjoy and understand poetry, have always been able to read [the Sonnets] as expressions of what they understand by the word *love*, without finding the masculine pronoun an obstacle.[146]

---

[141] The title of this collection derives from another image of Shakespearean shame in Sonnet 111.

[142] Auden, *The Dyer's Hand*, p. 186.

[143] Ibid., p. 206.

[144] Ibid., pp. 191–2.

[145] Auden, 'Introduction', p. xxix.

[146] Ibid., p. xxix.

This is difficult to defend, but it is not true to state that Auden 'dismissed the possibility of homosexuality in his preface',[147] or that, 'though anyone with a knowledge of Auden's biography might expect him to celebrate and endorse the homoerotic character of 1–126, he was absolutely determined not to do so'.[148] James Fenton has issued a persuasive defence of Auden, criticising the back-projection of 1980s and 1990s ideological values onto 1964, and demonstrating how Auden had spent many years acknowledging the Sonnets' homosexuality.[149] In the lecture he gave on 4 December 1946 at the New York School of Social Research, for example, he had averred that 'All this [Sonnets 119 and 120] suggests sexual infidelity, which wouldn't make sense if there hadn't been a prior sex relationship between Shakespeare and the young man'.[150] Whilst the Introduction does not go this far, it does follow the lecture in satirising those in the past who have tried to cover up and explain away the Sonnets' sexuality:[151]

> Confronted with the extremely odd story [the Sonnets] tell, with the fact that, in so many of them, Shakespeare addresses a young man in terms of passionate devotion, the sound and sensible citizen, alarmed at the thought that our Top-Bard could have any experience with which he is unfamiliar, has either been shocked and wished that Shakespeare had never written them, or, in defiance of common sense, tried to persuade himself that Shakespeare was merely expressing in somewhat hyperbolic terms, such as an Elizabethan poet might be expected to use, what any normal man feels for a friend of his own sex.[152]

Critics have overlooked how richly allusive this passage is, but it quotes Henry Hallam who 'wished that Shakespeare had never written them', and paraphrases Edmond Malone who had argued that this was the hyperbolical language of Elizabethan friendship. It even goes on to paraphrase George Chalmers, who had denied a queer reading on the basis of Shakespeare being 'a married man and a father'.[153] Having acknowledged that it is ludicrous to deny this aspect of the Sonnets, Auden turns his

[147] Smith, 'Shakespeare's Sonnets and the History of Sexuality', p. 22.

[148] Shakespeare, *Shakespeare's Sonnets*, ed. Duncan-Jones, p. 80.

[149] Fenton, *The Strength of Poetry*, pp. 206–7.

[150] Auden, *Lectures on Shakespeare*, p. 95. It is important to note that this is not the verbatim text of Auden's lecture but pieced together from his own and his auditors' notes, with Kinney's interventions.

[151] In the lecture, Auden observes: 'Most of these sonnets were addressed to a man. This can lead to a variety of nonsensical attitudes from exercises in special pleading to discreet whitewashing', ibid., p. 86.

[152] Auden, 'Introduction', pp. xxviii–ix.

[153] Ibid., p. xxix. See Chapter 3.

focus elsewhere, but this does not mean that his argument for love as a 'mystery' is mere obfuscation. Fenton insists that the mystical aspect of *eros* was a profoundly meaningful one for Auden, as his account of first meeting Chester Kallman suggests.[154] I would also want to go back to one of Auden's stated reasons for not allowing the Sonnets to be claimed entirely by the 'Homintern', namely that this would potentially negate the historical experience of Shakespeare's readers: 'men and women ... have always been able to read [the Sonnets] as expressions of what they understand by the word *love*, without finding the masculine pronoun an obstacle'. Auden's evasion of the Sonnets' sexuality in this essay may well have had a damaging effect. As Duncan-Jones points out, 'Not until the American Joseph Pequigney's *Such is My Love* in 1985 was a homoerotic reading of *Shakespeare's Sonnets* positively and systematically championed'.[155] But although Pequigney himself recognises Auden as an obstacle,[156] he also sounds very much like Auden when he writes that,

> Just as readers of homosexual orientation can find their own amorous impulses and responses reflected in the verse of a Donne or a Sidney, so can those of heterosexual bent find theirs given consummate expression in Shakespeare's love lyrics to the young man. Thus they perform the valuable service of revealing how much alike the two modes of loving can be, the considerable extent to which they are effectively indistinguishable.[157]

What Auden's 'Introduction' also does for the Sonnets is to liberate them from the constraints of the sequence, and his objections remain powerful for any reader today: 'The only semblance of order is a division into two unequal heaps', apparently divided between a young man and a dark-haired lady, although there might be more than one of each. Whilst there are batches that clearly belong together, some appear to have been driven apart (77 and 122 on the gift of a table book).[158] Moreover, he finds the arrangement psychologically unconvincing: 'It is not, it seems to me, possible to believe that, *after* going through the experiences described in Sonnets 40–42, Shakespeare would write either Sonnet 53 ("In all external

---

[154] In 1939, Auden wrote of having experienced 'a Vision of Eros ... a revelation of creaturely glory ... the glory of a single human being'. Although sex was involved, 'physical desire is always, and without any effort of will, subordinate to the feeling of awe and reverence in the presence of a sacred being: however great his desire, the lover feels unworthy of the beloved's notice', quoted in Mendelson, *Later Auden*, p. 31.

[155] Shakespeare, *Shakespeare's Sonnets*, ed. Duncan-Jones, p. 81.

[156] Pequigney records Auden's opinion, stated at a party in January 1964, that 'it won't do just yet to admit that the Top Bard was in the homintern', *Such is My Love*, pp. 79–80.

[157] Ibid., p. 74.

[158] Auden, 'Introduction', p. xxi.

grace, you have some part,/ But you like none, none you, for constant heart") or 105', which praises the beloved as 'constant in a wondrous excellence'.[159] Finally, Auden glances at the poems with which Shakespeare apparently chose to conclude the sequence, 153 and 154: 'Any writer with an audience in mind knows that a sequence of poems must climax with one of the best. Yet the sequence as we have it concludes with two of the worst of the sonnets, trivial conceits about, apparently, going to Bath to take the waters.'[160] Auden concludes that the Quarto was not authorised by Shakespeare: 'Though Shakespeare may have shown the sonnets to one or two intimate literary friends … he wrote them, I am quite certain, as one writes a diary, for himself alone, with no thought of a public.'[161] If they must be launched upon a wider audience, Auden argues, Shakespeare can at least expect his readers to act responsibly, which means not constructing elaborate biographical fictions but 'consider[ing] the Sonnets themselves'. Acknowledging his debt to Empson (and implicitly criticising Riding and Graves), Auden speculates on the kind of reader that the 'genuine artist' wants:

> He hopes they will study the text closely enough to spot misprints. Shakespeare would be grateful to many scholars, beginning with Malone, who have suggested sensible emendations to the Q text. And he hopes they will read with patience and intelligence so as to extract as much meaning from the text as possible. If the shade of Shakespeare has read Professor William Empson's explication of 'They that have power to hurt and will do none' (Sonnet 94), he may have wondered to himself, 'Now, did I *really* say that?', but he will certainly be grateful to Mr Empson for his loving care.[162]

Auden's own 'loving care' emerges through his discussion of the Sonnets' musicality,[163] and their rhetorical variety. He singles out Sonnets 5 and 116 for their alliteration ('Then were not summer's distillation left,/ A liquid prisoner pent in walls of glass'; 'Let me not to the marriage of true minds/ Admit impediments'). To demonstrate the Sonnets' 'mastery of every possible rhetorical device', he takes 116 and quotes extensively from C. S. Lewis's analysis of Sonnet 18 ('Shall I compare thee to a summer's day'), as

---

[159] Ibid., p. xxii.
[160] Ibid.
[161] Ibid., pp. xxi, xxii, xxxv.
[162] Ibid., p. xix.
[163] This relates to the larger critical movement in the 1930s to celebrate Shakespeare's plays as 'dramatic symphonies'. See Taylor, *Reinventing Shakespeare*, pp. 239–40.

demonstrating 'the avoidance of monotony by an artful arithmetical variation of theme or illustration'.[164]

Of course, this is rather dry stuff for any reader, let alone the 'foolish
and idle' whom Auden rebuked for coming to the Sonnets for biographical
titillation.[165] But in 1964 there was another way of experiencing Auden's
repudiation of the Quarto, whilst taking vicarious delight in Shakespeare's
sexual relations with both the Fair Youth and the Dark Lady. This was
Anthony Burgess's novel, *Nothing Like the Sun*, which described itself as 'A
Story of Shakespeare's Love-Life' but was also a meditation on the Sonnets.

Nothing Like the Sun: Darkening Shakespeare's Sonnets

Burgess's novel was written to commemorate the quartercentenary of
Shakespeare's birth, but its portrayal of the poet is hardly sentimental. In
a reading heavily indebted to Freud, Burgess splits Shakespeare in two.
There is WS, writer and superego, who is ambitious to progress in the
world and exercises discretion in his dealings with Southampton.[166] And
there is Will (invoking the Sonnets' frequent pun) who is subject to his
violent desire for boys, dark ladies and decadent aristocrats, and tormented
by both Puritan misgivings and venereal disease. Whilst Burgess draws on
the anti-romanticising approach of Joyce,[167] he substitutes *Ulysses'* preoccupation with *Hamlet* for the Sonnets, and his interest is more critical, in
both senses of that word, than biographical.

Like Auden, Burgess assumes that Shakespeare did not write the Sonnets
for publication. His WS values the privacy and exclusivity afforded by
the fetishised wooden chest[168] into which Southampton puts individual
Sonnets as he receives them:

[164] Auden, 'Introduction', p. xxvii. Auden here quotes from Lewis' analysis in *English Literature in the Sixteenth Century*, p. 507.
[165] Auden, 'Introduction', pp. xx–xxi.
[166] Burgess explains the decision to use initials: 'I called Shakespeare WS because too many connotations cluster round the full name; it needs to be purged of all the harmonics of greatness in a novel which has no concern with greatness', 'Genesis and Headache', p. 35.
[167] In the Foreword, Burgess acknowledges that he has taken the plot of Anne cuckolding Shakespeare with his brother, Richard, from *Ulysses*. For further discussion of Burgess's debt, see Stinson, *Anthony Burgess Revisited*.
[168] This imagined chest recurs in a number of recent biographical fictions of Shakespeare, for example, the 1998 film *Shakespeare in Love*, which tantalisingly positions the chest behind Shakespeare in the opening credits, or Robert Winder's *The Final Act of Mr Shakespeare* (2010), in which the chest goes up in flames along with the first Globe theatre. It probably dates back at least as far as William Henry Ireland's fictitious chest.

the sheaf of sonnets in the camphorwood box grew thicker. Those were poems by which he would never make any public name as a sonneteer: they were for one reader's eyes only. Sidney had told the world of his wrecked love for Lady Penelope Devereux, bonny sweet Robin's sister, now poor Penny Rich; Daniel had published his *Delia* and Drayton's *Idea* was going from hand to hand; but, though there were rumours of Mr WS's 'sugared sonnets among his private friends', those rumours must never sharpen into exterior knowledge. There were some things that must remain secret.[169]

The value of this chest is partly created by the precarious existence which the Sonnets suffer outside it. One is thrown onto a table, wafted by a breeze from the casement window to the floor, and then trodden upon by Southampton.[170] Another is caught in a domestic scuffle: '[WS] wrestled with his father for possession of thirteen lines (a sonnet thus incomplete being most unlucky), and then the paper tore … His father bit his bottom lip, looking now on his son, now on the rent and deformed sonnet.'[171] But if this frailty seems to valorise the processes by which the Sonnets will be made more durable, through preservation in the chest and pub-lication in a book, both solutions are viewed as acts of betrayal. Rather than preserving the Sonnets' singularity, the chest contributes to their adulteration: 'Jealously, WS saw other poems than his own, but certainly there was that first sonnet.'[172] Moreover, one theory about how the Sonnets get into print is that they are snatched from thence: 'Was it not perhaps dirty Chapman … who had, putting his own poems in that spice-smelling box, stolen in spite and jealousy and run in glee to Field?'[173] WS is clearly horrified at the idea of the Sonnets being published: 'poems I have written for friends have been thumbed by dirty hands'.[174] But as though to torture him further, Burgess inserts his own fake Sonnet into the novel as one of the first that Shakespeare writes:

> Fair is as fair as fair itself allows,
> And hiding in the dark is not less fair.
> The married blackness of my mistress' brows
> Is thus fair's home for fair abideth there.
> My love being black, her beauty may not shine
> And light so foiled to heat alone may turn.
> Heat is my heart, my hearth, all earth is mine;

---

[169] Burgess, *Nothing Like the Sun*, p. 126.
[170] Ibid., p. 108. This happens again at p. 180.
[171] Ibid., pp. 20–1.
[172] Ibid., p. 106.
[173] Ibid., pp. 174–5.
[174] Ibid., p. 171.

Heaven do I scorn when in such hell I burn.
All other beauty's light I lightly rate.
My love is as my love is, for the dark.
In night enthroned, I ask no better state,
Than thus to range, nor seek a guiding spark.
    And childlike I am put to school of night
    For to seek light beyond the reach of light.[175]

This sonnet is a credible early Shakespearean work for a number of reasons.
It plays on the possibility that at least one of the Sonnets, 145 ('Those lips
that love's own hand did make') is very early, dating back to 1582, and
Shakespeare's courtship of Anne Hathaway. The comparative ordinariness
of this lyric had long suggested to critics, before Andrew Gurr's defence of
the poem, that it was 'Perhaps not Shakespeare's'.[176] Burgess's fake sounds
like an apprentice piece on the paradox of dark as fair which Sidney
had made famous in *Astrophil and Stella*, and which recurs in 'genuine'
Shakespeare Sonnets such as 132: 'Then will I swear beauty herself is black,/
And all they foul who thy complexion lack.' Similarly, the line 'Heaven do
I scorn when in such hell I burn' convinces as a first draft of the conclusion
of 129: 'To shun the heaven that leads men to this hell.'

It was not until the Foreword of the 1982 edition that Burgess owned
up to having invented this sonnet. Whilst one consequence of this imitation is to remind the reader of the potential openness of the Shakespearean
poetic canon – it is certainly possible that new Sonnets might be found –
another is to make the reader doubt his/her ability to determine what a
'Shakespeare' sonnet looks like, and the presence of this fake may cast
lesser known poems into suspicion. I found myself checking Sonnet 91
as quoted: 'Thy love is better than high birth to me,/ Richer than wealth,
prouder than garments' cost,/ Of more delight than hawks or horses be …',
for it sounded too pedestrian to be 'Shakespeare'. Moreover, Burgess does
not protect the integrity of the canon by destroying the fake. Rather, this
sonnet has a robust existence, circulating among Shakespeare's acquaintance in Stratford until it falls into the hands of its author who acknowledges it as his own, though it remains outside the batch that an anonymous
agent is trying to publish. In this way, Burgess further undermines the
integrity of the Quarto by suggesting that some Sonnets are omitted.[177] At

---

[175] Ibid., pp. 17–21.
[176] Shakespeare, *The Works of Shakespeare: Sonnets*, ed. Knox Pooler, p. 137, and Gurr, 'Shakespeare's
First Poem: Sonnet 145'.
[177] For further discussion of Burgess's fake, in the context of Shakespeare's writing process, see my
article, 'Shakespeare's Sonnets and the Claustrophobic Reader'.

the same time, Burgess's brio in producing a fake relies on the comparatively recent canonicity of the Sonnets. When the Sonnets were deemed spurious or supplemental in the late eighteenth century, as we saw in the case of William Henry Ireland, they were never counterfeited: they have to be genuine to produce what is fake.

Burgess also undermines the notion of a sequence (and thereby indirectly the authority of the Quarto) through the order in which they are written. Ignoring for a moment those fragments of Sonnets that articulate Shakespeare's consciousness in the novel,[178] the order of composition is x ('Fair is as fair'), 20, 91, 1, 8, 104,[179] 129, 107, 111 and 110. The invention of nearly all of these Sonnets is driven by Shakespeare's relationship with Southampton. They begin as a meditation on his beauty that slips into a daring expression of love (91, 20). They become a financially motivated act of persuasion (1, 8), and then a more earnest attempt to reconcile with Southampton after their falling out (107, 110, 111). The Dark Lady Sonnets are not seen to be written in the novel, occupying a kind of shadow existence, as when WS tells Southampton that he is welcome to his mistress: 'Take too, I say, what I have writ for her, by her unread. Add them to the odorous fellowship of that spicy chest. Take this sonnet also, of the perils of lust (hark to the dog's panting; "had, having and in quest to have").'[180] By this means, Burgess explains how the two collections, Fair Youth and Dark Lady, came to be published together, but he also makes a distinction between those artful sonnets that patronage requires, and those WS writes for the release of his passion – and these are not straightforwardly divided between addressees. Early on, before meeting the Dark Lady, WS acknowledges: 'And there was this damnable love, this ravishment of the senses, bursting into jealousy that, in the quietness of his own chamber, he must unload into verse to be torn up after.'[181] Interestingly, Sonnet 129 'of the perils of lust' belongs to neither Fair Youth nor Dark Lady, and neither homosexual nor heterosexual passion specifically. Its

---

[178] There are unacknowledged quotations from 87 which recurs as a song ('Farewell, farewell, my blessing,/ Too dear art thou for any man's possessing' (pp. 72–3)), 29 ('I cannot waste my whole life in longing for this man's art and that man's scope' (p. 97)), 94 ('Power to hurt and he would do it' (p. 110)), and 146 ('my soul, centre of my sinful earth' (p. 159)). The fact that Burgess constructs all of Shakespeare's language from early modern lexis makes these Sonnet quotations far less obtrusive than they were in, for example, Harris's *Shakespeare and his Love*.

[179] The dating of this Sonnet is difficult to judge. WS remembers having written it in the early days before his falling out with Southampton, and quotes himself ' "To me, fair friend, you never can be old, For as you were when first your eye I eyed' (oh, vile!) 'Such seems your beauty still'" (Burgess, *Nothing Like the Sun*, p. 161).

[180] Ibid., p. 157.

[181] Ibid., p. 112.

centrality to Burgess' conception of WS's personality, rather than his biography, is reflected by the way in which its phrases linger in his mind. At the most violent period of his relationship with Fatimah, 'To her to rail, beat, near-kill', WS describes their relationship as 'a burning hell of pleasure' (which also recalls Sonnet 144), and again as 'a wretched dim hell of mine own making, spent, used, shameless, shameful'.[182] Finally, towards the end of the novel, he observes: 'It was the agony of knowing that it was departed, all the insanity of former love (had, having and in quest to have).'[183]

But if Burgess' novel downplays the creation of the Dark Lady Sonnets, the attention he turns to the figure of the Dark Lady will be one of the novel's most radical acts, and one from which he would later distance himself in his non-fictional biography, *Shakespeare* (1970). Here he claims:

> It is best to keep the Dark Lady anonymous, even composite. Shakespeare was a long time in London, and we cannot think that he limited himself to one affair. The Sonnets make statements of permanent validity about some of the commonest experiences known to men – obsession with a woman's body, revulsion, pain in desertion, resignation at another's treachery. Shakespeare was no John Keats mooning over Fanny Brawne, but a realist aware of self-delusion, the tugging of the black and the white spirits, and the irresistible lure of the primal darkness that resides in all women, whether white or black.[184]

It is worth overlooking the extraordinary misogyny of this assertion to consider how Burgess' novel opens up the range of possible identities for the Dark Lady.

She is first called up by the quotation from Sonnet 130, which stands as an epigraph:

> My mistress' eyes are nothing like the sun,
> Coral is far more red than her lips' red,
> If snow be white, why then her breasts are dun,
> If hairs be wires, black wires grow on her head …

This disavowal of conventional flattery aptly introduces Burgess' fictional biography of Shakespeare,[185] whilst focusing on the unconventional

---

[182] Ibid., pp. 154–5.

[183] Ibid., p. 208. Burgess seems also to have been haunted by this phrase: 'I know of no deeper disgust than that expressed in the phrase "had, having and in quest to have" where the poet seems to hear himself panting like a dog after a bitch in heat', *Shakespeare*, p. 130.

[184] Ibid., p. 131.

[185] Andrew Biswell suggests that the title 'is intended as a warning. It implies, with a fair degree of humility, that the fakeries of Burgess's language are a dim candle in comparison with the brighter Shakespearean sun, and that reading a fictionalised biography is a poor substitute for immersing

mistress who will fuel his verse. A number of Dark Ladies follow. These are the dark-haired, dark-eyed girls, some sexually promiscuous, others chaste, whom WS woos in Stratford. But as he enters the more diverse metropolitan cultures of Bristol and then London, the Dark Lady is no longer fair-but-dark but racially dark, represented first by the black prostitutes he meets in a brothel, and then the mysterious, 'brown'-skinned beauty, Fatimah, also known as Mistress Lucy. Burgess is here drawing on the work of G. B. Harrison who had argued in 1933 that the Dark Lady was a 'Black Woman', 'a courtesan, notorious to fashionable young gentlemen of the Inns of Court who took their pleasures in Clerkenwell'. His evidence was the mention in a Gray's Inn entertainment of one 'Lucy Negro Abbess de Clerkenwell', as well as testimonies to the existence of black prostitutes in London.[186] In the same year as Burgess's novel came out, however, Leslie Hotson argued that 'Lucy Negro' was actually Lucy Morgan, a fair-skinned gentlewoman of the Queen *c.* 1579–81, who fell into disgrace and was condemned to Bridewell for prostitution in 1600, before returning to her brothel in Clerkenwell: she was 'black' only in her deeds.[187]

The appearance of Hotson's disproving of the Lucy Negro theory just after Burgess's novel was published might explain why the latter distanced himself from this aspect of the novel in his 1970 biography, but Burgess seems to have had a genuine interest in the racial implications of the Sonnets' language of blackness.[188] He challenges readers in 1960s Britain, still predominantly white and experiencing the first influx of immigration from British colonies, to rethink their definitions of female beauty through Shakespeare's responses:

> If English men were white, [WS] thought, then must she be called black; but black she could not in truth be called, rather gold, but then not gold, nor royal purple neither, for when we say colours we see a flatness, as of cloth, but here was flesh that moved and swam on the light's tide, ever changing in hue but always of a richness that could only be termed royal; her colour was royalty. For her hair, it coiled in true blackness; her lips were

---

ourselves in the deeper waters of the original plays and poems', *The Real Life of Anthony Burgess*, pp. 284–5.

[186] Harrison, *Shakespeare at Work, 1592–1603*, pp. 310–11. The two most obviously indebted passages in *Nothing Like the Sun* are James Burbage's account of Lucy's origins, and the gossip Southampton relates, pp. 138–9, 141–2.

[187] Hotson, *Mr W. H.*, pp. 238–55, 254.

[188] In the screenplay he wrote for a Hollywood musical about Shakespeare's life, *Will!*, and later in his novel *Enderby's Dark Lady* (1984), the Shakespearean heroine is no longer a 'brown' woman hailing from the East Indies, but a 'black' African, born into slavery. For further discussion, see Franssen, *Shakespeare's Literary Lives*, p. 149.

thick; her nose not tightened against the cold air, like an English nose, an Anne nose, not pinched as at the meagreness of the sun, but flat and wide.[189]

This passage includes an intriguing reworking of Sonnet 20, replacing the male addressee's 'all hues in his controlling' with the black woman's ability to engross all colours, 'ever changing in hue'.

That said, there is still much to trouble us in *Nothing Like the Sun*'s representation of the Dark Lady. Although initially distinguished from prostitutes, Fatimah effectively becomes one through WS's assumptions about her, as well as through their physical and financial transactions. Having forced himself upon her, WS regrets to find that he has not taken her virginity: '[this] disappointment makes a kind of anger which makes a kind of savagery. But I possess her in a terrible joy, the appetite growing with the act of feeding, which astonished me. And in the end I coldly see that I have a mistress. And a very rare one'.[190] This is a truly chilling appropriation of Sonnet 130's 'I find my love as rare …'. Moreover, Fatimah/Lucy is not only relentlessly objectified sexually, but Burgess invokes Orientalist stereotypes which dehumanise her even as they make her a goddess, and which silence her even as they fill WS with words: 'naked, gold, glowing, burnished, burning, the sun, all desire of him … he would be possessed of all time's secrets and his very mouth grow golden and utter speech for which the very gods waited and would be silent to hear'.[191] And yet, Burgess' inclusion of black women into early modern London, into Shakespearean biography and into the Sonnet narrative is progressive for the time. As Anne Hathaway acknowledges, 'There are little poems, and some are to men and some are of a black woman'.[192] It would be another three decades before this proposition would be given any more serious academic attention.

The Black Woman Behind the Dark Lady in the 1990s

The racial implications of the term 'dark' in early modern lyric poetry began to gain critical traction in the 1990s. In *Things of Darkness: Economies of Race and Gender in Early Modern England* (1995), Kim F. Hall exposed and challenged

---

[189] Burgess, *Nothing Like the Sun*, pp. 57–8.
[190] Ibid., p. 150.
[191] Ibid., p. 9. For further discussion of Burgess's dualistic vision, including the paradigm of goddess/whore, see Belastegui, 'Negativity and Dialogical Play in *Nothing Like the Sun*', p. 31.
[192] Burgess, *Nothing Like the Sun*, p. 171.

literary criticism's traditional (and almost pathological) insistence that blackness means nothing beyond its antithesis to 'whiteness'; that is, in the absolute insistence on a merely aesthetic basis for blackness in the Renaissance, a practice that extends even to reading direct references to Africa as mere signs of physical beauty.[193]

Hall takes as an example Stephen Booth's glossing of 'black' in his edition of Shakespeare's Sonnets, whose meaning is 'only (and simply) established in an agonistic context with the word "fair"', and carries no racial meaning.[194] Hall's own focus is on the 'poetics of color' in the sonnet sequence, specifically Sidney's *Astrophil and Stella*, rather than any literal inter-racial encounter. She explores the tropes of female blackness which emerge from the white male aristocrat's need 'to negotiate involvements with the sexual, racial and "linguistic" difference brought about by increased travel abroad'.[195] Nevertheless, these tropes do include some obvious crossover with Shakespeare's Dark Lady Sonnets. The recurrent image of the male poet 'lightening' the dark lady, and thereby proving his linguistic mastery over her, is present through its presumed failure in Sonnets 130 and 147, but also its success in Sonnet 127:

> In the old age black was not counted fair,
> Or if it were, it bore not beauty's name;
> But now is black beauty's successive heir,
> And beauty slandered with a bastard shame:
> For since each hand hath put on nature's power,
> Fairing the foul with art's false borrowed face,
> Sweet beauty hath no name, no holy bower,
> But is profaned, if not lives in disgrace.
> Therefore my mistress' eyes are raven black …

Hall notes how blackness represents a positive contrast to that treacherous white beauty which is only created by cosmetics, and the way in which 'just as poets begin to depict Petrarchism as an empty and devalued currency, they turn to the language of blackness, which becomes an unexplored and endlessly fertile space for poetic invention'.[196] More pernicious than the representation of darkness in Shakespeare's Sonnets, Hall argues, is their valorisation of whiteness, which is implicated in England's colonialist enterprises and, specifically, its participation in the slave trade. In

---

[193] Hall, *Things of Darkness*, p. 69.
[194] Ibid., pp. 69–70.
[195] Ibid., pp. 66, 64.
[196] Ibid., p. 116.

an article entitled ' "These bastard signs of fair": Literary Whiteness in Shakespeare's Sonnets', Hall observes that

> The desirability and overvaluation of a seemingly abstract whiteness in conjunction with images linking blood, family and property interests … has material effects in that it upholds a system of power which increasingly licences the exploitation of people perceived as non-white.[197]

In this reading of the procreation/Fair Youth Sonnets, issues of race are suddenly illuminated where historically one had not expected to find them, opening up new questions about how the two 'sequences' relate to one another.

These questions were also central to another seminal essay, published in 1993, Margreta de Grazia's 'The Scandal of Shakespeare's Sonnets' – indeed, the essay cites Hall's PhD among its footnotes. Whilst keeping faith with the Malonean bipartite division, de Grazia redistributes the scandal from the homosexuality of the Fair Youth Sonnets to the miscegenation of the Dark Lady collection. Beginning, like Hall, with the social concerns of the procreation Sonnets, specifically the desire to maintain an unpolluted aristocratic bloodline, de Grazia detects a turn at Sonnet 127,

> with the shocking declaration that 'now is blacke beauties successive heire' … As if a black child had been born of a fair parent, a miscegenating successor is announced, one who razes fair's lineage ('And Beautie slandered with a bastard shame') and seizes fair's language ('beauty hath no name') – genealogy and etymology.[198]

Whilst de Grazia's reading is mainly concerned to distinguish between the early modern categories of 'pederastic love of a boy', which maintains the status quo, and the gynerastic lust which produces 'a waste of shame', it also insists upon greater critical receptivity to the racial implications of darkness:

> Tradition has been ever slower to entertain the possibility that these poems express desire for a black woman rather than desire for a boy. But the important work that is being done on England's contact with Africa and on its cultural representations of that contact is making it increasingly difficult to dissociate in this period blackness from racial blackness – black from blackamoor.[199]

---

[197] Hall, ' "These bastard signs of fair" ', p. 66.
[198] De Grazia, 'The Scandal of Shakespeare's Sonnets', pp. 45–6.
[199] Ibid., p. 162.

Finally, in his essay, '"Be Dark but Not Too Dark": Shakespeare's Dark Lady as a Sign of Color', Marvin Hunt extended the implications of this critical work to explore a more literal interpretation of the Dark Lady's darkness. Like de Grazia, he goes back over the reception history of the Sonnets to demonstrate how current interpretations are limited, arguing for a critical semiotics of colour that has traditionally included 'white', 'brown' and 'black', but where 'brown' means only the darker colouring of the European Caucasian. It is only as 'black' that the Dark Lady 'becomes semiotically if not literally a figure of radical cultural and racial otherness'.[200] Hunt pursues this figure through mid-seventeenth-century poems written to celebrate black women, and perceives some of the same conventions in the Dark Lady Sonnets, for example the language of drowning in an ocean that destroys all difference, as in Eldred Revett's poem, 'One Enamou'rd on a Black-Moor'.[201] At the same time, Hunt suggests that the Dark Lady Sonnets might reflect sympathetically on the status of African slaves in Shakespeare's England through a further re-interpretation of Sonnet 127, specifically line 7: 'Sweet beauty hath no name, no holy bower'. Hunt explains that the slave was considered nameless until s/he was given a Christian name in the process of baptism which also meant that they were free. This created tension between slave owners and the clergy who felt it their duty to baptise and save souls, meaning that the former might ban their slaves from entering a church at all, as implied by Sonnet 127. More generally, Hunt finds that

> in the commonplace imagery of freedom and imprisonment, tyranny and flight, inclusion and isolation, and slavery and liberation of the final movement of his sonnet cycle Shakespeare exploits a discourse of slavery in later Elizabethan England, a discourse that presents the poet-speaker and his fair accomplice, at least at the level of imagery, as slaves of a slave.[202]

But if this argument opens up our understanding of the Dark Lady in interesting ways, it also raises issues to do with reading these poems as a 'sequence'.

Hunt suggests that his argument about Sonnet 127 is potentially 'compromised by sonnet 128', given that playing the virginals was a specif-ically courtly form of musical performance, unlikely to have been practised by a former slave. Hunt calls upon Heather Dubrow's argument (discussed in the Introduction) that Sonnet 128 is 'misplaced' in the Quarto and is

---

[200] Hunt, '"Be Dark but Not Too Dark"', p. 371.
[201] Ibid., pp. 380–2.
[202] Ibid., pp. 385–6.

really about the Fair Youth to defend his reading.[203] Yet this has been seen as a weakness in his argument. Paul Franssen defends the inclusion of Sonnet 128 among the Dark Lady Sonnets on the basis that it 'shows openly physical desire for lips and kisses, a topos otherwise found only in those sonnets traditionally linked with the Dark Lady'. But he also warns that

> This attempt at preserving the Dark Lady's colour risks disintegrating her altogether: for if we reassign this sonnet to the Fair Friend, there is no telling how many others could also be reassigned. As I have suggested, the deconstruction of the Dark Lady as the sole addressee of sonnets 127–54 is not in itself problematic, but it does undermine the notion of a single Dark Lady, of whatever skin colour, that Hunt takes as his starting point.[204]

I am not sure that Hunt's argument does require a single Dark Lady, but this concern that all characterisation within the sequence will be destroyed by its disruption is telling. What we would potentially lose in terms of narrative is surely outweighed by the possibility of individual Sonnets having a wider and deeper resonance, becoming more culturally and historically situated, as advocated by Hall above.

In terms of creative appropriation, the late twentieth-century novel has tended to explore the Dark Lady in terms of Hunt's 'brown' category – as Jewish or Italian, most often in the person of Aemilia Lanyer,[205] whilst contemporary poetry has tended to parody the Sonnets' canonical status but has not investigated their racial politics. Harryette Mullen's 'Dim Lady', an adaptation of Sonnet 130, published in *Sleeping with the Dictionary* (2002), is an intriguing case in point. Identifying as an African American poet, Mullen constructs a 'black voice' in collections such as *Tree Tall Woman* and *Muse & Drudge*,[206] exploring how 'the speech of African Americans reflects our historic separation from mainstream culture and our critical perspective on the language of power. As descendants of slaves in the land of the free, we're accustomed to paradox'.[207] Moreover, the poem that precedes 'Dim Lady' in the collection locates her Sonnet adaptation in this racially and linguistically charged atmosphere. 'Denigration' is a brilliant and disturbing play on the n-word, exposing the negative connotations of

---

[203] Ibid., p. 387, fn. 14.

[204] Franssen, *Shakespeare's Literary Lives*, pp. 151–2.

[205] See, for example, Erica Jong's *Serenissima* (1997) in which the Dark Lady is Jewish, or Grace Tiffany's later novel, *Paint* (2013), in which Emilia darkens her skin to make herself look more Italian.

[206] See her discussion with Daniel Kane of the ways in which race has informed her work, 'An Interview with Harryette Mullen'.

[207] See Henning, 'Conversation with Harryette Mullen: B to D'.

words aurally but not etymologically linked, such as 'niggardly', 'niggling', 'neglect' and 'renege'. It begins with the challenge: 'Did we surprise our teachers who had niggling doubts about the picayune brains of small black children who reminded them of clean pickaninnies on a box of laundry soap?'[208] When we come to the next poem, and the title 'Dim Lady', in which 'Dark' obviously lingers, we might expect something similar. However, 'Dim', meaning low-lit, is contrasted with the luminescence not of the sun, as in Shakespeare's Sonnet, but of man-made light: 'My honeybunch's peepers are nothing like neon.' The natural comparisons of Sonnet 130 (sun, coral, snow) are replaced with garish, artificial products – the wipe-clean tablecloths in a pizza parlour, the Liquid Paper that whites over a mistake. Thus, the overwhelming focus of the parody is on an ugly, disposable, consumerist culture in which the Shakespearean Sonnet is debased. This debasement may make the Sonnet more accessible for young, modern audiences, but it avoids any deeper engagement with the contrast between ideal female beauty, coded extreme white, and the material reality which is darker and may be black. This is particularly notable in Mullen's adaptation of the line, 'If snow be white, why then her breasts are dun', 'dun' being glossed as a grey-brown colour, offering instead 'If Liquid Paper is white, her racks are institutional beige', 'beige' carrying no obvious racial undertones and undermining the contrast between white and dark. Extremes of white femininity do lie behind the poem. The speaker states that 'I don't know any Marilyn Monroes', and later avers that s/he prefers his/her beloved over any 'platinum movie idol'. But again, the whiteness referred to here, like the Liquid Paper, comes from a bottle. In this respect, Mullen's poem might resonate with Shakespeare's theme of the artificiality of white beauty which uses cosmetics to create the impression of whiteness, but it does nothing to valorise blackness by comparison. Even the term 'Slinkys', which has been identified as a racial allusion, turns out not to be really dark but the colour of 'dishwater'.

Mullen's avoidance of this aspect of Sonnet 130 certainly poses interesting questions, for, as Randall Couch suggests:

> Inevitably the reader tests alternatives: wouldn't the pragmatic equivalent of the sonnet's argument, for a black speaker, be to contest an idealized blackness in favour of a pale beloved? How would that rewrite identity into the blazon tradition? Might a black writer ventriloquize a white persona?

---

[208] Mullen, *Sleeping with the Dictionary*, p. 19. Mullen discusses her methodology in this poem in 'Conversation with Harryette Mullen: B to D'.

Could the poem's speaker be critiquing a hierarchy of skin tones among African Americans?[209]

But once again, a better understanding of the circulation of Shakespeare's individual Sonnets can enhance our interpretation of the specific allusion. In Timo Müller's recent book, *The African American Sonnet: A Literary History* (2018), Shakespeare's Sonnet 130 can be found as a source for 'the first African American love sonnet explicitly devoted to a black person'.[210] In 1899, Samuel A. Beadle 'a slave-born lawyer from Mississippi [and] the first African American who published a sonnet sequence', concluded his collection *Sonnets to My Love*, with the following lyric:

> Who is the queen of my fancy? Well,
> My friend would you really like to know?
> She is not yellow, white nor gray, and so
> Must be something else. I'm afraid to tell,
> Since all that's mean between heaven and hell,
> Abhor the colour black. She's cherub, though,
> And all the fair and the impartial know,
> She is a beautiful, beautiful angel.
> I care not what your prejudice, you'll love
> Her in your heart, when the light of her dark eyes,
> Beam on you, like the flash of stars above
> A dark and rolling cloud; her form complies
> With all the art the Grecian sculptors prove:
> 'Her voice?' A chord escaped from paradise.[211]

Here, Beadle borrows from Sonnet 130 by listing the beloved's perceived deficiencies, before celebrating his love for her. He replaces the negative, 'I love to hear her speak, yet well I know/ That music hath a far more pleasing sound', with a final line which reinstates the divine praise that Shakespeare rejected. Beadle also shows a sensitivity to the fair–dark opposition of Shakespeare's other Sonnets, in the line 'And all the fair and the impartial know ...', so that fairness becomes a moral quality that does not inhere in whiteness. It is fascinating that at the beginning of the century, we can find a more radical deployment of the racial politics of this Sonnet than one hundred years later, and that the question of those racial politics themselves is more obvious and needs less defence. Müller observes that 'The African features of Shakespeare's beloved were rarely acknowledged by nineteenth-century readers, but for Beadle they provide an important

[209] Couch, 'A Eurydice Beyond my Maestro', n.p.
[210] Müller, *The African American Sonnet*, p. 25.
[211] As quoted by Müller, ibid.

precedent that serves to legitimize his articulation of black love in a traditionally white form'.[212]

By the end of the twentieth century, Shakespeare's Sonnets have enabled the expression of a greater range of sexual and racial identities than at any other time in their history, and their responsiveness to 'minority' experiences has become a crucial aspect of their success. And yet, it is also true that what we think of as new and innovative and even radical in our thinking about the Sonnets has usually already been thought of or argued a century before. If we had a better appreciation of the Sonnets' critical and creative history, we might appreciate all that we have collectively forgotten about them.

[212] Ibid., p. 26.

Conclusion
But Thy Eternal Summer Shall Not Fade, 1998–2019

To conclude this study of the Sonnets' afterlife, I would like to consider how even the most familiar/banal Sonnet responds to (and is refashioned by) changing cultural and political pressures in the twenty-first century. The consideration of the individual lyric at the expense of the biographical narrative is fundamental to this renewal of critical and creative meaning.

> Shall I compare thee to a summer's day?
> Thou art more lovely and more temperate.
> Rough winds do shake the darling buds of May.
> And summer's lease hath all too short a date:
> Sometime too hot the eye of heaven shines,
> And often is his gold complexion dimmed;
> And every fair from fair sometime declines,
> By chance, or nature's changing course, untrimmed:
> But thy eternal summer shall not fade,
> Nor lose possession of that fair thou ow'st,
> Nor shall death brag thou wander'st in his shade
> When in eternal lines to time thou grow'st:
> > So long as men can breathe or eyes can see,
> > So long lives this, and this gives life to thee.

As I write, Sonnet 18 is perhaps the most famous Shakespeare Sonnet in British popular culture, regularly topping lists of 'Most Romantic Shakespeare Sonnets' and chosen to represent him in *The People's Favourite Poems* (2018).[1] Its status is also attested to within the academy: in *A Companion to Shakespeare's Sonnets* (2007), Michael Schoenfeldt links it with Sonnet 116 as 'among the most famous descriptions of the tenderness and authenticity which love is capable of producing'.[2] But whilst Sonnet 18 seems to testify

---

[1] When Gary Dexter recently offered members of the British public the chance to pay for him to recite their favourite poem, he chose Sonnet 18 as his representative 'Shakespeare'. See *The People's Favourite Poems*, p. 4.
[2] Schoenfeldt, 'Introduction', p. 4.

to the timelessness of Shakespeare's Sonnets – a synechdoche for what we mean by 'Shakespeare's Sonnets' – it has been susceptible to considerable critical and creative change in the last two decades.

In the film, *Shakespeare in Love* (1998), directed by John Madden from a screenplay by Marc Norman and Tom Stoppard, the romantic plot and poetic text mainly derive from *Romeo and Juliet*; 'Shall I compare thee to a summer's day?' is the only Sonnet included.³ Shakespeare's impulse to write it comes during a rehearsal at the Rose in which Lady Viola, disguised as Thomas Kent, in the part of Romeo, is expressing his love for Rosaline. Shakespeare warns Kent not to put too much passion into the speech: 'Don't spend it all at once'.⁴ The verb 'spend', in the context of Shakespeare advising a beautiful youth not to waste his love, recalls the procreation Sonnets, and yet Shakespeare exits to write Sonnet 18 for Lady Viola, implying his desire to leave the public and gender-confused world of the early modern stage, in favour of a private, aristocratic world of courtly romance. Moreover, although it is first Thomas who receives the Sonnet, the fact that Shakespeare has directed it to Viola 'by the hand of Thomas Kent' clarifies that he has no intention of sending sonnets to a boy. The scene quickly shifts to Lady Viola in her bedchamber reading the poem in Shakespeare's hand over which the camera lingers covetously.

But why choose Sonnet 18? The most obvious reason is familiarity – the screenwriters assume that British and American audiences will take pleasure in the moment of its conception and be able to recall the lines as read. The 'tenderness' and 'authenticity' which Schoenfeldt finds in the Sonnet also carry a powerful romantic charge which generates audience pleasure, and which seems to authenticate the film's portrait of Shakespeare as 'the poet of love'. More cynically, this is a lyric whose fame has elevated it above the Quarto sequence and any biographical narrative about Shakespeare. Its absence of gender pronouns makes it particularly blank in terms of Shakespeare's presumed sexuality, but it generally reads as heterosexual in our culture (a consequence of its interpretative history since the nineteenth century). A modern audience is more likely to identify its terms of admiration, 'Thou art more lovely', 'darling buds of May' and 'thy eternal summer', with female beauty, and its repeated emphasis on fairness, 'And every fair from fair sometime declines', seems to point directly to the actress

³ The film also shows some basic indebtedness to the 1941 novel, *No Bed for Bacon*, by Caryl Brahms and S. J. Simon, which also gives a privileged position to Sonnet 18, by having this occupy the closing lines of the novel. The 1998 film does allude to another Sonnet, no. 17, when Shakespeare speaks of his love to Thomas Kent, 'Oh, if I could write the beauty of her eyes! I was born to look in them and know myself'. However, the homoeroticism of the ensuing kiss is quickly foreclosed as he discovers Thomas's true identity, and this 'procreation' Sonnet, with its implied male addressee, has been altered to 'her eyes'.
⁴ *Shakespeare in Love* (1998).

playing Viola. *Shakespeare in Love* has been condemned by academic critics for its denial of Shakespeare's 'homosexuality' in the shaping of his life and career,[5] and the choice of Sonnet 18 acts repressively here, distorting the truth of Shakespeare's biography.

Sixteen years later, Sonnet 18 is still primarily identified with Shakespearean heterosexuality, but the reception of the Sonnet has changed significantly. Lee Hall's adaptation of *Shakespeare in Love*, first performed on stage in 2014, opens with Shakespeare struggling to write the Sonnet:

WILL: Shall I compare the.

> The ...
>
> *The company create Will's desk. They assemble around the desk and Will takes his place. Throughout the play, wherever possible, the company observe the action when they are not part of it.*
>
> Shall I compare ... thee? Shall I compare thee! ... to a ... to a ...?
>
> Shall I compare thee to a ... sum ... a sum ... a something, something ...
>
> Damn it.
>
> Shall I compare thee to a mummer's play?
>
> Shall I compare thee ... to ... an autumn morning? An afternoon in springtime? Zounds.
>
> *This is not right either ...*[6]

The delight we are presumed to take in the spectacle of Shakespeare suffering from writer's block is not new (see Shaw's *Dark Lady*), though it has rarely been associated with the Sonnets. Nor is there anything radical in the idea that Shakespeare wrote Sonnets professionally, and for commission, rather than to express heartfelt emotions – we have seen this idea discussed by John Payne Collier and Gerald Massey in the mid-nineteenth century. Nor is Marlowe's intrusion new. In the 1998 *Shakespeare in Love*, it was Marlowe who had to rescue Shakespeare from *Romeo and Ethel the Pirate's Daughter*, and here again he intervenes in the Sonnet:

MARLOWE: A summer's day.
SHAKESPEARE: What?
MARLOWE: A summer's day. Start with something lovely, temperate, and thoroughly trite. Gives you somewhere to go.[7]

If we know anything about the early years of Shakespeare's poetic career, it is galling that Marlowe should come in and complete the line, given the number of times that 'Come live with me and be my love' would

---

[5] See Iyengar, 'Shakespeare in Heterolove'.
[6] Hall, *Shakespeare in Love*, p. 3.
[7] Ibid., p. 4.

be reprinted by 1601 at the expense of other *Passionate Pilgrim* lyrics by Shakespeare. But what is more radical about Hall's rewriting is the attention that it gives to the Sonnet's ability to adapt to different speakers and different contexts. This Sonnet has only ever tenuously belonged to its author.

When Shakespeare and Lady Viola 'in real life' block out the balcony scene of *Romeo and Juliet*, Viola is waiting to be seduced by Shakespeare's words and his mind goes blank. Marlowe has to prompt him: 'Shall I compare thee ...?' Thus, an all-purpose sonnet, conceived for no apparent reason, is co-opted by Shakespeare himself as a means of wooing his beloved. Even here, the denigratory comments keep coming. When Shakespeare turns to Marlowe for his approval of line 2, the latter comments: 'It's not Philip Sidney'.[8] The sense of a sonneteering tradition that the film had completely overlooked is re-admitted, generating a Shakespeare whose anxiety of influence extends to poetry as well as drama. It turns out that Shakespeare has invented no more than this, and so Marlowe has to improvise, feeding Shakespeare the lines which he duly recites. Shakespeare's growing confidence under Marlowe's mentoring enables him to produce the final couplet, but the ten lines they have produced are clearly Marlowe's, generating audience laughter around Viola's breathless praise: 'Only you could have conceived such a thing.'[9]

Sonnet 18 subsequently reappears at least three more times, in comic and tragic variations. It is appropriated by Lady Viola in response to her enforced marriage, when she observes 'My summer's lease is all too brief', thereby demonstrating how the line may become the reader's.[10] It is also the song performed whilst Shakespeare and Viola consummate their love; their 'petit mort' coinciding with the repeated refrain 'And summer's lease hath all too short a date./ Too short a date'.[11] This is an intriguing reflection of recent critical arguments about the Sonnet. In 2006, Brian Crew explored the erotic implications of the poem's imagery of 'growth' and 'decline', suggesting that 'the conventional reading is dependent on its opposition to a bawdier possibility that may appear absent but which in fact informs the whole sonnet', and that the male speaker's addressee was potentially his own penis.[12] Whilst the play does not go this far, it does reveal the erotic

[8] Ibid., p. 29.
[9] Ibid., p. 31.
[10] Ibid., p. 42.
[11] Ibid., p. 56.
[12] Crew, 'Rewriting/Deconstructing Shakespeare', pp. 69–70. Crew also takes as an example Tom Stoppard's earlier rewriting of the Sonnet in *Travesties* (1974).

connotations of a language that appeared far more chaste in the 1998 film, and exposes the value of a deconstructionist reading which depends on removing the Sonnet from its presumed context and sequence. A further extension of this creative displacement occurs in the play when Sonnet 18 is used as an elegy for the dead Marlowe:

> SONG – 'BUT THY ETERNAL SUMMER'
> But thy eternal summer shall not fade
> Nor lose possession of,
> Nor lose that fair thou ow'st,
> Nor shall death brag thou wander'st in his shade.[13]

The Sonnet's promises of immortality are fully ironised here: Marlowe's 'authorship' of this Sonnet has been forgotten, and the only one that Shakespeare's Sonnets memorialises is the poet himself. The breakdown of lines also explores the difficulty of using language to articulate grief, even as there is some degree of consolation in the restoration of the familiar rhyme 'fade'/'shade'. At the same time, the reapplication of an 'hetero-sexual' love poem to mourn Shakespeare's love for Marlowe awakens some of the homoerotic charge which 'the Sonnets' carry with them, whilst opening up Sonnet 18 to further reinscription.

Hall's approach to the re-voicing of Shakespeare's Sonnets potentially owes much to the work of innovative poets since the turn of the century, who have explored the outrageous claims made by the Sonnets about Time, whilst playfully and even anarchically exposing some of their hidden resonances.[14] Philip Terry's *Shakespeare's Sonnets* (2010) uses Oulipean techniques to re-imagine nearly the whole of the Quarto sequence, and his version of Sonnet 18 devotes itself to the brevity of fame promised by advertising, and to the spectacle of drinking oneself to death ('Shall I compare thee to a Smirnoff ad?'). Its conclusion also exploits the affective power of failing to complete the line:

> Nor shall death brag thou sup in his shade
> When in immortal lines like these thou glowest:
> So long as men can drink and take a piss,
> So long lives thine in this.[15]

---

[13] Hall, *Shakespeare in Love*, p. 74.
[14] There is unfortunately no space here to explore the influence of the linguistically innovative sonnet on the contemporary reinterpretation of Shakespeare's Sonnets. See Jeff Hilson's important 'Introduction' to *The Reality Street Book of Sonnets*, pp. 8–17, and the Shakespeare-influenced lyrics in this collection by Harryette Mullen and Aaron Shurin.
[15] Terry, *Shakespeare's Sonnets*, p. 16.

More recently, the collection *On Shakespeare's Sonnets: A Poets' Celebration* (2016), edited by Hannah Crawforth and Elizabeth Scott-Baumann, has commemorated the quartercentenary of Shakespeare's death by commissioning members of the Royal Society of Literature to rewrite a Shakespeare Sonnet. As Colin Thubron notes in the Preface to these reworkings, 'The sonnets' confidence in poetic immortality – that "eyes not yet created" will forever read these words – is seldom stressed: a by-product, perhaps, of our age of foreboding'.[16] Yet the collection also contains a remarkable range of tonal as well as formal approaches to individual Sonnets. P. K. Kavanagh takes on Sonnet 18 by confronting it critically but affectionately, with the opening assertion: 'Exaggeration is the role of art!'. Sonnet 116 inspires three adaptations by Gillian Clarke, Carol Ann Duffy and Elaine Feinstein, intriguingly suggestive of the appeal this Sonnet has historically had for women writers. The prevailing mood of their responses varies considerably – plangent, cynical, try-hard romantic – but all acknowledge the difficulty of Shakespeare's ideal: 'Our two heads on one pillow; I awake/ to hear impediments scratch in the room/ like rats.'[17]

In line with these creative endeavours are the new critical efforts to focus on individual lyrics (and not always the most familiar Sonnets), freed from the constraints of a biographical and/or sequential context. A recent collection of critical essays, *The Sonnets: The State of Play*, edited by Hannah Crawforth, Elizabeth Scott-Baumann and Clare Whitehead (2017) demonstrates all of these virtues and Colin Burrow's essay, 'Shakespeare's Sonnets as Event', is particularly suggestive in its application of the early modern meaning of 'event' as 'a contingent future occurrence, which could turn out one way or another':

> For Shakespeare one danger and perhaps also a delight of a lyric poem is the way it addresses more occasions that its author can imagine. The audience of a lyric can only be partially anticipated, since a lyric is both an interpersonal event and a document which can go astray. This means in turn that the 'event' (in the early modern sense of 'the outcome') of lyric poetry is uncertain. A poem might be created as an act of address to one beloved, but once it is published – in the loose sense of being witnessed by anyone other than its author and its apparent addressee – it can have a force and effect which is entirely unpredictable by its author.[18]

---

[16] 'Preface', in Crawforth and Scott-Baumann, *On Shakespeare's Sonnets*, p. xii.
[17] 'CXVI' by Carol Ann Duffy, in ibid., p. 62.
[18] Burrow, 'Shakespeare's Sonnets as Event', p. 102.

This book, *The Afterlife of Shakespeare's Sonnets*, has explored some of the ways in which the Sonnets have gone astray historically, through print and manuscript, and the kinds of creative responses they have generated, far beyond any expectations Shakespeare can have had about them. In the process, it has suggested a number of changes to the way that we think about the Sonnets. First and foremost, it demonstrates that the Sonnets have a significant history outside of the Quarto, in both its 1609 and 1780 editions, and that what we recognise as a Shakespeare Sonnet is historically contingent. Readers had particular reasons for preferring *The Passionate Pilgrim* or Benson's *Poems*, when they did so, and the canonicity of the Quarto and of the 154 Sonnets contained within it was not a foregone conclusion. Indeed, it took far longer for the Sonnets to become 'Shakespearean' than studies have previously allowed, which might cause us to rethink the processes of canonising Shakespeare more generally.

This book has also argued that we need to treat Malone's bipartite division of the Quarto into Sonnets addressed to a man, and those to a woman, as the historically situated editorial intervention that it is, rather than a timeless truth which needs to be passed on to (and indeed imposed upon) readers today. Whilst the strong identification of the Sonnets with Shakespearean 'homosexuality' has performed an important cultural function in providing readers with a canonical means of expressing male–male desire, it has also led to frantic efforts to interpret the Sonnets allegorically, which have obscured the subtlety of individual lyrics and their inherent polyvocality. Although a biographical reading of 'the sequence' has had an important role to play historically, in terms of encouraging aesthetic appreciation of the Sonnets at a time when they had little status, it now seems appropriate, given the Sonnets' extraordinary canonicity, to heed Paul Edmondson and Stanley Wells' call for 'limited and precise biographical readings of individual poems'.[19]

Moreover, by shifting the use we make of a biographical approach to the Sonnets, we can make important discoveries about the *literary* relationships that brought them into being. This book has argued that the Earl of Pembroke was an influential early reader of the Sonnets, but further exploration of less august members of Shakespeare's literary circle could also prove illuminating. In her recent discussion of Michael Drayton's engagement with Shakespeare in draft, Meghan C. Andrews suggests 'that Shakespeare's writing practice was more collective than we have imagined, reflecting his partaking in intellectual engagement and conversational

---

[19] Edmondson and Wells, 'The Plurality of Shakespeare's Sonnets', abstract.

exchange'.[20] The work that continues into Shakespeare's involvement with the Inns of Court, particularly the Middle Temple, promises to further enrich our sense of how the Sonnets socialised with other poems, poets and readers.

Finally, this book has argued that the wonderfully rich creative tradition of alluding to and adapting Shakespeare's Sonnets – which is born out of hostility and resentment as well as love – depends partly on their individual histories which exist apart from (though they also intersect with) the history of the *Sonnets*. To try to delimit the interpretative possibilities of these Sonnets by fitting them back into 'the sequence', and fixing their gender and sexuality, as has happened with Sonnet 18, is misguided and destructive. For the Sonnets to continue finding readers in the twenty-first century, they need to be dispersed, fragmented and re-voiced. At the same time, an understanding of what they have meant as single lyrics can only enrich this creative process. It is this cultural history of individual Sonnets, as well as the lyrics themselves, that we should not allow to fade.

---

[20] Andrews, 'Michael Drayton, Shakespeare's Shadow', 293.

References

Abrams, Richard, 'Rereading Shakespeare: The Example of Richard Brathwait', *Shakespeare Survey* 60 (2007), 268–83

Acker, Faith, 'John Benson's 1640 *Poems* and Its Literary Precedents' in *Canonising Shakespeare: Stationers and the Book Trade, 1640–1740* ed. Emma Depledge and Peter Kirwan (Cambridge: Cambridge University Press, 2017), pp. 89–106

Ackroyd, Peter, *Dickens* (London: Minerva, 1991)

Alden, Raymond MacDonald, 'The 1640 Text of Shakespeare's Sonnets', *Modern Philology* 14.1 (May 1916), 17–30

Alexander, Catherine M. S., 'Province of Pirates: The Editing and Publication of Shakespeare's Poems in the Eighteenth Century' in *Reading Readings: Essays on Shakespeare Editing in the Eighteenth Century* ed. Joanna Gondris (Madison: Fairleigh Dickinson University Press, 1998), pp. 345–65

Alexander, William, *Aurora: Containing the first fancies of the Authors youth* (London: n.p., 1604), STC 337

Allingham, William (ed.), *Nightingale Valley: A Collection of Choice Lyrics and Short Poems. From the Time of Shakespeare to the Present Day* (London: Bell and Daldy, 1860, 1862)

Allot, Robert (ed.), *England's Parnassus* (1600) ed. Charles Crawford (Oxford: Clarendon Press, 1913)

Alpers, Paul J., 'Empson on Pastoral', *New Literary History* 10.1 (1978), 101–23

Andrews, Meghan C., 'Michael Drayton, Shakespeare's Shadow', *Shakespeare Quarterly* 65.3 (2014), 273–306

Anger, Suzy, 'George Eliot and Philosophy' in *The Cambridge Companion to George Eliot* ed. George Levine (Cambridge: Cambridge University Press, 2001), pp. 76–97

Armstrong, John, *Sonnets from Shakespeare: By Albert* (London: n.p., 1791)

Auden, W. H., *The Dyer's Hand & Other Essays* (London: Faber & Faber, 1963)
'Introduction', *The Sonnets* ed. William Burto (London: New English Library Ltd., 1964)
Lectures on Shakespeare ed. Arthur Kinney (London: Faber & Faber, 2000)
Letters from Iceland (New York: Faber & Faber, 1937)

Baker, David, 'Cavalier Shakespeare: The 1640 *Poems* of John Benson', *Studies in Philology* 95.2 (1998), 152–73

Barnes, Barnabe, *Parthenophil and Parthenophe Sonnettes, madrigals, elegies and odes* (London: n.p., 1593), STC 1469

Barrett Browning, Elizabeth, *Aurora Leigh* ed. Kerry McSweeney (Oxford and New York: Oxford University Press, 1993)

    The Brownings' Correspondence ed. Philip Kelley and Ronald Hudson (Winfield: Wedgestone Press, 1988)

    Selected Poems ed. Margaret Forster (Baltimore: Johns Hopkins University Press, 1988)

Bate, Jonathan, *Romantic Ecology: Wordsworth and the Environmental Tradition* (London and New York: Routledge, 1991)

    (ed.), *The Romantics on Shakespeare* (London: Penguin, 1992)

    Shakespeare and the English Romantic Imagination (Oxford: Clarendon Press, 1986)

Bate, Walter Jackson, *John Keats* (London: Chatto & Windus, 1963, 1979)

    The Stylistic Development of Keats (London: Routledge and Kegan Paul, 1945, 1958)

Beal, Peter, *Index of English Literary Manuscripts* (London and New York: R. R. Bowker & Co., 1980), 2 vols.

Bednarz, James P., 'Canonizing Shakespeare: *The Passionate Pilgrim, England's Helicon* and the Question of Authenticity', *Shakespeare Survey* 60 (2007), 252–67

    Shakespeare and the Poets' War (New York: Columbia University Press, 2001)

Beilin, Elaine V., '"The Onely Perfect Vertue": Constancy in Mary Wroth's *Pamphilia to Amphilanthus*', *Spenser Studies* 2 (1981), 229–45

Belastegui, Nuria, 'Negativity and Dialogical Play in *Nothing Like the Sun*' in *Anthony Burgess and Modernity* ed. Alan R. Roughley (Manchester and New York: Manchester University Press, 2008), pp. 21–37

Bell, Ilona, '"The Autograph Manuscript of Wroth's *Pamphilia to Amphilanthus*' in *Re-Reading Mary Wroth* ed. Paul Salzman and Marion Wynne-Davies (New York and Abingdon: Routledge, 2015), pp. 171–82

    'Rethinking Shakespeare's Dark Lady' in *A Companion to Shakespeare's Sonnets* ed. Michael Schoenfeldt (Oxford: Blackwell, 2007), pp. 293–313

    'Sugared Sonnets Among their Private Friends: Mary Wroth and William Shakespeare' in *Mary Wroth and Shakespeare* ed. Paul Salzman and Marion Wynne-Davies (New York and Abingdon: Routledge, 2015), pp. 9–24

Bell's Edition of Shakespeare's Plays, as they are now performed at the Theatres Royal in London (London: n.p., 1774), 2nd edition, 5 vols.

Bellew, John, *Poets' Corner: A Manual for Students in English Poetry* (London: n.p., 1868)

Bennett, Andrew, *Romantic Poets and the Culture of Posterity* (Cambridge: Cambridge University Press, 1999)

Billington, Josie, *Elizabeth Barrett Browning and Shakespeare* (London: Bloomsbury, 2012)

Bishop, Robert, *Robert Bishop's Commonplace Book: An Edition of a Seventeenth-Century Miscellany* ed. David Coleman Redding, PhD thesis, University of Pennsylvania, 1960

Biswell, Andrew, *The Real Life of Anthony Burgess* (Basingstoke and Oxford: Picador, 2005)

Blaine, Marlin E., 'Milton and the Monument Topos: "On Shakespeare", "Ad Joannem Roüsium", and *Poems* (1645)', *Journal of English and Germanic Philology* 99.2 (April 2000), 215–34

Boaden, James, *On the Sonnets of Shakespeare identifying the Person to whom they are Addressed; and Elucidating Several Points in the Poet's History* (London: Thomas Rodd, 1837)

Bodenheimer, Rosemarie, *The Real Life of Mary Ann Evans: George Eliot, Her Letters and Fiction* (Ithaca and London: Cornell University Press, 1994)

Bond, Garth, 'Amphilanthus to Pamphilia: William Herbert, Mary Wroth, and Penshurst Mount', *Sidney Journal* 31.1 (Spring 2013), 51–80

Booth, Stephen, *Shakespeare's Sonnets Edited with Analytic Commentary* (New Haven and London: Yale University Press, 1977)

Brahms, Caryl and S. J. Simon, *No Bed for Bacon* (London: Black Swan, 1941, repr. 1999)

Brathwait, Richard, *The Poet's Willow or, The Passionate Shepherd* (London: n.p., 1614), STC 3578

Brennan, Michael G., 'Creating Female Authorship in the Early Seventeenth Century: Ben Jonson and Lady Mary Wroth' in *Women's Writing and the Circulation of Ideas: Manuscript Publication in England, 1550–1800* ed. George L. Justice and Nathan Tinker (Cambridge: Cambridge Univeristy Press, 2002), pp. 73–93

Breton, Nicholas, *Brittons Bowre of Delights* (1591) ed. Hyder Edward Rollins (Cambridge, MA: Harvard University Press, 1933)

The Pilgrimage to Paradise (London: n.p., 1592), STC 523.09

Briggs, Julia, 'Virginia Woolf Reads Shakespeare or, Her Silence on Master William', *Shakespeare Survey* 58 (2005), 118–29

Brown, Charles Armitage, *Shakespeare's Autobiographical Poems: Being His Sonnets Clearly Developed with His Character chiefly drawn from his Work* (London: James Bohn, 1838)

Brown, Richard, *James Joyce and Sexuality* (Cambridge: Cambridge University Press, 1985)

Browne, William, *Britannia's Pastorals* (London: n.p., 1616), STC 3915

Browning, Elizabeth Barrett, *Aurora Leigh and Other Poems* ed. John Robert Glorney Bolton and Julia Bolton Holloway (London: Penguin, 1995)

Burgess, Anthony, 'Genesis and Headache' in *Afterwords: Artists and their Novels* ed. Thomas McCormack (New York: Harper Row, 1969), pp. 28–47

Nothing Like the Sun: A Story of Shakespeare's Love-Life (London: Vintage, 1988)

Shakespeare (London: Jonathan Cape, 1970)

Burnham, Michelle, '"Dark Lady and Fair Man": The Love Triangle in Shakespeare's Sonnets and *Ulysses*', *Studies in the Novel* 22 (1990), 43–56

Burrow, Colin, 'Editing the Sonnets' in *A Companion to Shakespeare's Sonnets* ed. Michael Schoenfeldt (Oxford: Blackwell, 2007), pp. 145–62

'Life and Work in Shakespeare's Poems' in *Shakespeare's Poems* ed. Stephen Orgel and Sean Keilen (New York: Garland, 1999)

'Shakespeare's Sonnets as Event' in *The Sonnets: The State of Play* ed. Hannah Crawforth, Elizabeth Scott-Baumann and Clare Whitehead (London: Bloomsbury, 2017), pp. 97–116

Butler, Martin, *Theatre and Crisis 1632–1642* (Cambridge: Cambridge University Press, 1987)

Bysshe, Edward, *The Art of English Poetry* (London: n.p., 1702)

Caines, Michael, *Shakespeare and the Eighteenth Century* (Oxford: Oxford University Press, 2013)

Campbell, Gordon, 'Shakespeare and the Youth of Milton', *Milton Quarterly* 33.4 (1999), 95–105

Campbell, James S., '"For you may touch them not": Misogyny, Homosexuality, and the Ethics of Passivity in First World War Poetry', *English Literary History* 64.3 (1997), 823–42

Oscar Wilde, Wilfred Owen and Male Desire: Begotten, Not Made (Basingstoke: Palgrave Macmillan, 2015)

Campbell, Thomas, *Specimens of the British Poets; with Biographical and Critical Notices and An Essay on English Poetry* (London: John Murray, 1819), 7 vols.

Cannan, Paul D., 'The 1709/11 Editions of Shakespeare's Poems' in *Canonising Shakespeare: Stationers and the Book Trade, 1640–1740* ed. Emma Depledge and Peter Kirwan (Cambridge: Cambridge University Press, 2017), pp. 171–86

'Early Shakespeare Criticism: Charles Gildon, and the Making of Shakespeare the Playwright-Poet', *Modern Philology* 102.1 (2004), 35–55

'Edmond Malone, *The Passionate Pilgrim* and the Fiction of Shakespearean Authorship', *Shakespeare Quarterly* 68.2 (2017), 139–71

Carey, John, *The Intellectuals and the Masses: Pride and Prejudice among the Literary Intelligentsia, 1880–1939* (London: Faber & Faber, 1992)

Caveney, Geoffrey, '"Mr W. H.": Stationer William Holme (d. 1607)', *Notes & Queries* 62.1 (2015), 120–4

Chalmers, George, *An Apology for the Believers in the Shakespeare-Papers, which were exhibited in Norfolk-Street* (London: n.p., 1797)

A Supplemental Apology for the Believers in the Shakspeare-Papers Being a Reply to Mr Malone's Answer (London: n.p., 1799)

Chamberlayne, William, *Eromena: or, the Noble Stranger: A Novel* (London: n.p., 1683), Wing/ 1611: 32

Pharonnida: A Heroick Poem (London: n.p., 1659), Wing C/1866

Chedgzoy, Kate, *Shakespeare's Queer Children: Sexual Politics and Contemporary Culture* (Manchester and New York: Manchester University Press, 1995)

Cheney, Patrick, *Shakespeare, National Poet-Playwright* (Cambridge: Cambridge University Press, 2004)

Chernaik, Warren, 'Books as Memorials: The Politics of Consolation', *Yearbook of English Studies* 21 (1991), 207–17

Choice Thoughts from Shakspere (London: George Routledge & Sons, 1866)

Churchyard, Thomas, *The Mirror of Man, and Manners of Men* (London: n.p., 1594), STC 5242

Clare, John, *John Clare: The Oxford Authors* ed. Eric Robinson and David Powell (Oxford and New York: Oxford University Press, 1984)

The Natural History Prose Writings of John Clare ed. Margaret Grainger (Oxford: Clarendon Press, 1983)

Clark, David Lee, 'Shelley and Shakespeare', *PMLA* 54.1 (1939), 261–87

Claussen, Nils, '"Hours Continuing Long" as Whitman's Rewriting of Shakespeare's Sonnet 29', *Walt Whitman Quarterly Review* (2009), 131–42

Clifton, Robin, 'Sir William Portman' (2004), *Oxford Dictionary of National Biography* online

Coiro, Ann Baynes, 'Fable and Old Song: *Samson Agonistes* and The Idea of a Poetic Career', *Milton Studies* 36 (1998), 123–52

'Poetic Tradition, Dramatic' in *Milton in Context* ed. Stephen B. Dobranski (Cambridge: Cambridge University Press, 2010), pp. 58–67

Cole, Sarah, *Modernism, Male Friendship and the First World War* (Cambridge: Cambridge University Press, 2003)

Coleridge, Samuel Taylor, *Biographia Literaria* ed. John T. Shawcross (Oxford: Clarendon Press, 1967), 2 vols.

Coleridge's Miscellaneous Criticism ed. Thomas Middleton Raysor (London: Constable & Co., 1936)

Marginalia ed. George Whalley in *The Collected Works of Samuel Taylor Coleridge* (London and Princeton: Routledge & Kegan Paul/Princeton University Press, 1980), 5 vols.

The Notebooks of Samuel Taylor Coleridge ed. Kathleen Coburn (London and New York: Routledge & Kegan Paul, 1961), 8 vols.

Table Talk ed. Carl Woodring in *The Collected Works of Samuel Taylor Coleridge* (London and Princeton: Princeton University Press, 1990), vol. 1

Connaughton, Michael E., 'Richardson's Familiar Quotations: *Clarissa* and Bysshe's *Art of English Poetry*', *Philological Quarterly* 60 (1981), 183–95

Connor, Francis X., 'Shakespeare, Poetic Collaboration and *The Passionate Pilgrim*', *Shakespeare Survey* 67 (2014), 119–30

Cook, John, *King Charles His Case* (London: n.p., 1649), Wing /C6025

Corcoran, Neil, *Shakespeare and the Modern Poet* (Cambridge: Cambridge University Press, 2010)

Corns, Thomas N., 'Thomas Carew, Sir John Suckling, and Richard Lovelace', in *The Cambridge Companion to English Poetry: Donne to Marvell* ed. Thomas N. Corns (Cambridge: Cambridge University Press, 1993), pp. 200–20

Couch, Randall, 'A Eurydice Beyond my Maestro: Triangular Desire in Harryette Mullen's "Dim Lady"', www.asu.edu/pipercwcenter/how2journal/archive/online_archive/v2_4_2006/current/in_conference/couch.html, accessed 18 April 2019

Craft, Christopher, '"Descend and Touch and Enter": Tennyson's Strange Manner of Address', *Genders* 1 (1988), 83–101

Crawforth, Hannah and Elizabeth Scott-Baumann (eds), *On Shakespeare's Sonnets: A Poets' Celebration* (London and New York: Bloomsbury, 2016)

Crawforth, Hannah, Elizabeth Scott-Baumann and Claire Whitehead (eds), *The Sonnets: The State of Play* (London and New York: Bloomsbury, 2017)

Crew, Brian, 'Rewriting/Deconstructing Shakespeare: Outlining Possibilities, Sometimes Humorous for Sonnet 18' in *Spanish Studies in Shakespeare and His Contemporaries* ed. José Manuel González (Newark: University of Delaware Press, 2006), pp. 69–70

Crosman, Robert, 'Making Love Out of Nothing At All: The Issue of Story in Shakespeare's Procreation Sonnets', *Shakespeare Quarterly* 41.4 (1990), 470–88

Culler, A. Dwight, 'Edward Bysshe and the Poet's Handbook', *PMLA* 63.3 (1948), 858–85

Curran, Stuart, *Poetic Form and British Romanticism* (Oxford: Oxford University Press, 1990)

Currie, Joy, '"Mature Poets Steal": Charlotte Smith's Appropriations of Shakespeare', *Shakespeare and the Culture of Romanticism* ed. Joseph M. Ortiz (Farnham: Ashgate, 2013), pp. 99–120

Cutts, John P. 'Two Seventeenth-Century Versions of Shakespeare's Sonnet 116', *Shakespeare Studies* 10 (1977), 9–15

Daniel, Samuel, *Delia. Contayning certayne sonnets: With the complaint of Rosamond* (London: n.p., 1592), 2nd edition, STC 6243.2

Das, Santanu, 'Reframing First World War Poetry: An Introduction' in *The Cambridge Companion to the Poetry of the First World War* ed. Santanu Das (Cambridge: Cambridge University Press, 2013), pp. 3–34

   Touch and Intimacy in First World War Literature (Cambridge: Cambridge University Press, 2005, repr. 2007)

Davenport-Hines, Richard, *Auden* (London: Heinemann, 1995)

Davidson, Graham, *Coleridge's Career* (Houndmills and London: Macmillan, 1990)

Davison, Francis, *A Poetical Rhapsody, containing, diverse sonnets, odes, elegies, madrigals, and other poesies* (London: n.p., 1602), STC 6373

Dawson, Giles E., *Four Centuries of Shakespeare Publication* (Lawrence: University of Kansas Libraries, 1964)

Decker, Christopher, 'Shakespeare and the Death of Tennyson' in *Victorian Shakespeare* ed. Gail Marshall and Adrian Poole (Houndmills and New York: Palgrave, 2003) 2 vols., vol. 2, pp. 131–49

   'Shakespeare Editions' in *Shakespeare in the Nineteenth Century* ed. Gail Marshall (Cambridge: Cambridge University Press, 2012), pp. 16–38

De Grazia, Margreta, 'The First Reader of *Shake-speares Sonnets*' in *The Forms of Renaissance Thought: New Essays in Literature and Culture* ed. Leonard Barkan, Bradin Cormack and Sean Keilin (London: Palgrave Macmillan, 2009), pp. 86–106

   'The Scandal of Shakespeare's Sonnets', *Shakespeare Survey* 46 (1993), 35–50

   Shakespeare Verbatim: The Reproduction of Authenticity and the 1790 Apparatus (Oxford: Clarendon, 1991)

Dellamora, Richard, *Masculine Desire: The Sexual Politics of Victorian Aestheticism* (Chapel Hill: University of North Carolina Press, 1990)

Depledge, Emma and Peter Kirwan (eds), *Canonising Shakespeare: Stationers and the Book Trade, 1640–1740* (Cambridge: Cambridge University Press, 2017)

Dexter, Gary, *The People's Favourite Poems* (London: Old Street Pub., 2018)

DiBattista, Maria, *Virginia Woolf's Major Novels: The Fables of Aesop* (New Haven and London: Yale University Press, 1980)

Dickens, Charles, *Bleak House, Norton Critical Edition* ed. George Ford and Sylvère Monod (New York and London: W. W. Norton, 1977)

The Letters of Charles Dickens ed. Madeline House and Graham Storey (Oxford: Clarendon Press, 1965–2002), 12 vols.

Our Mutual Friend ed. E. Salter Davies (Oxford: Oxford University Press, 1981)

DiPietro, Cary, 'Sex, Lies and Videotape: Representing the Past in *Shakespeare in Love*, Mapping a Future for Presentism', *Shakespeare* 3 (2007), 40–62

Shakespeare and Modernism (Cambridge: Cambridge University Press, 2006)

Dobson, Michael, 'Bowdler and Britannia: Shakespeare and the National Libido', *Shakespeare Survey* 46 (1994), 137–44

The Making of the National Poet: Shakespeare, Adaptation, and Authorship, 1660–1769 (Oxford: Clarendon Press, 1992)

Donne, John, *John Donne: The Complete English Poems* ed. C. A. Patrides (London: Dent, 1985)

Douglas, Lord Alfred, *Autobiography* (London: M. Seeker, 1919)

Dowland, John, *The First Booke of Songes or Ayres* (London: n.p., 1597), STC 7901

Drake, Nathan, *Literary Hours: or Sketches Critical, Narrative and Poetical* (London: n.p., 1798)

Shakspeare and His Times (London: n.p., 1817)

Drayton, Michael, *Englands Heroicall Epistles. Newly Enlarged. With Idea* (London: n.p., 1599), STC 7195

Ideas Mirrour: Amours in quatorzains (London: n.p., 1594), STC 7203

Drummond, William, *Poems* (Edinburgh: n.p., 1616), STC 1514

Dubrow, Heather, *Captive Victors: Shakespeare's Narrative Poems and Sonnets* (Ithaca and London: Cornell University Press, 1987)

'"Incertainties now crown themselves assur'd": The Politics of Plotting Shakespeare's Sonnets', *Shakespeare Quarterly* 47.3 (1996), 291–305

'Shakespeare's Undramatic Monologues: Toward a Reading of the Sonnets', *Shakespeare Quarterly* 32.1 (1981), 55–68

Dugas, Don-John and Robert D. Hume, 'The Dissemination of Shakespeare's Plays circa 1714', *Studies in Bibliography* 56 (2003–4), 261–75

Duncan-Eaves, T. C. and Ben D. Kimpel, *Samuel Richardson: A Biography* (Oxford: Clarendon Press, 1971)

Duncan-Jones, Katherine, 'Much Ado with Red and White: The Earliest Readers of Shakespeare's *Venus and Adonis* (1593)', *Review of English Studies* 44.176 (1993), 479–501

Ungentle Shakespeare: Scenes from his Life (London: Thomson Learning, 2001)

'Was the 1609 *Shakespeare's Sonnets* Really Unauthorised?', *Review of English Studies* 34.134 (1983), 151–71

'What are Shakespeare's Sonnets Called?', *Essays in Criticism* 47 (1997), 1–12

Dussinger, John A. 'Edwards, Thomas (*d.* 1757)' (2004), *Oxford Dictionary of National Biography* online

Edmondson, Paul and Stanley Wells, 'The Plurality of Shakespeare's Sonnets', *Shakespeare Survey* 65 (2012), 211–20

Shakespeare's Sonnets (Oxford: Oxford University Press, 2004)

Edwards, Paul, 'The Early African Presence in the British Isles' in *Essays on the History of Blacks in Britain from Roman Times to the Mid-Twentieth Century* ed. Jagdish S. Gundara and Ian Duffield (Aldershot: Avebury, 1992), pp. 9–29

Edwards, Thomas, *The Canons of Criticism ... and Sonnets* (London: n.p., 1765)

Eliot, George, *Adam Bede* ed. Carol A. Martin (Oxford: Oxford University Press, 2008)

The Complete Shorter Poetry of George Eliot ed. Antonie Gerard van den Broek (London: Pickering & Chatto, 2005), 2 vols.

The George Eliot Letters ed. Gordon S. Haight (London: Oxford University Press, 1956)

The Journals of George Eliot ed. Margaret Harris and Judith Johnston (Cambridge: Cambridge University Press, 1998)

Middlemarch (London: Vintage, 2007)

Middlemarch Notebooks: A Transcription ed. John Clark Pratt and Victor Neufeldt (Berkeley: University of California Press, 1979)

Ellis, George, *Specimens of the Early English Poets* (London: n.p., 1790)

Ellis, Steve, *Virginia Woolf and the Victorians* (Cambridge: Cambridge University Press, 2007)

Ellmann, Richard, *Oscar Wilde* (London: Penguin, 1987)

Empson, William, *Seven Types of Ambiguity* (London: Chatto & Windus, 1930)

Seven Types of Ambiguity (London: Pimlico, 2004)

Some Versions of Pastoral: A Study of the Pastoral Form in Literature (London: Chatto & Windus, 1979)

Engle, Lars, 'William Empson and the Sonnets' in *A Companion to Shakespeare's Sonnets* ed. Michael Schoenfeldt (Oxford: Blackwell, 2007), pp. 163–82

Erne, Lukas, '*Cupids Cabinet Unlock't* (1662), Ostensibly "By W. Shakespeare", in Fact Partly by John Milton' in *Canonising Shakespeare: Stationers and the Book Trade, 1640–1740* ed. Emma Depledge and Peter Kirwan (Cambridge: Cambridge University Press, 2017), pp. 89–106

'The Popularity of Shakespeare in Print', *Shakespeare Survey* 62 (2009), 12–29

'Print and Manuscript' in *The Cambridge Companion to Shakespeare's Poetry* ed. Patrick Cheney (Cambridge: Cambridge University Press, 2007), pp. 54–71

Shakespeare and the Book Trade (Cambridge: Cambridge University Press, 2013)

Erne, Lukas and Tamsin Badcoe, 'The Popularity of Poetry Books in Print, 1583–1622', *Review of English Studies* 65.268 (2006), 1–25

Eromena: Or, The Noble Stranger (London: n.p., 1683), Wing /1611

Evans, Willa McClung, *Henry Lawes: Musician and Friend of Poets* (New York: Modern Language Association of America, 1941)

'Lawes' Version of Shakespeare's Sonnet CXVI', *PMLA* 51.1 (1936), 120–2

Fairer, David, 'Shakespeare in Poetry' in *Shakespeare in the Eighteenth Century* ed. Fiona Ritchie and Peter Sabor (Cambridge: Cambridge University Press, 2012), pp. 99–117

The Famous Tragedie of King Charles I (London: n.p., 1649)

Feldman, Paula R. and Daniel Robinson, *A Century of Sonnets: The Romantic-Era Revival, 1750–1850* (Oxford: Oxford University Press, 1999, repr. 2002)

Fenton, Geoffrey, *Certaine Tragical Discourses* (London: n.p., 1567), STC 1356.1

Fenton, James, *The Strength of Poetry* (Oxford: Oxford University Press, 2001)

Ferry, Anne, *All in War with Time: Love Poetry of Shakespeare, Donne, Jonson, Marvell and Milton* (Cambridge, MA: Harvard University Press, 1975)

'Palgrave's "Symphony"', *Victorian Poetry* 37.2 (1999), 145–62

Fisher, J. W., ' "Closet-Work": The Relationship between Physical and Psychological Spaces in *Pamela*' in *Samuel Richardson: Passion and Prudence* ed. Valerie Grosvenor Myer (London: Vision Press Ltd, 1986), pp. 21–37

Flesch, William, 'The Ambivalence of Generosity: Keats Reading Shakespeare', *English Literary History* 62.1 (1995), 149–69

'Personal Identity and Vicarious Experience in Shakespeare's Sonnets' in *A Companion to Shakespeare's Sonnets* ed. Michael Schoenfeldt (Oxford: Blackwell, 2007), pp. 383–402

Flint, Kate, 'George Eliot and Gender' in *The Cambridge Companion to George Eliot* ed. George Levine (Cambridge: Cambridge University Press, 2001), pp. 159–80

Foster, Brett (ed.), *Bloom's Shakespeare Through the Ages: The Sonnets* ed. with an introduction by Harold Bloom (New York: Infobase, 2008)

Foster, Donald, 'Master W. H., R. I. P.', *PMLA* 102.1 (1987), 42–54

Foucault, Michel, *The History of Sexuality: Volume I. The Will to Knowledge* (New York: Vintage, 1978)

Fowler, Alastair, 'Genre and the Literary Canon', *New Literary History* 11 (1979), 97–119

Fox, Alice, *Virginia Woolf and the Literature of the English Renaissance* (Oxford: Clarendon Press, 1990)

Franssen, Paul, *Shakespeare's Literary Lives: The Author as Character in Fiction and Film* (Cambridge: Cambridge University Press, 2016)

Freeman, Arthur and Paul Grinke, 'Four New Shakespeare Quartos?', *Times Literary Supplement*, 5 April 2002, 17–18

Froula, Christine, 'Virginia Woolf as Shakespeare's Sister: Chapters in a Woman Writer's Autobiography' in *Women's Re-Visions of Shakespeare* ed. Marianne Novy (Urbana: University of Illinois Press, 1990), pp. 123–42

Fussell, Paul, *The Great War and Modern Memory* (Oxford: Oxford University Press, 1975)

Gager, Valerie L., *Shakespeare and Dickens: The Dynamics of Influence* (Cambridge: Cambridge University Press, 1996)

Garrington, Abbie, 'Early Auden', *Oxford Handbooks Online: Scholarly Research Reviews* (March 2016), www.oxfordhandbooks.com/view/10.1093/oxfordhb/9780199935338.001.0001/oxfordhb-9780199935338-e-91, accessed 18 April 2019

Gazzard, Hugh, 'Nicholas Breton, Richard Jones, and Two Printed Verse Miscellanies', *Notes & Queries* 62 (2015), 79–82

Gibson, Cheryl, '"'Tis not the meate, but 'tis the appetite": The Destruction of Woman in the Poetry of Sir John Suckling', *Explorations in Renaissance Culture* 20 (1994), 41–59

Gildon, Charles, *The Complete Art of Poetry in Six Parts* (London: n.p., 1718)

Gilead, Sarah, 'Ungathering "Gather ye Rosebuds": Herrick's Misreading of Carpe Diem', *Criticism* 27.2 (1985), 133–53

Ginsburg, Michal Peled, 'Pseudonym, Epigraphs, and Narrative Voice: *Middlemarch* and the Problem of Authorship', *English Literary History* 47.3 (1980), 542–58

Godwin, William, *Lives of Edward and John Philips, Nephews and Pupils of Milton* (London: Longman, 1815)

Goldberg, Jonathan, *Voice Terminal Echo: Postmodernism and English Renaissance Texts* (London: Routledge, 1986)

Gorji, Mina, *John Clare and the Place of Poetry* (Liverpool: Liverpool University Press, 2008)

Gosse, Edmund, *Critical Kit-Kats* (London: William Heinemann, 1896)

Guibbory, Achsah, 'Milton and English Poetry' in *A New Companion to John Milton* ed. Thomas N. Corns (London: John Wiley & Sons, 2016), pp. 71–89

Guillory, John, *Poetic Authority: Spenser, Milton and Literary History* (Columbia: Columbia University Press, 1983)

Gurr, Andrew, 'Shakespeare's First Poem: Sonnet 145', *Essays in Criticism* 21 (1971), 221–6

Hackett, Helen, *Shakespeare and Elizabeth: The Meeting of Two Myths* (Princeton and Oxford: Princeton University Press, 2009)

Hadfield, Andrew, *Edmund Spenser: A Life* (Oxford: Oxford University Press, 2012)

Haffenden, John, *William Empson: Among the Mandarins* (Oxford: Oxford University Press, 2005)

Hall, Kim F., '"These bastard signs of fair": Literary Whiteness in Shakespeare's Sonnets' in *Post-Colonial Shakespeares* ed. Ania Loomba and Martin Orkin (London and New York: Routledge, 2013), pp. 64–83

    Things of Darkness: Economies of Race and Gender in Early Modern England (Ithaca and London: Cornell University Press, 1995)

Hall, Lee, *Shakespeare in Love* (London: Faber & Faber, 2014)

Hallam, Arthur, *The Writings of Arthur Hallam* ed. T. H. Vail Motter (London: Oxford University Press, 1943)

Hallam, Henry, *Introduction to the Literature of Europe in the Fifteenth, Sixteenth and Seventeenth Centuries* (London: John Murray, 1837, repr. 1842), 4 vols.

Hammond, Gerald, 'Milton's "On Shakespeare"', *Southern Humanities Review* 20 (1986), 115–24

Hammond, Paul (ed.), *Shakespeare's Sonnets: An Original Spelling Text* (Oxford: Oxford University Press, 2012)

Hannay, Margaret P., *Mary Sidney, Lady Wroth* (Farnham: Ashgate, 2010)

Harris, Frank, *The Man Shakespeare and His Tragic Life Story* (London: Frank Palmer, 1909)

    Oscar Wilde: His Life and Confessions (New York: Brentanos, 1915)

    Shakespeare and His Love (London: Frank Palmer, 1910)

Harris, Jocelyn, *Samuel Richardson* (Cambridge: Cambridge University Press, 1987)

Harris, Wendell V., 'Canonicity', *PMLA* 106 (1991), 110–21

Harrison, G. B., *Shakespeare at Work, 1592–1603* (London: George Routledge & Sons, 1933)

Havens, Raymond Dexter, *The Influence of Milton on English Poetry* (New York: Russell & Russell, 1922, 1961)

Hayward, John, *The British Muse, or a Collection of Thoughts Moral, Natural and Sublime* (London: n.p., 1738)

Hazlitt, William, *Characters of Shakespear's Plays* (London: n.p., 1817, repr. 1818)
  The Collected Works of William Hazlitt ed. A. R. Waller and A. Glover (London: J. M. Dent, 1902–6), 13 vols.

Heffernan, Megan, 'Turning Sonnets into Poems: Textual Affect and John Benson's Metaphysical Shakespeare', *Shakespeare Quarterly* 64.1 (2013), 71–98

Henderson, George, *Petrarca: A Selection of Sonnets from Various Authors* (London: n.p., 1803)

Henning, Barbara, 'Conversation with Harryette Mullen: B to D', http://eoagh.com/conversation-with-harryette-mullen-from-b-to-d, accessed 18 April 2019

Herbert, George, *The English Poems of George Herbert* ed. Helen Wilcox (Cambridge: Cambridge University Press, 2007)
  The Works of George Herbert ed. F. E. Hutchison (Oxford: Clarendon Press, 1941, repr. 1964)

Herbert, William, *Poems, Written by the Right Honourable William Earl of Pembroke* ed. John Donne (London: n.p., 1660), Wing P1128
  The Poems of William Herbert, Third Earl of Pembroke ed. Robert Krueger, BLitt thesis, Oxford, 1961

Herrick, Robert, *The Complete Poetry of Robert Herrick* ed. Tom Cain and Ruth Connolly (Oxford: Oxford University Press, 2013)

Heywood, Thomas, *An Apology for Actors* (London: n.p., 1612), STC 13309

Hibberd, Dominic, *Owen the Poet* (Houndmills: Macmillan, 1986)
  Wilfred Owen: A New Biography (London: Weidenfeld & Nicolson, 2002)
  Wilfred Owen: The Last Year (London: Constable, 1992)

Higdon, David Leon, 'George Eliot and the Art of the Epigraph', *Nineteenth-Century Fiction* 23.2 (1970), 127–51

Hill, Aaron, *The Plain Dealer: Being Select Essays on Several Curious Subjects …* (London: n.p., 1730), 2 vols.

Hilson, Jeff (ed.), *The Reality Street Book of Sonnets* (Hastings: Reality Street, 2007)

History of the Works of the Learned (London: n.p., 1738)

Hobbs, Mary, 'Shakespeare's Sonnet II – A "Sugred Sonnet"?', *Notes & Queries* 224 (1979), 112–13

Hobday, C. H., 'Shakespeare's Venus and Adonis Sonnets', *Shakespeare Survey* 26 (1973), 103–9

Holland, Merlin, *Irish Peacock & Scarlet Marquess: The Real Trial of Oscar Wilde* (London and New York: Fourth Estate, 2003)

Honigmann, Ernst, *John Weever: A Biography of a Literary Associate of Shakespeare and Jonson* (Manchester: Manchester University Press, 1987)

Honigmann, E. A. J., *Milton's Sonnets* (London: Macmillan, 1966)

Hooks, Adam, *Anchora*, at www.adamghooks.net/2011/10/faking-shakespeare-part-1-passionate.html, accessed 18 April 2019

'Royalist Shakespeare: Publishers, Politics and the Appropriation of *The Rape of Lucrece* (1655)' in *Canonising Shakespeare: Stationers and the Book Trade, 1640–1740* ed. Emma Depledge and Peter Kirwan (Cambridge: Cambridge University Press, 2017), pp. 26–37

Hotson, Leslie, *Mr W. H.* (London: Rupert Hart-Davis, 1964)

Houston, Natalie M., 'Anthologies and the Making of the Poetic Canon' in *A Companion to Victorian Poetry* ed. Richard Cronin, Alison Chapman and Antony H. Harrison (Oxford: Blackwell, 2007), pp. 361–77

'Valuable by Design: Material Features and Cultural Value in Nineteenth-Century Sonnet Anthologies', *Victorian Poetry* 37.2 (1999), 243–72

Howarth, Peter, 'Poetic Form and the First World War' in *The Cambridge Companion to the Poetry of the First World War* ed. Santanu Das (Cambridge: Cambridge University Press, 2013), pp. 51–68

Hume, Robert D., 'Before the Bard: "Shakespeare" in Early Eighteenth-Century London', *English Literary History* 64.1 (1997), 41–75

Hunt, Leigh and Samuel Adams Lee (eds), *The Book of the Sonnet* (London: Sampson Low, Son & Martson, 1986), 2 vols.

Hunt, Marvin, '"Be Dark but Not Too Dark": Shakespeare's Dark Lady as a Sign of Color' in *Shakespeare's Sonnets: Critical Essays* ed. James Schiffer (New York: Garland, 2000), pp. 369–89

Hutchison, Coleman, 'Breaking the Book Known as Q', *PMLA* 121.1 (2006), 33–66

Hyde, H. Montgomery, *Famous Trials 7: Oscar Wilde* (Harmondsworth: Penguin, 1962)

Ingleby, C. M., L. Toulmin Smith and F. J. Furnivall (eds), *The Shakspere Allusion-Book: A Collection of Allusions to Shakespeare from 1591 to 1700* rev. John Munro and Edmund Chambers (London: Humphrey Milford, 1932) 2 vols.

Ireland, Samuel, *Miscellaneous Papers and Legal Instruments under the Hand and Seal of William Shakespeare: including the Tragedy of King Lear and a small fragment of Hamlet* (London: n.p., 1796)

Ireland, William-Henry, *The Confessions of William Henry Ireland* (London: n.p., 1805)

Isherwood, Anne, 'Cut Out "into little stars": Shakespeare in Anthologies', PhD thesis, King's College, London, 2014

Iyengar, Sujata, 'Shakespeare in Heterolove', *Literature Film Quarterly* 29.2 (2001), 122–7

Jackson, MacDonald P., 'Francis Meres and the Cultural Contexts of Shakespeare's Rival Poet Sonnets', *Review of English Studies* 56.224 (2005), 224–46

'Vocabulary and Chronology: The Case of Shakespeare's Sonnets', *Review of English Studies* 52.205 (February 2001), 59–75

Jackson, Russell, 'Oscar Wilde and Shakespeare's Secrets' in *In the Footsteps of Queen Victoria* ed. Christa Jansohn (Munster and London: Lit Verlag, 2003), pp. 301–14

Jacobs, Mark, 'Contemporary Misogyny: Laura Riding, William Empson and the Critics – A Survey of Mis-History', *English: Journal of the English Association* 64 (September 2015), 222–40

Jaggard, William (ed.), *The Passionate Pilgrim by W. Shakespeare* (London: n.p., 1599), STC 22342

Jagger, Nicholas, 'William Chamberlayne' (2004), *Oxford Dictionary of National Biography* online

John, Juliet, 'Dickens and Hamlet' in *Victorian Shakespeare* ed. Gail Marshall and Adrian Poole (Basingstoke: Palgrave Macmillan, 2003), vol. 2, pp. 46–60

Jones, William R., '"Say They Are Saints Although That Saints They Show Not": John Weever's 1599 Epigrams to Marston, Jonson and Shakespeare', *Huntington Library Quarterly* 73.1 (March 2010), 83–98

Jonson, Ben, *Every Man Out of Humour* ed. Helen Ostovich (Manchester: Manchester University Press, 2001)

Jowett, John, 'Shakespeare Supplemented' in *The Shakespeare Apocrypha* ed. Douglas A. Brooks (Lampeter: Edwin Mellen, 2007), pp. 39–73

Joyce, James, *The Critical Writings of James Joyce* ed. Ellsworth Mason and Richard Ellmann (London: Faber & Faber, 1959)

Ulysses ed. Declan Kiberd (London: Penguin, 1992)

Kane, Daniel, 'An Interview with Harryette Mullen' in *The Cracks Between What We Are and What We Are Supposed to Be: Essays and Interviews* by Harryette Mullen (Alabama: University of Alabama Press, 2012), pp. 204–12

Kastan, David Scott, *Shakespeare and the Book* (Cambridge: Cambridge University Press, 2001)

Kearsley, George (ed.), *The Beauties of Shakespeare; selected from his Plays and Poems* (London: n.p., 1783)

Keats, John, *The Letters of John Keats 1814–1821* ed. Hyder Edward Rollins (Cambridge: Cambridge University Press, 1958), 2 vols.

The Poems of John Keats ed. Mariam Allott (London: Longman, 1970)

Keevak, Michael, *Sexual Shakespeare: Forgery, Authorship, Portraiture* (Detroit: Wayne State University Press, 2001)

'Shakespeare's *Queer* Sonnets and the Forgeries of William Henry Ireland', *Criticism* 40.2 (1998), 167–89

Kerrigan, John, 'Shakespeare, Elegy, and Epitaph, 1557–1640' in *The Oxford Handbook of Shakespeare's Poetry* ed. Jonathan F. S. Post (Oxford: Oxford University Press, 2013), pp. 225–44

'Wordsworth and the Sonnet: Building, Dwelling, Thinking', *Essays in Criticism* 35 (1985), 45–75

Kesson, Andy and Emma Smith (eds.), *The Elizabethan Top-Ten: Defining Print Popularity in Early Modern England* (London: Routledge, 2013)

Keymer, Thomas, 'Shakespeare in the Novel' in *Shakespeare and the Eighteenth Century* ed. Fiona Richie and Peter Sabor (Cambridge: Cambridge University Press, 2015), pp. 118–40

Kilgour, Maggie, *Milton and the Metamorphosis of Ovid* (Oxford: Oxford University Press, 2012)

King, Edmund G. C., '"A Priceless Book to Have Out Here": Soldiers Reading Shakespeare in the First World War', *Shakespeare* 10 (2014), 230–44

Kingsley-Smith, Jane, 'The Failure of Shame in Shakespeare's Sonnets', *Review of English Studies* 69.289 (2017), 237–58

'"Let Me not to the Marriage of True Minds": Shakespeare's Sonnet for Lady Mary Wroth', *Shakespeare Survey* 69 (2016), 277–91

'Shakespeare's Sonnets and the Claustrophobic Reader: Making Space in Modern Fiction', *Shakespeare* 9.2 (2013), 187–203

Kirwan, Peter, '"Complete" Works: The Folio and All of Shakespeare' in *The Cambridge Companion to Shakespeare's First Folio* ed. Emma Smith (Cambridge: Cambridge University Press, 2016), pp. 86–102

Shakespeare and the Idea of Apocrypha: Negotiating the Boundaries of the Dramatic Canon (Cambridge: Cambridge University Press, 2015)

Knight, Jeffrey Todd, 'Making Shakespeare's Books: Assembly and Intertextuality in the Archives', *Shakespeare Quarterly* 60.3 (2009), 304–40

Knights, L. C., 'Shakespeare's Sonnets' in *Elizabethan Poetry: Modern Essays in Criticism* ed. Paul J. Alpers (London, Oxford and New York: Oxford University Press, 1967), pp. 274–97

Knoepflmacher, U. C., 'Fusing Fact and Myth: The New Reality of *Middlemarch*' in *This Particular Web: Essays on Middlemarch* ed. Ian Adam (Toronto: University of Toronto Press, 1975), pp. 43–72

Knox, Vicesimus, *Elegant Extracts* (London: n.p., 1789, repr. 1801)

The Poetical Epitome, or Elegant Extracts Abridged from the Larger Volume (London: J. Johnson, 1807)

Knox-Shaw, Peter, '*To the Lighthouse*: The Novel as Elegy', *English Studies in Africa* 29.1 (1986), 31–50

Lamb, Charles, 'On the Tragedies of Shakespeare, Considered with Reference for Their Fitness for Stage Representation' (1811) in *The Romantics on Shakespeare* ed. Jonathan Bate (London: Penguin, 1992), pp. 111–27

Lamb, Mary Ellen, '"Can you suspect a change in me?": Poems by Mary Wroth and William Herbert, Third Earl of Pembroke' in *Re-Reading Mary Wroth* ed. Katherine R. Larson and Naomi J. Miller with Andrew Strycharski (New York: Palgrave Macmillan, 2015), pp. 53–68

'"Love is not love": A Lyric Exchange between William Herbert, Third Earl of Pembroke, and Benjamin Rudyerd, the Inns of Court, and Shakespeare's Sonnet 116', *Shakespeare Quarterly* 70 (Fall 2019)

Lamos, Colleen, *Deviant Modernism: Sexual and Textual Errancy in T. S. Eliot, James Joyce and Marcel Proust* (Cambridge: Cambridge University Press, 1998)

Landry, Hilton, 'Malone as Editor of Shakespeare's Sonnets', *Bulletin of the New York Public Library* 67.7 (1963), 435–42

Lanier, Douglas, 'Encryptions: Reading Milton Reading Jonson Reading Shakespeare' in *Reading and Writing in Shakespeare* ed. David M. Bergeron (Newark and London: Associated University Press, 1996), pp. 220–50

Laoutaris, Chris, 'The Prefatorial Material' in *The Cambridge Companion to Shakespeare's First Folio* ed. Emma Smith (Cambridge: Cambridge University Press, 2016), pp. 48–67

Laurie's Graduated Series of Reading Lesson Books: Cheap and Abridged Edition for Elementary Schools (London: Longmans, Green & Co, 1866)

Lauritsen, John, *The Shelley-Byron Men: Lost Angels of a Ruined Paradise* (London: Pagan Press, 2017)

Lawrance, Hannah, 'Mrs Browning's Poetry', *British Quarterly Review* 42 (1865), 359–84

Lee, Hermione, *Virginia Woolf* (London: Chatto & Windus, 1996)

Lee, John, 'Shakespeare and the Great War' in *The Oxford Handbook of British and Irish War Poetry* ed. Tim Kendall (Oxford: Oxford University Press, 2007), pp. 134–52

Lee, Sidney, *The Passionate Pilgrim Being a Reproduction in Facsimile of the First Edition 1599* (Oxford: Clarendon Press, 1905)

  Shakespeares Sonnets: Being a Reproduction in Facsimile of the First Edition (1609) (Cambridge, MA: Harvard University Press, 1905)

Leighton, Angela, *Elizabeth Barrett Browning* (Bloomington: Indiana University Press, 1986)

Leishman, J. B. (ed.), *The Three Parnassus Plays (1598–1600)* (London: Ivor Nicholson & Watson Ltd, 1949)

Levenback, Karen, *Virginia Woolf and the Great War* (Syracuse: Syracuse University Press, 1999)

Lewalski, Barbara K., *The Life of John Milton* (Oxford: Blackwell, 2003)

Lewis, C. S., *English Literature in the Sixteenth Century excluding Drama* (Oxford: Clarendon Press, 1954)

Linche, Richard, *Diella, Certaine Sonnets, adioyned to the amorous Poeme of Dom Diego and Ginevra* (1596), STC 17091

Ling, Nicholas (ed.), *England's Helicon* (1600), STC 237.16

Lodge, Sara, 'Contested Bounds: John Clare, John Keats, and the Sonnet', *Studies in Romanticism* 51.4 (2012), 533–54

Lofft, Capel, *Laura: or an Anthology of Sonnets* (London: n.p., 1813–14)

Lootens, Tricia, *Lost Saints: Silence, Gender and Victorian Literary Canonization* (Charlottesville and London: University of Virginia Press, 1996)

Luke, David, 'Gerhart Meyer and the Vision of Eros: A Note on Auden's 1929 Journal' in *'The Language of Learning and the Language of Love': Uncollected Writings, New Interpretations* ed. Katherine Bucknell and Nicholas Jenkins (Oxford: Clarendon Press, 1994), pp. 103–11

Lynch, Kathleen M., *Jacob Tonson, Kit-Cat Publisher* (Knoxville: University of Tennessee Press, 1971)

Lyons, Tara L., 'Shakespeare in Print before 1623' in *The Cambridge Companion to Shakespeare's First Folio* ed. Emma Smith (Cambridge: Cambridge University Press, 2016), pp. 1–17

Magnusson, Lynne, 'Thomas Thorpe's Shakespeare: "The Only Begetter"' in *The Sonnets: The State of Play* ed. Hannah Crawforth, Elizabeth Scott-Baumann and Clare Whitehead (London: Bloomsbury, 2017), pp. 33–54

Malcolmson, Cristina, *George Herbert: A Literary Life* (Houndmills and New York: Palgrave Macmillan, 2004)

Malone, Edmond, *An Inquiry into the Authenticity of Certain Papers and Instruments … attributed to Shakspeare, Queen Elizabeth and Henry, Earl of Southampton* (London: n.p., 1796)

(ed.), *Supplement to the edition of Shakspeare's Plays published in 1778 by Samuel Johnson and George Steevens. In two volumes* (London: n.p., 1780)

Marcus, Jane, *Art & Anger: Reading Like a Woman* (Columbus: Ohio State University Press, 1988)

Marder, Louis, *His Exits and His Entrances: The Story of Shakespeare's Reputation* (Philadelphia: J. B. Lippincott, 1963)

Marotti, Arthur F., 'Folger MSS V.a.89 and V.a.345: Reading Lyric Poetry in Manuscript' in *The Reader Revealed* ed. Sabrina Alcorn Baron (Washington, Seattle and London: Folger Shakespeare Library, 2001), pp. 45–57

Manuscript, Print, and the English Renaissance Lyric (Ithaca and London: Cornell University Press, 1995)

'Shakespeare's Sonnets as Literary Property' in *Soliciting Interpretation: Literary Theory and Seventeenth-Century English Poetry* ed. Elizabeth D. Harvey and Katharine Eisaman Maus (Chicago and London: University of Chicago Press, 1990), pp. 143–73

'Shakespeare's Sonnets and the Manuscript Circulation of Texts in Early Modern England' in *A Companion to Shakespeare's Sonnets* ed. Michael Schoenfeldt (Oxford: Blackwell, 2007), pp. 185–203

Marshall, Gail, *Shakespeare and Victorian Women* (Cambridge: Cambridge University Press, 2009)

Martin, Peter, *Edmond Malone, Shakespearean Scholar: A Literary Biography* (Cambridge: Cambridge University Press, 1995)

Massey, Gerald, 'Shakspeare and His Sonnets', *Quarterly Review* 115 (1864), 224–50

Shakspeare's Sonnets Never Before Interpreted: His Private Friends Identified (London: Longmans, Green & Co., 1866)

Masten, Jeffrey, *Textual Intercourse: Collaboration, Authorship, and Sexualities in Renaissance Drama* (Cambridge: Cambridge University Press, 1997)

Matz, Robert, 'The Scandals of Shakespeare's Sonnets', *English Literary History* 77 (2010), 477–508

Mayer, Jean-Christophe, 'Transmission as Appropriation: The Early Reception of John Benson's Edition of Shakespeare's *Poems* (1640)', *International Shakespeare Conference* 2014

McDowell, Nicholas, 'Milton's Regicide Tracts and the Uses of Shakespeare' in *The Oxford Handbook of Milton* ed. Nicholas McDowell and Nigel Smith (Oxford: Oxford University Press, 2009), pp. 252–71

McMullan, Gordon, *The Politics of Unease in the Plays of John Fletcher* (Amherst: University of Massachusetts Press, 1994)

Shakespeare and the Idea of Late Writing: Authorship in the Proximity of Death (Cambridge: Cambridge University Press, 2007)

Melchiori, Giorgio, 'Barksted, William' (2004), *Oxford Dictionary of National Biography* online

Mendelson, Edward, *Later Auden* (London: Faber & Faber, 1999)

Meres, Francis, *Palladis Tamia. Wits Treasury being the Second Part of Wits Commonwealth* (London: n.p., 1598), STC 17834

Middleton, Thomas, *Thomas Middleton: The Collected Works* ed. Gary Taylor, John Lavagnino and John Jowett (Oxford: Oxford University Press, 2010)

Milton, John, *The Complete Poetry and Essential Prose of John Milton* ed. William Kerrigan, John Rumrich and Stephen M. Fallon (New York: Random House, 2007)

    The Complete Prose Works ed. Don M. Wolfe *et al.* (New Haven: Yale University Press, 1953–82)

    The Complete Shorter Poems ed. John Carey (Harlow: Longmans, 2007)

    Milton's Sonnets ed. E. A. J. Honigmann (London and New York: Macmillan and St Martin's Press, 1966)

    Paradise Lost ed. Alastair Fowler (London and New York: Routledge, 2013)

Miner, Earl, *The Cavalier Mode from Jonson to Cotton* (Princeton: Princeton University Press, 1971)

Mitchell, Judith, 'George Eliot and the Problematic of Female Beauty', *Modern Language Studies* 20.3 (1990), 14–28

Modiano, Raimonda, 'Coleridge as Literary Critic: *Biographia Literaria* and *Essays on the Principles of Genial Criticism*' in *The Oxford Handbook of Samuel Taylor Coleridge* ed. Frederick Burwick (Oxford: Oxford University Press, 2009), 204–16

Morgan, Paul, '"Our Will Shakespeare" and Lope de Vega: An Unrecorded Contemporary Document', *Shakespeare Survey* 16 (1963), 118–20

Morgan, Thaïs E., 'Victorian Effeminacies' in *Victorian Sexual Dissidence* ed. Richard Dellamora (Chicago and London: University of Chicago Press, 1999), 109–26

Morse, David, *High Victorian Culture* (Houndmills: Macmillan, 1993)

Mullen, Harryette, *Sleeping with the Dictionary* (Berkeley, Los Angeles and London: University of California Press, 2002)

Müller, Timo, *The African American Sonnet: A Literary History* (Jackson: University of Mississippi Press, 2018)

Murphy, Andrew, *Shakespeare for the People: Working Class Readers 1800–1900* (Cambridge: Cambridge University Press, 2008)

    Shakespeare in Print: A History and Chronology of Shakespeare Publishing (Cambridge: Cambridge University Press, 2003)

Myer, Valerie Grosvenor, '"Well Read in Shakespeare"' in *Samuel Richardson: Passion and Prudence* ed. Valerie Myer Grosvenor (London: Vision Press, 1986), pp. 126–34

Nagle, Christopher C., *Sexuality and the Culture of Romanticism in the British Romantic Era* (Houndmills and New York: Palgrave Macmillan, 2007)

Najarian, James, *Victorian Keats: Manliness, Sexuality and Desire* (Basingstoke: Palgrave Macmillan, 2002)

Nardo, Anna, *Milton's Sonnets and the Ideal Community* (Lincoln and London: University of Nebraska Press, 1979)

Neely, Carol Thomas, 'The Structure of English Renaissance Sonnet Sequences', *English Literary History* 45.3 (1978), 359–89

Nelson, Megan Jane, 'Frances Turner Palgrave and *The Golden Treasury*', PhD thesis, University of British Columbia, 1985

Nicholson, Catherine, 'Commonplace Shakespeare: Value, Vulgarity, and the Poetics of Increase in *Shake-speares Sonnets* and *Troilus and Cressida*' in *The Oxford Handbook of Shakespeare's Poetry* ed. Jonathan Post (Oxford: Oxford University Press, 2013), pp. 185–203

Nicoll, Allardyce, 'Shakespeare in the Bibliotheca Bodmeriana', *Shakespeare Survey* 9 (1956), 81–5

Noel-Tod, Jeremy, 'W. H. Auden' in *Great Shakespeareans: Joyce, T. S. Eliot, Auden, Beckett* ed. Adrian Poole (London and New York: Continuum, 2012), pp. 105–48

Norman, Marc and Tom Stoppard, *Shakespeare in Love* (London: Faber & Faber, 1998)

North, Marcy L., 'The Sonnets and Book History' in *A Companion to Shakespeare's Sonnets* ed. Michael Schoenfeldt (Oxford: Blackwell, 2007), pp. 204–22

The Norton Anthology of English Literature ed. M. H. Abrams *et al.* (New York: W. W. Norton & Co., 1962), vol. 1

The Norton Anthology of English Literature: The Sixteenth Century and Early Seventeenth Century ed. M. H. Abrams *et al.* (New York: W. W. Norton & Co., 2012)

Novy, Marianne, *Engaging with Shakespeare: Responses of George Eliot and Other Women Novelists* (Iowa City: University of Iowa Press, 1998)

Nunokawa, Jeff, '*In Memoriam* and the Extinction of the Homosexual', *English Literary History* 58.2 (1991), 427–38

O'Callaghan, Michelle, 'William Browne' (2004), *Oxford Dictionary of National Biography* online

O'Neill, Michael, 'The Romantic Sonnet' in *The Cambridge Companion to the Sonnet* ed. A. D. Cousins and Peter Howarth (Cambridge: Cambridge University Press, 2011) pp. 185–203

O'Neill, Stephen, *Shakespeare and YouTube: New Media Forms of the Bard* (London and Oxford: Bloomsbury, 2014)

Owen, Harold, *Journey from Obscurity: Wilfred Owen 1893–1918: Memoirs of the Owen Family* (London and New York: Oxford University Press, 1963)

Owen, Wilfred, *Wilfred Owen: The Complete Poems and Fragments* ed. Jon Stallworthy (London: Chatto & Windus, 2013)

Owen, W. B. J., *Understanding the Prelude* (Penrith: Humanities EBooks, 2007)

Oya, Reiko, ' "Authenticating the Inauthentic": Edmond Malone as Editor of the Apocryphal Shakespeare', *Shakespeare Survey* 69 (2016), 324–34

'"Talk to Him": Wilde, His Friends, and Shakespeare's *Sonnets*', *Critical Survey* 21.3 (2009), 22–40

Palgrave, Francis, *The Golden Treasury of the Best Songs and Lyrical Poems in the English Language* (London and Cambridge: Macmillan & Co., 1861)

The Golden Treasury ed. Christopher Ricks (London: Penguin, 1991)

Palgrave, Gwenllian F., *Francis Turner Palgrave: His Journals and Memories of His Life* (London and New York: Longmans, Green & Co, 1899)

Parker, Michael P., "'All are not born (Sir) to the Bay": "Jack" Suckling, "Tom" Carew, and the Making of a Poet', *English Literary Renaissance* 12 (1982), 341–68

Parsons, A. E., 'A Forgotten Poet: William Chamberlayne and *Pharonnida*', *Modern Humanities Research Association* 45.3 (1950), 296–311

The Passionate Pilgrim in *Shakespeare's Poems* ed. Katherine Duncan-Jones and H. R. Woudhuysen (London: Cengage Learning, 2007), pp. 385–418

Paterson, Don, *Reading Shakespeare's Sonnets: A New Commentary* (London: Faber & Faber, 2010)

Patmore, Coventry, *The Children's Garland from the Best Poets* (London: n.p., 1862)

Patterson, Annabel, 'Milton's Heroic Sonnets' in *A Concise Companion to Milton* ed. Angelica Duran (Oxford: Wiley-Blackwell, 2007), pp. 78–94

Pequigney, Joseph, *Such Is My Love: A Study of Shakespeare's Sonnets* (Chicago and London: University of Chicago Press, 1985)

Percy, Thomas (ed.), *Reliques of Ancient English Poetry Consisting of Old Heroic Ballads, Songs, and Other Pieces of our earlier Poets, chiefly of the Lyric kind* (London: n.p., 1765, repr. Dublin, 1766), 2 vols.

Perkins, David, *The Quest for Permanence: The Symbolism of Wordsworth, Shelley and Keats* (New Haven and London: Harvard University Press, 1959)

Phelan, Joseph, *The Nineteenth-Century Sonnet* (Houndmills and New York: Macmillan, 2005)

Phillips, Edward, *The Mysteries of Love and Eloquence* (London: n.p., 1658), Wing P2066

Phfister, Manfred, 'Route 66 and No End: Further Fortunes of Shakespeare's Sonnet 66', *Linguaculture* 2 (2010), 39–50

Pitman, Reverend J. R. (ed.), *The School-Shakespeare: or, Plays and Scenes from Shakspeare, illustrated for the use of Schools* (London: n.p., 1822)

Pointner, Frank Erik, 'Bardolatry and Biography: Romantic Readings of Shakespeare's Sonnets' in *British Romantics as Readers* ed. Michael Gassenmeier (Heidelberg: Universitätsverlag C., 1998), pp. 117–36

Poole, Adrian, *Shakespeare and the Victorians* (London: Bloomsbury, 2014)

Poole, Josua, *The English Parnassus, or, a Helpe to English Poesie* (London: n.p., 1657), Wing/P2814

Poole, Roger, '"We all put up with you Virginia": Irreceivable Wisdom about War' in *Virginia Woolf and War* ed. Mark Hussey (Syracuse: Syracuse University Press, 1991), pp. 79–100

Pope, Alexander, *The First Epistle of the Second Book of Horace Imitated* (London: n.p., 1737)

Prince, F. T., *The Italian Element in Milton's Verse* (Oxford: Richard West, 1980)

Quiller-Couch, Arthur (ed.), *The Oxford Book of English Verse 1250–1900* (Oxford: Oxford University Press, 1900, 1919)

Rasmussen, Eric, 'Publishing the First Folio' in *The Cambridge Companion to Shakespeare's First Folio* ed. Emma Smith (Cambridge: Cambridge University Press, 2016), pp. 18–29

'The Year's Contribution to Shakespeare Studies: Editions and Textual Studies', *Shakespeare Survey* 52 (1999), 302–26

Ravenscroft, Edward, *Titus Andronicus, or The Rape of Lavinia* (London: n.p., 1687), Wing S2949

Regan, Stephen, 'Auden and Shakespeare' in *W. H. Auden in Context* ed. Tony Sharpe (Cambridge: Cambridge University Press, 2013), pp. 266–74

Richardson, Samuel, *The Cambridge Edition of the Correspondence of Samuel Richardson: Correspondence with George Cheyne and Thomas Edwards* ed. David E. Shuttleton and John A. Dussinger (Cambridge: Cambridge University Press, 2013)

    Clarissa, or the History of a Young Lady ed. Angus Ross (London: Penguin, 1985)

    The History of Sir Charles Grandison ed. Jocelyn Harris (London: Oxford University Press, 1972), 3 vols.

Riding, Laura, *Anarchism is Not Enough* (1928) ed. Lisa Samuels (Berkeley, Los Angeles, and London: University of California Press, 2001)

Riding, Laura and Robert Graves, *A Survey of Modernist Poetry and A Pamphlet Against Anthologies* ed. Charles Mundye and Patrick McGuinness (Manchester: Carcanet, 2002)

Rinaker, Clarissa, 'Thomas Edwards and the Sonnet Revival', *Modern Language Notes* 34.5 (1919), 272–7

Ritchie, Fiona, *Women and Shakespeare in the Eighteenth Century* (Cambridge: Cambridge University Press, 2014)

Ritchie, Fiona and Peter Sabor (eds.), *Shakespeare in the Eighteenth Century* (Cambridge: Cambridge University Press, 2012)

Robbins, R. H., 'A Seventeenth Century Manuscript of Shakespeare's Sonnet 128', *Notes & Queries* 212 (1967), 137–8

Roberts, Josephine A., '"The Knott Never to Bee Untide": The Controversy Regarding Marriage in Mary Wroth's *Urania*' in *Reading Mary Wroth* ed. Naomi J. Miller and Gary Waller (Knoxville: University of Tennessee Press, 1991), pp. 109–32

Roberts, Sasha, *Reading Shakespeare's Poems in Early Modern England* (London: Palgrave Macmillan, 2003)

    'Reception and Influence' in *The Cambridge Companion to Shakespeare's Poetry* ed. Patrick Cheney (Cambridge: Cambridge University Press, 2007), pp. 260–80

Rollins, Hyder E. (ed.), *A New Variorum Edition of Shakespeare: The Sonnets* (Philadelphia and London: J. B. Lippincott & Co., 1944), 2 vols.

Rose, Jonathan, *The Intellectual Life of the British Working Classes* (New Haven and London: Yale University Press, 2001)

Rowse, A. L., *William Shakespeare: A Biography* (London: Palgrave Macmillan, 1963)

Rumbold, Kate, '"Alas, Poor YORICK": Quoting Shakespeare in the Mid-Eighteenth Century Novel', *Borrowers and Lenders: The Journal of Shakespeare and Appropriation* 2 (2006), www.borrowers.org.uga.edu/7151/toc

    Shakespeare and the Eighteenth-Century Novel: Cultures of Quotation from Samuel Richardson to Jane Austen (Cambridge: Cambridge University Press, 2016)

'Shakespeare's Poems in Pieces: *Venus and Adonis* and *The Rape of Lucrece* Unanthologized', *Shakespeare Survey* 69 (2016), 92–105

'"So Common-Hackneyed in the Eyes of Men": Banal Shakespeare and the Eighteenth-Century Novel', *Literature Compass* 4 (2007), 610–21

Sanderlin, George, 'The Repute of Shakespeare's Sonnets in the Early Nineteenth Century', *Modern Language Notes* 54.6 (1939), 462–6

Sanders, Julie, *Shakespeare and Music: Afterlives and Borrowings* (Cambridge: Polity Press, 2007)

Savoie, John, 'Monuments Men: Milton on Shakespeare', *Literary Imagination* 19.1 (2017), 19–29

Schaar, Claes, *Elizabethan Sonnet Themes and the Dating of Shakespeare's Sonnets* (Lund: Ohlsson, 1962)

Schalkwyk, David, *Speech and Performance in Shakespeare's Sonnets and Plays* (Cambridge: Cambridge University Press, 2002)

Scheil, Katherine West, *Imagining Shakespeare's Wife: The Afterlife of Anne Hathaway* (Cambridge: Cambridge University Press, 2018)

Schiffer, James, 'The Incomplete Narrative of Shakespeare's Sonnets' in *A Companion to Shakespeare's Sonnets* ed. Michael Schoenfeldt (Oxford: Blackwell, 2007), pp. 45–56

Schlegel, August Wilhelm von, *A Course of Lectures on Dramatic Art and Literature* trans. John Black (London: n.p., 1815), 2 vols.

Schoenbaum, Samuel, *Shakespeare's Lives* (Oxford: Clarendon Press, 1991)

Schoenfeldt, Michael, 'Introduction' in *A Companion to Shakespeare's Sonnets* (Oxford: Wiley-Blackwell, 2007), pp. 1–13

Schroeder, Horst, *Oscar Wilde, The Portrait of Mr W. H.: Its Composition, Publication and Reception* (Braunschweig: Technische Universität Carolo-Wilhelmina zu Braunschweig, 1984)

Schutte, William, *Joyce and Shakespeare: A Study in the Meaning of Ulysses* (Hamden: Archon Books, 1971)

Schwartz, Louis, *Milton and Maternal Mortality* (Cambridge: Cambridge University Press, 2009)

Scodel, Joshua, 'The Pleasures of Restraint: The Mean of Coyness in Cavalier Poetry', *Criticism* 38 (Winter 1996), 239–79

Scofield, Martin, 'Shakespeare and *Clarissa*: "General Nature", Genre and Sexuality', *Shakespeare Survey* 51 (1998), 27–44

Scott, Alison M., 'Tantalising Fragments: The Proofs of Virginia Woolf's *Orlando*', *Papers of the Bibliographical Society of America* 88.3 (1994), 279–351

Seward, Anna, *Letters of Anna Seward, written between the years 1784 and 1807* (Edinburgh: George Ramsay & Co, 1811), 6 vols.

The Shakspeare Allusion Book: A Collection of Allusions to Shakespeare from 1591–1700 ed. C. M. Ingleby, Lucy Toulmin Smith, Frederick James Furnivall and John James Munro (London: Humphrey Milford and Oxford University Press, 1932)

Shakespeare in Love dir. John Madden (Miramax, 1998)

Shakespeare in Love: The Love Poetry of William Shakespeare (London: Faber & Faber, 1999)

Shakespeare, William, *A Collection of Poems, viz. I. Venus and Adonis, II. The Rape of Lucrece, III. The Passionate Pilgrim, IV. Sonnets to Sundry Notes of Musick. By Mr. William Shakespear* ed. Bernard Lintott (London: n.p., 1709)

A Collection of Poems in Two Volumes, being all the Miscellanies of Mr William Shakespear, which were Publish'd by himself in the Year 1609, and now correctly Printed from those Editions. The First Volume contains, I. Venus and Adonis. II. The Rape of Lucrece. III. The Passionate Pilgrim. IV. Some Sonnets set to Sundry Notes of Musick. The Second Volume contains One Hundred and Fifty Four Sonnets, all of them in Praise of his Mistress. II. A Lover's Complaint of his Angry Mistress ed. Bernard Lintott (London: n.p., 1711)

The Complete Sonnets and Poems ed. Colin Burrow (Oxford: Oxford University Press, 2002)

The Globe Shakespeare: The Works of Shakespeare ed. William George Clark and William Aldis Wright (London and Cambridge: Macmillan & Co., 1866)

King Edward III ed. Giorgio Melchiori (Cambridge: Cambridge University Press, 1998)

Mr William Shakespeare Comedies, Histories and Tragedies ed. Edward Capell (1767–8), 10 vols.

The New Oxford Shakespeare: The Complete Works: Critical Reference Edition ed. Gary Taylor, John Jowett, Terri Bourus and Gabriel Egan (Oxford: Oxford University Press, 2017), 2 vols.

The New Oxford Shakespeare: The Complete Works: Modern Critical Edition ed. Gary Taylor, John Jowett, Terri Bourus and Gabriel Egan (Oxford: Oxford University Press, 2016)

The Norton Shakespeare ed. Stephen Greenblatt, Walter Cohen, Suzanne Gossett, Jean E. Howard, Katharine Eisaman Maus and Gordon McMullan (New York and London: W. W. Norton, 2015)

Pictorial Edition of the Works of Shakspere ed. Charles Knight (1839–41)

The Plays and Poems of William Shakespeare ed. James Boswell (London: n.p., 1821)

The Plays and Poems of William Shakespeare, in ten volumes ed. Edmond Malone (London: n.p., 1790)

The Plays of Shakspeare from the text of Dr S Johnson ed. Thomas Ewing (Dublin: n.p., 1771)

The Plays of William Shakspeare: in fifteen volumes ed. George Steevens (London: n.p., 1793)

Poems ed. John Benson (London; n.p., 1640), STC 22344

The Poems: Venus and Adonis, The Rape of Lucrece, The Phoenix and the Turtle, The Passionate Pilgrim, A Lover's Complaint ed. John Roe (Cambridge: Cambridge University Press, 2006)

Poems by William Shakespeare (London: n.p., 1804)

The Poems of Shakespear ed. George Sewell (London: n.p., 1725)

The Poems of Shakespeare ed. Alexander Dyce (London: Bell & Daldy, 1832, repr. 1857, 1866)

Poems written by Mr William Shakespeare ed. Thomas Evans (London: n.p., 1775)

Poems written by Shakespear ed. Francis Gentleman (London: n.p., 1774)

Shakespeare's Comedies, Histories, Tragedies and Poems ed. John Payne Collier (London: n.p., 1858)

Shakespeare's Poems ed. Katherine Duncan-Jones and H. R. Woudhuysen (London: Cengage Learning, 2007)

Shakespeare's Sonnets ed. Katherine Duncan-Jones (London: Thomas Nelson & Sons Ltd, 1997)

Shakespeare's Sonnets: An Original-Spelling Text ed. Paul Hammond (Oxford: Oxford University Press, 2012)

Shakespeares Sonnets: Being a Reproduction in Facsimile of the First Edition (1609) ed. Sidney Lee (Oxford: Oxford University Press, 1905)

Shakespeare's Sonnets edited with analytic commentary by Stephen Booth (New Haven and London: Yale University Press, 1977)

The Songs, Poems and Sonnets of William Shakespeare ed. William Sharp (London: n.p., 1885)

Songs and Sonnets by William Shakespeare ed. Francis Turner Palgrave (London and Cambridge: Macmillan & Co., 1865)

The Sonnets and A Lover's Complaint ed. John Kerrigan (London: Penguin, 1986)

The Sonnets of Shakespeare: From the Quarto of 1609 with Variorum Readings and Commentary ed. Raymond MacDonald Alden (Boston: Houghton Mifflin, 1916)

Supplement to the edition of Shakspeare's Plays published in 1778 by Samuel Johnson and George Steevens: In two volumes ed. Edward Malone (London: n.p., 1780)

Twenty of the Plays of Shakespeare, being the whole number printed in quarto during his life-time ed. George Steevens (London: n.p., 1766), 4 vols.

William Shakespeare: The Complete Works ed. Stanley Wells and Gary Taylor (Oxford: Clarendon Press, 1988)

Works edited by William George Clark, John Glover and William Aldis Wright (Cambridge and London: Macmillan & Co, 1863–6)

The Works of Shakespeare: In Seven Volumes ed. Mr Theobald (London: n.p., 1733)

The Works of Mr. William Shakespear. In Ten Volumes. Publish'd by Mr Pope and Dr Sewell (London: n.p., 1728)

The Works of Mr. William Shakespear. Volume Seventh. Containing Venus & Adonis. Tarquin & Lucrece And His Miscellany Poems ed. Charles Gildon (London: n.p., 1710)

The Works of Mr. William Shakespeare: in six volumes ed. Nicholas Rowe (1709) with an introduction by Peter Holland (London: Pickering and Chatto, 1999), 7 vols.

The Works of Shakespeare: Sonnets ed. C. Knox Pooler (The Arden Shakespeare, 1918)

The Works of William Shakespeare ed. James Orchard Halliwell-Phillips (London: n.p., 1865)

The Works of William Shakespeare: The Text Formed from an entirely New Collation of the Old Editions ed. John Payne Collier (London: Whittaker & Co., 1843)

Shakir, Evelyn, 'Books, Death and Immortality: A Study of Book V of *The Prelude*', *Studies in Romanticism* 8.3 (1969), 156–67

Sharp, William, *The Songs, Poems and Sonnets of William Shakespeare* (London: Walter Scott, 1885)

Sharpe, Kevin, *Criticism and Compliment: The Politics of Literature in the England of Charles I* (Cambridge: Cambridge University Press, 1987)

Shaw, George Bernard, *Misalliance, The Dark Lady of the Sonnets and Fanny's First Play* (Cabin John: Wildside Press, 2008)

Shaw, Philip and Gail Marshall, 'Shakespeare and Poetry' in *Shakespeare in the Nineteenth Century* ed. Gail Marshall (Cambridge: Cambridge University Press, 2012), pp. 113–28

Shawcross, John T., *The Arms of the Family: The Significance of John Milton's Relatives and Associates* (Lexington: University Press of Kentucky, 2004)

Shelley, Percy Bysshe, *The Complete Poetical Works of Percy Bysshe Shelley* ed. Thomas Hutchinson (London: Oxford University Press, 1952)

Sherry, Vincent, 'The Great War and Literary Modernism in England' in *The Cambridge Companion to the Literature of the First World War* ed. Vincent Sherry (Cambridge: Cambridge University Press, 2005), pp. 113–38

A Short Title Catalogue of Books Printed in England, Scotland, and Ireland first compiled by A. W. Pollard and G. R. Redgrave, 2nd edition rev. by W. A. Jackson and F. S. Ferguson, and completed by Katherine E. Pantzer (London: The Bibliographical Society, 1976)

Shrank, Cathy, 'Reading Shakespeare's Sonnets: John Benson and the 1640 *Poems*', *Shakespeare* 5 (2009), 271–91

Shyllon, Folarin, *Black People in Britain 1555–1833* (London: Oxford University Press, 1977)

Sidney, Sir Philip, *Syr P. S. His Astrophel and Stella* (London: n.p., 1591), STC 22536

Siegel, Carol, '"This thing I like my sister may not do": Shakespearean Erotics and a Clash of Wills in *Middlemarch*', *Style* 31.2 (1998), 36–59

Sillars, Stuart, *Structure and Dissolution in English Writing, 1910–1920* (Houndmills and New York: Macmillan, 1999)

Sinfield, Alan, *Alfred Tennyson* (Oxford: Basil Blackwell, 1986)
  The Wilde Century: Effeminacy, Oscar Wilde and the Queer Moment (New York: Columbia University Press, 1994)

Sircy, Otice C., '"The Fashion of Sentiment": Allusive Techniques and the Sonnets of *Middlemarch*', *Studies in Philology* 84.2 (1987), 219–44

Smillie, Robert, *My Life for Labour* (London: Mills & Boon, 1924)

Smith, Bruce R., 'Shakespeare's Sonnets and the History of Sexuality: A Reception History' in *A Companion to Shakespeare's Works, Volume 4: The Poems, Problem Comedies, Late Plays*, ed. Richard Dutton and Jean E. Howard (Oxford: Blackwell, 2005), pp. 4–26

Smith, Charlotte, *Elegiac Sonnets, and Other Essays* (Chichester: n.p., 1784)
  The Poems of Charlotte Smith ed. Stuart Curran (New York: Oxford University Press, 1993)

Smith, Emma and Laurie Maguire, 'What is a Source? Or, How Shakespeare Read His Marlowe', *Shakespeare Survey* 68 (2015), 15–31

Smith, Hallett, 'No Cloudy Stuffe to Puzzell Intellect: A Testimonial Misapplied to Shakespeare', *Shakespeare Quarterly* 1 (1950), 18–21

 The Tension of the Lyre: Poetry in Shakespeare's Sonnets (San Marino: Huntington Library, 1981)

Smith, James, *Samuel Richardson and the Theory of Tragedy: Clarissa's Caesuras* (Manchester: Manchester University Press, 2016)

Smith, Nigel, *Literature and Revolution in England, 1640–1660* (New Haven and London: Yale University Press, 1994)

Smyth, Adam, 'Commonplace Book Culture: A List of Sixteen Traits' in *Women and Writing c. 1340-c.1650: The Domestication of Print Culture* ed. Anne Lawrence-Mathers and Philippe Hardman (Woodbridge and Rochester: Boydell Press, 2010), pp. 90–110

 'Profit and Delight': Printed Miscellanies in England, 1640–1682 (Detroit: Wayne State University Press, 2004)

Snow, Edward A., 'Loves of Comfort and Despair: A Reading of Shakespeare's Sonnet 138', *English Literary History* 47.3 (1980), 462–83

Spenser, Edmund, *Amoretti and Epithalamion* (London: n.p., 1595), STC 23076

Spevack, Marvin, '*The Golden Treasury*: 150 Years On', *Electronic British Library Journal*, www.bl.uk/eblj/2012articles/article2.html, accessed 18 April 2019

Spiller, Michael R. G., *The Development of the Sonnet: An Introduction* (London and New York: Routledge, 1992)

Spink, Ian, *Henry Lawes: Cavalier Songwriter* (Oxford: Oxford University Press, 2000)

Spurgeon, Caroline F. E., *Keats' Shakespeare: A Descriptive Study Based on New Material* (London: Oxford University Press, 1928)

Squier, Charles L., *Sir John Suckling* (Boston: Twayne, 1978)

Stallworthy, John, *Wilfred Owen: A Biography* (London: Oxford University Press and Chatto & Windus, 1974)

Stallybrass, Peter, 'Editing as Cultural Formation: The Sexing of Shakespeare's Sonnets' in *Shakespeare's Sonnets: Critical Essays* ed. James Schiffer (New York: Garland, 2000), pp. 75–88

Stallybrass, Peter and Roger Chartier, 'Reading and Authorship: The Circulation of Shakespeare 1590–1619' in *A Concise Companion to Shakespeare and the Text* ed. Andrew R. Murphy (Oxford: Wiley-Blackwell, 2007), pp. 35–56

Stern, Tiffany, *Documents of Performance in Early Modern England* (Cambridge: Cambridge University Press, 2009)

Stevens, George Alexander (ed.), *The Choice Spirit's Chaplet: or, a Poesy from Parnassus* (London: n.p., 1771)

Stevens, Paul, *Imagination and the Presence of Shakespeare in Paradise Lost* (Madison: University of Wisconsin Press, 1985)

 'Subversion and Wonder in Milton's Epitaph "On Shakespeare"', *English Literary Renaissance* 19 (1989), 375–88

Stevenson, Randall, 'Woolf and Modernity: Crisis and Catoptrics' in *Virginia Woolf in Context* ed. Bryony Randall and Jane Goldman (Cambridge: Cambridge University Press, 2012), pp. 149–58

Stimpson, Catherine R., 'Reading for Love: Canons, Paracanons, and Whistling Jo March', *New Literary History* 21.4 (1990), 957–76

Stinson, John J., *Anthony Burgess Revisited* (Boston: Twayne, 1991)

Stone, Jr., George Winchester, 'Shakespeare in the Periodicals 1700–1740: A Study of the Growth of a Knowledge of the Dramatist in the Eighteenth Century', *Shakespeare Quarterly* 2 (1951), no. 3, 221–31, and no. 4, 313–28

Suckling, Sir John, *The Works of Sir John Suckling* ed. L. A. Beaurline and Thomas Clayton (Oxford: Clarendon Press, 1971), 2 vols.

Sullivan, Ceri, 'Disposable Elements? Indications of Genre in Early Modern Titles', *Modern Language Review* 102.3 (2007), 641–53

Swinburne, Algernon Charles, *Studies in Prose and Poetry* (London: Chatto & Windus, 1894)

Taylor, Gary, *Reinventing Shakespeare: A Cultural History, from the Restoration to the Present* (New York: Weidenfeld & Nicolson, 1989)

  'Some Manuscripts of Shakespeare's Sonnets', *Bulletin of the John Rylands Library* 68 (1985–6), 210–46

Taylor, Gary and John Jowett, *Shakespeare Reshaped, 1606–1623* (Oxford: Clarendon Press, 1993)

Tennyson, Alfred, *The Poems of Tennyson* ed. Christopher Ricks (London and New York: Longman and W. W. Norton, 1969)

Tennyson, Arthur Hallam, *Alfred Lord Tennyson: A Memoir by His Son* (London: Macmillan & Co., 1897), 2 vols.

Terry, Philip, *Shakespeare's Sonnets* (Manchester: Carcanet, 2010)

Thomas, Edward, *Collected Poems by Edward Thomas* ed. Walter de la Mere (London: Faber & Faber, 1961)

  The Collected Poems of Edward Thomas ed. R. George Thomas (Oxford: Clarendon Press, 1978)

Thompson, Anne and Sasha Roberts (eds.), *Women Reading Shakespeare 1660–1900: An Anthology of Criticism* (Manchester: Manchester University Press, 2012)

Trench, Richard Chevenix, *A Household Book of English Poetry* (London: Macmillan & Co. 1868)

Trillini, Regula Hohl, 'The Gaze of the Listener: Shakespeare's Sonnet 128 and Early Modern Discourses of Music and Gender', *Music & Letters* 89.1 (2008), 1–17

Van de Broek, A. G., 'Shakespeare, William' in *Oxford Reader's Companion to George Eliot* ed. John Rignall (Oxford: Oxford University Press, 2000), pp. 376–9

Vendler, Helen, *The Art of Shakespeare's Sonnets* (Cambridge, MA and London: Harvard University Press, 1997)

Voss, Paul J., 'Books for Sale: Advertising and Patronage in Late Elizabethan England', *The Sixteenth Century Journal* 29.3 (1998), 733–56

Walen, Denise, *Constructions of Female Homoeroticism in Early Modern Drama 1570–1662* (London and New York: Palgrave Macmillan, 2005)

Waller, Gary, *The Sidney Family Romance: Mary Wroth, William Herbert, and the Early Modern Construction of Gender* (Detroit: Wayne State University Press, 1993)

Wallerstein, Ruth, 'Suckling's Imitation of Shakespeare: A Caroline View of His Art', *Review of English Studies* 19.75 (1943), 290–5

Watson, Thomas, *Hekatompathia or Passionate Centurie of Love* (London: n.p., 1582), STC 25118a

Wells, Stanley, '"My Name is Will": Shakespeare's Sonnets and Autobiography', *Shakespeare Survey* 68 (2015), 99–108

Wells, Stanley, Gary Taylor, John Jowett and William Montgomery, *William Shakespeare: A Textual Companion* (Oxford: Clarendon Press, 1987)

White, R. S., *Keats as a Reader of Shakespeare* (London: Athlone Press, 1987)

Wilcher, Robert, *The Discontented Cavalier: The Work of Sir John Suckling in its Social, Religious, Political and Literary Contexts* (Newark: University of Delaware Press, 2007)

Wilde, Oscar, *The Collins Complete Works of Oscar Wilde* (Glasgow: Harper Collins, 1948, repr. 2008)

> *The Complete Letters of Oscar Wilde* ed. Merlin Holland and Rupert Hart-Davis (London: Fourth Estate, 2000)

> 'The Portrait of Mr W. H.' in *Complete Shorter Fiction* ed. Isobel Murray (Oxford and New York: Oxford University Press, 1979, repr. 1992)

Wilkes, Joanna, *Women Reviewing Women in Nineteenth Century Britain: The Critical Reception of Jane Austen, Charlotte Bronte and George Eliot* (London and New York: Routledge, 2016)

Williams, Rhian, '"Pyramids of Egypt": Shakespeare's Sonnets and a Victorian Turn to Obscurity', *Victorian Poetry* 48.4 (2010), 489–508

Williams, Wendy S., *George Eliot, Poetess* (Farnham: Ashgate, 2014)

Willoughby, Edwin Eliott, 'A Deadly Edition of Shakespeare', *Shakespeare Quarterly* 5.4 (1954), 351–7

> *A Printer of Shakespeare: The Books and Times of William Jaggard* (London: Philip Allan & Co., 1934)

Winder, Robert, *The Final Act of Mr Shakespeare* (London: Little, Brown, 2010)

Wood, Jane, 'Elizabeth Barrett Browning and Shakespeare's Sonnet 130', *Notes & Queries* (2005), 77–9

Woods, Gregory, *A History of Gay Literature: The Male Tradition* (New Haven and London: Yale University Press, 1998)

Woolf, Virginia, *The Diary of Virginia Woolf* vol. 3: *1925–1930*, ed. Anne Oliver Bell (London: Hogarth Press, 1980)

> *To the Lighthouse* (London: Vintage, 2004)

> *To the Lighthouse: The Original Holograph Draft* transcribed and edited by Susan Dick (Toronto and Buffalo: University of Toronto Press, 1982)

Wordsworth, William, 'Essay, Supplementary to the Preface' in *Poems by William Wordsworth, including Lyrical Ballads* (London: n.p., 1815)

> *The Letters of William and Dorothy Wordsworth: The Later Years* ed. Alan G. Hill (Oxford: Clarendon Press, 1978–88), 4 vols.

> *The Prelude, or Growth of a Poet's Mind* ed. Ernest de Selincourt (London: Oxford University Press, 1969)

Wordsworth, William and Samuel Taylor Coleridge, *Lyrical Ballads* (1805) ed. Derek Roper (Plymouth: Macdonald and Evans, 1982)

Woudhuysen, H. R., 'The Foundations of Shakespeare's Text', *Proceedings of the British Academy 125* (2004), 69–100

    Sir Philip Sidney and the Circulation of Manuscripts 1558–1640 (Oxford: Clarendon Press, 1996)

Wroth, Lady Mary, *The First Part of The Countess of Montgomery's Urania* ed. Josephine A. Roberts (Tempe: Arizona Center for Medieval and Renaissance Studies, 1995, repr. 2005)

    The Poems of Lady Mary Wroth ed. Josephine A. Roberts (Baton Rouge and London: Louisiana State University Press, 1983)

    The Second Part of The Countess of Montgomery's Urania ed. Josephine Roberts, completed by Suzanne Gossett and Janel Mueller (Tempe: Arizona Center for Medieval and Renaissance Studies, 1999)

Wynne-Davies, Marion, '"For *Worth*, Not Weakness, Makes in Use but One": Literary Dialogues in an English Renaissance Family' in *'This Double Voice': Gendered Writing in Early Modern England* ed. Danielle Clark and Elizabeth Clark (Houndmills: Macmillan, 2000), pp. 164–84

Zimmerman, Bonnie, '"The Mother's History" in George Eliot's Life, Literature, and Political Ideology' in *The Lost Tradition: Mothers and Daughters in Literature* ed. Cathy N. Davidson and E. M. Broner (New York: Frederick Ungar, 1980), pp. 81–94

Zwicker, Steven N., *Lines of Authority: Politics and English Literary Culture, 1649–1689* (Ithaca and London: Cornell University Press, 1993)

Index

Printed in the United States
by Baker & Taylor Publisher Services